LIBRARY OF HEBREW BIBLE/ OLD TESTAMENT STUDIES

561

Formerly Journal for the Study of the Old Testament Supplement Series

T&T CLARK • LIBRARY OF BIBLICAL STUDIES

THE VIOLENT GIFT

Trauma's Subversion of the Deuteronomistic History's Narrative

David Janzen

BLOOMSBURY
NEW YORK • LONDON • NEW DELHI • SYDNEY

Bloomsbury T&T Clark
An imprint of Bloomsbury Publishing Inc

1385 Broadway
New York
NY 10018
USA

50 Bedford Square
London
WC1B 3DP
UK

www.bloomsbury.com

First published 2012
Paperback edition first published 2013

Library of Congress Cataloging-in-Publication Data
A catalog record for this book is available from the Library of Congress

ISBN: HB: 978-0-567-43692-4
PB: 978-0-567-32335-4

Typeset by Forthcoming Publications Ltd (www.forthpub.com)

For Patricia,

whose writing is better than mine

CONTENTS

Abbreviations

AASF	Annales Academiae Scientiarum Fennicae
AB	Anchor Bible
ABD	David Noel Freedman, ed. *The Anchor Bible Dictionary*. 6 vols. New York, 1992
ABR	*Australian Biblical Review*
ABRL	Anchor Bible Research Library
AnBib	Analecta Biblica
ATANT	Abhandlungen zur Theologie des Alten und Neuen Testaments
ATD	Das Alte Testament Deutsch
BEATAJ	Beiträge zur Erforschung des Alten Testaments und des antiken Judentums
BETL	Bibliotheca Ephemeridum theologicarum Lovaniensium
Bib	*Biblica*
BibInt	*Biblical Interpretation*
BibOr	Biblica et Orientalia
BIS	Biblical Interpretation Series
BJS	Brown Judaic Studies
BLS	Bible and Literature Series
BO	Berit Olam
BWANT	Beiträge zur Wissenschaft vom Alten und Neuen Testament
BZAW	Beiheft zur Zeitschrift für die alttestamentliche Wissenschaft
CBC	The Cambridge Bible Commentary
CBQ	*Catholic Biblical Quarterly*
CBQMS	Catholic Biblical Quarterly Monograph Series
CHANE	Culture and History of the Ancient Near East
CRB	Cahiers de la Revue Biblique
DJD	Discoveries in the Judaean Desert
Dtr	The Deuteronomistic History
ESHM	European Seminar in Historical Methodology
ET	*Evangelische Theologie*
ET	English translation
FAT	Forschungen zum Alten Testament
FOTL	Forms of the Old Testament Literature
FRLANT	Forschungen zur Religion und Literatur des Alten und Neuen Testaments
GKC	*Gesenius' Hebrew Grammar*. Edited by E. Kautzsch and A. E. Cowley. Oxford, 1910

GTS	Gettysburg Theological Studies
HAT	Handbuch zum Alten Testament
HSM	Harvard Semitic Monographs
HAR	*Harvard Annual Review*
HTR	*Harvard Theological Review*
HUCA	*Hebrew Union College Annual*
IBHS	*An Introduction to Biblical Hebrew Syntax*. Bruce K. Waltke and M. O'Connor. Winona Lake, Ind., 1990
Int	*Interpretation*
ISBL	Indiana Studies in Biblical Literature
JBL	*Journal of Biblical Literature*
JBS	Jerusalem Biblical Studies
JPS	Jewish Publication Society
JSOT	*Journal for the Study of the Old Testament*
JSOTSup	Journal for the Study of the Old Testament Supplement Series
KAI	*Kanaanäische und aramäische Inschriften*. Edited by Herbert Donner. 3 vols. Wiesbaden: Harrassowitz, 1962–64
LCBI	Literary Currents in Biblical Interpretation
LHBOTS	Library of the Hebrew Bible/Old Testament Studies
LXX	Septuagint
LXX^{A}	Codex Alexandrinus
LXX^{B}	Codex Vaticanus
LXX^{L}	Lucianic Recension
MT	Masoretic Text
NAC	New American Commentary
NCBC	New Century Bible Commentary
NEBAT	Neue Echter Bibel Alten Testament
NIBC	New International Biblical Commentary
NIV	New International Version
NJB	New Jerusalem Bible
NRSV	New Revised Standard Version
NSBT	New Studies in Biblical Theology
OBO	Orbis Biblicus et Orientalis
OBT	Overtures to Biblical Theology
OTL	Old Testament Library
OTR	Old Testament Readings
OTS	Oudtestamentlische Studien
SBA	Stuttgarter biblische Aufsatzbände
SBL	Society of Biblical Literature
SBLDS	Society of Biblical Literature Dissertation Series
SBLSS	Society of Biblical Literature Semeia Studies
SBT	Studies in Biblical Theology
SBTS	Sources for Biblical and Theological Study
SE	*The Standard Edition of the Complete Psychological Works of Sigmund Freud*. Edited by James Strachey. 24 vols. London, 1955–74
SJLA	Studies in Judaism in Late Antiquity

SJOT	*Scandinavian Journal of the Old Testament*
StBL	Studies in Biblical Literature
STDJ	Studies on the Texts of the Desert of Judah
SubBib	Subsidia Biblica
TDOT	*Theological Dictionary of the Old Testament*. Edited by G. Johannes Botterweck and Helmer Ringgren. Translated by John T. Willis. 15 vols. Grand Rapids, 1977–2004
TynBul	*Tyndale Bulletin*
VT	*Vetus Testamentum*
VTSup	Vetus Testamentum Supplement Series
WBC	Word Biblical Commentary
WMANT	Wissenschaftliche Monographien zum Alten und Neuen Testament
ZAW	*Zeitschrift für die alttestamentliche Wissenschaft*

Chapter 1

THE VIOLENT GIFT: TRAUMA'S ABSENCE AND PRESENCE IN THE DEUTERONOMISTIC HISTORY

A. *The Trauma of Destruction and Exile*

It is "curious," as Thomas Römer and Albert de Pury understate it, that the "key events" of the destruction of Jerusalem and the temple and the forced migration to Babylon "occupy only a marginal and almost negligible place" in the Deuteronomistic History.[1] Even if one believes that 2 Kgs 23:26–25:30 is from the hand of an exilic redactor who brings a pre-existing edition up to date, one must still imagine that this redactor sees the destruction of Jerusalem and the exile as the negative culmination of Israel's history, and so even in such a redactional situation we might expect far more emphasis on the event. The siege and its accompanying death, famine, destruction, and forced migration, however, is narrated in the most laconic of prose. Here is the extent of the History's comment in 2 Kgs 25:1–11 on these horrific events:

> And in the ninth year of his [Zedekiah's] reign, in the tenth month on the tenth of the month, Nebuchadnezzar the king of Babylon and all his army came against Jerusalem and encamped against it and built siegeworks against it all around. And the city came under siege until the eleventh year of King Zedekiah. [In the fourth month?][2] on the ninth of the month,

1. Thomas C. Römer and Albert de Pury, "Deuteronomistic Historiography (DH): History of Research and Debated Issues," in *Israel Constructs Its History: Deuteronomistic Historiography in Recent Research* (ed. Albert de Pury, Thomas C. Römer, and Jean-Daniel Macchi; JSOTSup 306; Sheffield: Sheffield Academic, 2000), 24–141 (136).

2. Most scholars accept the addition of "in the fourth month" at the beginning of this sentence, a phrase taken from the LXX of Jer 52:6. Of all the textual witnesses to 2 Kgs 25:2, however, only the Syriac mentions a month number, and it is the fifth month, not the fourth. This is likely to be an addition of the Peshitta to 2 Kgs 25:2,

> famine seized the city and there was no food for the people of the land. Then the city was breached, and all the warriors [went out?][3] at night by way of the gate between the two walls which were around the king's garden (for the Chaldeans were all around the city) and they went toward the Arabah. The army of the Chaldeans pursued after the king and overtook him, and they seized the king and they brought him up to the king of Babylon at Riblah, and they passed judgment on him. They slaughtered the sons of Zedekiah before his eyes, and the eyes of Zedekiah he blinded, and he bound him in bronze fetters and brought him to Babylon. And on the fifth month on the seventh of the month, which was the nineteenth year of King Nebuchadnezzar the king of Babylon, Nebuzaradan the chief of the bodyguard, the servant of the king of Babylon, came to Jerusalem, and he burned the house of YHWH and the house of the king and all the houses of Jerusalem; every house of the great[4] he burned with fire. And all the army of the Chaldeans who were with the chief of the bodyguard pulled down the walls around Jerusalem. And Nebuzaradan the chief of the bodyguard exiled the rest of the people who were left in the city and the ones who had deserted to the king of Babylon and the rest of the multitude.[5]

since the Syriac also reads "fifth month" in Jer 39:2 and 52:6 (see Dominique Barthélemy, *Critique textuelle de l'Ancien Testament: 1. Josué, Juges, Ruth, Samuel, Rois, Chroniques, Esdras, Néhémie, Esther* [OBO 50/1; Göttingen: Vandenhoeck & Ruprecht, 1982], 423). We could read the lack of a month number as indicating that the ninth day is in the first month of Zedekiah's eleventh year (so, e.g., Marvin A. Sweeney, *I & II Kings: A Commentary* [OTL; Louisville: Westminster John Knox, 2007], 466). So while we would expect a month number here, the best textual evidence argues for its omission. Given that the Babylonians destroy the city in the fifth month (25:8), however, it may be that the siege ended shortly before that in the fourth month when the inhabitants finally ran out of provisions. After conquering the city, the Babylonians would have needed time to exile the population and collect the spoil before destroying it. See also Oded Lipschits, *The Fall and Rise of Jerusalem: Judah under Babylonian Rule* (Winona Lake, Ind.: Eisenbrauns, 2005), 80.

3. Most MT witnesses have no verb here in 2 Kgs 25:4, and this lack is clearly the most difficult reading. Jer 52:7 and 39:4 have each included verbs to gloss this difficulty (so Barthélemy, *Critique textuelle*, 423–24), as have some MT and LXX manuscripts here in 2 Kings. Some verb is clearly necessary here, however, and I have supplied יצא, along with some of the ancient witnesses; others add the verb ברח "to flee."

4. Reading בית here in the construct with the MT, Peshitta, Targum Jonathan, and Jer 52:13.

5. 2 Kgs 25:11 reads ההמון "the multitude," but Jer 52:15 reads האמון "the master workers, artisans." Jer 52:28–30 gives a different picture of the exile from 2 Kings, however, claiming that in 597, 587, and 582 combined only 4,600 Judeans in total were taken to Babylon. We find a distinctly different portrayal in 2 Kgs 24–25, and 24:13–16 presents a great number of exiles just for those taken to Babylon in 597. Moreover, 24:14, 16 has already referred to the artisans as החרש והמסגר.

This book will argue that, despite only a brief recounting of these traumatic events at the end of the History, the siege, famine, mass death, and forced migration in 2 Kgs 25 are not "marginal" in any way in Dtr, but rather that they should stand at the center of our interpretation of the work, albeit in two radically different ways. First, as an exilic work, the whole point of the History's narrative is to explain the horror of 586 B.C.E. by placing the siege, famine, mass death, destruction of Jerusalem, and forced migration to Babylon within an ethical framework that attempts to make sense of this trauma that the exilic readers have undergone. In what I will call the master narrative of Dtr, this suffering that the exiles endured and continue to endure in captivity is not without reason—indeed, from the standpoint of the master narrative, no suffering of Israel is—and can lead exilic readers, once they understand the logic in history that the master narrative advances, to a clearer understanding of truth, at least as the narrative portrays it. This, then, is the first of the two important ways that the trauma of 586 is central to an interpretation of Dtr, and the first stage of my argument, presented in the chapters that follow, will be directed at articulating the narrative's logic in history that explains this trauma. Making sense of these events, not to mention of the forced migration from Jerusalem and Judah in 597, the narrative presents Israel's suffering as a violent gift that leads readers to the truth of history.

I have borrowed the phrase "violent gift" from Aeschylus's *Agamemnon*, a play in which, as its eponymous character returns to Greece from his victory over Troy, the chorus speculates on the meaning of the history of suffering that the Greeks have endured during the war. If the historical realm is controlled by the gods, they conclude, then Zeus must intend a larger purpose to such horror:

> He leads mortals to understand
> that knowledge comes through suffering—
> he has established this as law.
> But in sleep drops into the heart
> the memory of pain;
> wisdom comes unwillingly.
> It is a violent gift (χάρις βίαιος), I suppose,
> from the gods on the awesome rowing bench. (*Agamemnon* 176–83)

From the standpoint of the master narrative of the Deuteronomistic History as well, the trauma endured by the survivors in exile has a larger purpose, and those who can see the logic that led to it have won, through great suffering, the truth that explains and controls Israel's fate. The insight that those who survived the forced migration to Babylon can glean from Dtr's narrative about the workings of history is their violent gift that can explain even the horrific suffering of the siege of Jerusalem and their removal from the land.

I mentioned above that the trauma of 586 is pivotal to our understanding of the History in two very different but important ways, and the second and more central stage of my argument in this book points out that we find interruptions of this master narrative's explanation of the logic that governs history, interruptions that subvert its explanatory logic that attempts to encapsulate the trauma of 586. Later in this chapter, I will argue that the History is an exilic work, and that if the author him or herself was not a survivor of the siege, famine, and forced migration, and a witness of the mass death that accompanied these events, then he or she was a member of a family within the exilic community forged by the massive psychic trauma that resulted from this horror. The nature of such trauma, and precisely how this affects the literary work of trauma survivors and their descendants, is the subject of Chapter 2. To briefly anticipate this later discussion, I will argue that while some survivors of massive trauma are able to articulate the events that caused the trauma, they are not able to do so by means of memory. Trauma can recur or intrude into the lives of those who suffer from it, but these recurrences are not the same thing as memories that form part of the autobiographical self. Such intrusions are not subject to conscious recall but recur in a manner dissociated from the self, unintegrated by the ego and its web of normal memories that it uses to make sense of the world. Trauma exists in the psychic lives of survivors and their descendants as something separate from the self and not controllable by it. When survivors of massive psychic trauma and even their descendants write of the events that caused the trauma, they find them impossible to articulate within the psychic worldviews that they use to explain their lives to themselves. Trauma is thus absent to the self, but powerfully, although uncontrollably, present in the way that it can impact the psyche and the literary works that survivors and their descendants produce. It is an autobiographical absence that cannot be captured or controlled in psychological or literary narrative.

I do not intend as part of this work to provide any kind of psychological profile of the author of the Deuteronomistic History; I will argue that he or she lived within the community of exiles in Babylon, and thus within a community shaped by massive psychic trauma, but this is an historical rather than a psychological argument. I am not arguing that the author suffered from Posttraumatic Stress Disorder or any other kind of trauma-related mental disorder. My examination of the History is based instead in what literary criticism refers to as trauma theory, and is a literary rather than a psychological investigation of the work. The second stage of my argument, the thesis of this work, builds upon the observations concerning the master narrative's explanation of history, and demonstrates that trauma interrupts and subverts this narrative, disputing its claim that the exilic community's trauma can be explained within a particular or any narrative, placed within a particular or any worldview. We find traumatic interruptions of the narrative when important concepts that the narrative uses and assumes to make its explanatory case—the way it portrays God, for example, or the way it portrays justice, Israel, punishment, and so on—are subverted. Trauma brings the language and concepts of Dtr's master narrative into question, renders them ambiguous, and even contradicts them, and so subverts the logic in history that the master narrative uses to explain the trauma that the exilic community has suffered. Trauma makes it impossible for the master narrative to present an air-tight, totalizing case that explains why the author's family and community, and potentially the author him or herself, have suffered in the way they have. Trauma puts the language and ethical worldview that the narrative uses to make sense of 586 on trial but renders no verdict. It is present as gaps or absences in this narrative, as it is within the psychological narratives (that is to say, within individuals' understandings of their selves) or literary narratives of survivors of massive psychic trauma and in the narratives of their descendants. Its intrusions into the narrative question, for example, the narrative's claim that God observes Israel's actions in history and then punishes and rewards them accordingly; they suggest instead that all of the nation's generations have been subject to punishment, regardless of their actions, and that such punishment cannot be clearly explained as the just reward for Israel's sin. Such traumatic absences and repetitions do not accept the language of ethical logic in which the master narrative tries to frame the trauma of the exiles, although these eruptions of trauma into the narrative offer no explanation of their own. It seems more to the point to write not of a traumatic narrative that offers a competing explanation of the logic in history that it subverts, but rather of a traumatic non- or anti-narrative that offers no logical explanation at all. Trauma does not see the mass death, suffering, and forced migration witnessed and experienced by the author, or at least by his or her family and community, as a "violent gift" that brings logical comprehension to history; trauma is in itself the violent "gift" that explodes into and radically challenges Dtr's master narrative's explanation of the exilic community's horrific experience, placing it in an endless trial with no conclusion. It is a violent gift only insofar as it does violence to the narrative's version of truth, fracturing it without offering any alternative totalizing explanation. So the second important way that trauma is pivotal to our understanding of the Deuteronomistic History is in its subversion of the History's narrative. The trauma of 586 is not "marginal" in the History—it is central to the master narrative's explanatory logic, and it is central to trauma's subversion of that logic.

As I mentioned above, I will discuss how trauma affects the literature of the survivors of massive psychic trauma and their descendants—what the field of literary criticism refers to as trauma theory—in Chapter 2. We will then be in a position not only to discuss the History's master narrative that attempts to provide a logical explanation of the trauma but also to show how trauma interrupts and subverts this narrative logic. The discussion of both the master narrative and the traumatic subversion of it will occupy Chapters 3 through 7, and each of these chapters will discuss one of the History's component books—Deuteronomy, Joshua, Judges, Samuel, and Kings[6]—beginning with a presentation of the master narrative in that book, followed by a discussion of the different ways that trauma interrupts and subverts that narrative, introducing gaps, ambiguity, and contradiction into the narrative's logic and linguistic concepts. The goal, in short, is to show how trauma is paradoxically present in the History as narrative absence.

Before I move to this discussion of trauma theory in Chapter 2, I will begin in section B below, as I have already mentioned, with a short defense of the unity and exilic date of the Deuteronomistic History, since I am arguing that the traumatic experience of the author, or at least of his or her family and community, explains the traces of the trauma that we find subverting the master narrative. The dating of the History deserves a book by itself, and if space here permits only a very short discussion of this topic, I at least find it necessary to provide the most basic reasons why it makes most sense to date the work to the exile, thus situating the composition of the History within a community of people who experienced massive psychic trauma. I am not arguing that the author him or herself survived the forced migration of 597 or the siege and forced migration of 586—although this is certainly within the realm of possibility—but I am arguing that he or she is at least the descendant of survivors and lived within a community shaped by this trauma. As we

6. By dividing my discussion up by the books of Dtr, I do not mean to imply that these books were original divisions. They were not, and the conquest narrative of Joshua, for example, really continues into Judg 1, just as the period of the judges continues into the account of Samuel and his sons in 1 Sam 1–7, and the career of David continues from 1 and 2 Samuel into 1 Kgs 1–2. Organizing my discussion by means of the books of Dtr as we currently find them is simply a matter of convenience.

will see in Chapter 2, trauma theory discovers the same kinds of traumatic absence in the literary works produced by second- and third-generation trauma survivors as in the writings by the survivors themselves.

B. *The Unity and Exilic Dating of Dtr*

1. *The Redactional School of Frank Cross*

Before we move to a discussion of trauma and its impact upon the narrative of Dtr, however, we need to survey at least briefly the reasons why it makes the most sense to see the History as a unified composition of the exilic period. Frank Cross's theory of a Josianic author (Dtr^1) and an exilic redactor (Dtr^2) of the Deuteronomistic History has the advantage of explaining the History's inclusion of both the eternal promise to David and the destruction of Jerusalem and final picture of the Davidide in exile, for he sees the eternal promise as a theme of the Josianic edition and the destruction and removal of the Davidide from power as the work of the redactor.[7] Cross proposes an original Deuteronomistic History, which he calls Dtr^1, written during the reign of King Josiah in support of and as propaganda for the religious reforms which the king began in the late seventh century. Cross identifies two major themes in Dtr^1: "the sin of Jeroboam," or the altars erected in the North following the split of the kingdom after Solomon's death that doom the North to destruction; and the unconditional covenant with the Davidides that promises this royal house an eternal kingship in Jerusalem. This Josianic author calls the North to submit to control of the Davidic monarchy and Judah to return to the covenant. In the exile, an editor (Dtr^2) retouched and reshaped the original version of the History in order to bring it up to date. The exilic additions blame the exile on the apostasy of Manasseh, Josiah's grandfather, and ignore the unconditional covenant with David.

Richard Nelson attempts to augment Cross's arguments for a double redaction, and argues that scholars must find "genuinely *contradictory* themes or tendencies" to establish redaction in the History.[8] He points to regnal formulae that differ before and after the account of Josiah;[9] to vocabulary and phraseology that he believes may be reliably used to

7. Frank Moore Cross, "The Theme of the Book of Kings and the Structure of the Deuteronomistic History," in *Canaanite Myth and Hebrew Epic: Essays in the History of the Religion of Israel* (Cambridge, Mass.: Harvard University Press, 1973), 274–89.

8. Richard D. Nelson, *The Double Redaction of the Deuteronomistic History* (JSOTSup 18; Sheffield: JSOT, 1981), 21–22 (my emphasis).

9. Ibid., 29–42.

distinguish Dtr[1] and Dtr[2]; to the movement between unconditional and conditional dynastic promises to the Davidides, the former indicating pre-exilic composition; and to a movement between theological optimism from the pre-exilic author to a "fatally flawed" view of Israel's history from the exilic editor.[10] None of these things are actually contradictory, however, and this may be part of the reason why, in a later article on the double redaction of Dtr, Nelson refers to "thematic dissonance" rather than contradictions as the basis for this redactional model.[11]

Richard Friedman supports Cross's position by arguing not only that Josiah is the "literary focus of the work,"[12] but that the characters of Josiah and Moses form an *inclusio* that points to the Josianic origin of the History. Moses smashes the golden calf "thin as dust" (Deut 9:1), the same wording that is used for Josiah's actions in regard to Jeroboam's altar (2 Kgs 23:15) and the Asherah in the temple (23:6). These are the only places in Dtr where this phrase is used. Moses says the law must be read every seven years "in the ears" of the people (Deut 31:11); 2 Kgs 23:2 says that Josiah reads the law "in their ears." While it may be questionable if Friedman has discovered enough overlap to point to an *inclusio* between the two figures, he certainly does produce additional evidence that points to Josiah as Israel's most highly regarded leader in Dtr.[13] Only Josiah in Dtr is said to act in regard to God with all his heart, soul, and mind, just as Moses commands Israel to love God in Deut 6:5 (2 Kgs 23:25); only Josiah out of all the kings carries out the instructions of Deut 12:2–4 to "smash" (נתץ) the Canaanite altars and "burn" (שׂרף) their idols (2 Kgs 23:4, 7, 12, 15). In Deut 31:26 "the writing of the law" is placed beside the ark, and we do not hear of it again until 2 Kgs 22:8.[14] The period covered by the History after the time of Josiah, argues

10. His argument on literary criticism is found in ibid., 43–98; his argument on the dynastic formulae on pp. 99–118; and the argument on theological differences on pp. 119–27. Quotation from p. 123.

11. Richard Nelson, "The Double Redaction of the Deuteronomistic History: The Case is Still Compelling," *JSOT* 29 (2005): 319–37.

12. Richard Elliott Friedman, *The Exile and Biblical Narrative: The Formation of the Deuteronomistic and Priestly Works* (HSM 22; Chico, Calif.: Scholars Press, 1981), 7. See also Hans-Detlef Hoffmann, *Reform und Reformen: Untersuchungen zu einen Grundthema der deuteronomistischen Geschichtsschreibung* (ATANT 66; Zurich: Theologischer Verlag, 1980), 312–13.

13. This, of course, does not mean that Josiah is the "literary focus of the work"; I would argue that it makes more sense to refer to the main themes of Dtr's narrative (I will introduce them fully in the next chapter) as the work's "focus" rather than a character whose life takes center stage in only two chapters.

14. Friedman, *The Exile*, 5–10.

Friedman, as well as some earlier passages, reflect the concerns of the exile, and so should be ascribed to Dtr^{2}. Other scholars who support Cross make further arguments for Josiah as the focus of the History. The bulk of Dtr, argues Nelson, is intensely interested in cultic reform, and so it is no surprise when this topic disappears after 2 Kgs 23, where Dtr^{1}'s narrative originally ended. The Deuteronomistic themes of the obedience to the law, centralization, and divine election of David and Jerusalem all culminate with Josiah. Josiah removes each of Manasseh's apostate cultic constructions, as well as those of Ahaz and the kings of Israel and Judah, and concludes Joash's repairs to the temple.[15] Gary Knoppers points out that while Dtr presents other kings as involved in cultic reform, heteropraxis (at least from a Deuteronomistic point of view) endures that Josiah must clear up, and so his status is enhanced.[16]

These arguments for redaction, however, often overlook a complexity of thought that can be ascribed to a single author. To begin with the idea of the supposed dissonance between the unconditional covenant with the Davidides, which Cross identified as one of the two main themes of Dtr^{1}, and the simultaneous presence of the loss of Davidide power because of the sins of Manasseh, even Nelson recognizes that there are difficulties with at least part of this argument. As he points out, all of the specifically conditional warnings come during the reign of Solomon (1 Kgs 2:4; 8:25; and 9:5). Solomon is threatened with the loss of the kingdom if he worships other gods, and his apostate actions result in the fulfillment of this warning. Each of these warnings refers to the "throne of Israel," which is a phrase found in Dtr only four other times, twice specifically in reference to the Northern Kingdom (2 Kgs 10:30; 15:12) and twice to the United Kingdom (1 Kgs 8:20; 10:9), but never in reference to Judah.[17] Solomon is punished for his apostasy, and his descendants do lose the throne of Israel, although they remain in power in Jerusalem, ruling only over the tribe of Judah, to which Dtr refers as their "fief."[18] And as Baruch Halpern points out, if Dtr^{1} truly did compose propaganda in support of Josiah's reforms, it would make far more sense for the author to say that Jerusalem and the Davidides could be threatened, thereby

15. Nelson, "The Double Redaction," 324–27.

16. Gary Knoppers, *Two Nations Under God: The Deuteronomistic History of Solomon and the Dual Monarchies* (2 vols.; HSM 52–53; Atlanta: Scholars Press, 1993–1994), 2:174.

17. Nelson, *Double Redaction*, 99–105.

18. For this translation of ניר see Ehud Ben Zvi, "Once the Lamp Has Been Kindled…: A Reconsideration of the MT *Nîr* in 1 Kgs 11:36; 15:4; 2 Kgs 8:19 and 2 Chr 21:17," *ABR* 39 (1991): 19–30.

providing a warning to those who might not support his reformation. Conditionality rather than unconditionality would make far more sense in such a scenario. Nor must we assume that conditionality of the covenant with David necessarily fits the period of the exile, since an exilic author could promote unconditionality as a way to support a Davidic restoration following the exile.[19] And Burke Long rightly argues that we should be cautious in putting too much weight on the inviolability of the unconditional covenant which God makes with David in 2 Sam 7, since in 1 Sam 2:30–36 God breaks an unconditional covenant which he had made earlier with the Elides.[20] There is no de facto contradiction between the unconditional covenant that God makes with David and the fate of the Davidides at the end of 2 Kings—after all, as Steven McKenzie points out, Athaliah is a non-Davidide who reigns in Jerusalem for seven years (2 Kgs 11:3–4), having removed the Davidides from the throne, but Dtr does not present this as a breach in the Davidic covenant[21]—and arguments that attempt to use this as a basis for redaction miss an important point regarding the way in which Dtr presents divine punishment. God can remove the Davidides from power, as during the time of Athaliah, in order to punish, and God can also make and break unconditional covenants, as the case of the Elides shows.

Or, to take another example of a theory of redaction that ignores theological complexity, for Cross and his followers the attribution of the exile to the sins of Manasseh, the grandfather of Josiah, is a creation of Dtr^2.[22] But, as Percy van Keulen argues, the message the narrative sends by blaming the exile on Manasseh is that even the king who enacts the most perfect repentance is unable to make up for this level of apostasy. "This message cannot have failed to have a great impact on an exilic audience: idolatry brings about irreversible disaster, so be not engaged in it."[23] Or the argument of Richard Friedman and others that Dtr^1 puts the blame of punishment on kings while Dtr^2 places the guilt for the exile on

19. Baruch Halpern, *The First Historians: The Hebrew Bible and History* (University Park, Pa.: Pennsylvania State University Press, 1988), 112–18.

20. Burke O. Long, *1 Kings with an Introduction to Historical Literature* (FOTL 9; Grand Rapids: Eerdmans, 1984), 16–17.

21. Steven L. McKenzie, "The Divided Kingdom in the Deuteronomistic History and in the Scholarship on It," in *The Future of the Deuteronomistic History* (ed. Thomas C. Römer; BETL 147; Leuven: Leuven University Press, 2000), 135–45 (139–43).

22. Cross, "The Themes of the Book of Kings," 285–86.

23. Percy S. F. van Keulen, *Manasseh Through the Eyes of the Deuteronomists: The Manasseh Account (2 Kings 21:1–18) and the Final Chapters of the Deuteronomistic History* (OTS 38; Leiden: Brill, 1996), 197.

the people[24] misses an important narrative point about leadership and apostasy within Israel, a matter that we will discuss in Chapter 2 as one of the main themes of the History's narrative, and in more detail in Chapter 7. The kings cause Israel to sin, and the narrative constantly uses the Hiphil of חטא to convey this idea, beginning with the condemnation of Jeroboam in 1 Kgs 14:16 and ending with the condemnation of Manasseh in 2 Kgs 21:10, 16. The people choose the monarchy in an attempt to be like the nations (1 Sam 8:5, 20), and as a result reject God as their king (8:7–8), for their human kings lead them in apostasy and cause them to commit the sin of the nations whom God wanted Israel to destroy. We shall see that, throughout Kings, God removes kings and dynasties for their sins and, eventually, the people for theirs, although it was the monarchy the people chose who caused them to sin.

Moreover, Gordon McConville argues that Cross is incorrect to maintain that Kings never suggests that there is no hope for the nation before the Manasseh narrative. (Cross's point is that Dtr[1], because it sees an unconditional covenant between God and the Davidides, maintains that God will not let Judah be destroyed.) McConville points out that Josiah's reforms appear in a well-established pattern of reform and apostasy. The earlier reforms do not ultimately produce positive results; Hezekiah, for example, is followed by Manasseh, and Asa by Joash and Ahaz.[25] Cross, in short, has missed an important ambiguity in the narrative's presentation of the Davidides in the earlier part of Kings, and by separating optimism toward and judgment of the Davidides and the South into different redactions, he has misread an important Deuteronomistic understanding of sin, the monarchy, and repentance. Apostasy, punishment, and salvation occur in a cycle throughout Dtr, and not merely in the book of Judges, as Knoppers, a member of the Cross school, points out.[26] Dtr's narrative makes the point that any royal house that causes the people to sin will be punished, and we have no reason to expect that the Davidides will be exempt from this dictum. The exile could simply be a temporary removal of the Davidides from power, as was the case during the time of Athaliah. After all, even in 2 Sam 7:14, God promises to punish the

24. E.g., Mordechai Cogan and Hayim Tadmor, *II Kings: A New Translation with Introduction and Commentary* (AB 11; New York: Doubleday, 1988), 206–7; Mark A. O'Brien, *The Deuteronomistic History Hypothesis: A Reassessment* (OBO 92; Göttingen: Vandenhoeck & Ruprecht, 1989), 227–34, 266–87; Antony F. Campbell and Mark A. O'Brien, *Unfolding the Deuteronomistic History: Origins, Upgrades, Present Text* (Minneapolis: Fortress, 2000), 19–20.

25. J. G. McConville, "Narrative and Meaning in the Book of Kings," *Bib* 70 (1989): 31–49 (44–46).

26. Knoppers, *Two Nations Under God*, 1:138–39, 166.

Davidides for sin, and does so as a result of Solomon's apostate high places in 1 Kgs 11–12. The question as to whether or not the narrative presents this punishment as permanent is a matter that we will take up in a later chapter.

Ultimately, to locate separate authors, or at least an author and redactor, on the bases that Cross and his followers propose is to misread complexity of thought within the narrative regarding the monarchs, people, apostasy, and divine punishment. The History's narrative presents complex ideas regarding the monarchy and Israel's leaders in general and their role in Israel's apostasy; about how much and what kind of sin will doom the people; and about the efficacy of reform and repentance following apostasy. These are all issues that we will explore in more detail beginning in the next chapter; my point here is simply that to mistake thematic complexity for thematic contradiction or dissonance can lead to the unnecessary creation of redactions that obscures the narrative's message.

2. *The Redactional School of Rudolf Smend*

Rudolf Smend's seminal article on redaction within the Deuteronomistic History examines seams in texts in Joshua and Judges. He argues, for example, that there is a clear break between Josh 1:6 and 7. The first of these verses demands courage of Joshua because the coming battle with the Canaanites will succeed, while 1:7 exhorts him to courage in the context of adherence to the law and limits success in battle to obedience to the law. So "courage" in 1:7 really means to make every effort to obey the law, while in 1:6 it means courage in battle. Joshua 1:8–9 continues the sense of 1:7, and so we can see 1:7–9 as the insertion of a redactor into a pre-existing history. Smend finds that the hand responsible for 1:7–9 also inserted 13:1bβ–6. He notes that 13:1a presents Joshua as old, just as 1:1 presents Moses as dead, and so draws readers back to 1:1. At the end of 13:6, God tells Joshua to allot the land to Israel as an inheritance, whereas in 13:7, Joshua is to divide the land as an inheritance. Smend believes that 13:6 seems to refer to Israel as a whole, whereas 13:7 specifies that the allotment is to be for the nine and a half tribes settling in the Cisjordan. All of this suggests, says Smend, that 13:1bβ–6 is an insertion into a text that originally moved from 13:1bα to 13:7.[27] Smend concludes that all of these passages were added by a redactor

27. Rudolf Smend, "The Law and the Nations: A Contribution to Deuteronomistic Tradition History," in *Reconsidering Israel and Judah: Recent Studies on the Deuteronomistic History* (ed. Gary N. Knoppers and J. Gordon McConville; SBTS 8; Winona Lake, Ind.: Eisenbrauns, 2000), 95–110 (96–102).

with a particular interest in the law, his DtrN, who sees the conquest of the land as dependent on obedience to the law. DtrN redacted DtrG (or DtrH, as Smend and his followers would later call the original edition of the history[28]), and Smend's article dates both the first version of the history and its redaction to the exile.

Walter Dietrich accepted and soon elaborated on Smend's proposal, and identifies four prophetic speeches in Kings that he concluded were all composed by the same author, and argued that some of them manifest additions from DtrN.[29] In Chapters 2 and 3 of *Prophetie und Geschichte*, he argues that the author of these prophetic passages was not DtrG, but a redactor who inserted the passages into pre-existing material. He refers to this newly identified redactor as DtrP, who must have redacted the History before DtrN, since the nomistic redactor has added material into passages from the prophetic editor. DtrG, DtrP, and DtrN are therefore all exilic compositions. DtrP develops DtrG's language and makes an explicit link between religious deterioration and political decline, something only implicit within the original version of the history.[30] Timo Veijola's examination of Samuel and Kings confirms Dietrich's analysis, and in his study of 1 Sam 20:12–17, 42b; 25; 2 Sam 21–24; and 1 Kgs 1–2 he finds all three of the hands Dietrich identified at work.[31] Veijola argues that DtrG is not anti-monarchical in its outlook as Martin Noth argues, but that DtrP is. DtrG, he claims, actually idealizes David and sees hope for a Davidic restoration, while DtrP portrays David as sinful, although willing to repent, and does not foresee a Davidic restoration. DtrN, finally, is critical of the monarchy, but signals a future for the Davidides so long as they keep the law.[32]

There has been little interaction on the part of the Smend school with the arguments of Cross and his followers, although the reverse is not

28. Smend's article uses the nomenclature of DtrG to refer to the first edition of the history; the change to DtrH appears to have been the suggestion of Walter Dietrich ("David in Überlieferung und Geschichte," *Verkündigung und Forschung* 22 [1977]: 44–48 [48 n. 11]).

29. Walter Dietrich, *Prophetie und Geschichte: Eine redaktionsgeschichtliche Untersuchung zum deuteronomistischen Geschichtswerk* (FRLANT 108; Göttingen: Vandenhoeck & Ruprecht, 1972), 28–31.

30. Ibid., 107–10.

31. Timo Veijola, *Die ewige Dynastie: David und die Entstehung seiner Dynastie nach der deuteronomistischen Darstellung* (AASF B/193; Helsinki: Suomalainen Tiedakatemia, 1975).

32. Ibid., 127–42; idem, *Das Königtum in der Beurteilung der Deuteronomistischen Historiographie: Eine redaktionsgeschichtliche Untersuchung* (AASF B/198; Helsinki: Suomalainen Tiedakatemia, 1977), 115–22.

true. Nelson's point about "genuinely contradictory themes" as the criterion for advancing arguments about redaction was actually a criticism of the Smend school,[33] and his point is a useful one in regards to this critique. Have Smend et alii discovered redactional hands or have they, like Cross et alii, mistaken complexity of thought for editing? Both Nelson and Thomas Römer point out that it seems odd to posit a nomistic redactor when obedience to the law is so clearly one of the main interests throughout the History, beginning most obviously in Deuteronomy, which contains a lawcode.[34] And Gary Knoppers argues that it is simply not clear according to this school how one chooses whether a passage belongs primarily to DtrH, because it is about history, or to DtrP because it is about prophecy, or to DtrN, because it is about law. The three themes are so tightly interwoven throughout the work that it is not clear at many places to which hand a given passage should be attributed. So in 2 Sam 7, for example, a prophetic oracle is central to the delivery of God's eternal covenant, and yet the school sees DtrP as anti-monarchical.[35]

If prophecy, history, and law are closely intertwined throughout the History, then the school must be able to show by means of the kinds of literary work Smend originally carried out that there is reason to assume literary seams demonstrating redaction. Smend, however, is not able to prove this conclusively. His attempt to find a seam between Josh 1:6 and 7 only works if one believes that a single author could not urge the same character to be strong and courageous in regard both to battle and keeping the law, and this is clearly within the realm of possibility. Moreover, 1:6 never actually specifies in what way in particular Joshua is to be strong and courageous. We could assume that the author refers to battle here, but it makes more sense to read 1:6 as interpreted by 1:7: if Joshua is strong and courageous and keeps the law, then he will cause Israel to inherit the land through battle, just as God promises in 1:6. This, after all, has been a constant refrain of Deuteronomy. Or in the case of Josh 13:1–7, there simply is no indication in the text that God speaks about all of Israel between 13:1bβ–6 in contrast to an explicit mention of the nine and a half Cisjordanian tribes in 13:7. Smend's claim that God twice commands Joshua to distribute the land in 13:6 and 7 ignores the fact that there is a difference between allotting in 13:6, where the verb

33. Nelson, *Double Redaction*, 21–22.

34. Ibid., 21; Thomas C. Römer, "The Book of Deuteronomy," in *The History of Israel's Traditions: The Heritage of Martin Noth* (ed. Steven L. McKenzie and M. Patrick Graham; JSOTSup 182; Sheffield: Sheffield Academic, 1994), 178–212 (186).

35. Knoppers, *Two Nations Under God*, 1:39.

נפל in the Hiphil refers to casting lots in order to reveal the divine will,[36] and the following task of dividing the land between the tribes, which Joshua will do once God's will is known in the matter. By postulating a redactor at these points, Smend misses, first, the intense insistence that the law must be followed for God to give and preserve the land for Israel. It is not courage in battle that Israel must exhibit to win the land in Joshua, it is obedience to divine command. He misses, second, the detail that the narrative presents when it comes to the presentation of the land to Israel. Joshua does not merely divide the land among the tribes according to his personal whim, he follows the instructions God gives, revealed through the casting of lots.

The same kinds of critique have been applied to Dietrich's attempt to identify a separate redactor in DtrP. Dietrich identifies only five phrases and expressions that DtrP uses differently than DtrG, van Keulen points out, while Erik Eynikel demonstrates the great overlap in vocabulary between DtrG and Dietrich's DtrP. The evidence for DtrP as a separate hand from DtrG is so scanty that one could argue just as easily that DtrG is responsible for the passages that Dietrich examines.[37] Dietrich himself actually admits that the language of DtrG and DtrP is too similar to distinguish with accuracy.[38] So Mark O'Brien rightly argues that we should be cautious in accepting Timo Veijola's applications of Dietrich's findings to Samuel and Judges, since we really have little basis for accepting their arguments for redactional hands.[39] Others who have adopted and expanded the analysis of this school have not made a better case for it—in fact, one of the tendencies of this school has been to multiply hands involved in the text, so that DtrN, for example, becomes a whole circle of redactional hands. It is this very redactional complexity, comments Iain Provan, that "prompts one to ask whether there is not something seriously wrong with the basic assumptions which lie behind it."[40] His comment is astute, for we have seen that the assumptions that lie behind it, beginning

36. This can be clearly seen by the use of נפל in the Hiphil in passages such as 1 Sam 14:42; Jon 1:7; Neh 10:35 [ET 34]; 11:1; 1 Chr 24:31; 25:8; 26:13–14.

37. Van Keulen, *Manasseh Through the Eyes of the Deuteronomists*, 21; Erik Eynikel, *The Reform of King Josiah and the Composition of the Deuteronomistic History* (OTS 33; Leiden: Brill, 1996), 27; cf. Dietrich's *Prophetie und Geschichte*, 88–95.

38. Dietrich, *Prophetie und Geschichte*, 110.

39. O'Brien, *The Deuteronomistic History Hypothesis*, 9. See Veijola, *Die ewige Dynastie* and *Das Königtum*.

40. Iain W. Provan, *Hezekiah and the Books of Kings: A Contribution to the Debate About the Composition of the Deuteronomistic History* (BZAW 172; Berlin: de Gruyter, 1988), 26.

with Smend's analysis, are such that redactional hands are created by eliminating the detail and complexity of thought wholly compatible within a narrative by a single author.

3. *Arguments for Multiple Pre-exilic Redactions*
Helga Weippert claims that the evaluations of the various monarchs in Kings demonstrate that there were two pre-exilic editions of Dtr (her RI from the time of Hezekiah and her Josianic RII), as well as a final exilic redaction (RIII).[41] Enzo Cortese has supplied the most frequently cited critique of Weippert's work.[42] He points out that her attempt to differentiate between the evaluation formulas for the Southern kings in her RI and RII fails in part because the distinction between the two is very small, and both formulas have language in common. Part of her attempt to distinguish between these two formulas is by arguing that RII compares the Southern kings to David while RI does not, but Cortese points out that only Asa, Hezekiah, and Josiah from her RII are compared to David, and that these three are the only ones within that swath of narrative to undertake cultic reforms. So these references to David are not evidence for redaction, they are indications of the narrative's theological interests. There is an even smaller difference in the language of the evaluations of the Northern kings in RI and RII, Cortese shows, and the differences in the evaluations of the Northern kings in RII are often greater than the differences between the evaluations in RI and RII.[43] And while Weippert isolates the verb כעס "to vex" as a distinctive component of the judgments of the Northern kings in RII, Cortese points out that this is used only of Omri, Ahab, and Ahaziah, three kings who follow foreign worship practices and increase apostasy. It is certainly not used for Joram and Jehu, who also fall within Weippert's RII, and who enact partial reforms. And Marvin Sweeney has shown that Weippert's attempt to see a distinctive judgment formula for the last four kings of Judah (those who fall in her RIII) ignores the similarities between those formulas and those of Manasseh and Amon. We can read Dtr's narrative at this point as trying to show readers that the "fathers" whose evil those last kings

41. Helga Weippert, "Die 'deuteronomistischen' Beurteilungen der Könige von Israel und Juda und das Problem der Redaktion der Königsbücher," *Bib* 53 (1972): 301–39.

42. Enzo Cortese, "Lo schema deuteronomistico per i re di Giuda e d'Israele," *Bib* 56 (1975): 37–52.

43. Provan makes the same critique of Weippert, arguing that she is in general too selective in her use of vocabulary from the different judgment formulas, with the result that some of the formulas that she assigns to the same redactor end up sounding very different (*Hezekiah in the Books of Kings*, 50–53).

imitate are the two kings who practice the same advanced apostasy as these kings.[44] Weippert, in short, has ignored theological messages from the narrative, misreading a complexity of Deuteronomistic judgment of royal actions as evidence for redaction.

Halpern and David Vanderhooft also make an argument for Hezekian, Josianic, and exilic editions of Dtr, an argument based on burial and ascension rather than evaluation formulae. Yet while they argue that Weippert's attempts to locate changes in redactors based on evaluation formulas depend on a mere "shift in diction,"[45] the same objection could also be applied to their own approach. Nadav Na'aman argues persuasively that when we find the kind of minor differences to which they point it is simpler to appeal to varieties in source material.[46] The authors—Dtr_1 and Dtr_2 for Na'aman—wrote so soon after some of the events described in Kings that they were not always dependent upon written sources, and so could supply details of the king mothers from Amon to Zedekiah, a change that Halpern and Vanderhooft attribute to the proclivities of different redactors. To write about earlier kings, the author depended upon written sources, and was not able to find all of the same information for each king. This is true as well for the death and burial formulas, since the narrative uses a stock phrase for the burial of kings before the time of Hezekiah. After his reign, Na'aman argues, the burial of the kings was transferred to the garden of Uzza, and this explains the shift in formula after Hezekiah's time, and so we need not point to a Hezekian redaction of the History.[47]

Iain Provan is another scholar who has pointed to Hezekiah as a high point in the History, and while he cannot truly be classified as a scholar who sees multiple pre-exilic editions of Dtr, his work does point to an important strength of scholars in this camp. Focusing on the judgment formulas in Kings, he finds that the ones applied to monarchs before Hezekiah center on the theme of high places, and that this theme reaches its apex in the narration of Hezekiah's reign. Dtr views the במות in the South up to the time of Hezekiah as Yahwistic, he writes, whereas those in the narrative after Hezekiah's time are always idolatrous.[48] Yet this

44. Marvin A. Sweeney, *King Josiah of Judah: The Lost Messiah of Israel* (Oxford: Oxford University Press, 2001), 35–36.

45. Baruch S. Halpern and David S. Vanderhooft, "The Editions of Kings in the 7th–6th Centuries B.C.E.," *HUCA* (1991): 179–244 (203).

46. Nadav Na'aman, "Death Formulae and the Burial Places of the Kings of the House of David," *Bib* 85 (2004): 245–54.

47. And Dtr provides Hezekiah with no burial formula, argues Na'aman, in order not to detract from the high regard in which the History portrays him (ibid., 252).

48. Provan, *Hezekiah in the Books of Kings*, 57–90.

first edition of the History was not written during Hezekiah's reign but during that of Josiah, argues Provan; we see a sharp difference in the way the narrative treats the themes of high places and the conditionality of covenant after the reign of Hezekiah, but not after the reign of Josiah. The portrayal of the unconditional covenant climaxes during Hezekiah's reign, not Josiah's, as do the comparisons of the king to David. Provan accepts that the first edition of the History was composed during Josiah's reign to support that king's reforms, but argues that it does so by holding Hezekiah up as the ideal for Josiah to imitate. An exilic redactor later brought the History up to date by narrating the period after Hezekiah's time and blaming the exile on Manasseh.[49]

Provan's analysis points to the clear affinities this camp has with the Cross school. Halpern and Vanderhooft specifically state that their work "harmonizes" that of Weippert and Cross,[50] and Weippert herself argues that her RII and RIII may be aligned respectively with Cross's Dtr^1 and Dtr^2.[51] One could also point to Sweeney's work, which largely falls within the Cross school, but which also makes tentative arguments supporting a Hezekian redaction as well as a Josianic one, while arguing that an entire Hezekian redaction cannot be fully reconstructed.[52] The scholars whose work we have just surveyed, however, point to changes in formulaic diction rather than in theme and theology in order to find a surer basis for redactional work within the History, although they have not succeeded, at times because, like the Cross and Smend schools, they misconstrue complexity of thought for evidence of redaction, and at times because they have ignored easier ways to explain the shifts in diction on which they rely for evidence.

Scholarship has largely rejected the center of Provan's argument for an edition of Dtr that originally culminates in Hezekiah's reign—the treatment of the במות theme—since it is simply not patent that the high places are uniformly portrayed as Yahwistic through the Hezekiah narrative and uniformly portrayed as foreign in the following section. The high places in 2 Kgs 23:8–9, in fact, are clearly Yahwistic shrines.[53] Provan's point, contra Cross, that the theme of the unconditional covenant with David culminates in the narrative of Hezekiah rather than that of Josiah is

49. Ibid., 99–113, 120–31, 171–73.

50. Halpern and Vanderhooft, "The Editions of Kings," 182.

51. Helga Weippert, "Das deuteronomistische Geschichtswerk: Sein Ziel und Ende in der neueren Forschung," *Theologische Revue* 50 (1985): 213–49.

52. Sweeney, *King Josiah of Judah*, 74–76, 177.

53. So, e.g., Knoppers, *Two Nations Under God*, 1:43; McKenzie, *The Trouble with Kings*, 121; van Keulen, *Manasseh Through the Eyes of the Deuteronomists*, 44.

an important corrective to the view of the Cross school. But like Cross's argument, this observation about the theme of unconditionality leads him to misread complexity of thought for evidence of redaction. Sweeney argues that while Dtr's narrative approves of Hezekiah's reforms, it compares him to David, but compares Josiah to Moses and Joshua. The point is to present Josiah as more than a perfect king, but as a perfect leader who avoids the flaws of even David.[54] Josiah's reforms surpass those of Hezekiah, Sweeney argues, because Josiah not only dismantles Solomon's high places, he destroys Jeroboam's altars as well, thereby healing the rift within the kingdom Solomon had originally caused.[55] Thus, the incomparability formula that Dtr presents for Hezekiah makes him incomparable in regard to his trust in God for protection of Jerusalem—and in fact, much of the Hezekiah narrative centers on the Assyrian siege of the city—while Josiah's incomparability formula in 23:25 presents him as incomparable in actions much more important in Dtr's narrative: cultic loyalty.[56]

4. *The Existence of the Deuteronomistic History*

In summary, then, we have seen that theories of redaction have a tendency to ignore theological complexity that can be attributable to a single author. Our survey of the attempts to find redactions in the History have ultimately led us to a conclusion that parallels Burke Long's observation that such attempts are based on very narrow variations in language and style that can replace theological nuance with invented redactors.[57] Both Long and Robert Wilson have further pointed out that the kinds of arguments that scholars have advanced for redactions do not remotely resemble the kinds of alterations to texts that we actually find from the ancient Near East, where it is impossible to detect the work of an editor unless one has two different editions of a work, one from before the editorial work and one after, to compare.[58]

54. As I will discuss in more detail in Chapter 7, it is Josiah's reform that Dtr's narrative presents as perfect, not his entire reign, since for the first 17 years of it he tolerates Manasseh's apostasy. And as we shall see in Chapters 3 and 4, Dtr's narrative does not present Moses and Joshua as perfect leaders either.

55. Sweeney, *King Josiah of Judah*, 31–32, 38–39.

56. Gary N. Knoppers, "'There Was None Like Him': Incomparability in the Book of Kings," *CBQ* 54 (1992): 411–31.

57. Long, *1 Kings*, 15–16.

58. Ibid., 18–19; Robert R. Wilson, "Unity and Diversity in the Book of Kings," in *"A Wise and Discerning Mind": Essays in Honor of Burke O. Long* (ed. Saul M. Olyan and Robert C. Culley; BJS 325; Providence: Brown Judaic Studies, 2000), 293–310 (302–3).

For some scholars, however, there is no Deuteronomistic History to talk about. For example, K. L. Noll argues that the Deuteronomistic language to which scholars point as evidence for the unity of the five books is simply the result of late glossing, and that there is no overarching narrative throughout them.[59] Nor, argues Richard Coggins, is there a distinctive Deuteronomistic language or ideology, for what we find in these five books is simply the general religious thought of ancient Israel.[60] Ernst Axel Knauf's argument moves in a similar direction, and although he writes that the term "Deuteronomistic" does refer to a literary style and a group of theological notions, he claims that there is such a "vast multiplicity" of these that they cannot tell us anything about authorship.[61] To put his argument another way, there is, as Hartmut Rösel argues, no unifying *leitmotif* that we can find within the specifically Deuteronomistic passages of the five books.[62]

One of the key arguments for the existence of a Deuteronomistic History as it is normally conceived, however, is the simple point that each book picks up at precisely the point in history where the previous one has left off. Deuteronomy ends with Moses' death, and that is where the book of Joshua begins. Joshua ends with the death of Joshua and the division of the land, although not with the complete extermination and dispossession of the Canaanites, as we shall see, and that is the situation with which Judges opens. First Samuel 1 begins at Shiloh, the place where Judg 21 ended in Israel's moral failure near the end of the period of the judges, and the opening chapters of 1 Samuel transition from the judges to the monarchy, a transition for which the final stories of Judges prepare readers (Judg 17:6; 18:1; 19:1; 21:25). As Serge Frolov points out, the cycle of apostasy that begins in Judg 13 does not end until 1 Sam 7 when Samuel defeats the Philistines who first attack in Judg 13, while Judg 1:1–2:6 is more closely linked to the subject of conquest that

59. K. L. Noll, "Deuteronomistic History or Deuteronomic Debate? (A Thought Experiment)," *SJOT* 31 (2007): 311–45 (esp. 323–25, 344).

60. Richard Coggins, "What Does 'Deuteronomistic' Mean?," in *Those Elusive Deuteronomists: The Phenomenon of Pan-Deuteronomism* (ed. Linda S. Schearing and Steven L. McKenzie; JSOTSup 268; Sheffield: Sheffield Academic, 1999), 22–35.

61. Ernst Axel Knauf, "Does 'Deuteronomistic Historiography' (DtrH) Exist?," in de Pury, Römer, and Macchi, eds., *Israel Constructs Its History*, 388–98 (389).

62. Hartmut N. Rösel, "Does a Comprehensive 'Leitmotif' Exist in the Deuteronomistic History?," in Römer, ed., *The Future of the Deuteronomistic History*, 195–211.

dominates the book of Joshua.[63] And 1 Kings begins with the end of David's reign, continuing the story of David's kingship which began in Samuel, as David instructs his heir in 1 Kgs 2:5–9 to deal with characters from the narrative of 2 Samuel. So the idea that each of these books was originally written and (largely) redacted independently of the others, even while each book after Deuteronomy picks up at precisely the point in history where the previous one left off, would appear to be so coincidental as to stretch credulity.

One could, of course, argue that this argument actually holds true for all of the books from Genesis through Kings and that they were all put together by the same editor. Reinhard Kratz, for example, claims that Deuteronomistic editing is a late phenomenon that began first in Samuel and Kings and appeared only later in Joshua and Judges, and combined the history of Israel in the Hexateuch with the history of Israel in the period of the monarchy.[64] And like Kratz, Konrad Schmidt sees Exodus as the real beginning of the history that ends in 2 Kings, since the History seems to see Israel's genesis in the exodus event.[65] Thomas Römer, however, rightly argues that the recapitulation of Tetrateuchal material in Deut 1–3 speaks against an earlier beginning to this historical narrative. This kind of repetition would be useless and unnecessary if an author or redactor were compiling a history that began with Exodus, Leviticus, and Numbers.[66] He argues as well that the book of Deuteronomy is tightly connected to what follows, and that we can in fact see a unity of thought and ideology that each book picks up at the point that the previous one leaves off.

Knoppers points generally to other similar characteristics of the books that provide evidence for their unity, such as prophecy and fulfillment; the division of history into periods; links between Deuteronomy and the

63. Serge Frolov, "Rethinking Judges," *CBQ* 71 (2009): 24–41. Marc Brettler has argued that there is so much literary and thematic overlap between Judg 1:1–2:10 and Joshua that it originally functioned as an appendix to Joshua ("Jud 1,1–2,10: From Appendix to Prologue," *ZAW* 101 [1989]: 433–35).

64. Richard G. Kratz, *The Composition of the Narrative Books of the Old Testament* (trans. John Bowden; London: T&T Clark, 2005), 153–215.

65. Konrad Schmidt, *Erzväter und Exodus: Untersuchungen zur doppelten Begründung der Ursprünge Israels innerhalb der Geschichtsbücher des Alten Testaments* (WMANT 81; Neukirchen–Vluyn: Neukirchener Verlag, 1999), 162–65.

66. Thomas C. Römer, "The Form-Critical Problem of the So-Called Deuteronomistic History," in *The Changing Face of Form Criticism for the Twenty-First Century* (ed. Marvin A. Sweeney and Ehud Ben Zvi; Grand Rapids: Eerdmans, 2003), 240–52 (246–47).

later books; allusions to the Davidic promise; and the Deuteronomistically worded speeches.[67] To this we could add the evidence of a number of stories that begin in one book and end in another: Moses' command to inscribe and read the law, given in Deut 27 and fulfilled in Josh 8; the story of the division of the land among the tribes in Josh 13–21 with notices that not all of the Canaanites were annihilated, and the attempts of the tribes to take fully the territories promised to them in this division in Judg 1; Israel's claim to want a king in order to be like the nations in 1 Sam 8, and the ironic way in which the kings cause Israel to be like the nations through their leadership in apostasy, explicitly stated in 2 Kgs 17 and 21; God's promise to remove the Elides from the priesthood in 1 Sam 2–3, finally fulfilled with the banishment of Abiathar in 1 Kgs 2; David's cursing of Joab in 2 Sam 3, also fulfilled in 1 Kgs 2 with his execution; and David's crafty misrepresentation to Solomon in 1 Kgs 2:8–9 of his promise to Shimei in 2 Sam 19:18b–23 that ends with Shimei's death as well.

Moreover, and perhaps most importantly, a unity of theme and material does exist for the books of Deuteronomy through Kings. Römer locates a *leitmotif* for this material, and one that distinguishes it from the preceding material of the Tetrateuch. The term "other gods" (אלהים אחרים) is a standard phrase in each of the books of the History, but elsewhere is found only in Chronicles, the deuteronomistic sections of Jeremiah, Hos 3:1, and twice in Exodus. The exile is also a motif of Dtr, and, except for Lev 26:27–33, there is no direct reference to it in the Tetrateuch. We find specific references to the exile as a threat or reality in Deut 4; 28; 30; Josh 23; Judg 18:30; 1 Sam 12; 1 Kgs 8; and 2 Kgs 17; 22–25.[68] To these two aspects of Dtr's *leitmotif* we can also add the specifically Deuteronomistic notion that intermarriage with foreigners will lead directly to apostasy, something enunciated in Deut 7:3–4; Josh 23:7; Judg 1:1–3:6; and 1 Kgs 11:1–13. There is no direct link between intermarriage with foreigners and apostasy in the Tetrateuch. In short, by isolating overlapping ideas that are prominent in Dtr but not in the Tetrateuch, we have in fact located a *leitmotif* to the History: intermarriage with Canaanites

67. Gary N. Knoppers, "Is There a Future for the Deuteronomistic History?," in Römer, ed., *The Future of the Deuteronomistic History*, 117–34 (132–33). See also his *Two Nations Under God*, 1:26–27 for a long list of the speeches in the History with Deuteronomistic wording.

68. Römer, "The Form-Critical Problem", 247–48, and idem, *The So-Called Deuteronomistic History: A Sociological, Historical and Literary Introduction* (London: T&T Clark, 2005), 40.

causes the worship of other gods, which results in exile. The combined aspects of this *leitmotif*, as we shall see in the following chapter, form aspects of one of the two main themes of the History's narrative.

The evidence of the biblical texts points most clearly to a break in sources between the books of Numbers and Deuteronomy. The summary of Deut 1–3, unique to the Pentateuch, is necessary because it marks the beginning of an originally independent work. The master narrative of the books of Deuteronomy through 2 Kings, which we shall examine in some detail in the first sections of Chapters 3–7, each of which focuses on one of the component books of Dtr, explains the history of Israel in the land in such a way as to emphasize to readers that the worship of other gods and cultic disloyalty to YHWH in general will lead to the loss of the land God has given to the nation. These connected Deuteronomistic motifs of intermarriage, apostasy, and exile are not as prominent throughout the book of Joshua, since we find there the story of the gift of the land, but it is central to the concluding two chapters of that book, warning Israel of the consequences of foreign worship once the giving of the land has largely been accomplished. The book of Judges provides many warnings like this, for the narrative of Judg 1–16 shows repeated examples of the nation losing control of the land, albeit not through exile, as punishment for their apostasy. These motifs predominate in Kings, where the narrative moves directly from the apostasy caused by the Northern kings to the exile of Israel in 2 Kgs 17, and then quickly to the exile of the South following the sins of Manasseh in 2 Kgs 21. The motif of the worship of foreign gods leading to the loss of the land plays the smallest role in Samuel, although the cycle of apostasy that began in Judg 13 continues into 1 Samuel and ends only when Samuel leads the people in right worship in 1 Sam 7, followed by the divine gift of victory over the Philistines.

The book of Samuel, however, manifests an important theme of Dtr's master narrative, which we shall also pursue in the following chapters, that of the failures of Israel's leadership that contribute to the people's cultic disloyalty to YHWH. In the narrative of Judg 3–1 Sam 8, the judges almost entirely fail to put an end to apostasy; the priests fail to lead right Yahwistic worship in 1 Sam 2–4; and finally the monarchy, which Israel chooses in 1 Samuel so that it can be "like the nations" (8:5, 20), fails because it makes Israel like the nations in their worship of other gods (2 Kgs 17:7–8, 11, 15; 21:2, 9, 11). Much of the narrative in Samuel after God's choice of David in 1 Sam 16 may seem superfluous to the master narrative's explanation of the exile by means of these themes, especially because the Succession Narrative of 2 Sam 9–20 and 1 Kgs 1–2 paints

David in such a poor light. This, however, does not mean that this document was a post-Deuteronomistic insertion,[69] for as Sweeney argues, portraying David in a poor light results in elevating Josiah by contrast as the one king who finally exhibits perfect loyalty to God in the narrative. And since David is not a perfect figure in Dtr's narrative, his flaws and successes prepare readers for his descendants in Kings, some of whom will act well and some of whom will not. The negative portrayal of Solomon at the end of the Succession Narrative prepares readers for his later cultic sins that Josiah must correct in order to heal the breach in the kingdom that it caused.[70] Samuel is a book about Israel's poor motivations for its choice in leadership and its decisive step toward the apostasy that will lead to exile in its choice of the monarchy, which from its beginning to its end largely acts poorly. So the book of Samuel as well is part of the central narrative focus on apostasy as the explanation for exile that we will articulate in more detail in following chapters.

As for the date of the composition of the Deuteronomistic History, it would seem easiest to place it, with Martin Noth, in the exilic period, sometime after the last event it narrates, which took place in 562 B.C.E. Even while the character of Moses prophesies a return from exile in Deut 30:1–10, the History includes no concrete details of post-exilic events, such as a return under the Persians or the rebuilding of the temple or the resettling of Yehud or the exclusion of the North from the post-exilic cult. So, like Rainer Albertz, I find attempts like those of Raymond Person to assign passages in the History to various parts of the post-exilic period unconvincing, simply because there are no clear allusions to any specific post-exilic event.[71]

Finally, in terms of intended audience, it makes most sense to see Dtr as a work composed for the exilic community rather than for the Judeans who remained in the land following 586, for the predictions of the nation's destruction in the narrative before 2 Kgs 25 tend to discuss the

69. For this argument, see John Van Seters, *In Search of History: Historiography in the Ancient World and the Origins of Biblical History* (New Haven: Yale University Press, 1983), 277–91. Van Seters argues that the portrayal here of the turmoil in the House of David, David's cowardice in regard to the Bathsheba and Uriah incident, and the concluding bloodbath at the hands of Solomon actually attack the Deuteronomistic ideal of a sure house for David.

70. Sweeney, *King Josiah of Judah*, 108–9.

71. Rainer Albertz, "Why a Reform Like Josiah's Must Have Happened," in *Good Kings and Bad Kings* (ed. Lester L. Grabbe; ESHM 7; LHBOTS 393; London: T&T Clark International, 2005), 27–46 (37–38). See also Raymond F. Person, Jr., *The Deuteronomic School: History, Social Setting, and Literature* (SBL Studies in Biblical Literature 2; Leiden: Brill, 2002).

exiles as if they made up the entirety of the nation. That is, there is no notion in passages like Deut 4:25–31; 28:64; 30:1–10; or 1 Kgs 8:46–51 that any people at all will remain in the land when the exile occurs. Dtr's narrative, in short, mainly portrays the exiles as the entirety of the remnant of Israel, and so we should see it as composed for them.

I realize that many scholars, particularly American ones, are committed to something like Cross's redactional theory, and the short space at my disposal to make an argument for unity of composition may have seemed insufficient to them. As we shall see in the following chapter, however, the literary manifestations of trauma in the works of second- and third-generation descendants of trauma survivors are just like those in the works of the survivors themselves. As a result, even if one wishes to argue that the bulk of Dtr was produced during the reign of Josiah, this would put the Josianic author only a few generations after the massive Assyrian devastation of Judah in 701, one that annihilated the nation and was arguably a more devastating invasion than the one that culminated with the destruction of Jerusalem in 587.[72] Even if the majority of the History had been written during the reign of Josiah, that is, its narrative would still be arguing that the traumatic disasters that Israel had suffered in its past and could again suffer in its future are explainable. And since the descendants of trauma survivors produce literature with the same characteristics of the survivors themselves, even dating most of the Deuteronomistic History to the reign of Josiah would lead us to expect a work in which trauma intrudes into and subverts the narrative's explanatory logic in the ways in which we will describe in the following chapters. Nonetheless, the complexity of narrative style and thought present within the Deuteronomistic History points to a work that was composed by a single author reliant to some degree on older sources that have been well integrated into the present work. Lacking good evidence to the contrary, we must also conclude that it was written in the exilic period.

72. For brief descriptions of Assyria's massive devastation of Judah in 701 see Ephraim Stern, *Archaeology of the Land of the Bible*. Vol. 2, *The Assyrian, Babylonian, and Persian Periods* (ABRL; New York: Doubleday, 2001), 7–10; and Amihay Mazar, *The Archaeology of the Land of the Bible, 10,000–586* B.C.E. (ABRL; New York: Doubleday, 1992), 438. For the devastating effects on Judah's population, see Nadav Na'aman, "Population Changes in Palestine Following Assyrian Deportations," *TA* 20 (1993): 104–24 and Israel Finkelstein, "The Archaeology of the Days of Manasseh," in *Scripture and Other Artifacts: Essays on the Bible and Archaeology* (ed. Michael D. Coogan, J. Cheryl Exum, and Lawrence E. Stager; Louisville, Ky.: Westminster John Knox, 1994), 169–87.

Chapter 2

TRAUMA THEORY AND ITS APPLICATION TO THE STUDY OF THE DEUTERONOMISTIC HISTORY

A. *The Study of Trauma in Mental Health Fields*

1. *Effects of Exposure to Trauma*

Before we continue with the discussion of the Deuteronomistic History, we must turn to the basic aspects of trauma theory, since this is going to prove essential to the reading of the History that will follow. The study of trauma has proven influential in a number of fields, and since our interest is applying trauma theory to a literary work, our main focus in the discussion of trauma in this chapter will be on its use within the study of literature. Much of what we will discover about the use of trauma studies within literary criticism will be made clearer by first examining the origins and effects of trauma in the human psyche, and so I open this chapter with a brief discussion of the developments within various mental health fields that led to the contemporary understanding of Post-traumatic Stress Disorder (PTSD). As we shall see, the notion most basic to the understanding of PTSD is that individuals who have suffered massive psychic trauma have developed a disorder that affects the manners in which they view reality and organize their lives. The trauma they have undergone becomes the organizing principle of their lives and yet, paradoxically, they themselves do not truly know this, and do not truly know the trauma itself. The trauma becomes the void center around which their lives grow, since this voidness is unknown to the subject. The argument that this book pursues here does not assume that the author of the Deuteronomistic History suffered from PTSD—although I believe this to be a possibility—but simply uses trauma theory as a tool of literary criticism that can help us make sense of the History. The opening section of this chapter is not an attempt to psychoanalyze the author, but to establish a groundwork to help us better understand the use of trauma theory in the field of literary criticism, something that I will examine in section B. In section C I will then be able to apply these conclusions to the Deuteronomistic History and show how we can use trauma theory to identify trauma's subversion of Dtr's master narrative, a program that I will then pursue in detail in the following chapters.

According to the text revision of the fourth edition of the *Diagnostic and Statistical Manual of Mental Disorders* (*DSM-IV-TR*), individuals have been exposed to psychic trauma if they have experienced events that involved or threatened death or serious injury or a threat to "physical integrity," and responded with intense fear, helplessness, or horror. They can be said to be suffering from PTSD if they experience a combination of symptoms of intrusion, constriction, and hyperarousal more than a month following the trauma. Intrusive symptoms include recurrent recollections or dreams of the event; acting or feeling as if the event were still occurring, in the forms of flashbacks, hallucinations, and the like; and intense psychological distress or physiological reactivity at exposure to cues that resemble the event. These are all, clearly, symptoms of the trauma intruding on individuals' lives to the extent that sufferers have no control over the symptoms. The constrictive symptoms, on the other hand, involve avoidance of stimulae associated with the trauma, as well as a general feeling of numbness. They include efforts to avoid thoughts, feelings, activities, places, and people associated with the trauma; an inability to recall important aspects of the trauma; a feeling of detachment from others, as well as a restricted range of feelings; and a sense of a foreshortened future. Finally, the symptoms of hyperarousal include an exaggerated startle response; hypervigilance; difficulty sleeping; and outbursts of anger. These, like all of the intrusive and most of the constrictive symptoms, are all beyond the conscious control of the trauma victim.[1] Among the various specific stressors known to produce post-traumatic states are natural disasters, participation in warfare, the experience of mass violence against civilians, rape, torture, and child abuse. John Briere's survey of psychiatric studies of PTSD concludes that among the events that increase the likelihood of the severity of the disorder are intentional acts of violence, physical injury, extent of combat exposure in war, witnessing death, degree of the grotesqueness of death witnessed, and sexual victimization.[2] Among those who have experienced massive psychic trauma—extensive exposure to the kinds of stressors

1. Task Force on DSM-IV, *Diagnostic and Statistical Manual of Mental Disorders* (4th ed., text revision; Washington: American Psychiatric Association, 2000), 463–64, 467–68.

2. John Briere, *Psychological Assessment of Adult Posttraumatic States: Phenomenology, Diagnosis, and Measurement* (2d ed.; Washington: American Psychological Association, 2004), 10–26 and 30–32. References to the studies in question may be found on pp. 30–32.

that Briere describes—the symptoms of PTSD do not abate, but continue for decades.[3] *DSM-IV-TR* also adds that "[t]he disorder may be especially severe or long lasting when the stressor is of human design,"[4] as in the case of siege and warfare.

The study of trauma in the field of psychoanalysis developed as an outgrowth of Jean-Martin Charcot's nineteenth-century investigations of hysteria. Sigmund Freud, a student of Charcot, credited him with being the first to recognize hysteria as a mental disease and thus as something that should be studied and treated, rather than dismissing the patient as a "malingerer."[5] It was in fact Freud who first saw a connection between hysteria and what he and other psychoanalysts called the "war neuroses" in subjects who fought in World War I. In *Beyond the Pleasure Principle*, published two years after the war, Freud refers to the "traumatic neurosis" observed in those exposed to combat, and notes that it involves intrusion into the dream lives of the victims. Just as in the case of those who suffer from hysteria, Freud points out, the repetitive return of the trauma in dreams causes the patient to become "fixated" to the trauma, thereby upsetting the normal healing nature of dreams.[6] Arguably a more important contributor to the early study of psychic trauma was Pierre Janet, another student of Charcot's and a rival of Freud's. Janet's work of 1889, *L'automatisme physiologique*, proposed a theory of *désagrégation* (a word normally translated into English as "dissociation"), in which neurotic ideas and processes "could become detached from the mainstream of consciousness, whereupon they had the power to form neurotic symptoms."[7] For Janet, personality is the harmonious functioning of memories with the mental processes that synthesize this information in the light of previous memories. It is this constant synthesizing of new experiences with old memories that allows the individual to adapt to the environment. Janet argues, however, that it is possible that "psychological misery" will block new memories from entering this synthesis, and cause them instead to exist in a subconscious (Janet was the first to use this term), thereby adversely affecting the personality.[8] Janet later expanded this theory, stating that a traumatic event becomes an obstacle

3. Judith Lewis Herman, *Trauma and Recovery* (New York: Basic, 1992), 87.
4. Task Force on DSM-IV, *Diagnostic and Statistical Manual*, 464.
5. Sigmund Freud, "Charcot", in *SE*, 3:11–39 (19–20).
6. Sigmund Freud, *Beyond the Pleasure Principle*, in *SE*, 18:7–64 (12–14).
7. Campbell Perry and Jean-Roch Laurence, "Mental Processing Outside of Awareness: The Contributions of Freud and Janet," in *The Unconscious Reconsidered* (ed. Kenneth S. Bowers and Donald Meichenbaum; New York: John Wiley & Sons, 1984), 9–48 (9–10; quote on p. 10).
8. Ibid., 28–34.

beyond which individuals cannot psychologically move, blocking their adaptation to a changing outside world. For Janet, memory is, in essence, the telling of an autobiographical story, but those who have been exposed to trauma cannot associate the traumatic event with their own life narratives contained in previous memories, and so cannot assimilate the event. They simply do not remember the trauma; rather, it reproduces itself through hallucinations and the like. Such reenactments are not truly memories, since the individuals have not integrated the event and do not have voluntary access to it, and so "[i]t is only for convenience that we speak of it as a 'traumatic memory.'"[9]

Like Freud, Janet argues that sufferers of trauma become "attached" (Freud's word is "fixated") to the trauma. Because they do not understand where their current terror comes from, they find it difficult to understand other life experiences.[10] Dissociation produces a break in the life narrative of memory that can permanently affect the individual. The trauma remains un-understood, but continually intrudes upon the subject's life. Freud also noted, at nearly the same time that he was writing *Beyond the Pleasure Principle*, that the "uncanny" involves the involuntary, repetitive, and compulsive return of something "which is able to stand over against the rest of the ego.... In the pathological case of delusions of being watched, this mental agency becomes isolated, dissociated from the ego...."[11] This has been caused by "the urge towards defence which has caused the ego to project that material outward as something foreign to itself."[12] When he describes the "inner compulsion to repeat" as one of the manifestations of the uncanny,[13] one is reminded not only of the fixation to trauma in dreams that Freud would soon describe in *Beyond the Pleasure Principle*, but also of Janet's explanation of the dissociation caused by trauma, which involves the repetitive intrusion of the trauma and the failure to assimilate the experience to the ego. Psychic trauma returns not as memory that one can recall, but instead compulsively, and it uncannily intrudes upon the self as something separate from it.

9. Pierre Janet, *Psychological Healing: A Historical and Clinical Study* (trans. Eden Paul and Cedar Paul; 2 vols.; London: George Allen & Unwin, 1925), 1:660–63; quote on p. 663.

10. Bessel A. van der Kolk and Onno van der Hart, "The Intrusive Past: The Flexibility of Memory and the Engraving of Trauma," in *Trauma: Explorations in Memory* (ed. Cathy Caruth; Baltimore: The Johns Hopkins University Press, 1995), 158–82 (164).

11. Sigmund Freud, "The Uncanny", in *SE*, 17:219–52 (235).

12. Ibid., 17:236.

13. Ibid., 17:238.

The eventual inclusion of PTSD as a disorder in *DSM-III* in 1980 was thanks in part to the renewed interest in the effects of trauma following the Vietnam War.[14] Empirical studies of the post-Vietnam era pointed to the intensity and quantity of traumatic events as part of the explanation for differing intensities of symptoms of PTSD. One study of Vietnam veterans found a strong correlation between PTSD and participation in wartime atrocities and/or the experience of a sheer number of combat stressors, such as coming under enemy fire, being wounded, and seeing a friend killed in action.[15] A study conducted in the 1980s of World War II American prisoners of war found that half of them still suffered from PTSD forty years after the war, and that one of the strongest predictors of this was the experience of torture while a POW.[16] In these and other studies of the intensity of the traumatic experience,[17] the dissociative effects of trauma remained its most telling aspect. Writing in 1985 about the entry on PTSD in the upcoming *DSM-IV*, a number of scholars pointed to the emerging fact that trauma largely did not seem to diminish over time, an idea that had only recently been discovered. The "traumatic event continues to be stressful because it is outside of the realm of the individual's experience. This leads to the inability to process the meaning of the event(s) in the person's cognitive schema of the world."[18] It is dissociation, in short, that accounts for the continuing power of trauma in the victims' lives. The inability to assimilate the experience means that it exercises its power over individuals precisely because they cannot know or control it. Traumatic memories are thus "timeless and ego-alien."[19]

The consequences for these findings in the study of literature produced by trauma survivors are important. As we shall see, it is the influence of the intrusive and constrictive symptoms of trauma particularly that have struck scholars who read the literature of trauma survivors. When the

14. Herman, *Trauma and Recovery*, 26–28.

15. Naomi Breslau and Glenn C. Davis, "Posttraumatic Stress Disorder: The Etiologic Specificity of Wartime Stressors," *American Journal of Psychiatry* 144 (1987): 578–83.

16. Nancy Speed et al., "Posttraumatic Stress Disorder as a Consequence of the POW Experience," *Journal of Nervous and Mental Disease* 177 (1989): 147–53.

17. For references to other such studies on survivors of trauma conducted in the 1980s, see Herman, *Trauma and Recovery*, p. 57.

18. Bonnie L. Green et al., "Posttraumatic Stress Disorder: Toward DSM-IV," *Journal of Nervous and Mental Disease* 173 (1985): 406–11 (408).

19. Bessel A. van der Kolk, "Trauma and Memory," in *Traumatic Stress: The Effects of Overwhelming Experience on Mind, Body, and Society* (ed. Bessel A. van der Kolk, Alexander C. McFarlane, and Lars Weisaeth; New York: Guilford, 1996), 279–302 (295).

trauma cannot truly be known, and when this unknowability becomes the center of the lives of those affected by massive traumatic events for decades following their survival, we would expect to see reflections of this in the literature produced by those who have survived. The compulsive and uncontrolled return of these non-memories that cannot be assimilated to one's life narrative, the continual failure to account for these intrusions, the constrictive effects of the consequent psychological numbing, and the sheer difficulty of trying to express this trauma through language will all be reflected in the literature of those trauma survivors who choose to write. As we shall see in section B of this chapter, these writers cannot be said to write about the trauma, since the trauma cannot ultimately be known; they write instead around the trauma. And this is also the case for the descendants of trauma sufferers; Nanette Auerhahn and Dori Laub, both of whom have extensive clinical experience treating survivors of the Holocaust and their children, as well as with the Fortunoff Video Archive for Holocaust Testimonies at Yale University, find that massive psychic trauma "shapes the internal representation of reality of several generations, becoming an unconscious organizing principle passed on by parents and internalized by their children."[20] We turn now to the effect of massive trauma on descendants of survivors.

2. *Trauma in Descendants of Survivors and in Traumatic Communities*

The effects of massive psychic trauma go beyond the lives of those who survived, and are also transmitted to their children. One study of children of Holocaust survivors, for example, observes that

> The children of survivors show symptoms which would be expected if they actually lived through the Holocaust.... They seem to share an anguished collective memory of the Holocaust in both their dreams and fantasies reflective of recurrent references to their parents' traumatic experiences. These children wake up at night with terrifying nightmares of the Nazi persecution, with dreams of barbed wire, gas chambers, firing squads, torture, mutilation, escaping from enemy forces and fears of extermination.[21]

The same study concludes that "[t]he children also come to feel that the Holocaust is the single most critical event that has affected their lives,

20. Nanette C. Auerhahn and Dori Laub, "Intergenerational Memory of the Holocaust," in *International Handbook of Multigenerational Legacies of Trauma* (ed. Yael Danieli; New York: Plenum, 1998), 21–42 (22).

21. Harvey A. Barocas and Carol B. Barocas, "Wounds of the Fathers: The Next Generation of Holocaust Victims," *International Review of Psycho-Analysis* 6 (1979): 331–41 (331).

although it occurred before they were born."[22] In a review and discussion of several hundred articles and dozens of doctoral dissertations written from the 1960s to the 1990s on the transmission of traumatic effects of the Holocaust to the second generation of survivors in North American families, Irit Felsen writes that the study of these descendants does not provide evidence of psychopathology—members of the second generation do not develop psychological disorders because their parents underwent psychic trauma, in other words—but suggests rather that we should discuss the transmission of trauma in terms of personality development. Individual psychic development is determined by both self-definition and one's relatedness to others, and in normal development these two processes facilitate each other in the production of healthy individuals. In the context of development within an environment in which one must relate to parents, not to mention other family and community members, who suffered massive psychic trauma, development will reflect this context, and this is especially so within cultures that stress relatedness and interdependency within family and community.[23]

Worldview is inherited largely from family and wider community, and when both have been exposed to trauma, the second generation will also be affected. Members of this generation find themselves repeating and reenacting aspects of their parents' trauma. They become obsessed with the lack of memory and the uncanny repetition of the trauma in their parents' lives, identifying with these victims while seeing an unbridgeable gap between themselves and their parents.[24] Because their parents have not themselves integrated the trauma into their autobiographical memories, the second generation feels the effect without directly experiencing the trauma that has caused it. As in the cases of their parents, the signifier—the effects of the trauma—are present, while the referent—the trauma itself—remains outside of conscious knowledge.[25] In fact, Ilany Kogan, based on her extensive clinical work with children of Holocaust survivors, has concluded that their parents' trauma "was retained as a

22. Ibid., 336.

23. Irit Felsen, "Transgenerational Transmission of Effects of the Holocaust: The North American Research Perspective," in Danieli, ed., *International Handbook*, 58–63; quote on p. 43.

24. Marianne Hirsch, "Marked by Memory: Feminist Reflections on Trauma and Transmission," in *Extremities: Trauma, Testimony, and Community* (ed. Nancy K. Miller and Jason Tougaw; Urbana, Ill.: University of Illinois Press, 2002), 71–91 (71–76).

25. Erin McGlothin, *Second-Generation Holocaust Literature: Legacies of Survival and Perpetration* (Studies in German Literature, Linguistics, and Culture; Rochester, N.Y.: Camden House, 2006), 10.

discordant, encapsulated event [by the second generation], out of reach of reason, insight or reflection. It had the power to eclipse life or induce a break in life's procession via solitary re-enactments or permeation of life as a whole."[26] Studies of families of Holocaust survivors show psychological and psychosomatic effects in the second and third generations of survivors. The descendants live in the shadows of their parents' and grandparents' untellable unknown pasts, and become obsessed with traumatic details that their ancestors cannot relate to them and that the descendants cannot imagine.[27]

Whole communities can be affected by trauma, and Kai Erikson, in his own studies of communities destroyed by disaster and in his survey of research done on other such communities, has found no examples of such trauma creating increased senses of communal bonds or other positive effects.[28] Nor should this be surprising. As Erikson has observed in his study of communities that have undergone trauma, it is the community that provides context for individuals and can cushion pain; when all or most of the individuals of a community suffer massive trauma, the community itself will be profoundly and negatively affected.[29] Disasters that befall entire communities will fracture the social group, observes Erikson, and dominate the way the community sees itself and the imagery it uses.[30]

Communities can, of course, try to take control of traumatic events, whether they have affected individuals or the entire society, and fit them into existing social worldviews and stories in order to make the trauma understandable—attempt, in other words, to control the trauma by creating a recognizable narrative for it.[31] As Kalí Tal points out in discussing the literature and art surrounding the Vietnam War, trauma shatters

26. Ilany Kogan, *The Cry of Mute Children: A Psychoanalytic Perspective of the Second Generation of the Holocaust* (London: Free Association, 1995), 4.

27. For examples of two such family histories, see Gabriele Rosenthal et al., "The Collective Trauma of the Lodz Ghetto: The Goldstern Family," in *The Holocaust in Three Generations: Families of Victims and Perpetrators of the Nazi Regime* (ed. Gabriele Rosenthal; trans. Catherine Johnson; London: Cassell, 1998), 51–68; and, in the same volume, Waltraud Schade et al., "Shared and Divided Worlds: The Stern Family," 95–117.

28. Kai Erikson, "Notes on Trauma and Community," in Caruth, ed., *Trauma*, 183–99.

29. Kai Erikson, *A New Species of Trouble: Explorations in Disaster, Trauma, and Community* (New York: W. W. Norton & Co., 1994), 230–35.

30. Ibid., 236–37.

31. Kalí Tal, *Worlds of Hurt: Reading the Literatures of Trauma* (Cambridge: Cambridge University Press, 1996), 6.

survivors' worldviews, and so makes communication of the trauma, done within language that has meaning and significance only within the context of a worldview, impossible. This is why trauma survivors who try to create narratives of trauma often express so much frustration with the limitations of language.[32] As Tal shows, however, the stories of the war produced by those who did not participate in combat tend to conform to pre-existing national narratives.[33] The trauma is then erased within stories that do not actually address it, but subsume it within narratives of the struggle of good against evil and the like.

As we move now to examine attempts to represent trauma in literature, we will find that trauma survivors and their descendants tend to portray the world as chaotic and unpredictable, lacking any moral authority, and portray trauma itself as ultimately unrepresentable and unexplainable, beyond the scope of language. The master narrative of the Deuteronomistic History, as we shall see in the first sections of the following chapters, takes a much different approach, and places a high value on the ability of language to explain past and present. The benefit of using trauma theory in order to read Dtr, as literary critics have used it to read other texts, is that it detects traces of trauma that have slipped into—or perhaps we should say behind—the main narrative of the History, traces that subvert the master narrative's attempt to provide an explanation for the exilic community's trauma. The traces of trauma are not themselves truly narrative, as we shall see, but rather eruptions into the master narrative of the History that have not been integrated into this narrative, just as trauma is not integrated into personal narrative yet intrudes uncontrollably in the lives of survivors and their descendants.

I would again urge readers who remain committed to a Josianic dating for the bulk of the History not to dismiss this argument about the effects of trauma on Dtr's narrative merely for historical reasons. As we have seen, the effects of trauma reach beyond those who suffer them to following generations and affect whole communities. Readers who remain unconvinced by my arguments for dating in the previous chapter can still attribute the origin of the traces of trauma in the text that will be outlined in the following chapters to the Assyrian invasion of 701 that destroyed Judah. Within such a framework of dating, it is well within the realm of possibility that a descendant of a survivor of that mass slaughter and destruction of Judah would have written a piece of literature bearing unmistakable traces of trauma. And again, even given my stance on the

32. Ibid., 121–24.
33. Ibid., 115–53, and see especially pp. 146–53.

place and date of composition of the History, I cannot say if it was composed by a survivor of the mass migration of 597, or by a survivor of the siege of Jerusalem and the mass migration of 586, or by a descendant of one of those survivors who lived in the traumatized community in Babylon. The literature of trauma survivors and of their descendants, we shall see in the following section, manifests trauma similarly. My argument in the following chapters is thus only that the History betrays the influence of trauma, and that reading the text through the lens of trauma theory—the concept to which we now turn—helps us make better sense of the writing's structure, gaps, imagery, and presentations of particular stories. It would certainly be possible to read these findings as the effects of trauma that occurred in a different historical period than the one for which I have argued, although, as the previous chapter indicates, it makes most sense to place the author among the community of survivors of the trauma of 586.

B. *The Literary Study of Trauma*

1. *Trauma's Resistance to Narrative*

The dissociative and intrusive effects of massive psychic trauma discussed in the previous section of the chapter are inevitably manifested in the literature of survivors and their descendants. Just as Janet wrote that we speak only for the sake of convenience of traumatic memories, we can say that there truly is no literature of trauma, since trauma will resist incorporation into a textual narrative precisely because it resists incorporation into personal narratives. Elie Wiesel may well be the best known author of the Holocaust, yet he himself denies that he writes about it.[34] It is precisely for this reason, writes Terence Des Pres, that silence is at the center of Wiesel's art.[35] "We all knew that we could never, never say what had to be said, that we could never express in words, coherent, intelligible words, our experience on an absolute scale," states Wiesel. "This is the concentration camp language. It negated all other language and took its place."[36] In response to Wiesel's famous statement that "there is no such thing as literature of the Holocaust, nor can there be,"

34. Cited in Terrence Des Pres, "The Authority of Silence in Elie Wiesel's Art," in *Confronting the Holocaust: The Impact of Elie Wiesel* (ed. Alvin H. Rosenfeld and Irving Greenberg; Bloomington: Indiana University Press, 1978), 49–57 (50).

35. Ibid., 55.

36. Elie Wiesel, "Why I Write," in Rosenfeld and Greenberg, eds., *Confronting the Holocaust*, 200–206 (201).

Alvin Rosenfeld argues that this claim reflects "the deep anguish and immense frustration of the writer who confronts a subject that belittles and threatens to overwhelm the resources of his language."[37] Quite so. If trauma cannot be understood, it cannot be put into language in order to communicate what it is. If there is no language to express trauma, then it seems inappropriate to write of traumatic literature, but we will use the term for convenience's sake.

Because massive trauma has not been assimilated into memory and personal narrative and yet proves a powerful force, it is present, paradoxically, in its very absence to memory, knowledge, and language. Testimony to trauma, as Shoshana Felman puts it, is composed of "bits and pieces of a memory that has been overwhelmed by occurrences that have not settled into understanding or remembrance." As a result, she continues, such testimony cannot offer "a completed statement, a totalizable account of those events. In the testimony, language is in process and in trial, it does not possess itself as a conclusion, as the conclusion of a verdict or the self-transparency of knowledge."[38] Or, as Efraim Sicher describes the characters in the fiction of Holocaust survivor Aharon Appelfeld, their trauma "forms a determining lacuna in the narrative space–time continuum; Appelfeld's survivors carry the Holocaust within them as a void that fragments personality…."[39]

At the heart of trauma lies something—or a lack of a thing—to which survivors have no direct access themselves. If it cannot be assimilated into their own personal narratives, their attempts to express trauma in a narrative that readers can make sense of will clearly be frustrated. Writing of the literature of genocide composed by the children and grandchildren of survivors, Walter Kalaidjian points out that merely attempting to relate faithfully the historical events of the traumatic experience in narrative "would simply mask the properly nonlinguistic event of trauma's 'speechless terror.'"[40] Michael Rothberg argues that attempts to represent trauma can fall into the trap of "narrative fetishism"—attempts to create

37. Alvin H. Rosenfeld, "The Problematics of Holocaust Literature," in Rosenfeld and Greenberg, eds., *Confronting the Holocaust*, 1–30 (4).

38. Shoshana Felman, "Education and Crisis, or the Vicissitudes of Teaching," in *Testimony: Crises of Witnessing in Literature, Psychoanalysis, and History* (ed. Shoshana Felman and Dori Laub; New York: Routledge, 1992), 1–56 (5).

39. Efraim Sicher, "The Burden of Memory: The Writing of the Post-Holocaust Generation," in *Breaking Crystal: Writing and Memory After Auschwitz* (ed. Efraim Sicher; Urbana, Ill.: University of Illinois Press, 1998), 19–88 (23).

40. Walter Kalaidjian, *The Edge of Modernism: American Poetry and the Traumatic Past* (Baltimore: The Johns Hopkins University Press, 2006), 41.

an understandable narrative that will inevitably remove the traces of the trauma itself.[41]

Survivors of massive psychic trauma often claim that they have nothing believable to report, since their experience quite literally defies belief. The "familiar rhetorical pattern" of reports of Holocaust survivors in Claude Lanzmann's massive documentary *Shoah*, writes Lea Fridman, is one of denial that what they experienced can be believed or even described. Here is an excerpt from a representative example from a survivor who was interviewed at Auschwitz for the documentary: "There were two huge ovens. It was terrible. No one can describe it. No one can recreate what happened here. Impossible? And no one can understand it. Even I, here, now. I can't believe I'm here. No, I just can't believe it. It was always this peaceful here. Always. When they burned 2,000 people—Jews—every day, it was just as peaceful."[42] Lanzmann must constantly coax the interviewees to speak in the film, for language constantly fails them. What this work discovers, writes Fridman, is a "resistance to language itself."[43] This unbridgeable gap between language and belief on one hand and the reality of trauma on the other is something that authors of traumatic literature frequently point to. "We never actually stopped trying to say something, even in moments of greatest torpor," writes Appelfeld. "But all we succeeded to emit was a stutter, or worse, familiar traditional words and fabrication." Or Primo Levi: "Today at this very moment as I sit writing at a table, I am not convinced that these things really happened." Or Charlotte Delbo: "I am no longer sure that what I have written is true, but I am sure that it happened."[44]

As the last quote shows particularly, the case is not always that the authors of traumatic literature cannot recall the events that caused the massive psychic trauma (although this is the case for some trauma survivors, and is suggested to some degree by the quote from Levi); the impossibility that they face instead is in situating the trauma within an explanatory narrative so that they can make truth claims about it and explain and make sense of it. In Levi's case, the trauma he suffered is so foreign to his ego that he cannot believe it, is unwilling to make truth claims about it. This failure of personal and social narrative, and thus of

41. Michael Rothberg, "Between the Extreme and the Everyday: Ruth Klüger's Traumatic Realism," in Miller and Tougow, eds., *Extremities*, 55–70 (66–67).

42. Lea Wernick Fridman, *Words and Witness: Narrative and Aesthetic Strategies in the Representation of the Holocaust* (Albany: State University of New York Press, 2000), 59.

43. Ibid., 60.

44. Quote from Appelfeld from ibid., 67; quotes from Levi and Delbo from p. 87.

language itself, to assimilate and describe and make truth claims about massive trauma, thus situating it within an accessible explanatory narrative, points as well to the uncontrollable nature of the experience. The Jewish characters of Appelfeld's novella *Badenheim 1939*, for example, participating in a music festival on the eve of World War II, feel that the words they use—words such as "understanding" and "clarity," not to mention "Jew"—have completely controllable meanings. They inhabit, writes Langer, "a verbal world like this, where the dictionary, as it were, still stands on a shelf in the Garden of Eden."[45] Their opinions about language do not change, even at the end of the story, as they board the cattle cars for "relocation." The novella thus ends up with a "double narrative," argues Fridman, which "alludes to the struggle around expression and its impossibility." The horror which all of these characters are about to encounter remains unspoken as a "foregrounded silence"; since it is impossible to believe, it is inevitably unspoken.[46] The characters' language becomes loaded with irony—they refer to the purity of the Polish air, for example, an elliptical reference to the gas that will kill them. In the end, the characters can no longer describe the world to make it coherent and situate themselves in it.[47] Nor is this surprising. Trauma, as we have seen so far, resists narrativization and is really a gap in narrative rather than narrative itself. Because trauma simply is not integrated into the worldviews people use to make sense of things, it cannot be a part of any explanatory narrative, and so it naturally moves to absence, rendering attempts to narrativize it ultimately futile. By its very nature, trauma resists and subverts the common or stereotypical language of narrative, making "familiar traditional words" merely "fabrication."

2. *Trauma and Literary Repetition*

The presence of trauma's absence leads not only to an unmooring of language from the notions of experience and belief, but to a loss of the connection between past, present, and future. To refer back to Janet's work, the power of trauma is so great and so unassimilatable that fixation to this unknown past prevents survivors from linking their present selves to that past event. It becomes the uncanny as Freud describes it, constantly repeating in the life and literature of the survivors, even though they have no direct access to it. In the case of one Holocaust survivor,

45. Laurence L. Langer, "Aharon Appelfeld and the Language of Sinister Silence," in *Admitting the Holocaust: Collected Essays* (Oxford: Oxford University Press, 1995), 125–37 (127).
46. Fridman, *Words and Witness*, 34.
47. Ibid., 40–43.

writes Laub, her fixation to her trauma was so great that she experienced her current family as "unempathetic strangers...because of their refusal to substitute for, and completely fit into, the world of parents, brothers and children that was so abruptly destroyed."[48] Her fixation to her trauma, in short, so dominated her life that her murdered family was far more real to her than her current, living one. This traumatic past, moreover, is constantly real in the present, more real than present events often seem. In Peter Balakian's poem "The History of Armenia," the history of the Armenian genocide does not just belong to the poet's grandmother's past in Armenia, but to the present of both survivor and third-generation descendant in New Jersey:

> When I told her
> I was hungry, she said
> in the grocery store
> a man is standing
> to his ankles in blood,
> the babies of East Orange
> have disappeared[49]

In the same way, Langer points to Delbo's memoire of her experience in Auschwitz and life following liberation, in which she writes that she does not live with Auschwitz but "beside it. Auschwitz is there, fixed and unchangeable, but wrapped in the impervious skin of memory that segregates itself from the present 'me.'"[50] Her work bears out this separation of traumatic time from lived, narrative time, and so Rothberg writes that in her work she "provides a stunning image of the doubleness of trauma's belated temporality: the past is at once completely present, because trauma stops time, and completely distant, because such time is not susceptible to transformation."[51] As we saw in the previous section of this chapter, the traumatic past can seem even more real to survivors than the present, and this is in part because traumatic memories, unlike those under conscious recall, do not change over time. They are constant, present, and powerfully uncontrollable, and this constant intrusion of the past inevitably finds its way into traumatic literature.

Intimately linked to this aspect of trauma and its void presence in literature is its repetition. The traumatic past can seem more real than the

48. Dori Laub, "An Event Without a Witness: Truth, Testimony and Survival," in Felman and Laub, eds., *Testimony*, 75–92 (78).

49. See Kalaidjian, *The Edge of Modernism*, 31–32.

50. Quoted in Laurence L. Langer, *Holocaust Testimonies: The Ruins of Memory* (New Haven: Yale University Press, 1991), 5.

51. Rothberg, "Between the Extreme and the Everyday," 65.

present because of its constant intrusion into the life of the survivor, and this too is represented in traumatic literature. For example, in William Heyen's poem "Kotov" about a Russian Jew who survives a German gas van and escapes death, the poem's refrain, "Only Kotov," which each time introduces the theme of escape while everyone else in the van dies, is the "verbal repetition that marks a symptomatic return of the trauma."[52] Or in Anthony Hecht's poem "The Book of Yolek," a summer walk in the woods recalls a forced march of Jewish children to a concentration camp. The five year old Yolek, who died in the camp, will always return in the life of the survivor: "Wherever you are, Yolek will be there, too. / His unuttered name will interrupt your meal." The ordinary life of the camp survivor here is converted into "uncanny cryptonyms of genocide."[53] Or, to take another example, the traumatic past of the character of Rosa, a Holocaust survivor in Cynthia Ozick's novella *The Shawl*, constantly intrudes upon her present life in Miami, where "the streets were a furnace, the sun an executioner," where the beach is "littered with bodies" and "locked behind barbed wire," near a hotel through which Rosa moves past "cooks in their meat-blooded aprons." This work as a whole, writes Langer, plays on the myth that the traumatic past can be forgotten, and that time can heal and redeem the future. Rosa's traumatic past is continually intruding on her present. When she writes letters to her niece Stella in English, she seems like an immigrant who has adapted to life in America; yet she also continues to compose letters in Polish to her daughter Magda who died in the camps. As she repetitively lives in the trauma of Magda's death, fantasizing about what her dead daughter would be like had she survived, she is advised to forget, but says, "For me there's one time only; there's no after."[54]

These aspects of trauma in literature—not only the dominance of and fixation to the traumatic past in the present, and the closely related repetition of trauma, but also the unknowable void at the center of experience that radically throws the ability of narrative and even language to convey trauma into question—all appear in the works of the children and grandchildren of survivors of massive trauma as they do in the literature of the survivors themselves. Traumatic narratives by descendants of survivors are themselves testimony to the powerful and continual repetition of trauma in literature. Given what we saw in the previous section of this chapter, this should not be surprising. These later generations are also

52. Kalaidjian, *The Edge of Modernism*, 73.

53. See ibid., 75–77.

54. Laurence L. Langer, "Myth and Truth in Cynthia Ozick's 'The Shawl' and 'Rosa,'" in *Admitting the Holocaust*, 139–44.

fixated to and obsessed by the present absence of trauma in their parents and grandparents. The lack of a personal memory of the trauma that the earlier generation suffered forms its own void of trauma, and these children and grandchildren of survivors will fictionally reconstruct parts of this lost memory.[55] Rivkah Miriam, the Israeli poet who is a daughter of Holocaust survivors, writes in an essay that she "imbibed the Holocaust experience with my mother's milk."[56] In their prose especially, writes Hanna Yaez, second-generation survivors emphasize their own and others' attempts to work through communal and familial trauma, highlighting such issues as intrusive traumatic anxieties and fears and the legacy of suffering they have received.[57] The failure of narrative and language to describe the traumatic event to later generations leaves those generations with a need to imagine that past, and Erin McGlothin describes those attempts as producing literature with the same tell-tale traumatic aspects that the survivors themselves produce. These literary forays result "in a narrative crisis in which narrative voice fractures, protagonists multiply in a compulsion to repeat, temporality is suspended, and generic conventions are transgressed or radically reshaped."[58] In a helpful example of all of these characteristics, McGlothin examines the collection of short stories called *Elijah Visible* by the second-generation Holocaust survivor Thane Rosenbaum. While each of the stories is independent of all of the others—there is no narrative development between them, in other words—the protagonists of each of the stories bears the name Adam Posner. The result, then, is that each story acts as a revision, but not a continuation, of the preceding ones; each narrative tries to overcome trauma while merely reenacting it without understanding.[59] If each narrative is a repetitive attempt to understand the parental trauma, each fails, and the work as a whole fractures the narrative voice which cannot reach its goal. The trauma is repeated in every story rather than comprehended, and the past lived over and over again.

Because the Holocaust in particular inflicted massive psychic trauma not merely on a collection of Jewish individuals but on Judaism as a whole, Ellen Fine actually writes of a "collective memory" of Judaism in respect to the trauma. Jewish writers, she argues, whether or not they

55. Efraim Sicher, "The Burden of Memory: The Writing of the Post-Holocaust Generation," in Sicher, ed., *Breaking Crystal*, 19–88 (29–30).

56. Quoted in ibid., 24.

57. Hanna Yaez, "Inherited Fear: Second-Generation Poets and Novelists in Israel," in Sicher, ed., *Breaking Crystal*, 160–69 (161).

58. McGlothin, *Second-Generation Holocaust Literature*, 12.

59. Ibid., 57–65.

or their families directly experienced the Holocaust, emphasize the hidden histories of their community that govern the present, the absent memory that is so full of gaps, and the guilt of being alive while others died.[60] Narratives of trauma, whether written by survivors or their descendants, collapse past, present, and future because of the very nature of trauma. The trauma becomes the constantly repeated past that supplants the present, suspending temporality. There is no comprehension of the trauma itself, merely its constant unknowable presence.

3. *Trauma and the Collapse of Ethics and Language*

Having now touched on the most important characteristics and features of traumatic literature, we have some sense of what it means to read a text through the lens of trauma theory. As we have already seen, however, traumatic narratives—really traumatic non-narratives—can be reworked by the social group in which they are spoken in order to appropriate them into pre-existing communal narratives. We need not think of such a process as something deliberately sinister; this is merely an attempt to take an experience that is not believable or understandable—nonexperience, as Langer puts it—and rework it into something that is. The events that give rise to massive psychic trauma are so incredible, in the most basic etymological sense of that word, that Auschwitz has been described as an "antiworld" because it is easier to believe that such horror does not happen on our planet.[61] Commentators on the Holocaust, Langer points out, sometimes find a need to infuse the trauma with language of heroism and martyrdom that flies in the face of the testimony of those who actually survived it. Attempts to create understandable narratives and language for trauma inevitably appeal to the ethical worldviews through which such narratives can make sense of and explain the trauma; Langer's argument is that ethical distinctions simply do not apply to the traumatic experience or attempts to represent it textually. In the case of the Holocaust the Nazis made moral life and language impossible. In one example Langer draws upon to illustrate this point, a Holocaust survivor recounts how, upon arrival at Auschwitz, he was sent to the right with his brothers, while his parents, chosen for murder, were sent to the left. Having no idea what this separation meant, he sent his younger brother after his parents. "I am—I feel like I killed him.... I wonder what my mother and father were thinking, especially when they all...when they all went into the crematorium. I can't get it out of my head." By feeling

60. Ellen S. Fine, "Transmission of Memory: The Post-Holocaust Generation in the Diaspora," in Sicher, ed., *Breaking Crystal*, 185–200 (189–94).

61. Laurence L. Langer, "Introduction," in *Admitting the Holocaust*, 3–12 (4–6).

guilt, the survivor accepts blame for an act in which he had no responsibility. He does so because he relies on an ethical system in trying to formulate the experience, while simultaneously demonstrating in his testimony the futility of relying on it.[62]

To take another example, Marek Edelman, a surviving leader of the Warsaw ghetto uprising, describes how, when the Germans appeared in the ghetto's children's hospital to remove the patients to Treblinka, a Jewish doctor was poisoning the children. Edelman writes, "She saved these children from the gas chamber. People thought she was a hero." Here again is the ethical language of heroism that phrases actions in terms of right and wrong. Langer, though, rightly argues that this testimony points not to the question of whether or not the act of poisoning the children was or was not heroic, but to "the poverty of traditional moral vocabulary when we address the subject of human conduct during the destruction of European Jewry."[63] Sara Nomberg-Przytyk writes that "in Auschwitz there was nothing more important than trying to help your fellow sufferers and yet, at the same time, how immoral it was to decide whose suffering should be alleviated and whose should continue unabated. Who had given us the right to condemn or save another? In Auschwitz there was no fairness in the merciless struggle for survival."[64] There quite literally was no fairness in any way in Auschwitz. Language, which by its very nature depends on making distinctions, is unable to cope with the absence of morality, of distinguishing between right and wrong, in trauma. Many survivors of massive trauma, then, "inhabit two worlds simultaneously: the one of 'choiceless choice' *then*; the other of moral evaluation *now*. Harmony and integration are not only impossible—they are not even desirable."[65]

Attempts to place trauma into an understandable narrative in an understandable language and thereby to make it correspond to a familiar worldview must inevitably efface the trauma with "narrative fetishism" and write it over with the non-traumatic language of moral evaluation. Attempts to tell stories of heroism and martyrdom, of ethical action in the face of trauma do not actually deal with the trauma at all, since survivors had only "choiceless choices" to make, although heroic stories are narratives that cultures find comforting to relate. The irony of the title

62. Laurence L. Langer, "Beyond Theodicy: Jewish Victims and the Holocaust," in *Admitting the Holocaust*, 25–30; quote on p. 29.

63. Laurence L. Langer, "A Tainted Legacy: Remembering the Warsaw Ghetto," in *Admitting the Holocaust*, 31–40 (32).

64. Cited in Laurence L. Langer, "The Literature of Auschwitz," in *Admitting the Holocaust*, 89–107 (102).

65. Langer, *Holocaust Testimonies*, 83 (emphasis in the original).

of William Styron's novel *Sophie's Choice* is, of course, that the title character really has no choice to make when asked which of her children she would like to live and which to be gassed and burned. There is no good or right answer to such a question—the language of morality simply does not apply. In Appelfeld's novel *Tzili* the title character is exposed to language and moral slogans during the war that, in peacetime, might bring security: "If you want to you can"; "You have to forget. It's not a tragedy"; "Don't think about the past"; "A man, after all, is not an insect." Yet in the novel, Tzili never discovers a new language that can express her own view of reality, and each time she accepts one principle, she encounters an event to contradict it and so to undermine the stability of language. Ultimately, one of the characters says, "I'm declaring a cease-words. It's time for silence now."[66] We see here a kind of double narrative, like the one Fridman identifies in Appelfeld's *Badenheim 1939*. Attempts by characters in the narrative to ground their trauma in clear ethical concepts are undermined by the traumatic narrative that eludes these formulations. Trauma here is really an anti-narrative: ultimately it can point only to silence, not explanation.

The features of traumatic literature that we have discussed—the inability of language to describe trauma and language's unmooring from experience; the loss of connection between past and present; the continual repetition of the trauma as it erases temporality; and the inability to place trauma within an ethical and explanatory framework—are not merely conventions of traumatic writing. They are simply the available ways to try to represent what cannot be represented, even though such attempts will always fail. Such failures, though, are disconcerting to say the least, and it is easier to assert that the old worldviews and their ethical systems apply, that language always functions, and that narratives can always be told to explain and make sense of even the most horrific experience. It is no wonder that some traumatic literature directly challenges the cultural and literary traditions out of which the authors arise. We can see a failure of traditional literary forms of representation in Delbo's short story "Phantoms, My Companions," in which a narrator in a boxcar bound for Auschwitz is accompanied by characters from the history of French drama. But one by one they abandon her until, at the gates of Auschwitz, she is left alone with Alceste, Moliere's misanthrope. Yet even he leaves when he sees the horror of what is about to come, and the narrator must face Auschwitz alone, without the benefit of art.[67] I

66. Langer, "Aharon Appelfeld," 130–34.

67. For this summary and analysis, see Langer, "The Literature of Auschwitz," 93.

emphasize this rejection of cultural representations in the literature of trauma not only because it springs from the trauma sufferer's recognition of the failure of the ability of language and culture to understand the trauma, but because this assertion is naturally threatening to the culture and language and ethical systems in which survivors and their descendants find themselves, a matter of no small importance in this analysis of the Deuteronomistic History.

C. *Trauma and the Master Narrative of the Deuteronomistic History*

1. *Dtr's Master Narrative*

The question that we now face is how to apply these observations about the literature of trauma to the Deuteronomistic History. Most—although certainly not all—scholars would say that the History has a straightforward narrative line that controls the meaning of the horrors of 586 and makes truth claims about them, as well as the other foreign invasions in Judges, Samuel, and Kings that the Israelites suffer and that lead to the destruction of the Northern Kingdom. The narrative relates that God has punished Israel for its sins, and in the History it tells it relates how Israel has repeatedly disobeyed the law God has given, meeting prophetic warnings with further rounds of apostasy.[68] This certainly appears to be an ethical explanation of the disasters the exiles suffered, and it clearly puts a great deal of emphasis on the ability of language to convey the truth of trauma and control it in narrative and ethical logic. I will refer to Dtr's attempts to explain the exilic community's trauma through narrative and ethical logic as the work's master narrative, and what is 2 Kgs 21–25, after all, but the master narrative's attempt to draw upon the lessons of Israel's history that it has relayed since Deuteronomy in order to make ethical sense out of the trauma that the exilic community has suffered? The siege, famine, destruction and forced migration of 25:1–11 is preceded by the apostasy of Manasseh that he forced Judah to commit, an apostasy so grave that it was worse than that of the Canaanites (21:11) whom God had ordered to be annihilated from the land so that they would not teach Israel such cultic practices in the first place (Deut 7:1–6; 20:16–18). The History's narrative is clear all along that God meets

68. For scholars who follow Cross's theory of redaction, the Josianic historian does not explain the exile since he or she wrote this edition of the work before that took place. Nonetheless, even if we consider this writer and edition of the History to have existed, the writer explains earlier invasions and acts of destruction as divine punishment for disobedience, and Cross's exilic redactor simply extends that logic to the exile.

apostasy with invasion and destruction and loss of the land, and provides a history of Israel that makes this point. In this narrative, Israel's ethical choices determine its fate. The sin of Manasseh, in which Judah participates, causes the exilic community's trauma (2 Kgs 21:10–15; 22:14–17; 23:26–27; 24:1–4), which would thus appear to be fully encapsulated and explained by the master narrative.

My argument in this book is that while readers can trace this narrative explanation for the trauma the exilic community has suffered that I have just adumbrated—the siege, famine, mass death, and forced migrations of 597 and 586 are the just divine punishments for Israel's apostasy—and that this message or master narrative takes up the lion's share of the History, we find trauma erupting into this narrative to subvert and undermine its message. We can call this traumatic subversion of the master narrative a double narrative, using the description that Fridman attaches to Appelfeld's *Badenheim 1939*, where the master narrative's ethical explanation and linguistic clarity is rendered impossible by the subversive force of trauma. Trauma places language in process and on trial, as Felman argues, and it can come to no clear answers through language or narrative, whether autobiographical or literary, in order to represent itself. Dtr's master narrative has reached a verdict about the logic that explains the events of history, and this narrative attempts to control the trauma of massive death, starvation, and forced migration within an ethical explanation. Its ethical dictionary still stands on a shelf in the Garden of Eden, as Langer describes the view of the Jewish characters in Appelfeld's novella, but trauma interrupts this narrative to introduce ambiguity into its logical certainty and to throw its conclusions into doubt.

Since I will argue that trauma subverts Dtr's master narrative, we must have some idea of what the narrative itself claims before we can embark upon such an investigation. I will argue in the following chapters on the constitutive books of the History that the master narrative emphasizes two main ideas, and in the first sections of each of the following chapters I will provide concrete examples of them. The first idea—I will call it the first theme of the narrative—is that Israel's failure to remain loyal to YHWH in worship and obedience leads to punishment and, ultimately, the loss of the land. The narrative explains the exiles' trauma in large part by claiming the nation failed in this cultic and nomistic loyalty. Dtr's narrative works, as Martin Rose puts it, with a "logic in history" that makes sense of the exile,[69] and the History's narrative explains the order

69. Martin Rose, "Deuteronomistic Ideology and Theology of the Old Testament," in de Pury, Römer, and Macchi, eds., *Israel Constructs Its History*, 424–55 (447–48).

underlying the past to the exiles by relying, in large part, on this theme. Rose writes that by the phrase "logic in history" he means that "history is not marked by a profound absurdity, but that it is—in a certain perspective—completely reasonable ('logical')."[70] The trauma suffered by the exilic community is not the result of chance or divine caprice, but the result of the nation's failure to remain loyal to their divine suzerain. For most scholars who study the History these are fairly uncontroversial statements;[71] Martin Noth argued that the work does not portray history as a random series of events, but instead teaches the true meaning of history to Israel. The events of 586, like those of 722, are divine retribution rightly administered for Israel's failure to keep the law in its apostasy.[72] The History is thus a great confession of Israel's guilt, as both Gerhard von Rad and Rainer Albertz describe it, that justifies God's control of history and his actions toward Judah,[73] reading the history of the people through the lens of Deuteronomy's law and its warnings of the punishment that will result from apostasy or cultic disloyalty.[74] In short, the master narrative of Dtr appears to be about God's just control of history and his righteous judgment in the punishment of Israel, thus explaining that the guilt of the people and their leaders is the cause of both the horrific destruction of Jerusalem and the forced migration that followed.[75] And because God continually sends prophets to the people to

70. Ibid., 447.

71. The scholars who follow Cross, of course, would disagree that the History as a whole is written to explain the exile, since they believe the bulk of the work was composed during the reign of Josiah. But even Cross refers to "the sins of Jeroboam" as one of the main themes of his Dtr[1] ("The Theme of the Book of Kings," 279–81), and thus recognizes that even his Dtr[1] sees apostasy as a crime that merits destruction. We see here the same kind of logic to which Rose refers.

72. Martin Noth, *The Deuteronomistic History* (trans. Jane Doull et al.; JSOTSup 15; Sheffield: JSOT, 1981), 89, 91.

73. Gerhard von Rad, *Old Testament Theology* (trans. D. M. G. Stalker; 2 vols.; New York: Harper & Row, 1962–1965), 2:337; Rainer Albertz, *Israel in Exile: The History and Literature of the Sixth Century B.C.E.* (trans. David Green; SBL Studies in Biblical Literature 3; Leiden: Brill, 2004), 282.

74. E.g., Sweeney, *King Josiah of Judah*, 21; Albertz, *Israel in Exile*, 287; Preuss, *Old Testament Theology*, 1:211.

75. For this sort of summary see, among others, von Rad, *Old Testament Theology*, 2:342–43; Walter Dietrich, "Martin Noth and the Future of the Deuteronomistic History," in McKenzie and Graham, eds., *The History of Israel's Traditions*, 153–75 (168); Walther Zimmerli, *Grundriss der alttestamentlichen Theologie* (Theologische Wissenschaft 3; Stuttgart: Kohlhammer, 1972), 157–58; Claus Westermann, *Theologie des Alten Testaments in Grundzügen* (ATD Ergänzungsreihe 6; Göttingen: Vandenhoeck & Ruprecht, 1978), 185–86; Otto Kaiser, *Der Gott des*

warn them of the consequences of their cultic failure, the terrors of 722, 597, and 586 are merely the fulfillment of an oft-repeated and clear divine word spoken through the prophets.[76] This first theme of the History's narrative is broadly accepted in scholarship, and so is regularly represented in dictionary articles on Dtr and in introductions to biblical literature.[77] It also embraces the aspects of the *leitmotif* to which we pointed in the previous chapter as distinguishing Dtr from the Tetrateuch: the assertion that intermarriage with Canaanites causes the worship of "other gods," which will lead to destruction and exile. Israel, the single nation God has called, has failed to worship YHWH alone and to keep his law, and thus has failed to keep the land; the narrative presents intermarriage as the act that ultimately leads to the trauma the exiles have suffered.

These sorts of scholarly claims do seem straightforward. The idea that the master narrative is trying to explain history as the logical outcome of divine response to Israel's choices and is thus trying to explain the exilic community's trauma appears throughout Deuteronomy, for example, as Moses constantly exhorts the nation to obedience, warning that failure to keep the law and worship YHWH alone will lead to destruction from the land, while success will lead to prosperity. When Israel settles in the land in Judges, we find that the narrative explains its continual punishment through foreign invasion as the result of its continual rounds of apostasy. The narrative from this point on seems especially focused on cultic activities as the yardstick by which God judges the nation, and by the end of the History in Kings the narrative focuses on the monarchy's poor

Alten Testaments (Uni-Taschenbücher 1747; Göttingen: Vandenhoeck & Ruprecht, 1993), 128–30; J. Alberto Soggin, *Introduction to the Old Testament: From Its Origins to the Closing of the Alexandrian Canon* (trans. John Bowden; 3d ed.; OTL; Louisville: Westminster John Knox, 1989), 179–80.

76. So, e.g., Rose, "Deuteronomistic Ideology," 447–50; Nelson, *Double Redaction*, 123; Hans Walter Wolff, "The Kerygma of the Deuteronomistic Historical Work," in Knoppers and McConville, eds., *Reconsidering Israel and Judah*, 62–78 (64); Soggin, *Introduction to the Old Testament*, 180–81; Walter Dietrich, *Prophetie und Geschichte* (FRLANT 108; Göttingen: Vandenhoeck & Ruprecht, 1972), 107; Albertz, *Israel in Exile*, 297; Werner H. Schmidt, *Old Testament Introduction* (trans. Matthew J. O'Connell; 2d ed.; New York: de Gruyter, 1995), 143–44.

77. E.g., Bernhard W. Anderson, *Understanding the Old Testament* (4th ed.; Englewood Cliffs, N.J.: Prentice–Hall, 1986), 183–84; Schmidt, *Old Testament Introduction*, 140–41; Kent Harold Richards, "Deuteronomist," in *Harper's Bible Dictionary* (ed. Paul J. Achtemeier; San Francisco: Harper & Row, 1985), 219; John J. Collins, *Introduction to the Hebrew Bible* (Minneapolis: Fortress, 2004), 184–85; Norman K. Gottwald, *The Hebrew Bible: A Socio-Literary Introduction* (Philadelphia: Fortress, 1985), 138–39; Steven L. McKenzie, "Deuteronomistic History," *ABD* 2:160–68 (161–62).

leadership in causing apostasy among the people as the explanation for the destruction of both the Northern and Southern Kingdoms, and so as the explanation of the exiles' trauma.

Yet while the consensus of scholarship on Dtr acknowledges the central role that the History's narrative places on absolute cultic loyalty to YHWH, not all scholars believe that the central criterion for explaining history here is cultic. Noth himself argued that Dtr's narrative displays a negative view of some aspects of the cult. Deuteronomistic emphasis on a centralization of cult entails a drastic cultic reduction, he argued, and the History in general is not terribly interested in cultic matters, seeing sacrifice as legitimate but "peripheral," and portraying the temple primarily as a place of prayer.[78] Yet cult is important throughout the History. Dtr portrays the temple in Jerusalem "as the culmination of Israel's history," writes Gary Knoppers, and by centralizing sacrifice in the temple, the narrative empowers the temple as a cultic center.[79] More to the point, however, the narrative's explanatory logic of history is cultically dependent: Israel is ultimately judged by its worship and sacrifice,[80] and it is no coincidence that some scholars, and not only followers of Cross's redactional theory, see the highlight of the History in the cultic reform of Josiah in 2 Kgs 23.[81] Josiah's "repentance" in 2 Kgs 23, exhibited through his cultic reform, is the only action in the whole History that Dtr's narrative adjudges to be done for God with "all his heart and with all his soul and with all his might, according to all of the law of Moses" (2 Kgs 23:25), which is precisely the attitude to the law that Moses exhorts in Deut 6:4–6.

Like Thomas Römer, I will argue below that Dtr's narrative insists on Israel's fidelity to the law if the nation is to keep the land,[82] although the

78. Noth, *The Deuteronomistic History*, 92–95.

79. Gary N. Knoppers, "Prayer and Propaganda: Solomon's Dedication of the Temple and the Deuteronomist's Program," in Knoppers and McConville, eds., *Reconsidering Israel and Judah*, 370–96 (372–74).

80. Halpern, *The First Historians*, 220–28.

81. So Albertz, *Israel in Exile*, 301–2; idem, "In Search of the Deuteronomists: A First Solution to a Historical Riddle," in Römer, ed., *The Future of the Deuteronomistic History*, 1–17 (8–9); Hoffmann, *Reform und Reformen*, 269–70; Andrew D. H. Mayes, "Deuteronomistic Ideology and the Theology of the Old Testament," *JSOT* 82 (1999): 57–82 (67); Gottfried Vanoni, "Beobachtungen zur deuteronomistischen Terminologie in 2 Kön 23,25–25,30," in *Das Deuteronomium: Entstehung, Gestalt, und Botschaft* (ed. Norbert Lohfink; BETL 68; Leuven: Uitgeverij Peeters, 1985), 357–62; Knoppers, *Two Nations Under God*, 2:174–75; Sweeney, *King Josiah of Judah*, 21–177; Nelson, *Double Redaction*, 122.

82. Römer, "The Book of Deuteronomy," 186.

narrative equates this nomistic fidelity to YHWH's law with cultic fidelity to YHWH. The narrative does not precisely explain this equation, although it is certainly explainable. I have argued elsewhere that the narrative uses right worship of and sacrifice to YHWH to the exclusion of any other god to signal Israel's assent to the validity of the entire law. Insofar as Israel rightly worships YHWH alone and does not commit apostasy, Israel signals its acceptance of God's authority to the exclusion of any other, and therefore acknowledges God's right to impose a law upon the nation. The narrative can thus assume that where sacrifice is being rightly done, the law is being obeyed and can see in Israel's cultic failure, a failure that explains the exilic community's trauma, a nomistic failure as well.[83]

The equation of cultic and nomistic fidelity to God, particularly in the opening of the History in Deuteronomy, is clearest in the narrative's use of "love." References to the necessity of Israel to love God in Deuteronomy (6:5; 7:9–10; 10:12–13; 11:1, 13, 22; 13:2–6 [ET 1–5]; 19:8–10; 30:6–10, 15–20) are linked to calls to obey the law and to calls to worship YHWH alone.[84] Von Rad argues that Deuteronomy locates an inner or "spiritual" sense of the law, and thus sums up the entire law in 6:5 as the single command to love God.[85] "Love" in ancient Near Eastern political language is how vassals express their loyalty to their suzerains. Love of a vassal for a suzerain appears as ancient Near Eastern political language as early as the Mari correspondence, and is frequent in the Amarna letters.[86] In the latter, it appears as referring to general vassal loyalty to the Pharaoh and in reference to the vassal's loyalty to the Pharaoh in the face of local rebellion against Egypt.[87] It reflects the

83. David Janzen, *The Social Meanings of Sacrifice in the Hebrew Bible: A Study of Four Writings* (BZAW 344; Berlin: de Gruyter, 2004), 132–50, esp. 136–37.

84. The connections between love and obedience to the commandments are found in 6:1–9; 7:9–10; 10:12–13; 11:1–32; 13:2–5 [ET 1–4]; 19:8–10; 30:6–10, 15–20; connections between love and the worship of YHWH alone in 6:1–5; 11:13–17, 22–28; 13:2–5 [ET 1–4]; 30:15–20. When we compare these two lists we see that there is some overlap, reflecting the connection the narrative draws between the necessity to obey all of the law and to worship YHWH alone.

85. Von Rad, *Old Testament Theology*, 1:201.

86. William L. Moran, "The Ancient Near Eastern Background of the Love of God in Deuteronomy," in *The Most Magic Word: Essays on Babylonian and Biblical Literature* (ed. Ronald S. Hendel; CBQMS 35; Washington: The Catholic Biblical Association of America, 2002), 170–81 (172–73).

87. Akkadian uses the verb *râmu* and cognate words to express love or loyalty within the context of a treaty, as North West Semitic uses רחם (see below). For an example of the use of *râmu* to express vassal loyalty to Pharaoh in the Amarna letters, see, e.g., 53.40–51; 83.43–51; 114.59–69; 138.71–80.

suzerain's regard for and support of his vassal as well.[88] This is also Neo-Assyrian political language that Esarhaddon directs toward his vassals,[89] and it is attested as part of the treaty vocabulary of North West Semitic, appearing in one of the treaties from Sefire in reference to the relationship between vassals and suzerain.[90] For the narrative of Dtr, then, there is no necessary conflict between cultic and nomistic loyalty, since absolute fealty in both areas expresses absolute loyalty to God as Israel's sole suzerain. To love YHWH means to be loyal to him and so to have regard for his authority to impose demands on Israel, his vassal. Israel acknowledges his status as suzerain through their worship of him alone, and they express this loyalty ethically by adhering to his commands. Deuteronomy, with a lawcode at its center, places strong emphasis on love as loyalty expressed ethically through obedience to the law,[91] while the rest of Dtr's narrative primarily presents loyalty as signaled through rightly practiced monolatry. Recognizing this, Hans-Detlef Hoffmann argues that Dtr is primarily a history of the cult, and sees a cycle of cultic reforms, both installing and removing apostate apparatuses, as its prominent feature.[92] And John Van Seters, while acknowledging a variety of

88. E.g., in the Amarna letters, see 123.23–24; 158.36–38.

89. Esarhaddon makes his vassals swear their loyalty to Ashurbanipal, his heir, in their treaty: "You will love Ashurbanipal, the crown prince, the son of Esarhaddon, king of Assyria, your lord, as your own lives" (D. J. Wiseman, *The Vassal-Treaties of Esarhaddon* [Iraq 20; London: The British School of Archaeology in Iraq, 1958], 49–50).

90. Matiel refers to his vassals as רחמן "friends" (*KAI* 224.8); the word is cognate with the root רחם "to love." Besides רחם (the root אהב is not well attested outside of Hebrew in North West Semitic languages), North West Semitic treaties also use נפש, לבב, and צדק in political senses that call upon a vassal to express loyalty to his suzerain, and so further reflects the language of Deuteronomy. For a discussion, see Udo Rüterswörden, "Die Liebe zu Gott im Deuteronomium," in *Die deuteronomistischen Geschichtswerke: Redaktions- und religionsgeschichtliche Perspektiven zur 'Deuteronomismus'-Diskussion in Tora und Vorderen Propheten* (ed. Markus Witte et al.; BZAW 365; Berlin: de Gruyter, 2006), 229–38 (235–37).

91. So Jeffrey H. Tigay, *Deuteronomy: The JPS Torah Commentary* (Philadelphia: Jewish Publication Society, 1996), 76–77; Richard D. Nelson, *Deuteronomy: A Commentary* (OTL; Louisville: Westminster John Knox, 2002), 91; Hermann Spieckermann, "Mit der Liebe im Wort: Ein Beitrag zur Theologie des Deuteronomiums," in *Liebe und Gebot: Studien zum Deuteronomium* (ed. Richard G. Kratz and Hermann Spieckermann; FRLANT 190; Göttingen: Vandenhoeck & Ruprecht, 2000), 190–205 (193).

92. Hoffmann argues that Dtr's narrative employs the cult as the criterion for its judgment of history, and that is why it is important to study Josiah's reforms within the larger context of them throughout Dtr (Hoffmann, *Reform und Reformen*, 22–24).

themes throughout the History as a whole, ultimately sees Dtr's narrative as a story that isolates Israel's identity in the laws and in its loyalty to God.[93]

As the main theme of Dtr's narrative, the failure of vassal loyalty through right worship and obedience to all of the law is central to the logic of history that it presents to the exiles to explain their trauma. Ultimately, this narrative logic relates closely to Israel's identity as the narrative sees it, for the History focuses readers' attention on the nation's fate as solely linked to its loyalty to its divine suzerain. This first main theme of Dtr's explanatory narrative is closely related to the second: Israel's failure in loyalty to God is profoundly influenced by the failures of their leaders. The failure of Israel's leadership to enforce vassal loyalty among the people helps to explain the exiles' trauma, as well as the punishments that earlier generations of Israel have undergone. By the end of Kings, the narrative concludes that the monarchy forces the people into the cultic disloyalty that explains the readers' trauma, and the narrative as a whole emphasizes how influential the leaders of Israel have been in the failure of Israel's cultic life throughout its history.

It is rare to see scholars discuss the leadership of Israel as a main theme of the History's narrative,[94] even though stories about the leaders of Israel and the success and failure of their leadership occupy a fair portion of the History. While the importance and prominence of this second theme is eminently clear in the evaluative comments on the individual monarchs' cultic failures and successes in Kings, the mere space that the History devotes to the actions and speeches of Moses, Joshua, the judges, the prophets, and the kings of the united monarchy who appear even before we come across the regular repetition of evaluative comments in Kings tells us that leaders are an important focus of the master narrative's interest. I will argue in the chapters below that the failures of Israel's leaders are more numerous than often recognized, if only because the narrative voice tends to avoid evaluative language in regard to Israel's leaders before the time of the divided monarchy.

The contrast between the negative reforms of Manasseh and the positive ones of Josiah is only the greatest contrast of many cycles of reforms throughout Dtr that go back to the narrative of Deut 9 (p. 154).

93. See Van Seters, *In Search of History*, 307–14 for the variety of themes that he sees operating in Dtr as a whole. The paratactic construction that he identifies at the heart of the narrative's composition does not rely on a single theme for unity within the work (pp. 320–21), but for his conclusion regarding the centrality of cult and law see p. 359.

94. Although see Sweeney, *King Josiah of Judah*, 31–32.

Readers are not always provided with an interpretive key by the narrator that evaluates the actions of every leader within Israel. We may be told that Josiah "did what was just in the eyes of YHWH" (2 Kgs 24:2), but what about Gideon, who makes an ephod after which Israel prostitutes themselves (Judg 8:27)? What about Jephthah, who burns up his daughter as a sacrifice to YHWH (Judg 11:34–39), despite the law's prohibition of such an action in Deut 12:29–31? The narrator does not explicitly evaluate their actions. (Nor is this unusual for biblical literature, for, outside of Kings, narrators rarely pass judgment on characters' actions.)[95] Readers, as they make their way through Dtr, must often make their own evaluative judgments of Israel's leaders, but they will be able to make them only insofar as they have rightly absorbed the first theme's emphasis on the role of loyalty and the lack of it to the divine suzerain in the explanation of history. By forcing readers to make such judgments without explicit narrative guidance, the narrative really forces readers to inculcate the cultic logic that it presents as determining history. Once readers have learned to use this logic to correctly evaluate Israel's rulers, they can then see how correct the narrative's evaluations of Israel's final rulers truly are.

2. *Summary of the Master Narrative's Main Concepts*

In order to pursue these two themes, the master narrative clearly puts faith in the ability of language to convey a meaning for the trauma and so to control it. Dtr's narrative thus depends on stable meanings for various concepts that it uses in its presentations of its two main themes. I list the definitions of some of these concepts that the narrative uses here, filling in the entries to the ethical dictionary that the narrative draws upon in its attempts to explain the trauma. It is precisely this language, these concepts or assumptions, that trauma itself subverts as it subverts the logic the narrative uses to explain history and, ultimately, the exilic community's trauma. In the second parts of the following chapters that focus on each individual book of Dtr we will see exactly how this logic and the linguistic concepts on which it is based are subverted, and so we must be clear as to how the master narrative uses this language before we can see how trauma interrupts the narrative to subvert and undermine it.

a. *God.* We can say, first, that the master narrative views God as the just divine suzerain. God has clearly revealed his expectations for Israel's conduct and placed them in a treaty or covenant framework. I have

95. Shimon Bar-Efrat, *Narrative Art in the Bible* (Sheffield: T&T Clark International, 2004), 28–30.

already mentioned the general scholarly consensus that the master narrative views God as just, and this consensus is not a surprise. God himself, in the song that he directs Moses to teach Israel in order to explain the exile and destruction to them, states that "his work is perfect, and all his ways are just," that he is "without deceit, righteous and upright" (Deut 32:4). Moses tells Israel that God "is not partial and does not take a bribe" (Deut 10:17), and tells them as well that God will keep the covenant with Israel, and thus will acknowledge their vassal loyalty to him and punish those who do not keep the law he has given them (7:9–10). David, in the context of explaining God's salvation of him because of his obedience to divine command (2 Sam 22:21–31) says that "the word of YHWH is pure" (22:31). God's justice in punishing and saving Israel is clearly seen throughout the master narrative, as we can see in the narrative's explanations for why the North and Samaria were destroyed in 2 Kgs 17:7–23 and why Judah and Jerusalem were destroyed in 21:1–15; in the speeches of Moses in Deuteronomy; in those of Joshua in Josh 23–24; in the master narrative's evaluative summary of the period of the judges in Judg 2:6–3:6; throughout the entire cycle of apostasy in Judg 2–16; and so on. There are some occasions, such as the disintegration of Israel in Judg 17–21, in which the master narrative provides no explanatory comment that describes the destruction of Israel as just punishment for the nation's sins; as in the case of the leadership theme, there are places where the narrator appears to urge readers to supply such evaluations by themselves. And as the suzerain who justly punishes and rewards his vassal for their adherence (or lack of it) to a clearly stated standard of behavior, the master narrative simply assumes that God's power is so great that he alone controls history and thus has untrammeled power to punish and reward. Readers can see this in the evaluative comments to which I have just referred, and God himself says this explicitly:

> There is no god except me.
> I kill and I make alive,
> I wound and I heal,
> and there is no one who delivers from my hand. (Deut 32:39)

b. *Justice.* In discussing what the master narrative assumes about God, we have been discussing related topics, one of which is justice. In Dtr's master narrative, justice is primarily a description of the way in which God interacts with Israel in history. When God treats Israel on the basis of their nomistic and cultic loyalty, a matter made clear in the law and in Moses' speeches that surround it, justice is being done. The blessings and curses of Deut 28 are concrete examples of just actions by God toward Israel based on their loyalty or disobedience. When 2 Kgs 17 and 21 explain the destructions of the Northern and Southern Kingdoms by means of the people's violation of the law, something described almost solely in terms of cultic disloyalty, these explanations are examples of God's justice in history.

c. *Israel.* The most obvious comment to make about the nation of Israel from the point of view of Dtr's master narrative is that YHWH has a unique relationship with this people. Israel is chosen: "Only your ancestors did YHWH love, and chose their descendants after them, you, from all the peoples of the earth" (Deut 10:15; cf. also 4:37; 7:6–7; 14:2; 26:18; 32:8–9). The master narrative uses "Israel" to refer to the single nation formed by the tribes (unless the narrative is specifically referring to the Northern Kingdom), not necessarily the way that we might expect a writer of the Babylonian exile, 150 years after the destruction of Samaria and the disappearance of the Northern Kingdom, to use the name. Israel is one people linked to one land under the law given to them by one God.[96] As a nation, it has its origins outside of Canaan, and is strictly forbidden from intermarrying with Canaanites, since this leads to apostasy and thus punishment (Deut 7:1–6; 20:16–18; Josh 23:6–13; Judg 2:6–3:6; 1 Kgs 11:1–11). In the History's master narrative, Israel is, of course, a series of successive generations that the narrative sometimes defines in relationship to each other: the generation that witnessed the exodus and the lawgiving at Horeb, for example, dies off and is followed by the generation whom we encounter at the beginning of Deuteronomy who will conquer the land (Deut 1:34; 2:16); this conquest generation dies off and is followed by the one who worships the Canaanite gods (Judg 2:10); and so on. To some degree, Israel is really treated as a single character in the story. The nation sins as one (e.g., Deut 1:26–28; 9:8, 12; Judg 2:11–13; 2 Kgs 17:7–23; and so on), and the covenant God makes with Israel assumes that the nation as a whole will be rewarded or punished based on their collective loyalty or disloyalty (e.g., Deut 4:21–27; 7:12–16, 26; 8:17–20; 28:1–69; Josh 23–24; Judg 2:6–3:6; 2 Kgs 17:7–23; and so on).

96. See, e.g., Rose, "Deuteronomistic Ideology," 444–46; Siegfried Herrmann, "Die konstruktive Restauration: Das Deuteronomium als Mitte biblischer Theologie," in *Probleme biblischer Theologie: Gerhard von Rad zum 70. Geburtstag* (ed. Hans Walter Wolff; Munich: Kaiser, 1971), 155–70 (158–62); A. D. H. Mayes, *Deuteronomy* (NCBC; Grand Rapids: Eerdmans, 1979), 57–58; Timothy A. Lenchak, *"Choose Life!": A Rhetorical-Critical Investigation of Deuteronomy 28,69–30,20* (AnBib 129; Rome: Pontificio Istituto Biblico, 1993), 237–41.

d. *Punishment.* Punishment in Dtr's master narrative is a manifestation of God's justice in history in response to Israel's failure in loyalty. The nation as a whole can receive punishment by foreign invasion (e.g., the individual movements of the cycle of apostasy in Judg 2–13) and removal from the land (the ultimate punishment, visited on both the Northern and Southern Kingdoms in 2 Kgs 17 and 25). God can also punish individuals, notably leaders of Israel, as, for example, he punishes Saul for his wrongly timed sacrifice in 1 Sam 13:2–14 and for his disobedience in 15:1–30.

The general pattern of punishment in the narrative, at least in the case of Israel as a whole, is that God will punish each generation for the sin that it commits. Moses tells Israel in Deut 29:16–27 [ET 17–28] that God will punish with the curses of Deut 28 the very generation who is disloyal to the covenant God has made with the nation. In 29:18–21 [ET 19–22] he says that God will punish those who ignore the instructions of the law, while "the next generation, your children who arise after you," will be amazed by the destruction that the sinful generation has received as a punishment, indicating that God will not wait until the next generation to punish.[97] He makes the same point in 7:9–10 when he says that God "repays the ones who hate him to his face to destroy him; he does not delay." (For these verses as the narrative's attempt to clarify Deut 5:9, see Chapter 3.) As soon as Israel enters and settles in the land in Judges, this is precisely what we see: God immediately punishes Israel with foreign invasion when they act in cultic disloyalty (Judg 3:7–8, 12–14; 4:1–3; 6:1–6; 10:6–9; 13:1), but when the narrative says nothing about the nation committing apostasy, it tells readers that "the land had rest" (3:11, 30; 5:31).[98] In readers' introduction to the punishment of Israel, the nation is punished with foreign invasion only because, "when the judge died, they acted corruptly more than their ancestors, to go after other

97. We should translate הדור אחרון in 29:21 [ET 22] as "the next generation," not "later generations" as Tigay (*Deuteronomy*, 281) and Duane Christensen (*Deuteronomy 21:10–34:12* [WBC 6B; Nashville: Thomas Nelson, 2002], 726) do. The definite article, the fact that דור appears in the singular, as well as the qualification that this particular generation is "your children who will arise after you," specify the next generation in particular. This is the only place in the Bible where we find this phrase with the definite article, and thus it emphasizes the specificity of the very next generation.

98. The one place that seems to be an exception to this pattern is 8:28, which states that "the land had rest" despite the fact that 8:27 claims that Israel "prostituted after" the ephod that Gideon made, which suggests some kind of idolatry. There is, however, no indication that any later generation suffers for this sin—God simply chooses not to punish the sinful one.

gods to serve them and to worship them" (Judg 2:19). It is these sinful generations, not the ones who are not reported to sin, who are punished with the foreign invasions that foreshadow the Babylonian invasion that causes the exiles' trauma. The curses of Deut 28 culminate with warnings of foreign invasion, as well as siege, famine, and exile (28:47–57, 64–67); this pattern of punishment begins in Judges and reaches its nadir in 2 Kgs 17 and 25. After Israel's repentance of its apostasy in 1 Sam 7, we again encounter the nation's apostasy in Kings, where we see further incidents of warfare in the context of apostasy (1 Kgs 14:25; 15:6, 16–22, 32; 19:15–18; 20:1–34; 22:29–36; 2 Kgs 3:4–27; 6:8–7:20; 8:12, 20–22, 28; 13:1–6, 20; 14:1–14; 15:18–20, 29; 16:1–9; 24:1–4, 8–17), as well as the ultimate destructions of the Northern and Southern Kingdoms for their cultic disloyalty (2 Kgs 17:1–23; 25:1–26). In this part of the History, almost every generation who worships foreign gods—and in Kings this almost always occurs because the monarchs cause them to do so—experiences warfare, although the narrative is largely focused on the removal from power of the kings and dynasties who are ultimately responsible for this sin.

So while we find that some scholars contrast the immediate and individual retribution in Chronicles with a very different portrayal of divine punishment in Dtr where, they argue, God can punish children for their parents' sin,[99] this is really not the picture with which Dtr's master narrative presents us. Moses tells Israel that God "does not delay" to punish, and the narrative bears this out, showing sinful generations from Judges through Kings, from Israel's entrance into the land to its removal from it, punished through foreign invasion and civil war. The notable changes that the Chronicler makes to stories from Dtr in terms of punishment are limited to how God treats individuals, not the nation: the split of the kingdom after Solomon's death in Chronicles is not attributed to his sin; the Chronicler does attribute sin to Asa to explain his illness in his old age (2 Chr 26:16–21); Josiah's death in battle is blamed on his disobedience (35:20–25); and so on.[100] The focus of explanation in Dtr's

99. E.g., von Rad, *Old Testament Theology*, 1:347–50; idem, *Das Geschichtsbild des Chronistischen Werkes* (BWANT 54; Stuttgart: Kohlhammer, 1930), 12–13; Robert North, "The Theology of the Chronicler," *JBL* 82 (1963): 369–81; Sara Japhet, *The Ideology of the Book of Chronicles and Its Place in Biblical Thought* (BEATAJ 9; Frankfurt am Main: Lang, 1989), 156–76; idem, *I & II Chronicles* (OTL; Louisville: Westminster John Knox, 1993), 1069.

100. See the examples provided by von Rad, *Old Testament Theology*, 1:348–49; Japhet, *The Ideology of the Book of Chronicles*, 165–76; Brian E. Kelly, *Retribution and Eschatology in Chronicles* (JSOTSup 211; Sheffield: Sheffield Academic,

narrative, however, is on why God punishes Israel and, thus, how the exile is to be explained, and in this matter, as we have seen, the narrative presents disloyal generations as being punished with foreign invasion.

e. and f. *Salvation and Repentance.* Dtr's master narrative links salvation and repentance. When Israel repents (שׁוב) of their cultic disloyalty and turns aside (סור) the foreign gods they worship, YHWH provides them with salvation from their foreign oppressors. This is what we see, for example, in the sequence of events in 1 Sam 7:3–11: "If you are repenting to YHWH will all of your hearts," Samuel says to Israel, "turn aside the foreign gods from your midst, and the Astartes, and set your hearts on YHWH and serve him alone, and he will rescue you from the hand of the Philistines" (7:3). The Israelites follow his instructions, and God saves them from their enemy. So salvation, like punishment, is a manifestation of God's justice in history, although in this case in response to Israel's repentance. This link between repentance and salvation makes perfect sense within the narrative's logic in history, for if God punishes vassal disloyalty with destruction, primarily through foreign invasion, then it stands to reason that God should reward a return to loyalty with salvation from foreign enemies. In Deut 30:1–5 Moses links the people's repentance in exile to their salvation in a return to the land, and Solomon asks God that, following the exiles' repentance, their enemies show them compassion (1 Kgs 8:46–53), a request that may well imply a return to the land, as Moses promised in Deut 30.[101] Scholarship, however, does not agree as to what future Dtr's narrative envisions for the exiles at the end of the History (a matter that we will discuss in Chapter 7 below), although some scholars argue that if the narrative suggests that Israel will return to the land from Babylon, then this will be based on repentance, just as Moses had predicted.[102]

g. *Prophecy.* Prophecy in Dtr's master narrative is largely the manner in which God communicates his will and specific commands to Israel. Moses, who repeats the law to Israel before they enter the land, describes himself as a prophet (Deut 18:15). God can communicate directly with

1996), 95–106; Ralph W. Klein, *1 Chronicles: A Commentary* (Hermeneia; Minneapolis: Fortress, 2006), 46–47.

101. So Mordechai Cogan, *1 Kings: A New Translation with Introduction and Commentary* (AB 10; New York: Doubleday, 2001), 287.

102. E.g., von Rad, *Old Testament Theology*, 1:346; Wolff, "The Kerygma of the Deuteronomistic Historical Work"; Donald F. Murray, "Of All the Years the Hopes—or Fears? Jehoiachin in Babylon (2 Kings 25:27–30)," *JBL* 120 (2001): 245–65.

people who are not prophets, like Joshua (in, e.g., Josh 1:2–9) or Solomon (in, e.g., 1 Kgs 3:1–14), although this is mainly accomplished through inquiry and/or the Urim and Thummim (e.g., Judg 20:18, 20, 23; 1 Sam 23:10–12; 2 Sam 2:1; and so on). In the master narrative it is the prophets, however, who provide divine warning to Israel and its leaders about the consequences of their failure to maintain vassal loyalty to God (e.g., Judg 6:7–10; 1 Sam 12:6–25; 13:13–14; 15:17–29; 2 Sam 12:1–15; 1 Kgs 11:29–39; 13:1–10; 14:6–16; 16:1–14; and so on), and these prophecies are fulfilled in the master narrative. Prophecy underlines God's justice, for through the prophets Israel is continually reminded of the necessity of the covenant loyalty they owe their divine suzerain and the punishment that will result from not maintaining it.

h. *History.* In the master narrative, history itself is the chronological forum in which God enacts justice and fulfills prophecy. It is the realm in which he exercises his power through justice. History in Dtr's narrative, as Horst Preuss puts it, "is a field of guilt and apostasy" in which God punishes the apostasy of which Israel is guilty.[103] God does not act capriciously, but observes Israel's actions and warns them of their failure, and only later intervenes to provide punishment and reward commensurate with their actions.

3. *Trauma and the Subversion of Dtr's Master Narrative*

In each of the following chapters on a constitutive book of Dtr, I will begin the chapter by providing concrete manifestations of the master narrative's two main themes. The narrative pursues these themes, of course, in order to communicate its logic in history that explains the exilic community's trauma to them through the use of stable linguistic concepts such as the ones that we have just examined. In the second section of each chapter, I will show how trauma erupts into this narrative to subvert or undermine this explanation of trauma and the linguistic concepts on which the explanation depends. The master narrative attempts to explain why the exiles underwent the experiences of forced migration, siege, famine, and the slaughter of their countryfolk; it uses the language of the concepts that we have just surveyed, in other words, to attempt to control the writer's and the community's trauma, to provide a clear and totalizing narrative and ethical basis that explains and thus encapsulates it. Trauma interrupts this explanatory narrative, however, to challenge these assumptions and negate this language, putting this speech on trial

103. Preuss, *Old Testament Theology*, 1:211.

and rendering it ambiguous, making any certainty in explanation impossible. We have seen already that trauma cannot be narrativized, whether the narrative is psychological or literary. This does not mean that trauma survivors and their descendants cannot speak or write about what happened, but it does mean that they will not be able to explain the trauma or encompass it in a narrative that attempts to make ethical truth claims about it. Trauma by its very nature cannot be integrated into explanatory narratives that make sense to sufferers, even if they might attempt to place it in an ethical or social context with which they are familiar. In this sense trauma is merely a gap, an absence that nonetheless exercises great unknown power over survivors and their descendants, especially if the descendants live within an entire community that has suffered massive psychic trauma. So despite the attempts of Dtr's master narrative, trauma eludes the narrative's linguistic control and challenges the very explanatory logic in which the narrative attempts to encapsulate it. If we wish, for the sake of convenience, to refer to this as a traumatic narrative—although it is really a non- or anti-narrative—then we have in the History a double narrative, the case that Fridman describes in her analysis of Appelfeld's *Badenheim 1939*. The dictionary of Dtr's master narrative may stand on a shelf in the Garden of Eden, where linguistic concepts and familiar theology can explain 597 and 586, but trauma radically challenges the concepts that the narrative employs to make this argument, leaving the narrative's clarity muddied and its ethical certainty ambiguous. The narrative's explanation of vast destruction and terror—God justly punishes Israel for their vassal disloyalty—is found wanting, and the trauma renders narrative unable to make the unbelievable believable.

I refer to trauma's interruption of Dtr's narrative as undermining or subversion. These traumatic interruptions are not really a narrative in and of themselves, for they offer no alternative explanation, no other framework in which to explain the horror suffered by the author's community and potentially by the author him or herself. Trauma is powerful precisely through its absence to memory and thought. When Charlotte Delbo writes that while she is not sure that her writing is true, she is sure that it happened, she means that she can find no framework of explanatory or ethical truth in which to situate her trauma. When Primo Levi writes that he is not convinced that the trauma he survived really happened, he refers to something that cannot be believed and that thus cannot have truth claims made about it. So in the History, trauma does not interrupt the master narrative in order to provide a competing explanation or truth claim, but to subvert the truth the narrative advances. Sometimes this subversion amounts to outright contradiction of the concepts or assumptions that the master narrative depends upon, although most of the time, as we shall see, it throws these concepts into ambiguity, questioning them in ways for which the master narrative provides no answers.

"Subversion" is not a term covered by biblical reference works, but scholars in the field do use it to describe aspects of biblical writings.[104] Among the few scholars who supply a definition for their use of the term is Rex Mason, who describes it as an attempt to overthrow power and its ideology.[105] Eric Siebert adopts the language of Bruce Lincoln and refers to subversive writing as "corrosive discourse" that eats away at the claims of authority of narrative voices; for Siebert it is propaganda that aims at "undermining, criticizing or otherwise 'corroding' an ideology, institution or individual."[106] It is this corrosive sense in which I am using the term to refer to trauma's eruption into the master narrative of Dtr, although I am not interested in using language that refers to authorial intention. Trauma itself is beyond conscious control or access, and so I do not find it worthwhile to discuss whether or not the author of the Deuteronomistic History meant to challenge the concepts that he or she depends upon to articulate the master narrative and its two themes. I am certainly not the first person to notice that the main concepts or assumptions of the History do not go unchallenged or unsubverted,[107] but for this investigation it is irrelevant as to whether or not this subversion was intended by the author.

Trauma brings the master narrative's language into question over and over, which is to say that trauma repeats in the History, a standard feature of traumatic literature. Sometimes the master narrative seems to control the trauma, as it does when it presents a detailed picture of the famine and degradation in a besieged city in the curses of Deut 28. Here, the famine that seizes the city in 586 is ethicized, since according to the

104. For a recent survey of the different ways in which biblical scholars understand subversion and apply it to the study of the texts, see Eric A. Siebert, *Subversive Scribes and the Solomonic Narrative: A Rereading of 1 Kings 1–11* (LHBOTS 436; New York: T&T Clark, 2006), 19–40.

105. Rex Mason, *Propaganda and Subversion in the Old Testament* (London: SPCK, 1997), 174.

106. Siebert, *Subversive Scribes*, 15–16.

107. E.g., see Robert Polzin, *Moses and the Deuteronomist: A Literary Study of the Deuteronomic History* (New York: Seabury, 1980), 59, where he refers to voices of "authoritarian dogmatism" and "critical traditionalism"; or see Lyle Eslinger's discussion of Solomon's prayer of 1 Kgs 8, which he sees as a voice subverting or undermining Deuteronomistic ideology (*Into the Hands of the Living God* [JSOTSup 84; BLS 24; Sheffield: Almond, 1989], 159–63, 177–78); or see Daniel Hawk's discussion of competing plot lines in the book of Joshua (*Every Promise Fulfilled: Contesting Plots in Joshua* [LCBI; Louisville: Westminster John Knox, 1991]).

prediction of these curses those who suffer the trauma have deserved it through their actions. In many places, however, the trauma repeats in Dtr and subverts the control that the master narrative tries to exert over it. As the trauma repeats into or beside the master narrative, it envisions suffering without explanation and punishment for no reason, and so subverts the language of God, justice, punishment, and so on that the master narrative uses to explain and ethicize the exile. Traumatic repetition collapses the generations of Israel, so that each generation can be portrayed as guilty, even though some commit no sin, and each generation of Israel can appear to suffer the same punishment as the exiles did, a subversion of concepts as basic to the narrative as "Israel" and "history." Intruding into the narrative and disrupting its argument, the trauma of the exilic community becomes the "one time only" that uncannily collapses time, the unique temporality that repeats and makes a mockery of the master narrative's chronology and understanding of history and divine justice.

Trauma's subversion of the master narrative of the History challenges and throws into ambiguity and radical questioning the notions that God is just; that the exiles' suffering is truly a punishment for disloyalty; that repentance has any effect at all on how God distributes salvation; or even that Israel consists of a succession of different generations, each making its own decisions in regard to its vassal duties that it owes to God and judged accordingly. Trauma collapses the narrative's understanding of history itself, since the "one time only" of trauma intrudes to deny the ethical weight that the narrative accords to history and the divine and human actions within it. It makes it impossible for the narrative to explain the exiles' trauma to them in any clear and final sense. For the traumatic intrusions that we can observe in the History, the narrative language of ethical explanation fails. No conclusions as to history, God, Israel, justice, punishment, and so on are available to trauma, and in the final chapters of Kings, where we might expect to find the narrative's clearest explanation of the exilic community's trauma—since these chapters deal with the actions that lead directly to the trauma of 586—we encounter merely ambiguity. By the end of the History, that is, the narrative itself finally and ultimately collapses through trauma's subversion of it.

It is in fact trauma's subversion of the narrative's explanation in the final chapters of the History, 2 Kgs 21–25, that we find uncannily anticipated or foreshadowed in the earlier parts of Dtr. In these concluding chapters, trauma intrudes as narrative absence to suggest that God does not punish disloyal generations or reward loyal ones; that God does not meet repentance with salvation; that, in fact, God does not seem able or willing to distinguish between different generations or their varying degrees of loyalty to him at all; or that such distinctions simply do not influence how he treats Israel. Trauma's suggestion here, uncannily anticipated many times at earlier points in Dtr, is that there simply is no logic in history and thus no explanation for trauma. God fails to punish the generations of Judah that Manasseh, Amon, and even Josiah, for the first 17 years of his reign, cause to sin in a manner worse than that of the Canaanites (while Josiah is not directly accused of causing the people to sin, he does nothing to reverse Manasseh's apostasy until his eighteenth year [2 Kgs 22:3]), a period that could have lasted as long as 74 years.[108] God also refuses to recognize Josiah's perfect act of repentance (2 Kgs 23:25–27),[109] an act that returns the people to vassal loyalty to God. It is possible to read the stories of the final four kings of Judah who follow Josiah as stating that no one of them ever reinstates apostasy, at least not to the point of causing the people to practice it and thus to act in cultic disloyalty to their divine suzerain. When God thus executes judgment and inflicts punishment on Judah in 586, it is possible for readers to conclude that the people have been living in cultic loyalty for 35 years,[110] longer than a generation, that is, after Josiah returned them to cultic loyalty. We could conclude that God has punished the wrong generation for the sins that Manasseh causes Judah to commit, perhaps because God cannot distinguish between the generations or between the guilty and the loyal; or that God does not punish the guilty and does not save those who have returned to vassal loyalty—that, in short, acts of vassal loyalty or disloyalty may have no effect on how God treats Israel. These perfectly possible explanations subvert the narrative's explanation for the trauma, and it is these traumatic gaps and subversions of the narrative in 2 Kgs 21–25 that uncannily repeat throughout Dtr.

108. Manasseh reigns for 55 years (2 Kgs 21:1) and Amon for two (21:19). Manasseh's sin continues for another 17 years in the first part of Josiah's reign until he enacts his reforms (22:3). Readers are not told, however, at what point in his reign Manasseh institutes his apostasy.

109. The narrative is clear that Josiah "repented (שׁב) to YHWH with all his heart, with all his soul, and with all his might, according to all of the law of Moses" (23:25). No other figure in Dtr is ever said to act towards God with all of his heart, soul, and might, although Moses commanded this attitude to God in Deut 6:4–5. This unique description of Josiah, then, suggests that he performs a perfect act of repentance.

110. Since Josiah's reign lasts 31 years, and since he returns Judah to cultic loyalty with his reform of his eighteenth year (2 Kgs 23:1–3), Judah worships rightly for the final 13 years of his reign. His successors rule for 22 more years (23:31, 36; 24:8, 18), and none of them is said to cause the people to sin.

Chapter 3

DEUTERONOMY: THE UNCANNY BEGINNING OF TRAUMA

A. *Law and Leadership: Dtr's Master Narrative in Deuteronomy*

1. *The First Theme: Nomistic and Cultic Loyalty*

To determine how trauma subverts the Deuteronomistic History's master narrative in Deuteronomy, we must first examine the narrative in this book, and this is where we begin in section A of this chapter, as we will in the following chapters on the other books of the History. The two main themes of Dtr's narrative are well reflected in the speech of Moses in 1:1–4:40 that opens the History. I will use this speech as an example, first, to focus on the theme of Israel's failure in its cultic and nomistic loyalty to God—in Deuteronomy, Moses presents the demands of this loyalty that Israel will ultimately fail to fulfill, and in the first speech we find a concrete example of this failure—and then to focus on the theme of the failure of Israel's leadership, which is less visible in Deuteronomy than in the later books. Moses is a very good leader in the narrative's eyes, but it does not present him as a perfect leader—even he is not said to express his loyalty to YHWH with all of his heart, soul, and mind as Josiah does, and his failure in leadership contributes to the divine punishment of one generation who is condemned, like the exiles, to die outside of the land. In both of these themes the narrative advances its explanation of the exiles' trauma.

The History opens with Moses speaking to Israel in Moab after the nation has captured the Transjordan and is about to enter the rest of the land. To begin by showing how this speech manifests the narrative's first theme, it is helpful to explain why 1:1–4:40 is part of a single composition—4:1–40, the end of the speech, is "commonly regarded" by scholars as being a later insertion into the History[1]—since this demonstration

1. So Patrick D. Miller, *Deuteronomy* (Interpretation; Louisville: John Knox Press, 1990), 20.

points to how, from the very opening of the narrative, readers are shown the consequences of failure in absolute vassal loyalty to God. A typical argument for Deut 4 as a later addition is that of Andrew Mayes, which claims that the transition from the history of Deut 1–3 to the paraenesis of ch. 4 is too abrupt; that the call to "hear" that opens ch. 4 begins new sections in Deuteronomy (cf. 5:1; 6:4; 9:1; 20:3; 27:9); and that chs. 1–3 do not focus on the law at all as ch. 4 does, and omits the major points of Israel's history on which 4:1–40 focuses (Horeb, exodus, and Baal-peor).[2] But even some scholars who argue that 4:1–40 is a late insertion point out that it has been closely edited to match the preceding material,[3] and as Richard Nelson, who argues that 4:1–40 is a later insertion, admits, if we remove ch. 4 then there is a rough transition between chs. 3 and 5.[4] Moreover, arguments that attempt to separate Deut 4 from the preceding three chapters of the speech miss the complexity of the message that the narrative presents in this speech as a whole, a message that goes to the heart of its two main themes.

The connection between Deut 1:1–3:29 and 4:1–40 is integral to the first main theme of the History's narrative. There is certainly no clear distinction—let alone contradiction—between Deut 1–3 and Deut 4 that compels us to see two different authorial hands at work. The entirety of Moses' first speech, on the contrary, makes perfect sense as a single unit within a narrative that uses Israel's past to explain its exilic present. The initial disobedience to divine command by the exodus generation, who sent spies into the land (1:22) rather than listen to God's order to "enter and take possession" (1:8), an order that Moses relays (1:21), is followed by that generation's fear of the inhabitants and their refusal to obey the divine command to enter the land (1:26–28). Their disobedience leads to their consequent loss of the land—God states that the whole generation will die out without possessing any of it (1:34–37)—and so is a story that coheres perfectly with the narrative's first main theme that disobedience to divine command, a grave failure in vassal loyalty, leads to loss of the land. This already points to the narrative's explanation of the exiles'

2. A. D. H. Mayes, "Deuteronomy 4 and the Literary Criticism of Deuteronomy," in *A Song of Power and the Power of Song: Essays on the Book of Deuteronomy* (ed. Duane L. Christensen; SBTS 3; Winona Lake, Ind.: Eisenbrauns, 1993), 195–224 (205–7).

3. E.g., Georg Braulik, *Die Mittel deuteronomischer Rhetorik: Erhoben aus Deuteronomium 4,1–40* (AnBib 68; Rome: Biblical Institute, 1978). One of Braulik's points throughout that work (and also, in a much more condensed form, in his *Deuteronomium 1–16,17* [NEBAT 15; Würzburg: Echter, 1986], 38–39) is that 4:1–40 has links only to the end of chs. 1–3.

4. Nelson, *Deuteronomy*, 61.

trauma. It is not until that disobedient generation dies off in 2:14–15 that God commands an invasion of the Transjordan (2:16–3:11), in which the new generation, the one Moses is addressing in Deuteronomy, meticulously follows the divine commands for battle, exhibiting a trust in God's power to defeat enemies and bestow the land on them that their parents did not. After Moses relates this history in Deut 1–3, 4:1 opens with ועתה "and now," showing that Israel's experiences in the past have relevance for their actions in the present.[5] Brevard Childs notes specifically that Israel's experience of judgment in chs. 1–3 is followed in ch. 4 by a command—"hear"—to learn from that experience and be obedient.[6] ועתה...שמע opens a new section, but it is a new section of the same speech that is tightly linked to what has preceded.[7] The ethical crisis of the first three chapters of the History, in which the generation that experienced exodus and lawgiving is forbidden from entering Canaan, is followed in ch. 4 by a call from God to the next generation who will enter the land to respond properly in ethical action if they wish to survive in the land.[8] Not having been present at Horeb, they need more precise instruction as to their suzerain's demands to avoid their parents' fate.

Dtr's master narrative, after all, is presenting a logic in history that links Israel's actions to its fate, providing examples of both vassal obedience and disobedience throughout the History. So it makes sense that, at its very opening, the narrative of Dtr would begin with a generation who has witnessed God's power to punish and to protect Israel in the land. The generation whom Moses addresses in Israel has seen their parents

5. So Miller, *Deuteronomy*, 20–21.

6. Brevard S. Childs, *Introduction to the Old Testament as Scripture* (Philadelphia: Fortress, 1979), 214.

7. As Moshe Weinfeld points out, there is a difference between the imperative of שמע when it appears without an object, where we expect to find it as an opening address for new sections (so Deut 6:4; 9:1; 20:3; 27:9), and when it appears with an object (as in 4:1), specifically an object that is the commandment that God has given to Israel. He also shows that "and now" frequently appears in Dtr to connect a story with the lesson that is to be drawn from it: e.g., Deut 10:12; Judg 9:16; 10:23, 25; 1 Sam 12:13; etc. (*Deuteronomy 1–11: A New Translation with Introduction and Commentary* [AB 5; New York: Doubleday, 1991], 199). See also Tigay, *Deuteronomy*, 42.

8. So J. G. McConville and J. G. Millar, *Time and Place in Deuteronomy* (JSOTSup 179; Sheffield: Sheffield Academic, 1994), 36. And, as Tigay points out, 4:1–40 is particularly interested in what has and has not been seen. So just as Israel has "seen" the events that Moses relates in chs. 1–3 (1:19, 30–31; 3:21), those who did not learn the proper lesson from the evidence of their eyes will not "see" the land (1:35–36). 4:3–4 makes the same point about Baal of Peor, and the language in 3:24 that refers to God's power is repeated in 4:6–7, 32–39 (*Deuteronomy*, 42).

die outside of the land as punishment for disobedience to their divine suzerain; they have also witnessed God's power to give them land. This is the situation of chs. 1–3. Now, in 4:1–40, Moses begins his instructions as to the specific things this and future generations of Israelites must do to remain there. The narrative's message to the exiles is that Israel has from the beginning been aware of what kind of behavior God expects, and so the nation is clearly aware of which actions lead to prosperity in the land and which ones result in punishment and the loss of the land. The exiles, unfortunately, can see their fate in that of the disobedient exodus generation, who died outside of the land.

Now that the new generation in Moab has seen God's power to punish and to give land, Moses begins to direct them in 4:1–40 as to the details of vassal loyalty that will allow them to avoid their parents' fate. He has clear examples from the experiences of the two generations to point to in order to illustrate the difference between obedience and disobedience. The new generation he addresses in Moab will not keep the land if they do not follow every command that YHWH gives (4:1–2) and thus maintain absolute nomistic loyalty, something their parents failed to do when they abandoned their trust in God's power and refused to enter the land. They must avoid apostasy and thus maintain absolute cultic loyalty, in contrast to their parents who worshiped Baal of Peor (4:3–4). At the very opening of this paraenesis, we see the two kinds of vassal loyalty, cultic and nomistic, that dominate Dtr's narrative. So it is no wonder that Moses directs the new generation's attention to Horeb in 4:5–14; this will be the focus of his work in Deuteronomy, and becomes the focus of what this new generation is directed to do in order to survive in the land. The transition between chs. 3 and 4 is hardly abrupt, as Mayes claims; Deut 1–3 is a historical narrative that prepares readers for the paraenesis of Deut 4, where Moses emphasizes the necessity of both nomistic and cultic loyalty.[9] Their parents have failed at both counts: those who worshiped Baal of Peor were killed (4:3–4); and the rest, who disobeyed a direct divine command, also died outside of the land.[10]

Having reminded the Moab generation in Deut 1–3 of the consequences of vassal loyalty and disloyalty in regards to the land, Moses exposes them in Deut 4 to the conflation of nomistic and cultic loyalty to YHWH, the grounding of the narrative's logic that explains history. While

9. So E. Talstra, "Deuteronomy 9 and 10: Synchronic and Diachronic Observations," in *Synchronic or Diachronic? A Debate on Method in Old Testament Exegesis* (ed. Johannes C. de Moor; OTS 34; Leiden: Brill, 1995), 187–210.

10. For a longer discussion of this point, see J. Gary Millar, *Now Choose Life: Theology and Ethics in Deuteronomy* (NSBT 6; Leicester: Apollos, 1998), 74–80.

Moses emphasizes in 4:2 the need to keep each and every law ("You will not add to the word that I am commanding you and you will not take away from it"), 4:3–4 refers specifically to an instance of apostasy that led to destruction. Deuteronomy 4:5–14 returns immediately to the law that Israel received at Horeb and which it must keep, but 4:15–24 is a warning of Israel's destruction that will result from idolatry. As we discussed in Chapter 2, Dtr's narrative states that both absolute ethical and cultic loyalty to the divine suzerain are necessary if the nation is to survive in the land, and the different parts of the narrative vary as to which of these two kinds of loyalty they emphasize. In this speech, Moses moves back and forth between the two, but his talk of idolatry here is simply another way for the master narrative to point to the apostasy that has doomed the exilic readers, for 4:25–31 states that destruction from the land will occur because of idolatry, and the narrative presents the exiles of both the Northern and Southern Kingdoms as the result of apostasy taking the form of idolatry (1 Kgs 12:28–30; 2 Kgs 17:21–23; 21:11–15). That is, given the loss of the land at the end of the narrative in 2 Kings, the idolatry of which the master narrative warns in Deut 4 would appear to be in the service of the worship of other gods. Moses concludes his first speech in 4:32–40 by once again referring to both the necessity of complete cultic loyalty to YHWH (4:35, 39) and a command to keep the law (4:40). The use of the language of idolatry in 4:1–40 as a whole ultimately contrasts visible idols with an invisible God who, nonetheless, was audible at Horeb, where he commanded (4:12–20). This perhaps provides us with a clue as to the link between cultic and nomistic loyalty in the narrative: when Israel begins to worship other gods, they no longer acknowledge YHWH's authority to command, and so cultic disloyalty will inevitably be followed by nomistic disloyalty. Unlike the visible idols of the other gods, the invisible YHWH has the authority to command.[11]

The historical example of Deut 1–3 and the ethical lesson to be drawn from it in Deut 4 are directed to the new generation of Israel in Moab in the narrative context of Moses' speech, but the presentation of Israel's idolatry/apostasy and the punishment for this action as inevitable in 4:25–31 speaks also to an exilic audience. This idolatry that Israel will certainly commit—Moses begins this section by saying, "When you act corruptly and make an idol"[12]—will mean that "you will surely be

11. And so this is another link between the crimes of apostasy and idolatry in 4:1–40. See Braulik, *Die Mittel deuteronomischer Rhetorik*, 80–81.

12. Some scholars translate this conditionally; that is, with the sense of "If you act corruptly and make an idol…." E.g., see Weinfeld, *Deuteronomy 1–11*, 194; Gerhard von Rad, *Deuteronomy: A Commentary* (trans. Dorothea Barton; OTL; Philadelphia: Westminster, 1966), 47; Mayes, *Deuteronomy*, 155. But 4:25 begins

destroyed quickly from the land which you are about to cross the Jordan to possess" (4:26). The exilic readers have just received their first explanation from the master narrative for the destruction and forced migration they have undergone. So in Deut 1:1–4:40, the opening of the History, Moses tells the exiles that any disobedience by a generation of Israel to divine command—such as the exodus generation's failure to immediately respond to the divine command to enter the land, or their worship of Baal Peor—will be punished with death outside of the land, while obedience will be rewarded with land, and he warns that in the case of idolatry/apostasy the land will surely be lost. There is no need to divide Deut 1–4 up on the basis of authorship; the chapters work together well to manifest the most prominent and important theme in the Deuteronomistic History's narrative: it was the exilic community's failure to remain loyal to YHWH that explains the trauma they have undergone.

For reasons of space, I will not continue to examine each of Moses' speeches in Deuteronomy to flesh out this first theme of the master narrative, but will only briefly point out here that the emphasis on both cultic and nomistic loyalty in the first speech is apparent throughout Deuteronomy. Moses segues easily from injunctions to Israel that it must keep *all* of the law to injunctions that it remain absolutely cultically loyal to God, seeing obedience to each and every commandment as necessary if Israel is to survive. There are many references to the necessity to keep the law, and a number of them specify that the nation must keep all (כל) of it to survive: 5:29; 8:1; 11:8, 22, 32; 13:1 [ET 12:32], 19 [13:18]; 15:5; 19:9; 26:13; 27:1; 28:1, 14, 15; 29:28 [29:29].[13] In almost all of these cases, Moses exhorts fidelity to all of God's commands (מצוה or מצות), although 29:28 commands obedience to "all the words of the Torah," and 11:32 to "all the statutes and the judgment." As the appearance of this latter phrase in a place where we would expect to see "commands" suggests, "statutes and judgments" in Deuteronomy has the sense of the

with כי תוליד "When you beget," and the rest of the verbs in the sentence that follow it are in the perfect consecutive, thus signaling that these are events that will happen in a series. The perfect consecutive expresses "actions, events, or states, which are to be attached to what precedes, in a more or less close relation, as its *temporal* or *logical* consequence" (*GKC* ¶112a, emphasis in the original). Thus, since the sentence begins with כי תוליד, referring to what will happen in the future, והשחתם should be read as the temporal and/or logical consequence of the actions that follow.

13. In these verses, Deuteronomy almost always uses the phrase כל (ה)מצוה/יו or כל הדבר(ים). Many LXX versions of 11:13 read "if you will certainly obey all of his commandments (כל מצותיו)," but this is likely an attempt to replace the more difficult "if you will certainly obey my [Moses'] commandments (מצותי)," found in the MT and LXX[A].

divine command in general.[14] The use of כל in all of the passages cited above emphasizes the necessity of the absoluteness of Israel's nomistic fidelity if it wishes to keep the land. The historical review of Deut 1–3 at the beginning of Moses' speech prepares readers for precisely this. Disobedience to even a single divine command can result in the loss of the land, and this is why Moses begins the paraenesis of 4:1–40 with the exhortation that Israel neither add to nor subtract from the divine word.

That this injunction about the law in 4:2 is immediately followed by a warning of destruction caused by apostasy in 4:3–4 is typical of Deuteronomy. In 10:12–11:32, to take another example from the introduction to the lawcode, Moses tells Israel to keep all of the law in four different verses (10:13; 11:8, 22, 32). These commands are interspersed with the blessings Israel will receive for doing so (11:8–12, 14–15, 23–25), as well as with the warning that God will destroy Israel from the land if the nation commits apostasy (11:16–17). This is assumedly what Moses means when he says a blessing and curse has been laid before Israel, the blessing to follow from obedience to the law and the curse from disobedience and apostasy (11:26–28). He essentially characterizes disobedience of the law simply as apostasy and draws no discernable difference between the effects of keeping "all the commandment" and of keeping the law against apostasy alone. Deuteronomy 13:1–19 [ET 12:32–13:18], an example of this equation of cultic and nomistic fidelity from the lawcode itself, begins and ends with the command to obey all of the law (13:1 [ET 12:32], 19 [13:18]), but is focused entirely on the necessity to execute those within the nation who commit apostasy, even if it is an entire town. In this scenario, it seems that there is only one out of all the commandments in the lawcode that matters. The same is true in 28:69–29:28 [ET 29:1–29], an example from the conclusion to the lawcode, which ends with the injunction to obey all of the law (29:28 [ET 29]), while the passage as a whole focuses on the destruction of the nation as punishment for apostasy. The master narrative, in short, articulates no distinction between obeying all of the commandments and worshiping YHWH alone; it simply seems to equate nomistic and cultic loyalty to the divine suzerain, as we have already discussed.

So far, then, we have seen the first of the two themes the master narrative uses in order to explain the logic of history to the exiles. We pointed in the previous chapters to a *leitmotif* constructed of a series of related

14. See Norbert Lohfink, "Die '*ḥuqqîm umišpāṭîm*' im Buch Deuteronomium und ihre Neubegrenzung durch Dtn 12:1," *Bib* 70 (1989): 1–30; and Georg Braulik, "Die Ausdrücke für 'Gesetz' im Buch Deuteronomium," in *Studien zum Deuteronomium* (SBA 2; Stuttgart: Katolisches Biblewerk, 1988), 11–38.

motifs that mark out the History from surrounding biblical material, and we find them in Deuteronomy as aspects that contribute to this first theme of the narrative. In regard to the worship of "other gods" and exile, Deuteronomy tends to emphasize a more general destruction of the nation rather than specifically a forcible migration away from the land, although the latter is part of the larger portrayal of divine punishment for Israel's infidelity in places like 4:25–28; 28:64–68; and 30:1.[15] The motif of intermarriage as the cause of apostasy is also present in Deuteronomy, and is the focus of 7:1–6. We encounter this Deuteronomistic motif of intermarriage as leading to apostasy for the first time here, and this motif provides the rationale for the חרם that Israel must visit on the nations in their conquest of Canaan (so also 20:16–18). As a divine command, the genocide in Canaan is certainly one way that Israel can manifest its love of or loyalty to God, and Deut 7 is clearly structured much like 6:10–25, which itself is an attempt to make clear what love of God means.[16] As Dtr's narrative sees it, Israel will be unable to be loyal to YHWH if it does not kill off the Canaanites, for their continuing presence in the land will lead to cultic disloyalty and, thus, the loss of the land.

So that the exiles do not miss the master narrative's logic in history that explains the exile, the narrative of Dtr makes it clear that the lessons of the law that Moses teaches are not merely for the conquest generation in Moab. The call that Moses makes to nomistic and cultic loyalty in Deuteronomy is, in the context of the narrative, a call to the conquest generation that still waits in Moab, but it is also addressed to all of the following generations of Israel, including the one in exile. One way in which this is conveyed in the speeches of Moses that open the History is through a conflation of the different generations of Israel. In the first speech, Moses addresses the conquest generation as if they had been at

15. For the connections that the narrative draws in Deuteronomy between the worship of other gods and the destruction of the people and/or exile from the land, see 6:14–15; 8:19–20; 28:14–68 (and note that 28:14, while the conclusion to the list of blessings, leads into the curse section with a reference to "other gods"); 29:17–27 [ET 18–28]; 30:17–18. Deut 11:26–28 connects apostasy to curses described elsewhere in the book, but does not explicitly specify exile or destruction.

16. Both 6:10–25 and 7:1–26 open with the same phrase—"When YHWH your God brings you into the land"—followed by commands that echo the Decalogue in 6:12–18 and 7:2–11. So Norbert Lohfink, *Das Hauptgebot: Eine Untersuchung literarischer Einleitungsfragen zu Dtn 5–11* (AnBib 20; Rome: Pontifical Biblical Institute, 1963), 154–57, 180–81. In both passages, this is followed by blessings for obedience (6:18–19 and 7:12–15), and then by a question answered by material that echoes earlier parts of the passage (6:20–25 and 7:17–26). See Nathan MacDonald, *Deuteronomy and the Meaning of "Monotheism"* (FAT 2/1; Tübingen: Mohr Siebeck, 2003), 108.

Horeb (1:6), and as if they had been old enough at that time to govern, spy out the land, and fight as warriors (1:9–18, 19–36, 41–46), even though 1:39 makes it clear that at the time of which Moses speaks in Deut 1 the conquest generation was far too young for this. The exodus generation who witnessed the theophany at Horeb is dead by the time the speeches of Deuteronomy begin. 2:14–15 makes it clear that the punishment of the exodus generation for disobeying the divine command to enter the land announced in 1:34–35 has been realized: all of that generation but Caleb has died before they could possess the land. The conflation of generations is taken even farther than this by Moses, who addresses even later generations when he refers to Sihon's and Og's land as being "across the Jordan" (3:8)—it is, of course, only "across the Jordan" to those who already live to the west of the river.[17] There is a rhetorical strategy at work here: this conflation of the generations puts each generation of Israel, including the exiles, at the brink of decision with the conquest generation in Moab. Moses' seeming ignorance as to the difference between different generations can be read as an attempt to frame the call to vassal loyalty as a decision that each generation of Israel must make.[18] To emphasize the "emphatic contemporaneity"[19] of this call to loyalty, Deuteronomy uses the word יום 62 times in the context of the decision for loyalty to YHWH.[20] The "today" of decision for the generations of Israel is every day, including the present of the exiles. Thus, in Deut 1–4, the journey undertaken by the exodus generation becomes a journey of the conquest generation. The past for Dtr's narrative always has present relevance, for the same logic consistently governs history.[21]

From the standpoint of the narrative, the decisions that the following generations of Israel will make in the History will generally be the wrong ones. This is clear enough already in Deut 4:25–31; 30:1–10; and 31:16–29, all of which foresee with absolute certainty Israel's future cultic

17. So Susan Slater, "Imagining Arrival: Rhetoric, Reader, and Word of God in Deuteronomy 1–3," in *The Labor of Reading: Desire, Alienation, and Biblical Interpretation* (ed. Fiona C. Black, Roland Boer, and Erin Runions; SBLSS 36; Atlanta: Society of Biblical Literature, 1999), 107–22 (109–10).

18. E.g., see Miller, *Deuteronomy*, 67; von Rad, *Deuteronomy*, 55; Braulik, *Deuteronomium 1–16,17*, 49.

19. This wording from Gerhard von Rad, *The Problem of the Hexateuch and Other Essays* (trans. E. W. Trueman Dicken; London: SCM, 1984), 29.

20. For the listing of the appearances of יום in Deuteronomy in the context of loyalty to God, see McConville and Millar, *Time and Place in Deuteronomy*, 43 n. 61.

21. So ibid., 48; Simon J. deVries, *Yesterday, Today and Tomorrow: Time and History in the Old Testament* (Grand Rapids: Eerdmans, 1975), 45.

failure. 4:25–31 refers to the punishment of exile for this failure, but also to the nation's future repentance in exile, which remains a possibility because of God's refusal to destroy the nation utterly. This bit of optimism is echoed and expanded in 30:1–10, which uses similar language,[22] and adds that God will return the exiles to the land after their repentance (30:4–5), and that at that time God will circumcise the hearts of Israel so that they will then keep the commandments and allow God to cause them to prosper in the land following their return (30:6–10). Deuteronomy 31:16–29[23] roots Israel's coming cultic disloyalty in the very nature of the nation (31:27); read together with 30:6–10, then, readers see that success in the land following a return from exile will be possible only because God will change Israel's natural "rebellion" and "stiff neck" (so Moses in 31:27) to an ability to keep the law.[24]

2. *The Second Theme: The Failure of Leadership*

Up to this point, I have addressed appearances of only the first of the master narrative's two themes in Deuteronomy, but the second, the failure of Israel's leadership, is also present in the book—although less prominently than the first—beginning with Moses' first speech. Moses exhorts Israel to faithfulness to their divine suzerain throughout the book; he calls himself a prophet (18:15), and the narrator states that he had an inimitable relationship with God (34:10).[25] I said above that I

22. For a comparison of the language of the two passages and the Deuteronomistic theology of repentance that they reflect, particularly in comparison with 1 Kgs 8:47–50, see Weinfeld, *Deuteronomy 1–11*, 215–16 and 223–24. See also Polzin, *Moses and the Deuteronomist*, 70.

23. Except for 31:14–15, with its reference to a "tent of meeting" that is not mentioned anywhere else in Deuteronomy, the rest of the chapter is an original part of the History, and includes ideas and vocabulary common to Deuteronomy and Dtr.

24. On the act of God to make obedience possible in 30:6–10 specifically, see Marc Zvi Brettler, "Predestination in Deuteronomy 30:1–10," in Schearing and McKenzie, eds., *Those Elusive Deuteronomists*, 171–88 (172–73); Tigay, *Deuteronomy*, 285; Nelson, *Deuteronomy*, 348–49; von Rad, *Deuteronomy*, 183–84; Mayes, *Deuteronomy*, 369.

25. It is commonly argued that 34:1a, 7–9 derives from P; for a recent defense of this position see Ludwig Schmidt, "P in Deuteronomium 34," *VT* 59 (2009): 475–94. Scholars find the origin of 34:10–12 more difficult to determine, however. Nonetheless, the only part of these verses that concerns us is 34:10 ("There never again arose in Israel a prophet like Moses, whom YHWH knew face to face"), and this is clearly Deuteronomistic. As Weinfeld points out, the incomparability formula that we see in the independent clause appears elsewhere in Dtr (1 Kgs 3:12; 2 Kgs 18:15; 23:25; see his *Deuteronomy and the Deuteronomic School* [Oxford: Clarendon, 1972], 359). And since each incomparability formula in Kings provides a rationale

would use the first speech of 1:1–4:40 to demonstrate both of the narrative's themes, and in this speech we see that even Moses is not perfect according to the narrative, and this lack of perfection bars him, like the exodus generation, from entering the land. When God first commands Israel to "enter and possess the land" (1:8), Moses, on his own initiative, delegates leadership responsibilities, taking the "heads of your tribes" and establishing them as "judges" (1:9–18). Yet the law of 16:18–20 states that Israel, not Moses, is to do this, and not until they enter the land, facts that Moses would already know, since in Deuteronomy he merely repeats the law he has already heard. He does not relay God's command to enter the land until 1:21,[26] after he has chosen the judges, suggesting that he is searching for others who will take the blame with him if Israel is defeated in the land. At this point Israel wants to spy out the land and Moses immediately approves of the idea. In fact, his response to Israel's plan to spy out the land—"The thing was good in my eyes" (1:23)—is much like Israel's response to his plan to choose judges—"The thing you have spoken to do is good" (1:14). Neither Moses nor Israel appears to be able or willing to check the bad decisions of the other. God seems to hold Moses as at least partly accountable for the spying mission and the fear that it creates in Israel, and so he suffers the same fate as that generation (1:37–38). His claim to Israel that God was angry with him "on your account" (1:37) sounds somewhat disingenuous, given that the picture he presents of the genesis of the spying mission in 1:22–23 seems to show him as potentially having veto power over the whole matter. "All of you came to me" with the plan to spy out the land, says Moses, "and the thing was good in my eyes." The first speech, then, at least implies that Moses had less trust in God's power to deliver the land than Moses says he did in 1:29–31, that he took the divine command as an opportunity to choose leaders who could share in the blame of potential failure, and that he enabled Israel in its disastrous spying mission rather than lead the nation in complete obedience to divine command.[27]

for what made the king incomparable (Solomon is wisest, Hezekiah exhibits the greatest trust, Josiah is best in terms of repentance), it makes sense to include also the dependent clause in 34:10 as from Dtr as well.

26. It is true that, in 1:6, Moses says that "God spoke to us" at Horeb to give the command to enter the land, but readers discover at 5:22–31 that God did not speak to Israel at Horeb after the Decalogue. Only Moses would have originally heard the command to enter the land.

27. Commentators, though, tend to avoid ascribing sin to Moses despite his punishment in 1:37–38, sometimes arguing that, although blameless, he suffers for the sin of his generation (e.g., Duane L. Christensen, *Deuteronomy 1:1–21:9* [WBC

If the mistakes of Moses that he relates in the opening speech seem minor—he chooses judges rather than waiting for Israel to do so later, and he only acquiesces to a plan for spying that Israel and not he developed—it emphasizes the larger point of Deut 1–4: loyalty to the divine suzerain must be absolute since even minor acts of disobedience can result in complete disaster as regards the nation's success in the land. As 1:22–23 seems to present the situation, had Moses refused the request to spy and not chosen spies from the tribes, the spying mission would not have proceeded. The minor failure of this leader has disastrous results for Israel as a whole. Should leaders take the decision-making process away from God for even a moment, and make even seemingly minor alterations to divine commands, disaster can result. And Moses seems to go on disobeying divine commands. When God tells Moses to enter into battle with Sihon and take his land (2:24–25), Moses again avoids immediately obeying the command, and again does something on his own initiative that at least implies he is less than confident in God's ability to deliver the land: he send messengers to Sihon asking for safe passage through his land (2:26–30). The text gives no indication that it is God's idea, and that Moses at least appears to want to avoid fighting here. And if this point too seems minor—after all, after God repeats the instructions to take Sihon's land in 2:31, Sihon comes out in battle, and Israel possesses his land—it is worthwhile noting that both Joshua and Jephthah will engage foreign enemies in dialogue in Josh 9 and Judg 11, with negative results in each case.

When we closely examine Moses' first speech at the very opening of the History, then, we find both of the narrative's main themes. Moses appears to bear some of the responsibility for the spying mission, and so he shares the fate of dying outside of the land.[28] The repetition of Israel's actions and fate in the portrayal of Moses not only highlights the narrative's theme of a failure in vassal loyalty leading to destruction, it uses Moses' failure of leadership to explain the exiles' trauma to them. They and their leader, Jehoiachin, now are in danger of dying outside of the land just like the exodus generation and Moses. Even seemingly minor errors on the part of a leader can have disastrous consequences for the whole nation. Deuteronomy foreshadows Josiah: he does to Jeroboam's

6A; Thomas Nelson, 2001], 32; Tigay, *Deuteronomy*, 17; Nelson, *Deuteronomy*, 29–30). His claim that he is punished "on your account" can be read this way, but the fact of the matter is that this claim is not one that the narrator or God endorse.

28. For the death of Moses outside of the land as reflecting a warning of the fate of Israel, see Dennis T. Olson, *Deuteronomy and the Death of Moses: A Theological Reading* (OBT; Minneapolis: Fortress, 1994), 18.

altar what Moses does to the golden calf (cf. Deut 9:1 and 2 Kgs 23:15); he alone smashes the Canaanite altars and burns their idols as Deuteronomy demands (cf. Deut 12:2–4 and 2 Kgs 23:4, 7, 12, 15); he alone reads the law "in the ears" of the people (cf. Deut 31:11 and 2 Kgs 23:2). It is thus no surprise that he alone fulfills the command of the Shema to be loyal to God with all of his heart, soul, and might (2 Kgs 23:25); even Moses does not do this in Dtr's narrative. Most of Israel's leaders, as we shall see, will not live up to even Moses' flawed leadership, and their failures in leading cultic loyalty in Israel will also manifest the narrative's logic in history that explains the exile. The punishments that Israel suffers in later stories in the History are due, the narrative explains, to their vassal disloyalty, but the leaders who fail to put a stop to it or who actually take the initiative in promoting it are partly to blame as well. By the time we reach the narrative in Kings, we will see the monarchy actively causing cultic disloyalty that will explain the exiles' trauma.

B. *The Uncanny Beginning of Trauma*

1. *The Traumatic Subversion of God, Moses, and the Law*

As we saw in the previous chapter, trauma resists narrativization and ethicization. It cannot be expressed in narrative because it literally cannot be known. This is not to say that those who have suffered massive psychic trauma can never speak or write of what they have witnessed, but it is to say that neither they nor their descendants seem able to explain what happened, to ground it in any kind of worldview or narrative or ethical system that they can use to make sense of it. Like Charlotte Delbo, they might be sure that what they experienced occurred, but they are unable to make any meaningful totalizing truth claims about it; like Primo Levi, they may be literally unable to believe that the trauma occurred. So while Dtr's master narrative may present a logic in history that attempts to explain fully and thus control the exilic community's trauma, trauma itself inevitably escapes such an attempt. Testimony to trauma, we have seen, simply has no way of making sense of it. Since trauma unsettles stereotypical language of narrative, we should not be surprised when we find it intruding with ambiguity that challenges and subverts the unambiguous language of concepts like God, justice, history, and so on that the narrative uses to provide an ethical explanation of trauma. Trauma is present, paradoxically, as narrative absence, as ambiguity and contradiction that slips into or behind the narrative to subvert its totalizing explanation and its logic in history that attempts to capture trauma. A stable explanation of events, especially an explanation that attempts to encompass events that admit of no ethical framework, will not totally succeed.

Trauma becomes the single unknowable time that, because it cannot be known, cannot be narrativized, and it will erupt into a narrative framework to subvert and unsettle its unambiguous linguistic concepts and explanations with ambiguity. Trauma intrudes upon Dtr's narrative in Deuteronomy to challenge and subvert some of the most basic claims that the narrative attempts to use to explain the trauma. By subverting the narrative's logical explanation and throwing its language into a trial without resolution, trauma prevents a totalizing explanation.

So we find the anti-narrative of trauma subverting the concepts that the master narrative uses to ground its logic in history that tries to explain the massive psychic trauma of the exilic readers to them. Dtr's narrative and its ethical logic of history rests on YHWH not simply as the power behind history but as its just director who rewards Israel's loyalty with blessings and its apostasy and disobedience with destruction. YHWH "does not show favor and does not take a bribe" (10:17); he is "perfect," "just," "faithful and without deceit," "righteous and upright" (32:4). However, God's actions in Deuteronomy are not entirely explainable in the context of a logical and just presentation of history. In the story of 9:8–10:11, for example, Israel, while still at Horeb, constructs and worships a golden calf. This mimics precisely the apostasy that Jeroboam will lead in 1 Kgs 12, and Israel's actions here prefigure this "sin of Jeroboam" that will result in the destruction of the Northern Kingdom.[29] Moses, unlike the kings of the North, burns the offending idol (ואשׂרף אתו באשׁ) and grinds it until it is "crushed to dust (דק לעפר)" (9:21), which is precisely what Josiah will do to Jeroboam's idol (2 Kgs 23:15) and to the idols with which Manasseh and other kings of Judah had defiled the temple (23:6, 11; cf. 21:7).[30] Moses' action, like Josiah's, is certainly positive, but there are a number of subversions of the narrative here. While Moses' action is not actually described as repentance as Josiah's reformation in 2 Kgs 23 is (23:25 summarizes Josiah's reformation by saying that he "repented [שׁב] to YHWH"), that is what it amounts to, for he puts a stop to Israel's cultic disloyalty as a good leader should according to the narrative. YHWH's intention to destroy the nation

29. For parallels between the story of the golden calf and Jeroboam's idol, see Weinfeld, *Deuteronomy 1–11*, 424; Braulik, *Deuteronomium 1–16,17*, 78; Mayes, *Deuteronomy*, 199–200. See Tigay, *Deuteronomy*, 98 for the placement of the golden calf story within the context of the sin of the exodus generation that Moses relates in 9:22–23.

30. 2 Kgs 23:15 says that Josiah "burned" Jeroboam's high place and "crushed it to dust"; 23:6 says he "burned" Manasseh's Asherah and "crushed it to dust"; 23:11 says he "burned with fire" the chariots of the sun that the kings of Judah had put in the temple.

(אשמידם) in 9:14 before Moses' action of repentance is understandable given the narrative's view of God, justice, and punishment, but we have already seen that God grants salvation when Israel repents or returns to vassal loyalty. YHWH's eventual decision to save and not destroy Israel because of the golden calf may be related to the act of repentance that Moses enacts, but the narrative makes no such explicit connection. Moses, in fact, seems to claim that it was not the destruction of the idol but his intercession for Israel during his forty days and nights on the mountain (9:25–29) that saved Israel: "YHWH listened to me that time also; YHWH was not willing to destroy you" (10:10). And Moses' intercession does not refer to repentance even once.[31] He tells YHWH instead that if he destroys Israel, the Egyptians will view him as weak; he tells God that they will conclude that Israel perished in the wilderness "because YHWH *was not able* to bring them to the land."

It is certainly possible to read the golden calf story as suggesting that God responds to repentance, Israel's return to vassal loyalty, but the story is ambiguous at this point. Trauma, remember, suggests, undermines, and subverts, but does not provide certain alternative explanatory conclusions. What trauma suggests here is that God does not respond to repentance, and that what makes him unwilling to destroy Israel despite their idolatry is Moses' argument that to destroy the nation risks YHWH's reputation as the one who controls history. It is quite possible, in short, to interpret this story as claiming that God saves Israel from destruction not because he is responding to repentance that reinstates vassal loyalty, but for a reason completely divorced from the narrative's logic in history, a reason that ignores and so subverts the narrative's understandings of God, justice, punishment, repentance, and salvation. It is also possible to conclude that God responds to Moses' leadership of repentance rather than his warning that God will appear weak, but the narrative does not say so. Trauma is present precisely in this ambiguity that results from an absence of narrative explanation. Trauma subverts the narrative by suggesting that salvation here ultimately has nothing to do with justice or ethics or the cultic action of repenting from idolatry—or, for that matter,

31. Weinfeld suggests that in this intercession Moses refers to the ancestors in 9:27 because the exodus generation is evil (*Deuteronomy 1–11*, 415), and so he prompts YHWH to recognize the fact that he should save the nation because not all generations of Israel are disloyal. Tigay suggests that this reference was meant to remind God of his oath to the ancestors (*Deuteronomy*, 103). In neither case, however, does Moses really provide a motivation to God to save Israel that makes sense in regard to the narrative's logic in history. God will judge the generations of Israel based on their loyalty, not the loyalty of their ancestors.

mercy, a concept that is never mentioned in the story—it has to do with YHWH's concern with his reputation. Justice is not being done as the narrative understands it; God is not acting like God as the narrative understands him. While readers might certainly see this flaw in God's justice as one that works in Israel's favor, it still questions the narrative's ethical framework of history, for it suggests (although does not explicitly claim) that Israel's actions in regard to vassal loyalty have no bearing on how God treats them. God is not acting, in short, as he should, and so trauma subverts the narrative's concepts of God, justice, punishment, repentance, and salvation. While this is a subversion of the narrative's logic in history that eventually results in a positive outcome for Israel, it foreshadows another subversion of these narrative concepts. Josiah's acts of repentance, narrated to remind readers of Moses' repentance here, are also ignored by God (2 Kgs 23:25–26), and that subversion of the narrative subverts its explanation for the exilic community's trauma. The narrative will blame the exile on the sins of Manasseh (2 Kgs 23:26), without clearly explaining why God does not respond to Josiah's repentance. The narrative's explanation of trauma is subverted in Deut 9–10 not because of its uncanny relationship to 2 Kgs 23, and because it suggests that Israel's acts of vassal loyalty and disloyalty cannot always explain why God acts the way he does.[32]

We can see the divine disregard for justice creating a clearly negative effect for Israel in the story of God's punishment of Moses in regard to the spying mission; as Olson argues, this is a matter central to the narrative of Deuteronomy, since Moses' death outside of the land is a constant possibility for future generations of Israelites,[33] and one with which the exiles can clearly identify. Yet Dtr's narrative never specifies Moses' sin, and only obliquely links it to Israel's desire to send spies into the land, an act that resulted in the Israelites' fear that prevented them from obeying God's command to enter the land. Even given our earlier discussion of the master narrative's presentation of this story, it is not entirely clear how Moses is responsible for Israel's sin. "*You* came near to me" with

32. Even if we decided that the narrative does not want to see Moses' action in destroying the idol as repentance on the part of this generation of Israel—after all, we find no explicit reference to Israel's repentance in the golden calf story—then we have a case where God should destroy the nation for idolatry but does not. Even in this interpretation, God ignores the dictates of justice and punishment and acts out of concern for his reputation alone. Here again, trauma suggests that Israel's actions of loyalty or disloyalty do not explain why God acts the way he does, and the narrative's logic in history is subverted.

33. Olson, *Deuteronomy and the Death of Moses*, 17–21.

the plan, Moses tells Israel (1:22); then "*you* were not willing to go up, and *you* rebelled against the command of YHWH your God, and *you* were contentious" (1:26–27). But, "*I* said to you, Do not tremble or be afraid of them. YHWH your God goes before you; he will fight for you, just as he did with you before your eyes in Egypt.... But in this matter none of *you* trusted YHWH your God" (1:29–30, 32). It is difficult to miss the second person plural verb forms that point to Israel's, not Moses', sin. If Moses should be considered as guilty and disloyal for countenancing the plan, then so should Joshua, who sends spies into the land entirely on his own initiative in Josh 2, yet he is charged with no crime and he is not punished.

One could read the text, as we did in the previous section of this chapter, as implying that Moses is Israel's human leader and thus that he bears a special obligation to bolster Israel's trust in God and to refuse to allow the spying mission. The point here again, however, is that the narrative never explicitly makes such an argument. It is clearly not impossible to say that this is the argument that the narrative wants to make, but it is not entirely clear, either. It is simply not clear why Moses is punished when Joshua, who undertakes a spying mission on his own initiative, is not. Right at the point where Moses' punishment—death outside of the land—parallels that of the exiles, whose punishment the narrative is trying to explain, we find ambiguity in the explanation. Nor is it clear why Moses is punished when Caleb, who was actually one of the spies (1:36), is rewarded for his trust in God to give the land to Israel. Because of the trust he exhibits, Caleb lives to enter the land (1:36) and actually receives a sizable portion of it as a reward for his trust (Josh 14:6–15), while Moses, who expresses exactly the same trust (Deut 1:29–31), is punished with death outside of the land. It is the very lack of explanation that provides the traumatic ambiguity and that subverts the narrative's concepts of God, justice, and punishment. Neither the narrator nor YHWH charges Moses with a crime;[34] God merely says to him, "You too will not enter there" (1:37). Nor is this punishment without explanation merely mentioned one time. God rejects Moses' plea for entrance to the land in 3:27–28, and Moses refers to his punishment as an example to warn Israel of God's anger in 4:21–24. Paul Kissling writes that at this point it sounds as if Moses is warning the Israelites that God punishes the

34. Deut 32:48–50 does charge Moses with a sin he committed at Meribath-qadesh, but this passage is from P, not Dtr. The link between Moses' punishment and the incident at Meribah in 32:48–50 corresponds to Num 20:12–13, and the assertion that Aaron died at Mount Hor parallels Num 20:20–28 and 33:38, all P texts. Deut 10:6 puts Aaron's death at Moserah. See Tigay, *Deuteronomy*, 518.

ones loyal to him as if they were disloyal, and so Israel must take care to do nothing that seems remotely disloyal,[35] but for God to treat the loyal as if they were disloyal suggests that he does not base his treatment on vassal loyalty. And since Moses' fate of dying outside of the land is the same fate as that faced by the exilic readers of Dtr, by the time these readers reach 2 Kgs 23, they might think back to this story and see it as an uncanny repetition of God's unexplained rejection of Josiah's repentance that returns Israel to proper loyalty to God. In that ultimate explanation of the exilic community's trauma, readers could conclude, as they can here in Deuteronomy, that God can punish with no regard to the loyalty exhibited by Israel.

There are ways that readers could explain the very different standards of justice that God applies to Moses and Caleb—they might assume, for example, that Moses bears ultimate responsibility for the spying mission because he was Israel's leader and Caleb was not. This will not be an explanation that will work in the case of Joshua, however, and at that point we come across an unbridged gap in the narrative explanation for why God punishes some people—like Moses and (potentially) the exilic readers—with death outside of the land. The narrative's distinction between those who maintain vassal loyalty and those who do not as the basis for punishment and reward is thrown into unresolved ambiguity and is uncannily repeated in God's refusal to acknowledge the loyalty of Judah that Josiah reinstates with his reforms. It is not insignificant that this punishment of Moses is mentioned three times near the very beginning of Dtr's narrative; right at the History's genesis, we find doubt that God judges rightly and that proper action on Israel's part in accordance with divine teaching will be enough to prevent destruction. The exiles' fate of death outside of the land will mirror that of Moses, and the story of Moses' punishment suggests that the narrative's structuring of history cannot provide explanatory logic for that grim fate. The master narrative's pictures of God, justice, and punishment simply fail as parts of a totalizing, air-tight explanation at this point; narrative explanation has become unexplained ambiguity that subverts the logic of just divine punishment that attempts to make sense of the exiles' trauma. Trauma does not absolutely deny that an explanation for Moses' punishment is possible that would make sense on the narrative's terms, but trauma's presence as absence in narrative explanation does subvert the narrative's truth claims about why God punishes.

35. Paul J. Kissling, *Reliable Characters in the Primary History: Profiles of Moses, Joshua, Elijah and Elisha* (JSOTSup 224; Sheffield: Sheffield Academic, 1996), 50.

Moses may be a failure (or, at least, not a perfect success) as Israel's leader from the standpoint of the master narrative, but from the standpoint of the narrative he still does provide Israel with the information regarding cultic and nomistic loyalty to God that they must choose to follow if they want to avoid disaster. In the narrative, the ethical choice that Moses lays before the people—"Choose life so that you and your descendants may live…in the land" (30:19–20)—is the core of the narrative's logic in history. Israel's failure to choose rightly, according to the narrative, logically explains the trauma. However, Moses' whole presentation of the law and of divine expectations is suspect. As we have already pointed out, when Moses tells the conquest generation in Moab that God has forbidden him to enter the land "on your account" (1:37), "because of you" (4:21), he may simply be disingenuous, denying the role that he played in permitting the spying mission. Since we can read the narrative as arguing that Moses' failure to lead properly allowed the spying mission to take place, this absence of narrative certainty opens the possibility that Moses has hidden the full truth from Israel, and has wrongly decided to interpret a just divine punishment of his actions as administered to him "because of you," and this means that Moses cannot always be taken at his word. This is, of course, not certain, but it is a possibility that absence of narrative explanation has raised. The gap in the narrative's explanation of Moses' punishment—itself a traumatic subversion of the narrative's concepts of God, justice, and punishment—raises the possibility that Moses does not explain why God punishes him because he is lying, or because he is not entirely clear as to why God punishes. Trauma, in short, has opened up the possibility that the words of Moses are not always trustworthy, either because he lies, or does not fully understand God's standards of justice, or both.

If the case is that Moses is ignorant of the reason for his punishment or is misleading Israel as to the reason for his fate, then his reliability as a narrator—and almost all of Deuteronomy is presented as his speech—is called into question, and the narrative's conception of prophecy as rightly directing Israel to salvation and life in the land is subverted. If Moses himself does not fully understand how God controls history, or if he is willing to misinterpret this logic in history, he would not appear to be the best choice to direct Israel in how to survive in the land. The ambiguity that trauma presses into Dtr's master narrative suggests that Moses' guidance is flawed, and thus that the logic in history that he sets forth at the beginning of the narrative, the ethical choice that he calls all of Israel's generations to make, is flawed. Given that the narrative explains the exilic community's trauma by saying that it was punishment for Israel's rejection of Moses' instructions, this ambiguity subverts the narrative's logic in history. If Moses lies about God's will or is not well-informed about it, then it is not clear that the cultic and nomistic loyalty that he exhorts really influences how God treats Israel. When Moses announces in 30:1–10 that God will meet repentance with salvation—a perfectly logical point to make, as I argued in the previous chapter, given his other statements about the results of vassal loyalty—while his own account of the golden calf story suggests that God does not take Israel's repentance into account, readers might conclude that he does not truly know how or why God acts. By the time they reach the story of Josiah, where God's refusal to recognize Josiah's repentance (the narrative's final explanation of the exiles' trauma) uncannily reflects Deut 9–10, they might wonder if Moses has entirely misrepresented how God moves history.

And there is another point at which Moses' ability to communicate rightly a logic in history that can explain trauma is called into question: he fails to explain the equation between cultic and nomistic loyalty to YHWH. Earlier in this chapter we saw how Moses moves easily in Deuteronomy from assertions that Israel must keep all of the law to assertions that cultic loyalty alone matters to assure Israel's survival in the land. These kinds of moves seem to make the point of the lawcode moot, especially when the divine judge indicates numerous times that the single law that will govern Israel's fate is that which deals with absolute loyalty to him. The lack of explanation as to the relation between cultic and nomistic loyalty challenges and subverts the narrative's historical logic that presents history and thus the exiles' trauma as explainable in terms of ethics and justice. Israel has two imperatives to obey, but the relationship between them and their potential contradiction—simply worshiping YHWH rightly in and of itself can potentially be read as obviating the need to obey any other commandment—has been left unexplained. Vassal loyalty to YHWH is at the heart of the narrative's logic in history, and Moses' failure to explain what is at best an ambiguous and at worst a contradictory exposition as to how to keep the land and avoid trauma suggests that he does not know or fully understand how God directs history, and so cannot explain the exiles' trauma at all.

In this absence of clear explanation, trauma subverts the narrative's claim that Israel clearly knows how it should act, and that it was the nation's failure to follow clear ethical instructions that explains the exilic community's trauma. Trauma will introduce precisely the same ambiguity into the narrative's explanation of the exiles' trauma in 2 Kgs 23:26–27, where God will explicitly ignore Josiah's perfect act of repentance that returns the people to cultic loyalty. In 2 Kgs 23, Josiah acts "according to all of the law of Moses"; the fact that this makes no difference to God suggests that the instructions Moses gives may not be entirely accurate. The possibility exists already in Deuteronomy that Israel's trauma is a result of Moses' ignorance or lies. Potentially, of course, it is also a result of God's failure to act in accordance with the law that he gave Moses. The narrative presents Israel's existence in the land as dependent upon following Moses' guidance as a true revelation of the way in which God directs history, and if Moses either lies about this or misrepresents it or does not understand it, or if God has little interest in ruling history as he had earlier said he would, then readers might expect most or all of the future generations of Israel to undergo trauma like that of the exiles, because in this case history would not be something that Israel could really know or influence through human action. Trauma suggests that this is a possibility—it does not offer this as an absolute and competing explanation, for that would make it a counter- rather than an anti-narrative—and so subverts the narrative's explanation for the exile. This intrusion of traumatic absence or ambiguity into the narrative not only subverts the narrative's portrayal of Moses, but also the narrative's portrayal of God and the justice and the punishment of which Moses speaks, since it is hardly clear that his explanations of such things should be trusted. Since Moses describes himself as a prophet (18:15), it can even be said to subvert the narrative's portrayal of prophecy as the sure communication of divine direction and warning. And, potentially, attempts by the exiles to follow Moses' instructions in order to return to the land might lead to disaster, since readers cannot be entirely sure if or when Moses speaks truthfully.

2. *The Subversive Repetition of Trauma*

As we saw above, Moses collapses the different generations of Israel who are all called to make the same choice for cultic loyalty. He refers to the generation who hears the law in the Transjordan and who will go on to conquer the land as if they were the same generation who experienced the exodus and who witnessed the theophany at Horeb. At a place like 5:3–4, then, we find this manner of expressing Israel's identity used to stress that all generations of Israel are equally responsible to make a moral choice that will determine the survival of the nation: "Not with our ancestors did YHWH make this covenant, but with us, we who are here this day, all of us who are alive." This fusing of different generations and time can be said to be part of the master narrative insofar as this calls each generation of Israel to ethical responsibility in regard to their loyalty to God.[36] This is why, Mayes argues, 5:3 contradicts the perspective of Deut 1–3, for in 5:3 Moses speaks to the generation in Moab as if they were the generation who stood at Horeb, even though readers know by 2:14–15 that the Horeb generation has died.[37] Of course, all of Moses' speeches in Deuteronomy are addressed solely to the generation in Moab rather than to their parents' generation, although this fact is not clear until 2:14–15.[38] As a result, Moses speaks to the conquest generation as if they were the ones who rebelled against God and were banned from the land in 1:22–40, as if it were their actions that were responsible for Moses' death in the Transjordan (1:37; 4:21), and as if they were the ones who committed the apostasy with the golden calf in 9:15–21 that almost led to Israel's complete destruction, despite the fact that this generation has committed no sin. Because the Deuteronomistic History opens with precisely this ambiguity, where a sinless generation is addressed as a generation who was disloyal to their suzerain and punished, trauma plants doubt from the very beginning of Dtr that there will be a clear distinction between loyal and disloyal generations. This throws doubt on any kind of logical and ethical explanation for the exilic community's trauma, which the master narrative is attempting to control and explain. When trauma presents Israel as a single generation constantly committing and suffering for the same act of disloyalty, it subverts the master narrative's concepts of Israel, history, punishment, and justice. Unlike the case of Deut 28, which claims that the trauma of siege, famine, and destruction that the exiles suffered can be explained through the ethical choice of the nation, Moses' comments that conflate the exodus and conquest generations suggest that God can confuse the ethical choices of one generation with those of the next. In these traumatic intrusions into the narrative, there is no real sense that Israel is a series of generations, or that history proceeds chronologically, or that it is only the exodus generation who is punished for the disobedience of God's command that they manifest; the "one time only" of traumatic repetition applies to every generation of Israel and continually repeats, regardless of the actions of any given generation, and so Moses speaks to

36. So, e.g., Miller, *Deuteronomy*, 67; McConville and Millar, *Time and Place in Deuteronomy*, 47; deVries, *Yesterday, Today, and Tomorrow*, 45–48.

37. Mayes, *Deuteronomy*, 165.

38. As early as 1:34–35, Moses says to his audience that God has sworn that "Not one of these people, this evil generation, will see the good land that I have sworn to give to your ancestors," but this oath still does not make it clear that Moses is actually speaking to the children of the evil Horeb generation rather than to that generation itself.

a sinless generation as if they were their parents' generation, guilty of sin and so condemned to die outside of the land.

That the narrative can sometimes actually distinguish between sinful and sinless generations is not the point; the point is that trauma intrudes to make this distinction ambiguous in Moses' speech and thus to fracture and render impossible any totalizing explanation for what the exilic readers have suffered. Readers can see well enough in the narrative of Deuteronomy that the conquest generation is not, in fact, punished for their parents' sin. Yet the very fact that Moses sometimes speaks as if he cannot tell the difference between the loyal and disloyal generations calls the narrative's certainty that the rebellious generations alone will be punished into question. Can Moses not always make this distinction? If he can, why does he address an innocent generation as if they were guilty of their parents' sin and received their parents' punishment of dying outside of the land? A narrative strategy of calling all generations of Israel to vassal loyalty does not really answer these questions, for Moses could easily do so without in any way suggesting that the generation in Moab is responsible for their parents' sin. Is Moses, as the inimitable communicator between God and Israel, simply mirroring a divine indifference or inability to distinguish between different generations and their punishments? Moses' speech at such points may merely seem confusing, but we should note here that in the final part of the explanation of the exilic community's trauma in 2 Kgs 21–25, God does not punish the sinful generations for the sin that Manasseh caused them to commit for some portion of his 55-year reign or during the 19 years between Manasseh's death and Josiah's reform when Judah continued in apostasy worse than that even of the Canaanites. God instead waits for 35 years after Josiah's perfect act of cultic repentance to punish a people who have not clearly been said to sin for decades.[39]

So the ambiguity that trauma introduces into Moses' words in Deuteronomy, where a generation who is never said to sin is punished as if they had, uncannily anticipates the subversion of the narrative's explanation of trauma at the end of the History. Statements such as Deut 24:16 that children are not to be put to death[40] for their parents' sin and that each person will be put to death for his or her own sins, and Moses' claim in

39. See Chapter 2 for the calculation of these figures.

40. Reading יומתו with the MT all three times that it appears in this verse rather than ימותו in the LXX, Samaritan Pentateuch, and Syriac. Following Nelson (*Deuteronomy*, 285), מות occurs far less frequently in the Hophal than in the Qal, and so the MT is the more difficult reading here.

7:9–10 that God "repays the ones who hate him to his[41] face, to destroy him; he does not delay to repay the one who hates him to his face" point to the clear idea that God punishes sinners and not a later generation for their sin. In this context, even 5:9 in the Decalogue, which states that God punishes "the iniquity of the ancestors upon the children, and upon the third and fourth generation for those who hate me" can be seen to refer to a punishment of later generations only if they continue their ancestors' sin.[42] Deuteronomy 7:9–10, which uses much the same language as 5:9–10, appears to be a narrative clarification of those verses from the Decalogue that interprets them as pointing to a punishment only of the guilty, not their progeny.[43] Dtr's narrative, that is, repeats the language of 5:9–10 in 7:9–10 in order to make the point that "the third and fourth generation" are punished because they continue the sin that their ancestors began. From the narrative's standpoint, as we discussed in the previous chapter, God punishes those who sin, not later generations, and in Judges, our first exposure to a consistent application of punishment for cultic disloyalty, the apostate generations are immediately punished by foreign invasions (3:7–8, 12–14; 4:1–2; 6:1–6; 10:6–9; 13:1), while the land has rest from war when the generations of Israel remain cultically loyal (3:11, 30; 5:31).[44] So when Moses speaks as if he and/or God are

41. The MT reads לשׂאניו אל־פניו, and the LXX, Samaritan Pentateuch, and Syriac read לשׂאניו אל־פנהם. The MT is the more difficult reading, however, since the LXX et al. have harmonized the suffix on the noun with the plural participle.

42. This was already the conclusion of some rabbinic sources (e.g., *b. Ber.* 7a; *b. Sanh.* 27b). Some modern scholars also support this conclusion; see the explanations in, e.g., Miller, *Deuteronomy*, 77; Weinfeld, *Deuteronomy 1–11*, 299; Mayes, *Deuteronomy*, 167; Tigay, *Deuteronomy*, 437.

43. While the Decalogue is an earlier source that the author has inserted into the History, 5:9–10 has so much language in common with 7:9–10 that the latter can be seen as an attempt to clarify the language from the inserted source in order to harmonize it with the narrative's understanding of God's punishment. Both passages use the phrase (ה)חסד לאהבי(ו) ולשמרי מצותו in order to refer to the way in which God treats those who love/are loyal to him and obey him (and 5:9 adds לאלפים between חסד and לאהבי, while 7:9 puts לאלף דור at the end of the phrase). Both passages also use לשׂנאי to refer to those who are not loyal to God. David Aaron rightly argues that 5:9 sounds so antithetical to Deuteronomistic theology that it was only included in the History because it was so well known (*Etched in Stone: The Emergence of the Decalogue* [New York: T&T Clark, 2006], 226), but in the context of Deuteronomy and the History as a whole, especially given the repetition of the language of 5:9–10 in 7:9–10, "the ones who hate me" in 5:9 are both the "ancestors" and their descendants "to the third and fourth generation."

44. As I mentioned in the previous chapter, Judg 8:28 says that the land had rest despite the fact that 8:27 claims that Israel "prostituted after" an ephod that Gideon

unable to distinguish between the actions and punishments of different generations, he uncannily anticipates the subversion of the narrative's explanation of trauma in 2 Kgs 21–25. We expect to see trauma repeating in the writings of survivors and their descendants as it becomes the single unknowable event that dominates their lives, and as trauma repeats in Dtr, its "one time only" undermines the distinctions in chronology—subverts the narrative's concepts of history and Israel, in other words—necessary for the narrative clearly to make its case that God justly observes Israel's actions and punishes and saves accordingly.

We find the same conflation of exodus and conquest generations and thus the same traumatic subversion of the narrative's concepts of Israel and history again in Deut 29, where Moses addresses the conquest generation in Moab as if they had been in Egypt and seen God's might (29:1–2 [ET 2–3]). Moses adds here that God has made Israel unable to understand, even until this day (v. 3 [ET 4]). He then moves Israel's story through the following 40 years to the recent victories over Sihon and Og that the conquest generation has experienced (vv. 4–7 [ET 5–8]). Throughout he addresses Israel in the second person plural, and moves from the experiences of one generation to another as if there were no difference between them. Moses makes the point in 29:8–14 [ET 9–15] that all generations are called to make an ethical decision for or against the covenant, and Moses warns that YHWH will punish apostasy with great destruction and exile (vv. 16–20 [ET 17–21]). Moses is clear here that God punishes those who have been disloyal and not the following generation; in fact, he says that the children of the sinful generation will see and learn from God's punishment of the generation who has sinned (vv. 18–21 [ET 19–22]). Moses continues to address the generation in Moab in the second person plural, until he begins talking about "the next generation, your children who will arise after you" in 29:21 [ET 22].[45] This might seem to be directed to the exiles' children—they are the ones who can see that God made Jerusalem like Sodom and Gomorrah (v. 22 [ET 23]) and who can thus conclude that God punished the exiles for their apostasy by destroying the land and exiling the nation (vv. 24–27

made. So in this case, the land has rest even though apostasy is occurring, but there is no claim that a later generation is punished for this sin.

45. As I argued in Chapter 2, we should read הדור אחרון in 29:21 [ET 22] as "the next generation" and not "later generations" as Tigay (*Deuteronomy*, 281) and Christensen (*Deuteronomy 21:10–34:12*, 726) do. The definite article, the fact that דור appears in the singular, and Moses' qualification that this generation consists of "your children who will arise after you" all emphasize the specificity of the particular generation that follows the sinful one.

[ET 25–28]). And while this seems to cohere with the narrative's logic in history that explains the trauma of 586, we must remember that in the narrative Moses is speaking to the sinless generation in Moab, accusing them of the exiles' sin just as he has accused them of their parents', for he says that "*your* children who will arise after *you*" will see the punishment of this sinless generation. The unique temporality of trauma collapses all time into trauma, and the exilic readers of the History can get the uncanny sense that each generation of Israel has suffered precisely the same trauma as the last. But this repetition of trauma subverts the narrative's explanation of it, for Moses here charges a guiltless generation—the one in Moab—with sins it has not committed, and so the narrative's concepts of justice and punishment are subverted.

By Deut 32:5, part of the Song of Moses, Israel is simply described as "a crooked and twisted generation." In some of these repetitive intrusions of trauma into the narrative, each generation is precisely the same: always crooked and twisted regardless of its acts of loyalty; and thus always at the brink of traumatic punishment, if not actually suffering it. This in itself subverts the later testimony of the narrative, which certainly does not accuse every generation of Israel of apostasy and wrongdoing, and certainly not the generation whom Moses addresses at the time he addresses it. And at the very least, the generations following the successful judges live without any recorded incident of apostasy (Judg 3:11, 30; 5:31), as do the generations of Israel between Saul and Solomon. As we have seen, however (and as we will discuss in some detail in Chapter 7), it does uncannily anticipate the absent presence of trauma in the narrative of 2 Kgs 21–25, where a potentially innocent generation is punished like a guilty one. The master narrative of Dtr may call each generation to the same ethical decision, but it is the trauma of the siege survivors and their descendants in exile that makes each generation guilty and each subject to the trauma of destruction. Scholars of traumatic literature, as we have seen, often refer to the trauma of the past as intruding on literary characters in their present; in Dtr, a piece of literature about the past, the trauma erupts and repeats into its narrative about the past. As a work about history, there is clearly chronology in the narrative, but the temporality of the trauma of siege and forced migration can seem to suspend this chronology as it repeats constantly in these intrusions into the narrative. Traumatic repetition does not subvert only the narrative's concept of history, but its concepts of justice, punishment, and Israel as a series of individual generations as well.

The master narrative provides some hope to the exilic community that they might produce a generation whom God will not accuse, even inadvertently, of sin and punish, for in 30:1–10 Moses states that when the nation has been exiled God will meet their repentance—which is a return to cultic loyalty—with a circumcision of their hearts that will lead to complete obedience. We will wait until Chapter 7 on Kings to discuss more fully what kind of hope the narrative extends to its exilic readers, but we can say here that the master narrative is clear in 4:25–31 that punishment and exile will be followed by repentance. Both this passage and 30:1–10 indicate that exile will happen—e.g., "When you beget children and children's children and become complacent in the land and have acted corruptly and make an idol.... I call the heavens and the earth as witnesses against you today that you will surely perish" (4:25–26).[46] The narrative here, as at the beginning of Deut 30, presents apostasy and exile not as a possibility for Israel but as a certainty.

Yet the good news for the exiles in 30:1–10 that God will reward repentance with salvation is tempered by a subversion of the narrative here, for as passages like 30:6–10 and 29:3 [ET 4] make clear, God has made it impossible for the pre-exilic generations of Israel to obey[47]—they are not able to understand, and God has not circumcised their hearts in order to make obedience possible. There is really no ethical choice for them to make, since they do not have the ability to make it. What the narrative of 30:1–20 as a whole, which Moses speaks to the conquest generation, guarantees for all generations of Israel until the exile is that they cannot obey, and so will be repetitively subjected to the trauma that the exilic generation will undergo. Not until the time of the exiles' repentance will God make obedience possible, and so the destruction and exile are practically accomplished facts, as God tells Moses in 31:16–21 in an introduction to the song Moses must teach Israel so it can stand as

46. Deut 4:25–31 begins, "*When* (כי) you bear children and children's children and have become complacent in the land and have acted corruptly and made an idol (ונושנתם והשחתם ועשיתם פסל)...." See *GKC* ¶158d, 164d–e for a temporal particle כי followed by a perfect consecutive as expressing causes already brought into effect.

47. Deut 29:3 [ET 4] reads, "YHWH has not given you a heart to know or eyes to see or ears to hear until this day (עד היום הזה)." This could mean either: (1) God still has not provided the audience with the ability to understand; or (2) God has just now given this ability to them. The argument that the second meaning is the most logical one because the new generation has now heard the law (e.g., Nelson, *Deuteronomy*, 340; Lohfink, *Das Hauptgebot*, 128 n. 5) misses the point that the verse is not about having the law, it is about having the ability to understand and to do it, which is precisely the point also of 30:6–10. The verse suggests rather the inability of all of Israel's pre-exilic generations to be able to understand and do the law (so Miller, *Deuteronomy*, 206; Ryan O'Dowd, *The Wisdom of Torah: Epistemology in Deuteronomy and the Wisdom Literature* [FRLANT 225; Göttingen: Vandenhoeck & Ruprecht, 2009], 93–94).

a “witness” against them. We see yet another traumatic gap in the master narrative’s logic of history: there is no choice for loyalty to the divine suzerain to be made, since God has made that impossible, a claim that subverts the logic that lies behind Moses’ endless exhortations to Israel to act rightly in order to avoid destruction. Yet in the context of 30:1–10 and 29:3 [ET 4], the people’s failure to keep the law and remain loyal to their divine suzerain does not really seem to explain the trauma; this can hardly be a failure when no real ethical choice is involved. The passage subverts the narrative’s concepts of God, justice, and punishment. God is not a God of justice as the narrative presents him; when there is no ethical choice to be made, there is no justice. Trauma, as we saw in Chapter 2, appears as an absence in a totalizing ethical explanation.

Chapter 4

JOSHUA: GOD'S FAILURE AND INJUSTICE

A. *The Master Narrative: Joshua's Failure and Israel's Land*

Unlike Deuteronomy, the book of Joshua actually pays little explicit attention to the theme of obedience to all of the law. God's initial command to Joshua in 1:7–8 to observe "all the law" and "this book of the law" reminds readers of the emphasis in Deuteronomy on obedience to the entire law, as does the story of its public inscription and reading in 8:30–35, but we find almost no other explicit references to nomistic fidelity in the book. In 22:5 Joshua tells the Transjordanian tribes to keep the law Moses commanded and to love (that is, be loyal to) YHWH, and in 23:6–8 he conflates the notions of total obedience to the law and complete cultic faithfulness just as Moses did in Deuteronomy, but the salvation history he recites in Josh 24 omits the theophany and lawgiving at Horeb. The focus of 23:7–8, 11–16 and 24:14–23 moves to cultic loyalty, and this is where the narrative's emphasis in terms of covenant fidelity will largely remain until the end of the History. From this point on in the narrative, the equation of absolute cultic fidelity and obedience to the law in Deuteronomy is largely subsumed by a focus on cultic loyalty alone.

As in the previous chapter, we begin our investigation of this part of the Deuteronomistic History with a survey of the master narrative and its main themes so that we can then move in section B to examine how trauma subverts them. The master narrative in Deuteronomy has much more to say about the first theme of the consequences of Israel's failure in absolute vassal loyalty to YHWH than about its second, the contributions of the failures of leadership in Israel's sin and punishment; this emphasis is reversed in Joshua, and so our investigation of the narrative here focuses on the failures of Joshua's leadership.

It would be wrong to claim that the narrative presents the totality of Joshua's leadership as a failure, and Richard Nelson argues that Dtr's narrative portrays Joshua as a good leader, for, writes Nelson, God appoints him to succeed Moses (Deut 3:21–22, 26–28; 31:1–8), and he proves to be a model of obedience to divine command and the law (Josh 5:10; 8:29, 30–35; 10:26–27).[1] While avoiding outright criticism of Joshua, however, the narrative provides more details about questionable decisions of leadership on his part than was the case for Moses. Although God promises Joshua victory in Canaan in 1:2–9, and although Joshua himself witnessed the earlier defeats of Sihon and Og in Deut 2:24 and 3:2 (and cf. Josh 1:3), his first real act as a military leader in Josh 2:1 is to replicate the spying mission of the exodus generation that caused them and Moses to die before entering the land. Like Moses, he avoids a divine command to enter the land (cf. Deut 1:8 and Josh 1:2), and instead embarks on a matter of his own choosing.[2] The mission certainly begins inauspiciously, since the only action the spies undertake is to go to the house of a prostitute and sleep there. The verb שכב that describes their actions in 2:1 likely does not suggest that they had sex with Rahab,[3] although the word choice here does "tantalize the reader with hints of impropriety,"[4] since it is not entirely clear why the spies would even go to the house of a prostitute in the first place.

While one could argue that the narrative views positively the inclusion of the Canaanite Rahab and her family in Israel, we need to remember the virulently anti-Canaanite motif of intermarriage that plays such an important role in the narrative's theme that deals with cultic loyalty. The command of genocide in Deut 7 is absolute, Moses repeats it in the law of Deut 20:16–18, and neither the narrator nor God ever indicate that the command of חרם should be set aside in Rahab's case. This is clearly not a minor issue for the narrative; Moses twice insists that leaving Canaanites

1. Richard D. Nelson, "Josiah in the Book of Joshua," *JBL* 100 (1981): 531–40; idem, *Joshua: A Commentary* (OTL; Louisville: Westminster John Knox, 1997), 30–31.

2. So also Aaron Sherwood, "A Leader's Misleading and a Prostitute's Profession: A Re-examination of Joshua 2," *JSOT* 31 (2006): 43–61 (49).

3. If the narrator meant to suggest that the spies did anymore than literally sleep there, we would expect to see שכב עם or שכב את or שכב אתה. See Yair Zakovitch, "Humor and Theology or the Successful Failure of Israelite Intelligence: A Literary-Folkloric Approach to Joshua 2," in *Text and Tradition: The Hebrew Bible and Folklore* (ed. Susan Niditch; SBLSS; Atlanta: Scholars Press, 1990), 75–98 (83); Elie Assis, "The Choice to Serve God and Assist His People: Rahab and Yael," *Bib* 85 (2004): 82–90.

4. Hawk, *Every Promise Fulfilled*, 63.

alive in the land will lead to apostasy and thus punishment. Given Josh 1:7–8, which renews Deuteronomy's repeated emphasis on keeping all of the law, and given Deut 1–3, where we saw that even a minor violation of divine command can lead to disaster for Israel, we should not jump to conclusions about the laying aside of the law of חרם here. Rather, we see a leader of Israel making suspect decisions that directly violate a divine command. While readers see Rahab acknowledging YHWH's power in 2:8–11, they do not see a consequent assertion of her cultic loyalty anywhere. Rahab, of course, has good reason to lie to the spies, and she pins her survival and the survival of her family on the oath she wants the spies to swear based on her faithful treatment of them (2:12–13). The spies, of course, are dependent upon her faithfulness, since the king of Jericho was alerted to their presence and now hunts for them (2:2–3). Her act of sparing their lives rather than turning them over to the king has an aspect of Pascal's wager to it: if Israel is successful in destroying Jericho, she has potentially saved her family; if not, she has not harmed herself at all. In 6:22–25, Joshua does indeed honor the oath the spies made with Rahab—and he does so on his own initiative, not because of any divine command—and so her family is saved. Notably, he does not try to justify her exemption from the חרם command by claiming that she and her family will be faithful Yahwists; the narrator reports only that Joshua made the decision to spare their lives "because they hid the messengers whom Joshua sent to spy out Jericho."[5] Rahab and her family remain alive, in short, because they did not spoil his spying mission that God did not command. And in honoring the oath, he has disobeyed God's absolute command of חרם from Deut 7 and 20, and has begun to sow the seeds of Canaanite presence, intermarriage, and apostasy.

Joshua's leadership is questionable not only in the Rahab story but in the story of the incorporation of the Gibeonites into Israel in Josh 9, as well. In this chapter, the narrative leaves readers with no doubt that this group of Canaanites deceives Israel. They lie about their Canaanite origins in 9:6, 11 in order to avoid the חרם that the Israelites inflict on Jericho and Ai (9:3), and support these lies by altering their physical appearance in 9:4–5, 12–13. Like Rahab they acknowledge YHWH's power (9:9–10, 24), and like Rahab they make no claim that they will worship him exclusively, or even at all. Given their lies in a situation reminiscent of that of Rahab, readers may ask themselves at this point in the story if she had not been similarly deceptive. In the Gibeonite story,

5. The MT of 6:17 provides the same rationale, but in this case directly from the mouth of Joshua. The LXX omits this reference to Joshua speaking in 6:17, however, and its shorter text is to be preferred.

the narrative at the very least suggests that Israelites should get divine approval before thinking of making a covenant with Gibeon and allow them to remain in the land: "The [Israelite] men[6] took from their [the Gibeonites'] provisions, but did not consult YHWH" (9:14). And it is specifically the leadership of Joshua[7] that is responsible for Israel's failure here in not subjecting the Gibeonites to חרם and instead acquiescing to their request for a ברית "covenant" (9:6, 11, 15), precisely what God forbade Israel to make with the Canaanites in Deut 7:2: "you will certainly make them חרם; you will not make a covenant (ברית) with them and you will not show them mercy." When Gibeon first approaches the Israelite camp, it is the Israelites[8] and not their leader who first respond skeptically to the request for a covenant (9:6–7). The Gibeonites do not answer the Israelites' question concerning the veracity of their story; they turn instead to Joshua and present a longer version of their deceptive story to him (9:8–13), and he grants their request for a covenant. Joshua 9:15 does not only repeat the term ברית, precisely what YHWH forbade Israel to make with the Canaanites, it also uses the root חיה, which Moses uses in Deut 20:16 in his repetition of the command to annihilate the Canaanites.[9] The implication in this story is that Joshua has again failed to carry out the order of חרם that God commanded. And lest readers miss this, the word "covenant" appears five times in the chapter as a whole (9:6, 7, 11, 15, 16). This is the only covenant that Israel is said to make with the Canaanites in the conquest period, and so, as we shall see in the following chapter on Judges, when God condemns Israel

6. The MT's אנשים is likely original. The LXX's οἱ ἄρχοντες "the leaders" may have been reading נשיאים, influenced by the recurrence of the same word in 9:15–21; it may also have been reading the same word as the MT but simply understood "men" as having the sense of "leaders," as in the case of Judg 8:15. See Barthélemy, *Critique textuelle de l'Ancien Testament*, 15.

7. The story of Josh 9 as it now appears refers to the influence of "the leaders of the congregation" (נשיאי העדה), but only in the sections that derive from the Priestly Writing and that are not originally part of the Deuteronomistic History. For 9:15b, 18–21 as deriving from P rather than Dtr, see esp. the arguments in Roy K. Sutherland, "Israelite Political Theories in Joshua 9," *JSOT* 53 (1992): 65–74.

8. The term איש ישראל is used collectively in 9:6 and 7, and so can be read simply as "the Israelites." See *GKC* ¶123a–b. The witnesses to the text frequently try to clarify this collective reading: the LXX of 9:6 translates the words as "Israel" (and some LXX versions translate "all Israel"); the ketib/qere of 9:7 provides a verb that has איש ישראל as its subject in both the singular (the qere) and plural (the ketib); and the LXX has changed the subject of that verb from the more difficult reading of the MT to "the children of Israel." See Nelson, *Joshua*, 121; Trent C. Butler, *Joshua* (WBC 7; Waco, Tex.: Word, 1983), 98.

9. See Hawk, *Every Promise Fulfilled*, 84–85.

in Judg 2:1–2 for having made a covenant with the Canaanites, Joshua must bear some responsibility for the punishment that follows.

As 9:14 presents the matter, it is Israel as a whole who eats of the Gibeonites' deceptive food and who does not consult YHWH, but it is Joshua specifically who makes the covenant with the Canaanites in 9:15a; even after he discovers their trickery in 9:16, he does not revoke the covenant or order their annihilation, but has them remain in Israel as "hewers of wood and drawers of water" (9:23).[10] In 9:26, Joshua "rescued them from the hand of the Israelites, and they did not kill them." Israel rather than Joshua in this story seems truly to understand what God wants; the Gibeonites themselves are aware of what "YHWH your God commanded Moses his servant,…to destroy all the inhabitants of the land" (9:24). It is Israel's leader alone here who is ultimately in the wrong. In the stories of Rahab and the Gibeonites, we find Canaanites who remain in the land, the first steps in the intermarriage, apostasy, and punishment of Israel that begin in Judg 2:1–3:6. As Moses warns in Deut 7:1–6, to allow Canaanites to survive in the land leads to intermarriage, which leads to apostasy and punishment, and he makes a similar argument in 20:16–18. Joshua's spying mission and his covenant with the Gibeonites are the first steps in a loss of the land that will affect more than one generation. It seems difficult to argue here that the stories of Rahab and the Gibeonites should be read as an amelioration of the divine command of Canaanite genocide. In fact, the narrative's summary of the conquest in 11:16–23 points to חרם as the goal of the battles with the Canaanites (11:20, 21), and states, following Deut 7:2, that "mercy" is the precise opposite of the חרם that "YHWH commanded Moses" (11:20).[11]

10. Andrew Mayes notes that the phrase "hewers of wood and drawers of water" is used only in Deut 29:10 [ET 11] and Josh 9:21, 23, 27. Deut 29, where Moses warns both Israel and its resident aliens within Israel to keep the covenant, uses the term to refer to the resident aliens, and so Mayes argues that that passage anticipates the incorporation of the Gibeonites in Josh 9 (see his "Deuteronomy 29, Joshua 9, and the Place of the Gibeonites in Israel," in Lohfink, ed., *Das Deuteronomium*, 321–25). Given the ordering of these passages, however, and an assumption of the command of genocide for the Canaanites in Josh 6–8, it would appear that there is a legitimate group of non-Canaanite resident aliens within Israel before the nation enters the land, and that, in Josh 9, Joshua has illegitimately tried to integrate the Canaanite Gibeonites into this group of non-Canaanite resident aliens whose presence is acceptable. The divine command of annihilation in Dtr applies to Canaanites alone; this is why the laws regulating conduct in war in Deut 20 command the annihilation only of Canaanites, not of people of any other nation.

11. The command that Moses relays in Deut 7:2 is that "you will certainly make them חרם, and you will not make a covenant with them, and you will not show them mercy (תחנם)." The narrator states in Josh 11:20 that "it was from YHWH to harden

The master narrative does not explicitly indicate these failures of Joshua's leadership to readers, but after the story of Moses there is little direct condemnation of Israel's leadership until the reign of Saul, and even after that little again until the end of Solomon's reign, with the exception of God's explicit censure of David in 2 Sam 12. Yet even without direct condemnation, it is clear enough, as we shall see, that there are major failures of leadership by the judges, Samuel, David, and even Solomon during the early part of his reign for which neither the narrative nor God offer any direct condemnation. As I suggested in Chapter 2, we can perhaps see a narrative strategy where readers learn to identify the failures of the leaders presented in the narrative through their increasing familiarity with Israel's failures of complete vassal loyalty to YHWH. Only by Kings does the narrative provide readers with a series of consistent evaluations of the nation's leadership to ensure that they have rightly understood the two main themes of the narrative and their interdependence. Poor leadership decisions in Joshua's case have prepared the way for future apostasy and destruction. As the narrative explains this, it is also in the process of explaining what causes the traumas that future generations of Israel—like the exiles—will suffer. This will become more explicit in Judg 1:1–3:6, where the narrative says that the survival of the Canaanites in the land leads to intermarriage, apostasy, and the punishment of foreign invasion, a punishment that foreshadows the one the exilic readers have experienced.

Certainly Joshua's exhortations to cultic and nomistic fidelity in Josh 22:1–5; 23; and 24 make him sound like Moses in the best sense, but we can note that even at points when he seems to lead Israel rightly, the narrative can subtly underline his failure in seemingly minor issues. For example, after Joshua has dealt with the sin of Achan in ch. 7 and saved Israel from destruction (and note 7:6, where he and the elders appear to inquire of God, something that they fail to do later in the case of the Gibeonites), and then has gone on to take Ai in ch. 8, he then leads the renewal of the covenant in 8:30–35, as Moses had commanded in Deut 27. This action of creating a written and public copy of the law is clearly not a minor point from the master narrative's point of view, for the nation's survival depends on absolute adherence to it. Joshua's seeming act of obedience here, however, only partially follows Moses' command in Deut 27:1–8 that Israel write the law on stones and sacrifice "on the day that you cross over the Jordan." Joshua does not get around to this until after the victory over Ai. Scribes at Qumran, or at least of the

their heart to meet Israel in battle so that [Israel] might make them חרם so there might be no mercy (תחנם) for them."

Vorlage of the text they used, observed this and moved the account of the writing of the law and the sacrifice from its original position at 8:30–35 and placed it after 5:1 in 4QJosh[a] so that it can still appear as if Joshua fulfills the command on the same day Israel crosses the Jordan.[12] Joshua's dilatory action here in a matter of great importance for the narrative lodges an act of disobedience within one of obedience, reminiscent of Moses' failure immediately to enter the land upon God's command in Deut 1:8, and of Saul's untimely sacrifice to YHWH in 1 Sam 13 that will cost him an eternal dynasty. The command of Deut 27 and Joshua's tardy fulfillment of it in Josh 8 includes not simply the public writing of the law, but a sacrifice as well; as we have already seen, nomistic and cultic loyalty are in some way equal in Dtr's master narrative. Joshua acts slowly, more slowly than Moses commanded, to bring the nation's focus to the law, the ground of their nomistic loyalty, and to lead them in sacrifice, the central expression of cultic loyalty. In Josh 8, the act of writing and reading the law to Israel is done at the wrong time, just as the sacrifice to YHWH is. Joshua's failure of leadership here is not a minor point for the narrative. Joshua puts less importance on pointing Israel to nomistic and cultic loyalty than he should, and it will be only a matter of time before Israel's leaders stop doing this entirely. His seemingly minor failure here is merely the first step down a slippery slope in the narrative that will culminate with the kings whose leadership in cultic disloyalty ultimately explains the exiles' trauma.

And this is not the only place where Joshua feels free to alter the commands he has been given. At the battle of Jericho, the paradigmatic event of the conquest,[13] Joshua changes the divine instructions for the destruction of the city that he receives. The LXX's shorter text of Josh 6 is to be preferred, in part because it is the shorter reading, and in part because it is the more difficult one. According to this more original text,

12. For the alteration of 8:30–35 by later scribes to make it fit its position in 4QJosh[a], thereby making the Qumran reading "suspiciously easier," see Nelson, *Joshua*, 116–18. Eugene Ulrich argues that the sequence of the act in 4QJoshua is "simple and unproblematic" because it follows Moses' command ("4QJoshua[a] and Joshua's First Altar in the Promised Land," in *New Qumran Texts and Studies: Proceedings of the First Meeting of the International Organization for Qumran Studies, Paris 1992* [ed. George J. Brooke; STDJ 15; Leiden: Brill, 1994], 89–104 [95–96]; Ulrich et al., *Qumran Cave 4–IX: Deuteronomy, Joshua, Judges, Kings* [DJD 14; Oxford: Clarendon, 1995], 145–46), but this is precisely one of the reasons that makes the placement in the MT the more difficult and thus preferred reading.

13. For Jericho as the paradigm of the conquest, see Millard C. Lind, *Yahweh is a Warrior: The Theology of Warfare in Ancient Israel* (Scottdale, Pa.: Herald, 1980), 82.

YHWH commands the warriors to go around the city in 6:2–3. But Joshua immediately tells the priests, a group God has not mentioned in his command, to order the people to circle the city (6:6–7).[14] In the divine command the trumpet blast is to signal the final shout (6:5), but the priests blow the trumpet as they circle the city (6:8–9), something that they continue to do for six days (6:11–14), although there is no suggestion in the divine command of 6:2–3 that the circling should happen more than once. (The MT has added to the text in order to resolve these gaps between God's commands and Joshua's alteration of them, providing divine sanction for circling the city for six days and the priests' continual blowing of the horns in 6:3–4.[15]) Joshua also changes the signal for the charge from a trumpet blast to his command (6:5, 16).[16] His changes delay the immediate charge that God's command implies, suggesting a similar distrust to that which he displayed when sending the spies to Jericho, and the final emphasis on his command suggests a claim on his part for control and responsibility for victory that, for the narrative, lies entirely with God.

In the narrative's presentation of him, Joshua is no Manasseh, but neither is he a Josiah. Joshua does not entirely trust YHWH (Josh 2 and 6), he reinterprets and supplants divine commands (Josh 6), he permits Canaanites to stay in the land and so helps to lay the basis for future punishment and apostasy (Josh 9 and 6:17, 22–23), and he disobeys the precise instructions of Moses in 8:30–35 in a matter of utmost importance for Israel's survival in the land. It is not that Joshua evinces no interest in the narrative in nomistic and cultic loyalty—indeed, he commands Israel both to keep the law (22:5; 23:6) and to worship YHWH alone (23:7–13, 16; 24:14–15), repeating Moses' claim that intermarriage will lead to

14. The MT and 4QJosh[a] also contain an insertion in 6:6 in which Joshua commands the priests to carry horns in front of the ark. This was inserted later in order to provide a basis for 6:8, where the priests do this even though God does not command it, and it also appears to draw from 3:6 (Nelson, *Joshua*, 86; see also Butler, *Joshua*, 66).

15. In the shorter and original version of the text in the LXX, the warriors are told to circle the city in 6:3a. The MT has added 6:3b, which commands this circling to happen once each day for six days, and 6:4, which adds the command that they circle the city seven times on the seventh day with the priests blowing the horns. These expansions were added in order to provide divine sanction for what happens in 6:8 and 13. This makes the MT the easier and longer reading, which is why we can tell that the LXX is original. In the LXX, the command to blow the horn and for the people to shout in 6:5 is to happen after the warriors have circled the city only once.

16. For a comparison of the MT and LXX in Josh 6, see Nelson, *Joshua*, 83–90. See also Kissling, *Reliable Characters in the Primary History*, 71–72.

apostasy and destruction (23:12–13)—but his repetition of the exodus generation's spying mission, his guilt in allowing Canaanites to survive in the land and of making a covenant with them, and his failure immediately to draw Israel's attention to the law and to lead them in Yahwistic sacrifice suggest a decline in leadership that will accelerate by the time we reach Judges. His failure is the first step toward the ultimate failure of Israel's kings, the leaders who guide the people to ruin in Dtr's narrative.

Despite his failures, however, God gives victory to Israel in battle. With the exception of the first battle against Ai, where YHWH explicitly fights against Israel (7:1–5), there are no accounts of Israelite losses. The battles are won by God (Josh 6:17; 8:1, 18; 10:8, 10, 30, 32, 42; 11:6, 8), and Israel simply carries out the command to slaughter and utterly destroy (6:17, 21, 24; 8:24, 26; 10:28, 30, 32, 33, 35, 37, 39, 40; 11:8, 11, 12, 14, 20, 21), sometimes burning the cities following the complete slaughter of חרם there (6:24; 8:19, 28; 11:11). The master narrative does not present these scenes as normal battles with casualties on both sides. There are no reported Israelite casualties at all (except in the first battle with Ai); in fact, after the battle with the five kings in 10:1–27, the narrative states that "*all* the people returned…in peace" (10:21).

And the liquidation of the Canaanites is not merely obedience to a divine command; in the logic of the narrative, by killing all of the Canaanites Israel will avoid future apostasy and disloyalty to their divine suzerain (Deut 7:1–6; 20:16–18), and so חרם is an act of vassal loyalty that, if properly carried out, should ensure future loyalty. When Israel is completely loyal to God, then it reaps the reward of life in the land, and the narrative in the conquest stories from Josh 1 to Judg 1 expresses this intimate connection between these two ideas with its use of ירשׁ in the Qal and Hiphil. In these chapters, ירשׁ in Qal always refers to Israel's possession of the land, whereas in Hiphil the verb refers to Israel exterminating (or, in some cases, failing to exterminate) the Canaanites.[17] As the

17. In Josh 1–Judg 1, ירשׁ in Qal always refers to the possession of the land, and it always takes land as its object (Josh 1:11, 15; 12:1; 13:1; 18:3; 19:47; 21:43; 24:4, 8). When it appears in the Hiphil, however, it is better to translate it as "to annihilate" rather than as "to dispossess, drive out." In cases where ירשׁ appears in the Hiphil in the conquest stories and where it is clear whether it refers either to merely driving out the Canaanites or annihilating them, it always has the sense of annihilation. In Josh 8:7, ירשׁ in the Hiphil refers to the annihilation of the inhabitants of Ai (for context, see 8:22, 26–28); in 13:12 it refers to the population in the Transjordan whom the Israelites annihilated (cf. 13:8–12 and Deut 2:34; 3:3 for the relevant context); in 14:12 it is a reference to God's promise in Deut 9:1–3 to destroy the Anakim; in 23:9 it refers to what God has already done to the Canaanites (and clearly, in the narratives of Joshua, they have been annihilated); and when

beneficiary of divine victory, the possession of the land as a gift is something that Israel has earned not with its fighting prowess but through its expression of loyalty to the divine suzerain. ירשׁ in Hiphil, referring to the liquidation of the Canaanites, is the obedient response that allows Israel to take ownership of the land (ירשׁ in Qal).

Israel's obedience in חרם, however, is not perfect, since in 13:13; 15:63; 16:10; and 17:13 we read that some of the individual tribes leave Canaanites alive in the land. Readers are left to wonder how well Israel has learned the lesson of the necessity of complete obedience to God, since the master narrative has already stressed that leaving Canaanites alive in the land is the first step on the road to apostasy and destruction. It is not until Judg 1 that readers learn that the decisions of the individual tribes to leave Canaanites alive in the land occur only after the death of Joshua (Judg 1:1). In the book of Joshua, though, readers are not yet aware of this chronological disjunction in Dtr's narrative, and it is at least possible that the narrative means to suggest that this failure on the part of Israel merely follows the bad example Joshua has set, making him at least partially responsible for these acts. If Joshua's leadership is not as destructive as that of the kings who will actually cause Israel to commit apostasy, it is a step in that direction.

But even once we omit these cases as examples of Joshua's flawed leadership in the narrative, his actions in the cases of Rahab and the Gibeonites undermine his final addresses to Israel in chs. 23 and 24.[18]

Joshua warns in 23:13 that God will not continue to do this on behalf of Israel, the verb is thus still referring to this annihilation. The unanimity of this evidence thus suggests that when it is unclear as to the sense of a particular occurrence of ירשׁ in the Hiphil in the conquest narratives, we should translate it as "annihilate." And given God's command to annihilate the Canaanites in Deut 7:1–6 and 20:16–18, this makes perfect sense. For a study of the general difference between and meanings of ירשׁ in the Qal and Hiphil, see Norbert Lohfink, "Die Bedeutungen von hebr. *jrš qal* und *hif*," *BZ* 27 (1983): 14–33.

18. It is clear enough that Josh 23 is a Deuteronomistic composition; following Nelson, *Joshua*, 255, we can observe the overwhelming presence of Deuteronomistic vocabulary and ideas. On this, see also Nelson, *Double Redaction*, 94–98 and Weinfeld, *Deuteronomy and the Deuteronomic School*, 320–21, 333–34, 336, 339–44, 347, 350, 357. There is much more controversy surrounding the Deuteronomistic origins of Josh 24, but this chapter in fact contains close parallels to the mini salvation histories related at places in Dtr like Judg 6:7–10; 10:10–16; 1 Sam 7:3–4; 10:17–19; 12:1–25 (so, e.g., Götz Schmitt, *Der Landtag von Sichem* [Stuttgart: Calwer, 1964], 17–21; C. Brekelmans, "Joshua xxiv: Its Place and Function," in *Congress Volume: Leuven 1989* [ed. J. A. Emerton; VTSup 43; Leiden: Brill, 1991], 1–9). It thus makes sense to argue that ch. 24 was in fact the original conclusion to Joshua in Dtr; see, e.g., Volkmar Fritz, *Das Buch Josua* (HAT I/7; Tübingen:

There he warns Israel of the consequences of the future cultic disobedience of the nation; but as the narrative has already subtly warned readers, poor leadership will play a not-insignificant role in the final collapse of the exile that its readers have experienced. In 22:5 and 23:6, Joshua provides two of the few references to the law in the book, warning, like Moses in Deuteronomy, of the necessity of obedience to all of it, and in 23:7–13 he returns readers to the first main theme of the narrative with its accompanying motifs: intermarriage will lead to apostasy and thus to destruction from the land. In 23:13–16 he repeats Moses' surety in Deuteronomy that apostasy will happen, and will be followed by destruction.[19] Gordon Mitchell notes that the language of 23:16 parallels that of 7:11 from the Achan story, where God allows an Israelite defeat (7:3–5) and threatens Israel itself with חרם (7:11–12) because Achan had stolen from the plunder at Jericho designated for the divine treasury (7:13–21). Only upon Achan's execution (7:24–26) does God allow Israel to resume their conquest. Both 23:16 and 7:11 refer to Israel "transgressing the covenant" that God has "commanded,"[20] and thus 23:16 points back to the case of Achan as part of the future warning for Israel. In that story, one man's theft of a mantle and a gold bar from the חרם of Jericho led to an Israelite defeat and to the divine warning that, because Israel "transgressed my covenant that I commanded them," the whole nation would become חרם unless they dealt with Achan's sin. Joshua 24 looks back to the Achan story as well, for Joshua begins his recounting of Israel's salvation history there in 24:2 with "Thus says YHWH, the God of Israel," the only other time besides 7:13 that the phrase appears in Joshua.[21] In both cases the phrase opens a warning about what Israel must do to avoid destruction, and again readers are subtly reminded of a story in which the sin of just one man warranted the

J. C. B. Mohr, 1994), 235–39; Wolfgang Richter, *Die Bearbeitung des "Retterbuches" in der deuteronomistischen Epoche* (BBB 21; Bonn: Hanstein, 1964), 45–47.

19. 23:16 begins by stating בעברכם, which clearly means "When you transgress…," and, like Deuteronomy, thus sees the occurrence of disobedience as leading to destruction as an absolute certainty. Given the exilic audience and the narrative's theology of history, this is an unsurprising claim. For -ב before an infinitive as introducing a temporal (rather than conditional) clause, see Paul Joüon, *A Grammar of Biblical Hebrew* (trans. and rev. T. Muraoka; 2 vols.; SubBib 14; Rome: Pontificio Istituto Biblica, 1991), ¶133c; *IBHS*, ¶11:2:5c; *GKC* ¶164g.

20. Gordon Mitchell, *Together in the Land: A Reading of the Book of Joshua* (JSOTSup 134; Sheffield: JSOT), 115.

21. So Brekelmans, "Joshua xxiv," 1. It appears before the short salvation histories of Judg 6:7–10 and 1 Sam 10:17–19 (p. 6).

destruction of the nation. Like ch. 23, it foretells Israel's future apostasy that will merit destruction (24:20),[22] and its language looks forward to other recitations of salvation history in the narrative that warn Israel of cultic failure.[23] From now on in Dtr's narrative, cultic loyalty will be the dominant metric by which YHWH judges Israel.

B. *The Traumatic Intrusions: God's Failure and Injustice*

1. *The Traumatic Subversion of God*

The book of Joshua reflects, as we have seen, the narrative's focus on the contributions of Israel's leadership to the punishment of the people, one of its two main themes, and Joshua's faults have grave negative consequences for Israel. Joshua has prepared the way for apostasy by allowing Canaanites to remain in the land, and thus he has prepared the way for God's righteous punishment of exile. Israel is certainly complicit in this failing according to the narrative, but readers can gain the unsettling feeling that God is complicit in this failing as well. The summary of the conquest in 11:16–23 states that Joshua took the whole land (11:16, 23), since it was God's will to make the Canaanites חרם (11:20, 21), and says that this was accomplished because "it was from YHWH to harden their heart to meet Israel in battle" (11:20). As Daniel Hawk points out, 11:16–23 also refers to the survival of the Gibeonites, the Canaanite people who trick Joshua into guaranteeing their survival, and so raises the question as to why God did not harden their hearts also.[24] It is true that Moses tells Israel in Deut 7:20–24 that the conquest will not be

22. The temporal translation of כי in the phrase כי תעזבו את־יהוה in 24:20 is not the only possible interpretation, since a conditional translation is also possible—i.e., we could translate "If you abandon YHWH" rather than "When you abandon YHWH"—but given the context of 24:19, where Joshua tells Israel that "You are not able to serve YHWH," the temporal reading makes the most sense. For כי as introducing temporal clauses, see Joüon, *A Grammar of Biblical Hebrew*, ¶166o; *IBHS*, ¶38:7a.

23. Brekelmans points to the similar salvation histories later in the narrative, all of which warn of or appear in the context of punishment for cultic failure (Judg 6:7–10; 10:10–14; 1 Sam 7:3–4; 10:17–19; 12:1–25). The verb עבד with YHWH or other gods as its object appears 14 times in Josh 24, and is found multiple times in the salvation histories of Judg 10; 1 Sam 7; 12 ("Joshua xxiv," 5–7). Brekelmans argues that these summaries of salvation histories with warnings of cultic failure disappear after 1 Sam 12 (pp. 7–8), but in fact they do appear later in the narrative directed at individual kings rather than at all of Israel (e.g., 2 Sam 12:7–12; 1 Kgs 11:31–39; 14:7–11; 16:2–4).

24. Hawk, *Every Promise Fulfilled*, 48–49. See also Eslinger, *Into the Hands of the Living God*, 45.

completed quickly, and that God will cause some Canaanites to remain for a period, lest the animals in the land pose a threat to Israel.[25] This, however, hardly accounts for the case of the Gibeonites, who are incorporated into Israel as forced labor. Leaving some Canaanites for an interim period to control the animal population before all the inhabitants are ultimately annihilated is one thing; to fail to intervene to prevent the incorporation of a Canaanite group into Israel is another. Moses was very clear in Deut 7 and 20, as we have seen, that leaving Canaanites in the land will lead to apostasy, and that apostasy leads to destruction. The master narrative has never explicitly said that God had a duty to harden Canaanite hearts, but given the claim in 11:20 that God hardened Canaanite hearts so Israel could enact חרם, one must wonder why he has not acted as fully as possible to rid the land of Canaanites and thus eliminate entirely the source of apostasy and the repetition of the punishment that successive generations of Israelites will suffer.

It is possible to conclude, then, that Canaanites remain in the land not only because of Joshua's failure with the Gibeonites, and not only because of the later failures of the individual tribes completely to annihilate the Canaanites in their allotments, but because of God's unexplained failure to harden the hearts of the Gibeonites. We find here a gap in the narrative's explanation at this very point of grave failure that points Israel towards apostasy and destruction. Did Israel's failure to consult God on the matter (an issue that 9:14 mentions explicitly) cause God to overlook or forget about the Gibeonites? Did God simply decide partially to revoke one of his commands without readers or Israel being informed of this? And if so, why revoke this particular command? The Gibeonites are Canaanites, and liars at that, and the narrative has told readers that

25. Josh 7:20–24 does not specify how long this period will be; Moses says only that YHWH will send הצרעה (a word that the versions render as "the hornet"; if cognate with צרעת, it could refer to a plague of skin disease) and will drive out the nations "little by little." Duane Christensen interprets this as an indication that the expulsion will take "generations" (*Deuteronomy 1–21:9*, 164–65); Moshe Weinfeld argues that this timeline contradicts the claim of Deut 9:3 that Israel "will exterminate them and destroy them quickly" (*Deuteronomy 1–11*, 375). We need not see this vague reference to time here as lasting terribly long; it is perfectly possible to read it as a prediction of the conquest narratives in Joshua and in Judg 1. In Josh 6–11, Israel defeats a series of Canaanite cities; in Judg 1, after the individual tribes have been assigned to their allotments, they are to go to their pieces of Canaan and finish off the job of extermination. Nor does Deut 7:22—"you will not be able to put a quick end to them"—really contradict 9:3, for the latter verse refers only to the quick extermination of the Anakim, not all of the Canaanites, and Josh 11:21–22 reports that the Anakim were quickly exterminated.

their presence in the land will cause Israel's apostasy and destruction. Does God want this to happen? Clearly, God's commitment to supporting Israel's cultic loyalty and survival in the land is called into question. We see no direct accusation that God wants to cause apostasy within Israel, but the traumatic absence in the narrative's explanation leaves this open as a possibility. Leaving Canaanites in the land, the first step on the road to the trauma and destruction of exile, is something that God could have prevented, and is a traumatic gap in narrative explanation that thus suggests that he, along with Joshua, shares culpability in this matter. The narrative's logic in history blames the exiles' trauma on Israel; trauma intrudes into this narrative to subvert this explanation with the suggestion (but not the outright claim) that God is in part to blame for the fate of the exilic community. Trauma only suggests this, of course; it is present as ambiguity or narrative absence, not as a competing narrative explanation.

Given, in fact, the assertions of Deut 29:3 [ET 4] and 30:6–10, which claim that God has not made it possible for Israel to follow the law—an assertion that Joshua reiterates in 24:19 when he tells Israel that "you cannot serve YHWH,"[26] and a claim that echoes his earlier certainty in 23:16 that apostasy will happen and Israel will "perish from the land"—readers can get the sense that God wants Israel to suffer from a divine punishment that he has made them incapable of avoiding. Such portrayals of God make nonsense of the many commands concerning nomistic and cultic loyalty that Moses gives in Deuteronomy—for example, "Choose life so that you will live" (Deut 30:19). It makes equal nonsense of the similar commands that Joshua gives in Josh 22:1–9 (e.g., "Watch carefully to do the commandment and the law that Moses the servant of YHWH commanded you" [22:5]),[27] or those he gives in ch. 23 (such as, "Be very firm to obey and do all that is written in the book of the law of

26. Joshua's assertion in 24:19 is so shocking ("perhaps the most shocking statement in the OT" [Butler, *Joshua*, 274]) that some scholars argue that the verse is a later insertion (e.g., Martin Noth, *Das Buch Josua* [HAT 1/7; Tübingen: J. C. B. Mohr, 1938], 105–6; Kurt Möhlenbrink, "Die Landnahmensagen des Buches Josua," *ZAW* 56 [1938]: 250–54). Joshua claims in 24:19 that it is YHWH's own holiness and jealousy that will make this impossible (see, e.g., Butler, *Joshua*, 274–75; Hawk, *Joshua*, 274–75), but no matter what reason makes obedience impossible, it flies in the face of the narrative's logic in history.

27. And the full exhortation of Joshua in 22:5 reuses common vocabulary in Moses' commands to covenant loyalty in Deuteronomy: "love your God" (Deut 6:5; 10:12; 11:1, 13, etc.); "walk in his ways" (Deut 5:30; 10:12; 11:22); and so on. For a complete list of the parallels, see Weinfeld, *Deuteronomy and the Deuteronomic School*, 332–36.

Moses" [23:6])[28] and ch. 24 (e.g., "Fear YHWH and serve him perfectly and in truth, and turn aside the gods that your ancestors served" [24:14]), all of which reflect common ideas in the master narrative in regard to the necessity of adhering to the divine suzerain's command. While the master narrative has diligently stated that Israel always has a choice in directing their vassal loyalty to YHWH, and thus can explain the exilic community's trauma through their failure to do so, trauma intervenes to throw this certainty into doubt. Trauma questions the narrative's portrayal of God as an impartial judge who distributes punishment to Israel only for the ethical actions that the nation has chosen, and suggests that God is rather the one who makes Israel incapable of choosing, and thus the one who punishes not for Israel's choice but for God's. This is not simply a subversion of the narrative's understandings of God, justice, and punishment, it is a subversion of the narrative's whole ethical explanation of how history works.

Nor is 11:16–23 the only suggestion that God deliberately acts to leave Canaanites in the land and thus ensure the destruction of Israel. The claims in Josh 21:43–45 are like those of 11:16–23: "YHWH gave all of the land to Israel"; the nation "possessed it and dwelled in it"; and "YHWH gave rest to them all around." They do make sense within the master narrative's presentation of the conquest,[29] but they gloss over the

28. The command that Joshua gives Israel here, in fact, repeats the same language as the command that God first gave to Joshua personally in 1:6–9, and is the first appearance of the phrase "the book of the law" since 8:30–35, when the law is written on stones.

29. Josh 11:16–23 does use חרם in the Hiphil in v. 20 to refer to what Joshua did to the Canaanites, but given the context of this section (and of the conquest narratives as a whole), this refers only to the specific towns that Israel fought. This is why 11:21 uses חרם to refer specifically to the absolute destruction of the Amorites—they alone have been completely killed off within Israel's borders. In the overall context of the narrative's presentation of the conquest, it is easiest to take the claims of 11:16–23 and 21:43–45 as referring to general ownership and to a general conquest that has left some Canaanites who remain and who eventually need to be annihilated. The narrative has noted at a number of earlier points that the conquest will consist of more than a quick defeat of the Canaanites. As early as Deut 7:20–24, Moses tells Israel that while God will "give" them the Canaanites who will be "destroyed," this is something that will not take place quickly (7:22). The claim of 21:43–45, like that of 11:16–23, can be taken in the general sense of the overwhelming victories that God has given to Israel over the armies of Canaan that have given the land to the nation. The narrative from Deut 7 through Judg 1 presupposes that minor work for the individual tribes remains, but that by Josh 11 the defeat of the Canaanites has been so massive that the land can be said to belong to Israel, and that the nation dwells in it.

work that Israel has yet to accomplish in settling the land, as well as the work that YHWH has not done in helping the nation eliminate the Canaanites. We know, of course, that some Canaanites remain in the land because of the failures of Joshua and Israel in the cases of Rahab and the Gibeonites, cases in which God has also failed to harden Canaanite hearts so that they might also be destroyed. In the section of the book devoted to the division of the land among the tribes, we read in 13:13, 16:10, and 17:13 that the tribes do not annihilate the Canaanites in their territories. (Not until Judg 1 do we learn that these references to the tribes' failures in the book of Joshua are achronological and do not occur until after Joshua's death.) While this is assumedly the fault of the tribes—17:13 is clear that the Manassites were powerful enough to wipe out the Canaanites, but simply did not—15:63 tells readers that the people of Judah "were not able to destroy" the Jebusites, leaving readers with the conclusion that God, responsible for Israel's victories under Joshua, did not supply the tribe with the ability to defeat the Canaanites. Joshua and Israel may be responsible for leaving Canaanites in the land, but God seems to bear some of this responsibility as well, both during the lifetime of Joshua and after, and in the case of 15:63, the blame would appear to fall on God alone.

As present as God is in granting victories in the battles of Josh 6; 8; and 10, he is absent in the cases of Rahab in ch. 6 and the Gibeonites in ch. 9, where he does not so much as announce divine disapproval of the covenants with the Canaanites he forbade in Deut 7.[30] It is true that 9:14 accuses the Israelites of failing to inquire of YHWH before Joshua makes the covenant with Gibeon, but God speaks to Joshua without prior inquiry in 1:1–9; 3:7–8; 4:1–3, 15–16; 5:2, 9; and so on, and so it is unclear why he does not choose to warn Joshua away from covenants with Rahab and Gibeon that will lay the basis for the punishments that God will visit on the nation. YHWH does not even warn against or punish the spying mission at the beginning of Joshua that leads to the covenant with Rahab despite the severe punishment of Israel and Moses for the spying mission at the beginning of Deuteronomy, just as God is absent in Judah's inability to drive out the Canaanites. In these cases, God must bear some complicity for the covenants that Israel has made,[31] and thus bear some responsibility for the apostasy that will follow. All of these cases of

30. See also L. Daniel Hawk, "The Problem with Pagans," in *Reading Bibles, Writing Bodies: Identity and the Book* (ed. Timothy K. Beal and David M. Gunn; Biblical Limits; London: Routledge, 1997), 153–63 (157–58).

31. See Eslinger, *Into the Hands of the Living God*, 25–54.

God's inaction, however, subvert Dtr's master narrative, which places responsibility for Israel's cultic failure and consequent destruction on the Israelites alone, and, like examples of God ignoring the law in Deuteronomy, they subvert claims that God is perfectly just.

Of all of the cases of God's absence or inaction in Joshua that we have just surveyed, the clearest point of divine failure is Judah's inability to destroy the Jebusites. As clear as the narrative's conquest accounts are in ascribing Israel's victories to God, there is no obvious explanation that fits with the master narrative for this failure that leaves Canaanites in the land. It is not impossible to explain this in reference to the narrative; we could point, for example, to Moses' assertion in Deut 7:20–24 that some Canaanites will remain until the land is fully settled by Israel so that the people are not overrun by wild animals, or Joshua's very different claim in Josh 23:13 that the Canaanites remain as "a snare and a trap." We could argue that, because Jerusalem is part of Benjamin's inheritance (15:8; 18:16, 28), God does not give Judah the power to exterminate the Jebusites so that the tribe would not settle in a city that does not belong to them[32]—perhaps Judah receives the city later because, according to Judg 1:21, Benjamin fails to exterminate the Canaanites there. (The MT's version of 15:63 states that "the Jebusites lived with the children of Judah in Jerusalem to this day," but the LXX omits "with the children of Judah," and this shorter reading is to be preferred.[33]) It is also possible, of course, to read this notice as suggesting that God, who continually granted victory to Israel in its conquest, was unable or did not want to do so. It is the very appearance of לא יכלו "were not able" in 15:63, a notice that will repeat in regard to Judah in Judg 1:19,[34] that seems so striking and highlights the explanatory gap in the narrative at this point. This absence of explanation and the consequent ambiguity of interpretation throw the master narrative's portrayal of God into question. Is God not

32. See Hawk, *Every Promise Fulfilled*, 104–5; J. Alberto Soggin, *Joshua: A Commentary* (trans. R. A. Wilson; OTL; London: SCM, 1972), 180.

33. See A. G. Auld, "Judges 1 and History: A Reconsideration," *VT* (1975): 261–85 (274–75); Nelson, *Joshua*, 185.

34. In Judg 1:19, "Judah was not able to exterminate the inhabitants of the plain" (reading with the LXX, Targum, and Vulgate, which contain the more difficult reading; see section A of Chapter 5 for this explanation). And the verse is clear that, although "YHWH was with Judah," this inability to conquer the plain is due to the inhabitants' military advantage: "they had chariots of iron." So even if we were to argue that Judah is not able to exterminate the Jebusites in Josh 15:63 because Jerusalem does not belong to them, the repetition of this failure in Judg 1:19 remains an unexplained failure.

powerful enough to annihilate? Has he briefly changed his mind about granting victory, acting inconsistently? Is he simply leaving the Canaanites in the land because he is preventing Israel from being loyal, reflecting Joshua's assertion to Israel that "you cannot serve YHWH" (24:19)? What, in fact, unites each of the cases of the divine failure to act—the failure to harden Gibeon's hearts, to give victory to Judah over the Jebusites, and to warn Joshua and Israel away from incorporating Canaanites into the nation—is this simple lack of explanation. This ambiguity, these gaps in the narrative, are trauma's interruption of totalizing explanation, and this traumatic subversion places the narrative's concepts on trial but provides no resolution. Readers can reasonably conclude that God may not always be powerful enough to help Israel in important ways, or may act inconsistently at important junctures, or may be acting to deprive Israel of ethical agency when it comes to the decisions of vassal loyalty that Israel must make to remain in the land. His curious unwillingness completely to destroy the Canaanites—whose presence leads to apostasy—is not explained, and as such is a lacuna in the narrative's attempt to fully explain the trauma. Like the comments of Moses and Joshua that point to Israel's simple inability to maintain covenant loyalty, it subverts the narrative's explanation of trauma through a just application of divine punishment. The presence of trauma's absence at these points in the narrative undermines the narrative's whole logic in history by subverting its concept of God as a just actor who responds to disloyalty with punishment. When God removes ethical choice, punishment can hardly be said to be just, and it makes Moses' and Joshua's exhortations to vassal loyalty seem ludicrous.

As a result, this ambiguity—this anti-explanation and anti-narrative—that we see subverts not only the master narrative's concept of God, but its concepts of justice and punishment as well. The ambiguity of trauma has erupted into the narrative and unsettled the certainty of the narrative's linguistic concepts. If God will not act consistently, or if he is arranging history so as to leave Canaanites in the land, thus making it impossible for Israel to avoid intermarriage and apostasy, then the narrative's conceptions of justice and punishment have also been subverted. If Canaanites remain in the land because of God's failures, and if this leads to intermarriage and apostasy as Moses has said it will, then it is hardly just for Israel to be punished. The ambiguity in the portrayal of God subverts the narrative's whole claim of Israel's ethical choice as determining its fate, and thus undermines its logic in history. God's failures seem to point to a divine desire that successive generations of Israelites suffer the same kind of trauma that the exiles did, since it is the presence of the Canaanites in the land that sets off the cycle of apostasy and punishment in Judges. It is no wonder that Joshua says in 24:19, as Moses did before him in Deut 29:3 [ET 4] and 30:6–10, that Israel will be unable to act in accord with the terms of its covenant with YHWH.

Trauma's subversion of the narrative is not total here—trauma, in short, does not offer a definitively different picture of God—but is present as absence in narrative explanation. It suggests and hints, but it does not present a totalizing explanation, or else it would be a narrative that competed with the master narrative. Joshua's statement to Israel in 24:19 that "you are not able to serve YHWH," for example, is surrounded by commands to the nation to do precisely that (24:14, 23) and by Israel's claims that it will do so (24:18, 21, 24), all of which appear to bolster the master narrative's point that Israel has choice in its vassal obedience—a point that Joshua clearly articulates in 24:15—and thus to bolster its logic in history. The narrative absence of trauma's ambiguity suggests that these claims are not true, but does not provide any kind of totalizing argument for opposite claims. Trauma is, by its very nature, an absence of narrative and explanation.

By the time we reach 2 Kgs 21–25, where God explicitly ignores Josiah's perfect act of returning Judah to cultic loyalty and instead chooses to punish the nation, readers may recall that, since the time of the conquest, God has appeared to work actively to leave Canaanites in the land, thereby sowing the seeds of apostasy for which he is punishing the nation. The failures of God that we have just enumerated, that is to say, uncannily anticipate God's failure in 2 Kings to recognize Josiah's act of repentance. Trauma suggests that God, from the time of Israel's entrance into the land, has been working to destroy Israel, and that he is willing to work outside of the narrative's logic in history and its concepts of God, justice, and punishment to do so. By the time readers reach the end of Kings, then, at the narrative's concluding explanation of the exiles' trauma, trauma suggests that God will not honor even a perfect act of repentance that returns Judah to cultic loyalty if this will prevent the destruction of the nation that he has promoted since the conquest. Yet it is hardly clear that this is the conclusion that we must come to, for trauma does not make this conclusion clear enough to be a competing narrative. The interpretation of the texts I have just presented is certainly an interpretive possibility that can help to make sense of passages in Joshua and of 2 Kgs 21–25, but it is not an interpretive certainty. It is the absence and fracturing of narrative certainty, which is the way in which trauma manifests its presence.

2. *The Achan Story: God's Injustice*

As in Deuteronomy, readers can receive the uncanny suspicion, a suspicion that subverts the claims of Dtr's narrative, that God is more interested in his reputation than in dealing justly with Israel. God does not warn Joshua against the spying or covenants that would have prevented some Canaanites from remaining in the land; the only direct warning and punishment that we actually see in Joshua is the case of Achan's theft of the objects of חרם that belonged in the divine treasury. God is, it seems, willing to allow Israel to muddle their way to apostasy and punishment, but immediately threatens the destruction of the entire nation because one man has stolen from him (7:11–12). The divine command in 7:15 to burn Achan and all that is his, apparently including his family,[35] is itself disturbing, since it is difficult to see what guilt his family could bear for his actions. Attempts to explain this command of 7:15 by arguing that the חרם that he has stolen has ritually contaminated his family and other belongings[36] tend to read concepts from the Priestly Writing and the Holiness Code into Dtr. The History is not concerned with issues of cultic purity and does not describe anything like P's rules of impurity contamination.[37] Even if Dtr's narrative did maintain the same system of ritual contamination as P, the argument that Achan's family, and thus Achan himself, have been contaminated by his contact with the mantle and precious metals that belong to God's treasury would still make no sense. It is true that in P the laity and even the Levites die when they come into contact with things designated as "most holy" (e.g., Num 1:51; 3:10, 38; 4:19; 8:19; 17:28 [ET 13]; etc.), but in P, objects that are "most holy" are found only in the sanctuary, which the objects of Achan's theft

35. The command in 7:15 that the thief be burned, אתו ואת־כל־אשר־לו "him and all that/who belong to him," seems to command the death of his family as well, and in 7:24 Achan's family is brought to the place where he is killed in 7:25.The LXX of 7:25, however, records only the death of Achan. As a result, it is not clear that Israel fully carries out the punishment that God demands in 7:15.

36. See, e.g., Joel S. Kaminsky, *Corporate Responsibility in the Hebrew Bible* (JSOTSup 196; Sheffield: Sheffield Academic, 1995), 67–95; R. E. Clements, "Achan's Sin: Warfare and Holiness," in *Shall Not the Judge of All the Earth Do What is Right? Studies on the Nature of God in Tribute to James L. Crenshaw* (ed. David Penchansky and Paul L. Redditt; Winona Lake, Ind.: Eisenbrauns, 2000), 113–26; Nelson, *Joshua*, 101–2.

37. As Eyal Regev argues, holiness is described in Deuteronomy as a quality of all of Israel, and so, unlike the Priestly Writing, the laity has relatively free access to the holy sanctuary ("Priestly Dynamic Holiness and Deuteronomic Static Holiness," *VT* 51 [2001]: 243–61). For a list of ten important differences between P's and Dtr's concepts of holiness, see pp. 245–53.

are not.[38] In P, there is no effect when what is common comes into contact with what is merely holy.[39] The very fact that Dtr does not make the same kind of distinction between holy and most holy should make us wary of reading notions of purity and holiness from P into Dtr's narrative.[40] Moreover, there is no notion in either P or Dtr that those who have merely secondary contact with what is holy or even most holy (that is, who come into contact with someone who directly handled such things) should die.[41] And if we were dealing with a case of ritual contamination, where mere secondary contact should result in death, then anyone who came into contact with the precious things in Jericho or anyone who touched those people should die, yet this is clearly not the case. In 7:22–23, after all, the messengers retrieve the stolen objects and bring them to the treasury.[42] The call for the destruction of Achan's family and his belongings and the threatened destruction of the whole nation, something put in motion by the death of the Israelite warriors at Ai (7:5), is simply a matter of divine concern for what belongs to God, and does not reflect any known divine command.

God's concern for his property is out of proportion when one considers the violations of the חרם command in the incidents of Rahab and Gibeon in which God has decided not to intervene, for they represent the first Canaanite presence in Israel that will, in its totality, lead to intermarriage, apostasy, and punishment. If God can warn in regard to the issue of Achan's crime, why can he not do so in regard to Joshua's and

38. Jacob Milgrom, *Leviticus 1–16: A New Translation with Introduction and Commentary* (AB 3; New York: Doubleday, 1991), 977.

39. Ibid., 978.

40. The only place at all in Dtr where we see a reference to the "most holy" is in the construction of the temple (1 Kgs 6:16; 7:50; 8:6). For P, however, the distinction between "holy" and "most holy" is extremely important because of that writing's intense interest in order and the problems of crossing holiness boundaries. See on this issue, e.g., Frank H. Gorman, Jr., *The Ideology of Ritual: Space, Time and Status in the Priestly Theology* (JSOTSup 91; Sheffield: Sheffield Academic, 1990), 39–45, 63–65.

41. This is not even an issue in P, because, as the passages from Numbers listed above indicate, laity who come into contact with the most holy die immediately. There is no opportunity for others to come into secondary contact with them. Dtr says nothing about such a case.

42. If one wanted to argue that the narrative assumes that priests but not laity can handle what is חרם and holy, just as in P the priests can enter the tabernacle because they are holy (Exod 29:1; Lev 8:31–9:7; Num 16:1a, 2–11, 16–22, 26, 35; 17:1–5 [ET 16:36–50]), then we must note that the "messengers" whom Joshua sends in 7:22 are not said to be priests. See also Jacob Milgrom, *Cult and Conscience: The Asham and the Priestly Doctrine of Repentance* (SJLA 18; Leiden: Brill, 1976), 34 n. 127.

Israel's missteps that are leading the nation to destruction? And the punishment God announces in the case of Achan also seems out of proportion to the crime. "Israel has sinned, and they have transgressed my covenant that I commanded them and they have taken from the חרם and they have stolen and they have acted deceptively and they have put them among their things" (7:11), God says to Joshua. God misrepresents the situation to Joshua, however, for "they" have not done these things; only one man has, and at 7:11 Israel is unaware of the crime. The narrator, in fact, makes precisely the same puzzling claim in 7:1. Commentators frequently note in this regard that God is making Israel take collective responsibility for Achan's individual action.[43] This is clearly true, but it is simply incorrect to say, as the narrative and God do, that Israel has sinned, since the nation itself has not. Noticing this, the LXX translators add to the original claim in 7:1 that "the Israelites rebelled in regard to the חרם" that "they took from the חרם." This then justifies the punishment against all of Israel in 7:5 and God's claim that "*they* have stolen" in 7:11, but this is precisely why the shorter MT is the more difficult reading in 7:1. Yet God's misrepresentation of the crime in regard to its perpetrator provides him with an explanation for his punishment of the whole nation, and this is why he has permitted Ai to defeat Israel: the people of Israel themselves now "are חרם" (7:12). It is true that Moses warns in Deut 7:25–26 that if the Israelites take gold and silver from the Canaanite idols "you will be חרם like it," and that Joshua's warning against theft from the חרם in Josh 6:18 sounds like Moses' in Deut 7:25.[44] Regardless of the fact that Achan's silver and gold does not originate from idols (7:21), the divine interpretation of the command concerning theft from the חרם in the Achan story apparently suggests that the sin of even one man, of which the rest of the nation remains ignorant, can result in the punishment of all of Israel, at least if the sin involves stealing from the divine treasury.

We can, in short, identify two unexplained divine consistencies in the Achan story. First, if God truly wishes Israel to avoid sin that can lead to punishment of the nation, why does he not directly intervene in other cases, like the incidents involving Rahab and the Gibeonites, that put

43. E.g., Nelson, *Joshua*, 105; Hawk, *Joshua*, 111; Hans Hertzberg, *Die Bücher Josua, Richter, Ruth* (ATD 9; Göttingen: Vandenhoeck & Ruprecht, 1985), 50.

44. If we read with the LXX rather than the MT in Josh 6:18, then Joshua warns Israel to avoid the חרם "lest you covet (תחמדו) and take (ולקחתם) from the חרם." The MT reads "lest you make חרם (תחרימו)" in place of "covet," which makes little sense. See Nelson, *Joshua*, 85, 87; Fritz, *Das Buch Josua*, 66, 67; Barthélemy, *Critique textuelle*, 4–5. The verbs "to covet" and "to take" thus occur in both Moses' and Joshua's warnings, as well as in Achan's confession in 7:21.

future generations of Israelites in danger? Second, why does God blame the whole nation for a sin that one man has committed? The warriors who died at Ai have suffered for the sin of one man; God either is unable to tell the difference between Achan and the rest of Israel when he blames the nation in 7:11, or he is simply looking for an excuse to destroy Israel. And just as there is no explanation for why God punishes Israel in this episode, there is no explanation for why all that belongs to Achan need be burned. The fact that the lacunae in the narrative include the lack of explanation for why God has made Israel חרם uncannily returns us to 2 Kgs 21–25, where, as we will discuss in Chapter 7, we find an equal lack of explanation for the trauma that God inflicts on a people that Josiah has already returned to cultic loyalty. Trauma's intrusion into the Achan story foreshadows its intrusion into the end of the History's narrative, subverting the master narrative's portrayal of God as a just actor "keeping steadfast love for the ones who love him and keep his commandment to the thousandth generation and repaying the ones who hate him to his face to destroy him" (Deut 7:9–10). In the Achan story, God seems more than willing to violate the narrative's concept of divine justice when he feels that his honor has been attacked. His concern for this particular violation of חרם contrasts with his unexplained absence of concern for the violation of the חרם law in the cases of Rahab and the Gibeonites, Israel's first steps to the intermarriage and apostasy that will destroy them. The concepts of justice and punishment are subverted in this story as Israel is punished without any explained reason. It is certainly possible to read the story of Achan and conclude that history is dominated by a God interested in himself rather than in justice or in Israel, and this possible conclusion opens the nation to the possibility of suffering trauma at any unpredictable time the deity might choose.

Joshua's appeal to God following the defeat at the hands of Ai, then, is entirely appropriate to this situation. Having no explanation for the defeat, he appeals not to God's sense of justice but to his vanity for his reputation before the nations (7:8–9), just as Moses did in the case of the golden calf (Deut 9:28–29).[45] Joshua meets God's anomistic action with

45. As Nelson (*Joshua*, 102) notes, the similarity in message in Josh 7:7–9 and Deut 9:28–29 is paralleled by similarities in the leaders' physical position during their entreaties to God (both Joshua and Moses are prostrate [cf. Deut 9:25]); the destruction of both the golden calf and Achan by fire (cf. Deut 9:21; in Josh 7:15, God commands that the offender be burned, although the LXX^{C}'s version of the story does not report that this actually happened); and the use of the verb שמד (cf. Deut 9:8; 10:11). It is difficult for the attentive reader not to think about Moses' petition upon reading Joshua's prayer here.

an appeal to him that has nothing to do with justice: if the Canaanites destroy Israel, "what will you do for your great name?" Readers can see God as willing to destroy the nation for a crime the nation has not committed, and may wonder if God will do so again. Second Kings 21–25, as we have already seen (and will discuss in more detail), makes the same suggestion, for there God punishes the nation decades after Josiah returns them to loyalty. History in the Achan incident is not structured by divinely mandated justice that follows a clear logic as Dtr's master narrative claims, but is at the whim of unpredictable and uncontrollable divine vanity that punishes the innocent and guilty alike. This not only subverts the narrative's explanation of trauma, but for the exilic readers it again opens the possibility that their actions may not affect how God acts in history, and thus suggests that the future might be no more than a constant repetition of trauma.

When we consider the stories of Achan, Rahab, and the Gibeonites as a whole within the context of the master narrative, they appear to be not so much about divine mercy for outsiders who acknowledge YHWH's power—and both Moses and the narrator have been clear that God does not intend Israel to show any "mercy" to the Canaanites (Deut 7:2; Josh 11:20)—but about divine indifference for the law and Israel's fate. For the narrator, unlike many modern readers, the stories of genocide are not problematic; "the smoke of burning towns and the stench of rotting flesh"[46] are signs of God's gift of the land and Israel's obedient response in חרם. What challenges and subverts the master narrative is the claim that God will make Israel חרם as punishment even in cases when Israel cannot reasonably have knowledge of a crime one of its members has committed. We have noted already that 23:16 looks forward to the certainty of Israel's apostasy and punishment through destruction and loss of the land, and that it parallels God's words of judgment against the nation that appear in 7:11 in the Achan story, words that condemn Israel for a sin that the nation has not committed. Joshua 23:16 thus becomes not only a prophecy of exile, it suggests further, like the Achan story and unlike the master narrative, that there is no just reason for the exile and that Israel will suffer for sins for which it could not reasonably be said to be held guilty. As I mentioned in the previous chapter on Deuteronomy, trauma in 2 Kgs 21–25 subverts the assertion that the trauma that the exilic community suffers can reasonably be attributed to the actions of the generations who succeed the religious reforms of Josiah. We find this same subversion in the passages that we have just discussed. Whereas

46. John Bright, *The Authority of the Old Testament* (Nashville: Abingdon, 1967), 243.

the narrative argues that the nation as a whole bears culpability for the siege, destruction, famine, and forced migration of the exile, Josh 23:16, with its reference to both the Achan story and the exiles' trauma, suggests that God will punish and destroy even when Israel as a whole has no moral agency in the matter. The subversions of the narrative's portrayals of God, justice, and punishment in this story are clear; we should add as well that the narrative's view of history as the forum in which God enacts justice has been placed under question by trauma. If there has not been justice in the past, there may be no reason to expect it in the future.

Israel's failures, even when they are not really failures by the narrative's standards of justice, are punished by making the nation itself חרם. What God does to the Canaanites by means of Israel is what God will do to Israel by means of Babylon. The repetition of details of the slaughter of the Canaanites (Josh 6:21; 8:21–26; 10:10–11, 20, 28, 30, 32, 33, 35, 37, 39, 40; 11:8, 11, 14), the burning of their cities (6:24; 8:19, 28; 11:11), and siege warfare (10:31, 34) would not fail to leave an impact on readers who themselves have survived a trauma just like this. In these stories of conquest, the exiles are not merely confronted with a story of the distant past but with the repetition of a realized trauma that their own community members have experienced. As in Deuteronomy, trauma collapses time, and so makes one of Joshua's central aspects—the taking of the land and the slaughter of the Canaanites—not just a warning of what could happen to Israel, but a repetition of what did happen to the exiles. What trauma suggests in the book of Joshua, however, is that what the exiles experienced is not explainable on the master narrative's terms.

Chapter 5

JUDGES: TRAUMA AS THE ESSENCE OF HISTORY

A. *The Master Narrative in Judges: Israel's Cultic and Leadership Failures*

Judges opens at a point when Israel has no leader, and the narrative portrays the nation acting in disobedience to God's command to annihilate the Canaanites, thus guaranteeing the apostasy and punishment of foreign invasion that dominate Judges and foreshadow the narrative's final explanation of the trauma of 586. Yet as the narrative relates the stories of the judges, it points out that the mere existence of leaders in Israel is not enough; judges who are disloyal to God only preside over a disloyal nation. Nonetheless, when the narrative presents Israel without a leader in Judg 17–21, the nation's cultic and nomistic disloyalty is perhaps even worse than is the case when poor judges are in charge. In these chapters, the nation is so disloyal that God begins to treat Israel like a foreign nation—in the civil war that closes the book, Israel is so foreign in its cult and ethical practices that God can use it like the foreign nations earlier in the book to punish itself. By these chapters as well, the narrative hints that a monarchy, at least a Davidic one, might lead Israel properly, but hints as well that readers should not expect too much from Judean leadership. By the time readers reach Kings, however, they will see that the poor leadership of the judges has merely foreshadowed the worse leadership of the monarchs, who contribute even more to Israel's punishment in Kings than the judges do in this book. The disloyalty of Israel and its leaders here simply foreshadows the exiles' fate and explains their trauma as the logical result of the cultic and nomistic disloyalty that the nation's leaders participate in.

When the book opens by initially presenting Israel without a leader of the nation for the first time—Judg 1:1 tells readers that Joshua is dead, and the chapter moves to describe the activities of the tribes with no mention of any leader—we find the nation quickly undermining the fidelity of the conquest generation. Moses and Joshua may not have been perfect, but we see a rapid decline of Israel when the nation has no leadership at all. After Israel's pledges of loyalty to God in Josh 23–24 and the death of Joshua, the tribes in Judg 1 do not wipe out (Hiphil of ירשׁ) the Canaanites from all of the land they have inherited. While Israel has "taken" (לקח) the land in the conquest (Josh 11:23) and has "defeated" (נכה) the kings in the land (Josh 10:40–41; 12:1, 6, 7), Israel does not "possess" (Qal of ירשׁ) all of the land immediately following the conquest (13:1), although YHWH promises to "exterminate" (Hiphil of ירשׁ) the remaining inhabitants (13:6; 23:5), so long as Israel does not intermarry with the Canaanites and worship their gods (23:13).[1] Judges 1 repeats some of the same assertions of the tribes' failures to exterminate the Canaanites completely that we have already come across in Joshua (we see references to these failures in Josh 13:13; 15:63; 16:10; and 17:13), although only in Judg 1:1 do we finally understand that these failures occur "after the death of Joshua." Judah is not able[2] to exterminate (Hiphil of ירשׁ) the inhabitants of the lowlands (Judg 1:19); Benjamin does not do so to the Jebusites who live in Jerusalem (1:21), despite the fact that Judah has already taken the city (1:8); nor do Manasseh (1:26–27), Ephraim (1:29), Zebulun (1:30), Asher (1:31–32), and Naphtali (1:33) annihilate all of the Canaanites in their inheritances. The Amorites actually appear to have the upper hand in their battles with Dan (1:34).

1. We should note that after allotting the inheritances to the tribes, the narrative states that "YHWH gave all the land to Israel that he had sworn to give to their ancestors, and they possessed it (Qal of ירשׁ) and dwelt in it" (21:43). This verse does not state that Israel exterminated all of the Canaanites from the land, a meaning that we would expect to see expressed by ירשׁ in the Hiphil (see the previous chapter for this as the meaning of the verb in the Hiphil in the conquest narratives), but rather that the major work of defeating the Canaanites had been accomplished. This distinction becomes an important one in the interpretation of the opening chapters of Judges.

2. יכלו is absent in most of the MT witnesses to 1:19, but the LXX, Targum, and Vulgate provide it. A finite verb is not absolutely necessary before להורישׁ (see *GKC* ¶114 l), but given its appearance in the versions and in the parallel text of Josh 15:63, it makes most sense to include it. Moreover, 1:19 states that "YHWH was with Judah," so the claim in the same verse that Judah was unable to defeat an enemy makes the inclusion of יכלו the more difficult reading. It is possible that the MT copyist simply followed the pattern of לא הורישׁ found seven times in 1:27–33. See also Robert G. Boling, *Judges: A New Translation with Introduction and Commentary* (AB 6A; Garden City, N.Y.: Doubleday, 1975), 58; Susan Niditch, *Judges: A Commentary* (OTL; Louisville: Westminster John Knox, 2008), 31; Hertzberg, *Josua, Richter, Ruth*, 152.

What Judg 1 adds to the picture from Joshua is a decline in the actions and fates of the tribes' failures now that they are without any kind of leadership. As Barry Webb shows, 1:1–2:5 may be divided into three sections, each introduced with the verb עלה "to go up," and each representing a progressive decline in Israel's actions and fate.[3] Judah "goes up" and does חרם to the Canaanites in 1:1–21,[4] and is largely faithful to YHWH's command to exterminate the Canaanites and largely successful in fully conquering its inheritance. The next section begins when Joseph "goes up" but depends for victory on a Canaanite informer, who then lives in Israel in 1:22–26. So, as Lawson Younger points out, the success of Judah is followed by the stories of the failures of Manasseh, Ephraim, and Zebulun, and the narrative tells us that the Canaanites live among them. Yet even worse are the following indictments of Asher and Naphtali, which say that they live among the Canaanites. Worst of all is the final case of Dan, who is actually oppressed by the Canaanites (1:34–35).[5] Following this progressive decline in the obedience of the Northern tribes to annihilate the Canaanites, a divine messenger "goes up" in 2:1–5 to indict Israel for permitting Canaanites to live among them. As Moses has warned, to allow the Canaanites to survive in the land leads to intermarriage, apostasy, and punishment, which is precisely the outcome the narrative in Judges goes on to relate. Clearly, life without a leader leads to self-destruction and cultic disloyalty.

On the other hand, the narrative has also already been warning readers that the mere presence of a leader is not in itself enough to protect Israel from apostasy and destruction. Judges 1, it is true, focuses on the failures of a leaderless Israel, and the most damning part of the narrative's presentation of the acephalous tribes is that, except in one case involving Judah, the Israelite tribes are able to annihilate the Canaanites but simply fail to do so. (Joshua 17:12–13 actually says that at first Manasseh was not able to annihilate some of the Canaanites, and even when the tribe grew stronger it did not do so.) Israel's failure to exterminate the Canaanites explains God's judgment in 2:1–5: "I said, '...As for you, do not make a covenant (ברית) with the inhabitants of this land; tear down

3. Barry G. Webb, *The Book of the Judges: An Integrated Reading* (JSOTSup 46; Sheffield: JSOT, 1987), 90–92.

4. The verb חרם appears in 1:17.

5. K. Lawson Younger, Jr., "Judges 1 in Its Near Eastern Literary Context," in *Faith, Tradition, and History: Old Testament Historiography in Its Near Eastern Context* (ed. A. R. Millard, James K. Hoffmeier, and David W. Baker; Winona Lake, Ind.: Eisenbrauns, 1994), 207–27 (215–20); idem, "The Configuring of Judicial Preliminaries: Judges 1:1–2:5 and Its Dependence on the Book of Joshua," *JSOT* 68 (1995): 75–92 (83).

their altars.' But you did not obey my voice." This use of ברית, however, points back to Joshua's failure in allowing the Canaanites in Judg 1 to remain in the land. None of the notices of the tribes' failures to annihilate the Canaanites refers to a covenant made with the inhabitants of the land; the only place in the narrative so far where Israel has made a ברית with the Canaanites is in Josh 9, where the term is used a number of times (9:6, 7, 11, 15, 16). In that passage, in fact, the people of Israel opposed the covenant (9:7); it was Joshua who was ultimately responsible for its creation (9:15) and who rescued the Gibeonites from Israel when the nation discovered that they were Canaanites and wanted to annihilate them (9:26), as the law directs. By making a covenant with Canaanites, an act God has explicitly forbidden in Deut 7:2, Israel begins to reap the curse God lays upon the nation for making that covenant: "I will not drive them out before you, and they will be adversaries to you and their gods will be snares to you" (Judg 2:3). Both the individual tribes who fail to exterminate the Canaanites and the past leader are thus at least partly responsible for the intermarriage and apostasy that follows. This emphasis on the failure of both nation and leader will repeat numerous times with increasing severity in Judges.

In Judges, it is not merely the nation who sins, but its leaders do too. To turn first to the nation's sin beyond its disobedience of the command to annihilate the Canaanites, we should note that the narrative of Judges focuses almost entirely on cultic loyalty—or, really, its lack—and says nothing at all about obedience to all of the law, at least not until the book's final chapters. The narrative in Judg 2–16 provides a series of concrete examples of how cultic disloyalty leads to foreign invasion and loss of control of the land, a clear foreshadowing of the end of the narrative in Kings that will blame the foreign invasions that destroy Israel and Judah on apostasy, making Judg 2–16 a clear part of the ethical explanation for the exilic community's trauma. Once the conquest generation dies (2:6–10), the cycle of apostasy begins, introduced in 2:11–23. Israel's worship of the gods of the peoples provokes YHWH's anger, resulting in a loss of control of the land to invaders. Israel's cry, but not repentance (שׁוב), results in YHWH's pity or change of heart (נחם), and therefore he raises up judges to save Israel, "but when the judge died, they repented (ישׁבו) and acted more corruptly than their ancestors, going after other gods to serve and worship them" (2:19). This cycle dominates Judg 2–16, and so the narrative's standard of judgment of Israel and their fate in the land here is entirely cultic. The presence of the Canaanites and intermarriage with them (see esp. 3:5–6) leads to apostasy and Israel's loss of control of the land throughout this first major section of the book.

And as 2:19 suggests, Israel's cultic disloyalty becomes worse throughout the narrative, and its leaders become progressively less effective in preventing apostasy and mediating God's salvation. As Moses has warned, God does not delay to punish those who act in disloyalty to him (Deut 7:9–10), and now, as Israel has settled on the land, we see God punishing the generations who worship other gods. The explanation for the exiles' trauma here is clear: apostasy leads to foreign invasion (3:7–8, 12–14; 4:1–2; 6:1–5; 10:6–9; 13:1); the land has rest only when Israel remains cultically loyal (3:11, 30; 5:31).[6]

Israel is not alone in its cultic disloyalty, however; some of the judges are failures in this arena as well. Following the story of Othniel (3:7–11), the first and only judge from Judah (see 1:11–13), we see a progressive deterioration of Israel and its judges. Ehud does not remove the פסילים "idols" to which 3:19 and 26 refer, an act that Deut 7:5, 25 insists that Israel carry out upon their arrival in the land. As Robert O'Connell suggests, this could explain the renewed apostasy following his judgeship.[7] While Deborah participates in the battle against the Canaanite oppressor, she also appoints a leader of the army who at first appears too cowardly to function well in that position (4:4–8). Gideon shows no trust in God's power to deliver (6:11–40; 7:9–14), turns his army to massacre Israelite towns (8:4–9, 13–17), and leads his people in idolatry (8:24–27). Jephthah sacrifices his daughter to God (11:29–40), an act prohibited by Deut 12:29–31, and also uses his army to fight against Israel (12:1–6). Samson, the last of the judges in the book, actually wants to marry a foreign woman (14:2), and he fails to deliver Israel from their oppressors,

6. The land has rest also when Israel "whores after" the ephod Gideon makes (8:27), a statement that certainly refers to cultic infidelity. The ephod itself may well have been draped over an idol, which was perhaps the real focus of the apostate worship to which the verb זנה points here (so, e.g., Trent C. Butler, *Judges* [WBC 8; Nashville: Thomas Nelson, 2009], 222; J. Alberto Soggin, *Judges: A Commentary* [trans. John Bowden; OTL; London: SCM, 1981], 160; Hertzberg, *Josua, Richter, Ruth*, 197; Lillian Klein, *The Triumph of Irony in the Book of Judges* [JSOTSup 68; BLS 14; Sheffield: Almond, 1988], 64–65). While the reference in 8:28 to the land having rest thus seems incongruous with the basic pattern of punishment following disloyalty, the narrative in Judges is drawing readers' attention to the punishment of the worship of other gods that will eventually destroy both Israel and Judah. In any case, we certainly do not see God punishing an innocent generation here.

7. Robert H. O'Connell, *The Rhetoric of the Book of Judges* (VTSup 63; Leiden: Brill, 1996), 84. Klein also notes that Ehud's assassination of Eglon is not accomplished with the aid of God's spirit, and that God is not involved at all in this act or in Ehud's prevarication beforehand that made it possible (*The Triumph of Irony in the Book of Judges*, 37–39).

an act that even the worst of his predecessors accomplishes. By this time, writes Cheryl Exum, the framework of the cycle of apostasy and deliverance has broken down, and the leadership of the judges has failed.[8]

For the master narrative, the mere presence of a leader in Israel, even leaders whom God has appointed, will not necessarily save the nation from invasion and exile. The narrative in Judges foreshadows the leadership of the monarchy that will take control of Israel's and Judah's cultic life and ultimately lead the people in the apostasy that causes the trauma the exiles suffer. Gideon actually leads the nation in idolatry as the kings will, and Jephthah makes an illegitimate child sacrifice that all of Israel celebrates. As I have argued elsewhere,[9] Jephthah's belief that YHWH will accept the sacrifice of his daughter flies in the face of the law of Deut 12:29–31, which forbids child sacrifice. Moreover, his daughter agrees with him, parroting his faulty reasoning: "My father, you have opened your mouth to YHWH; do to me even as it went out from your mouth" (11:36). From the master narrative's point of view, the daughter has every right to reject her father's vow and sacrifice, both of which are sins, and yet she meekly complies, thereby implicating herself from the narrative's perspective. The narrative also points to Israel's complicity in this sin, for 11:39–40 tells readers that Israel memorializes her participation in foreign sacrifice. "She became a statute in Israel," says the narrator; "four days every year the daughters of Israel go out to recount (לתנות) the daughter of Jephthah the Gileadite" (11:39–40). The only other time readers of the History encounter the verb תנה is in Judg 5:11, where it is used in the context of recounting "the righteous acts of YHWH" on behalf of Israel. Israel is complicit in Jephthah's crime for generations afterwards because the nation, like Jephthah and his daughter, has not learned to distinguish between good and bad sacrifice; because the nation, it would seem, equates the daughter's acquiescence to illegitimate sacrifice to the sorts of things that YHWH has done for Israel. Even if we understand the verb תנה here to have a neutral sense rather than the praise implied in its use in 5:11,[10] the only insight that the

8. J. Cheryl Exum, "The Centre Cannot Hold: Thematic and Textual Instabilities in Judges," in Knoppers and McConville, eds., *Reconsidering Israel and Judah*, 578–600 (580–81).

9. David Janzen, "Why the Deuteronomist Told About the Sacrifice of Jephthah's Daughter," *JSOT* 29 (2005): 339–57.

10. And we should most likely read the verb as having the sense of "recount." It has this sense in Rabbinic Hebrew (Marcus Jastrow, *Dictionary of the Talmud Babli, Yerushalmi, Midrashic Literature and Targumim* [New York: Pardes, 1950], 1681), Palestinian Aramaic (Joseph A. Fitzmyer and Daniel J. Harrington, *A Manual of Palestinian Aramaic Texts: Second Century B.C.–Second Century A.D.* [BibOr

narrative gives readers as to the daughter's character—and thus the basis that it suggests lies behind the recounting of her in Israel's annual festival—is her complicity in rather than condemnation of her father's crime.

Judges like Gideon and Jephthah are precursors of the cultic disloyalty that the kings will cause Israel to commit. Lillian Klein argues that the judges symbolize aspects or weaknesses of Israel,[11] and to this extent we can see the failures of the judges mirroring those of the people. Through those kinds of parallels, the narrative suggests that there is little difference between Israel and the poor leaders whom we see here. If the leadership of the nation is no better than Israel is, we can hardly expect it to keep the nation from cultic disloyalty, a fact that will clearly apply to the kings who, in the narrative's eyes, are responsible for leading the apostasy that dooms the exiles and thus explains their trauma. In the case of Gideon, both judge and nation are oppressed (cf. 6:3–5 and 6:11), both lament their need for deliverance (cf. 6:6 and 6:13), and, like Israel, Gideon manifests a strong reluctance to follow God (6:11–7:15).[12] The narrative of Jephthah draws parallels between Israel's self-interest and his own. Just as the elders of Gilead's need for a leader to free them from the Ammonites causes them to enter into negotiations with Jephthah (11:1–11), so Jephthah bargains with them in order to secure a position as ruler in Gilead, and then attempts to bargain with the king of the Ammonites (11:12–28), and finally bargains with God, offering him a burnt sacrifice in exchange for victory (11:30–31). Webb points out that the words of Jephthah's vow to YHWH in 11:30 echo those of his negotiation with Gilead in 11:9.[13] Just as Jephthah refuses to accept responsibility for his vow when he speaks to his daughter—"*you* have brought me very low, *you* have become my troubler" (11:35) he says to her when she comes out to meet him and he realizes that he has vowed to sacrifice her—so Israel, in 21:2–3, will refuse to accept responsibility for the חרם

34; Rome: Biblical Institute, 1978], 49.1.3), and Punic (Maurice Sznycer, *Les passage puniques en transcription latine dans le "Poenulus" de Plaute* [Études et commentaires 65; Paris: Klincksieck, 1967], l. 936). As Mikael Sjöberg points out, the use of the noun חק "statute" here suggests that this festival that recounts the daughter's willingness to be sacrificed became an official decree. When scholars translate תנה as "lament" in this story, he rightly warns, they lose the commemorative aspect of the verb and its presentation as a legal obligation. See his *Wrestling with Textual Violence: The Jephthah Narrative in Antiquity and Modernity* (The Bible in the Modern World 4; Sheffield: Sheffield Phoenix, 2006), 66.

11. Klein, *The Triumph of Irony*, 17–18.
12. So O'Connell, *The Rhetoric of the Book of Judges*, 163.
13. Webb, *The Book of the Judges*, 63, 74.

it commits in its warfare against Benjamin in ch. 20. Jephthah's cultic ignorance—he sacrifices his own daughter, even though the law prohibits such an act—reflects that of Israel throughout Judges, perhaps most especially in 17:1–13, where Micah sincerely believes that his idol and illegitimate priest[14] will please YHWH.[15] Jephthah's slaughter of his own daughter, moreover, parallels Gilead's slaughter of Ephraim, their kinsfolk, in 12:1–6,[16] just as his oath that leads to her sacrifice foreshadows Israel's "great oath" that precedes its self-slaughter in Judg 20.[17] Both Gideon and Jephthah, in fact, slaughter Israelites (8:4–17; 12:1–6), and so foreshadow the way that Israel as a whole will deal with Benjamin, Jabesh-gilead, and Shiloh in chs. 20–21.[18] For the master narrative, poor leadership is not better than no leadership at all, for some of the judges in the story do precisely the same things that Israel does all by itself. The failure of the judges merely foreshadows the greater failures of the kings who will appear in the narrative's final explanation of the exiles' trauma.

The narrative is not entirely pessimistic about leadership per se, however. Not all of the judges are cultically disloyal, and we see sinless generations of Israel living in cultic loyalty to YHWH during and after the periods of some of these leaders (3:11, 30; 5:31). And after the time of Samson, we encounter a leaderless Israel again in Judg 17–21 whose actions so clearly disobey the commands for cultic and nomistic loyalty that the narrative suggests that some kind of leadership is clearly necessary. Upon introducing the story of Micah in Judg 17–18, who builds an idol and has a Levite lead the cult of its worship, only to see both idol and illegitimate priest move to dominate the cultic life of Dan, the narrator comments that "in those days there was no king in Israel; all did what was right in their own eyes" (17:6; cf. similar references in 18:1; 19:1; and 22:25). O'Connell notes that beyond violating Moses' general

14. Micah's and Dan's priest is illegitimate because he is a descendant of Moses, not of Aaron (18:30).

15. As Klein notes, Jephthah is ignorant in other ways, as well, as his diplomacy with Ammon in 11:12–28 conflates Moabite, Ammonite, and Amorite historical figures and confuses Moab's and Ammon's national gods (*The Triumph of Irony*, 89).

16. So J. Cheryl Exum, "The Tragic Vision and Biblical Narrative: The Case of Jephthah," in *Signs and Wonders: Biblical Texts in Literary Focus* (ed. J. Cheryl Exum; Semeia; Atlanta: Scholars Press, 1989), 59–83 (72).

17. See Frank M. Yamada, *Configurations of Rape in the Hebrew Bible: A Literary Analysis of Three Rape Narratives* (StBL 109; New York: Lang, 2008), 96–97 n. 48. We hear about this oath in 21:5, although this verse tells us that Israel made it before its first battle with Benjamin.

18. So Gregory T. K. Wong, *Compositional Strategy of the Book of Judges: An Inductive Rhetorical Study* (VTSup 111; Leiden: Brill, 2006), 125–31.

instruction in Deut 12, the Micah story alone contains seven other actions that specifically disobey commands from the same chapter of Deuteronomy, including the construction of an illegitimate cultic site and the manufacture of an idol.[19] Gale Yee argues that the Micah story deals with the cultic disorder that has overtaken Israel, while Judg 19–21 portrays the social disorder that Israel's lawless character and the failure of its leaders have produced. In that story, a gang rape and murder produce an Israelite civil war and the near-extinction of one of the tribes, and the story concludes with the attempts to produce wives for Benjamin by destroying an Israelite town and desecrating the festival for YHWH at Shiloh.[20] While the narrative makes no reference to the necessity to obey all of the law, it is perhaps no coincidence that we find a picture of a largely anomistic nation in chs. 19–21 following an example of complete cultic disloyalty in chs. 17–18, an allusion to the narrative's earlier equation of cultic and nomistic loyalty in Deuteronomy. The narrative of Judg 17–21 as a whole, notes Gregory Wong, raises the question of why Israel did not act with the ferocity it did in chs. 19–21 when, in chs. 17–18, the nation did not unite to prosecute the Danites' idolatry. The nation seems far more interested in itself—in doing "what is right in their own eyes"—than in vassal loyalty to God.[21]

When Israel has poor leadership or none at all, says the narrative, it commits the sorts of actions that result in the trauma of destruction and exile. The Danites' idol and illegitimate priestly line remain until the destruction of the North (18:30). Without a leader, Israel becomes just like the foreign nations in its cult and moral actions—so much so, in fact, that the narrative suggests that God uses it like the foreign nations earlier in Judges who punished Israel. Just as God used the foreign nations to punish Israel, now Israel, who has become like a foreign nation, can punish itself in internecine slaughter. And just as the Canaanites were the focus of חרם in Joshua, now Israel is. When Israel acts like foreign nations in its cult and ethics, God will use it like one. So the narrative refers to Israel as committing חרם against Benjamin—although the word is not used in regard to what Israel does to this tribe, the population of Gibeah is put to the sword (20:37) and the city is burned (20:40), and

19. O'Connell, *The Rhetoric of the Book of Judges*, 236–37. For other places in the Micah story where we see an awareness of Deuteronomy's cultic laws, see Aydeet Mueller, *The Micah Story: A Morality Tale in the Book of Judges* (StBL 34; New York: Lang, 2001), 76–84.

20. Gale Yee, "Ideological Criticism: Judges 17–21 and the Dismembered Body," in *Judges and Method: New Approaches in Biblical Studies* (ed. Gale Yee; 2d ed.; Minneapolis: Fortress, 2007), 138–60.

21. Wong, *Compositional Strategy*, 71–74.

only 600 Benjaminites survive (20:47)[22]—and against Jabesh-gilead, where the term is used (21:11). Although YHWH has not commanded these acts of חרם, it seems that Israel's cultic disobedience has resulted in horrific acts that it carries out against its own members where it begins to destroy itself in חרם.

The very structure of Judges emphasizes the narrative's portrayal of Israel as becoming a foreign nation in its cultic life and in the sense of being a tool God can use to punish it. The double introduction of Judges in 1:1–2:5 and 2:6–3:6, argues Younger, is paralleled by the double epilogue. Israel's idolatry of 2:6–3:6 parallels its idolatry of chs. 17–18, and its wars of subjugation of the Canaanites in 1:1–2:5 have become its wars of destruction of itself in chs. 19–21.[23] And the narrative of 20:18–25, where Israel misinterprets oracles from YHWH and so is slaughtered by Benjamin, shows that God not only condones this kind of self-punishment that starts to wipe Israel from the land, but also helps it along.[24] Israel has not changed from the beginning of Judges to its end, and the judges, many of them failures as leaders, have been unable to change the nation. By the end of Judges, Israel is undergoing the same punishment for its cultic and nomistic disloyalty that it has suffered for the entire book, the same chain of events, according to the narrative, that explains the exiles' trauma. When Israel acts like the Canaanites, God will treat Israel like the Canaanites and subject them to חרם, even using Israel itself to carry out this punishment. So when the people, under the leadership of the monarchy, are accused of acting just like the nations in their cultic life (2 Kgs 17:8, 11, 15) or even worse (2 Kgs 21:9, 11), readers will not find God's response of punishment through foreign invasion and destruction surprising.

22. For a similar argument that the master narrative presents these acts of violence as constituents of חרם, see Robert G. Boling, "In Those Days There Was No King in Israel," in *A Light unto My Path: Old Testament Studies in Honor of Jacob M. Myers* (ed. Howard N. Bream, Ralph D. Heim, and Carey A. Moore; GTS 4; Philadelphia: Temple University Press, 1974), 33–48 (41–42) and Exum, "The Centre Cannot Hold." Wong also points to the similarities between the conquest of Ai, which results in חרם (Josh 8:26), in Josh 8 and the conquest of Benjamin in Judg 20 (*Compositional Strategy*, 57–70).

23. Younger, "Judges 1," 224.

24. As Israel prepares to fight Benjamin in order to punish Gibeah, they twice approach God for oracles about the war (20:18, 23). Their first question, "Who will go up for us first to fight with the Benjaminites?" receives the response, "Judah will be first," a response that is followed by the death of 22,000 Israelites (20:21). The second request for an oracle, "Will we continue to draw near to fight with the Benjaminites, our kin?" receives the response, "Go up to them," a response that this time is followed by the death of 18,000 Israelites (20:25).

But, again, the narrative in Judges is not entirely pessimistic about leadership, despite the failure of the judges that it chronicles; we have seen already that in the final chapters, where Israel is leaderless, the narrative suggests that a monarchy might provide right cultic and moral leadership. Judges 19–21 is part of the books' reflection upon Dtr's theme of the problem of right leadership. Moshe Weinfeld and others note that the references to the lack of a king as related to Israel's doing what is right in its own eyes reflects the language of Deut 12:8: "You will not do all that we are doing here today, all doing what is right in their own eyes."[25] As Israel's cultic and nomistic life collapses between the periods of leadership of individual judges, at times during their leadership, and, in chs. 17–21, after their leadership, Dtr's narrative in Judges points toward the possible benefits of a monarchy, and even a specifically Davidic rather than Saulide or Northern one. This is not only true in the final two stories of the collapse of Israel's cultic and nomistic loyalty, but throughout Judges. Weinfeld argues that 1:1–2:10 is in fact specifically composed to exalt Judah and its Davidic monarchy over the North, for in this prologue God tells Judah to fight the Canaanites first and guarantees them success (1:1–2); Judah executes Adoni-bezek in Jerusalem even before they take it from the Jebusites (1:7–8); and Judah conquers the Philistines (1:18) as Saul cannot.[26] Whereas Judah is able to take (לקח) Jerusalem, Judg 1:21 states that Benjamin, to whom Jerusalem has been allotted (Josh 18:28), does not exterminate (ירש) the Canaanites who live there, and so Saul's tribe contributes to the punishment that plagues Israel throughout Judges.[27] In this introduction to Judges, argues Theodore Mullen, only Judah does חרם (1:17), and only Judah is explicitly said to obey Moses (1:20), whereas the other tribes leave Canaanites in the land contrary to God's command.[28] Thus, argues O'Connell, the double prologue of 1:1–2:5 and 2:6–3:6 presents a

25. Weinfeld, *Deuteronomy and the Deuteronomic School*, 170–71; Boling, "In Those Days There Was No King in Israel," 33–48; Veijola, *Das Königtum*, 16–19, 25–29.

26. Moshe Weinfeld, "Judges 1:1–2:5: The Conquest Under the Leadership of the House of Judah," in *Understanding Poets and Prophets: Essays in Honor of George Wishart Anderson* (ed. A. Graeme Auld; JSOTSup 152; Sheffield: Sheffield Academic, 1993), 388–400 (398).

27. Weinfeld ("Judges 1:1–2:5," 396), E. Theodore Mullen, Jr. ("Judges 1:1–3:6: The Deuteronomistic Reintroduction of the Book of Judges," *HTR* 77 [1984]: 33–64 [46]), and Marc Zvi Brettler (*The Book of Judges* [OTR; London: Routledge, 2002], 101) argue that 1:21 has transferred an original notice of Judah's failure to capture Jerusalem to Benjamin, thereby deprecating Saul's tribe.

28. Mullen, "Judges 1:1–3:6," 53.

pro-Judah approach to leadership in Israel, just as the double conclusion of Judg 17–18 and 19–21 calls Israel to support a king from Judah rather than from Benjamin, let alone Gibeah, Saul's hometown, the town and tribe responsible for the gang rape and murder that trigger the civil war.[29] Northern leadership in general is portrayed as deficient in Judges; the only judge from Judah in the narrative is Othniel, the very first judge, who acts only as the tool of God to provide salvation to Israel from the punishment of foreign oppression, while all of the rest of the major judges are from the North, and they all preside over, and at times lead, cultic and moral decline in Israel.[30] The only actual king in the narrative, Abimelech, is a Northerner who slaughters his brothers and is quickly dethroned according to God's will (Judg 9), suggesting a "polemic against northern kingship." In Dtr's narrative, all of the Northern kings are responsible for maintaining the apostate sanctuary at Dan, and part of the point of the Micah story of chs. 17–18 is to mock the legitimacy of any sanctuary there.[31]

Beginning with the figure of Joshua, the master narrative has begun to argue that poor leadership will lead to cultic disloyalty. (Moses' failure in the narrative lies not in promoting apostasy or in creating conditions that lead to it, but rather in enabling the disobedience to a specific divine command that causes a generation to die outside of the land.) Bad leadership will eventually be a cause of cultic disloyalty, as in Joshua's case; bad leaders can go even further and actually lead the nation in apostasy, as in the case of Gideon. On the other hand, the narratives of the introduction and conclusion to Judges show that, without a leader, Israel behaves worse than it does with one.[32] With the exhaustion of the cycle

29. O'Connell, *The Rhetoric of the Book of Judges*, 229–31, 266–67, 297–99.

30. The narrative does not indict the judge Deborah of any wrongdoing, except perhaps in her questionable choice of Barak as a general, although it does describe a decline in Israel's state and fortunes during her rule: she must fight an enemy based in Hazor (4:2), a city the Israelites defeated in Josh 11; and not all of the tribes come out to support her (see Sweeney, *King Josiah of Judah*, 116–18).

31. Marc Brettler, "The Book of Judges: Literature as Politics," *JBL* 108 (1989): 395–418 (407–10); quote from p. 408. For Judg 17–18 as a polemic against the Northern apostate cult centers, see also Yairah Amit, *Hidden Polemics in Biblical Narratives* (trans. Jonathan Chipman; BIS 25; Leiden: Brill, 2000), 99–117. Amit also argues that chs. 19–21 can be read as an anti-Saulide polemic; see "Literature in the Service of Politics: Studies in Judges 19–21," in *Politics and Theopolitics in the Bible and Postbiblical Literature* (ed. Henning Graf Reventlow, Yair Hoffman, and Benjamin Uffenheimer; JSOTSup 117; Sheffield: JSOT, 1994), 28–40.

32. Amit suggests, in fact, that 1:1–2:5 mentions no leaders of Israel because the text wants readers to reflect on the problem of the lack of leadership in Israel after Joshua (*The Book of Judges*, 73–75).

of apostasy in Judges and the decline of Israel at its end, the master narrative suggests that a change in office of leadership might be beneficial—it hints at, but does not explicitly make, a causal link between the phrases "all did what was right in their own eyes" and "in those days there was no king in Israel"—but it also plants seeds of doubt in the readers' minds concerning the efficacy of this change. We learn not to expect much from leaders from Benjamin or Gibeah; we are prepared as well for the future failures of the Northern kings who will maintain an illegitimate sanctuary in Dan and cause Israel to sin. Nor does the narrative present Judah positively in every case—as Barry Webb argues, Judah does not wish to fight and initially opposes the judge in 15:9–20; in chs. 17–18 it is a Levite from Judah who is involved in cultic abuses; and in ch. 20 it is Judah who goes up first to fight Benjamin (just as it went up first in 1:1–2) and fails in battle.[33] We see a decline in Judah as in the other tribes, and it is simply not clear by the end of Judges that merely changing the kind of leadership in Israel will save the nation from its worship of other gods and exile.[34] And, of course, by the time we reach Kings we see that when Israel has a monarchy the people will simply end up doing what is right in the kings' eyes. The narrative explains that no leadership office, not even one where God can choose the leader, will successfully lead Israel unless the individual rulers enforce cultic and nomistic loyalty in Israel. Israel's fate under poor leaders in Judges simply foreshadows—and helps to explain—the trauma of 586.

B. *Trauma as the Essence of History in Judges*

1. *The Collapse of History: The Subversive Repetition of Trauma*

It is not a revelation to say that the History's narrative in Judges moves from dark to darker. It is a book "about loss," writes Don Hudson, a narrative that "chronicles and reflects a rapidly disintegrating society that was oblivious to a gradually disappearing God."[35] It is certainly difficult not to see the cycle of apostasy and the deterioration of Israel and its leaders throughout Judges this way, for they point to cultic disloyalty as the result of poor leadership in the narrative's past under Joshua, in its

33. Webb, *The Book of the Judges*, 201–2.

34. For arguments like mine that suggest the "in those days there was no king" formula in the conclusion of Judges cannot, given the whole context of the book, be read as wholeheartedly supporting kingship, see ibid., 210 and Klein, *The Triumph of Irony*, 141.

35. Don Michael Hudson, "Living in a Land of Epithets: Anonymity in Judges 19–21," *JSOT* 62 (1994): 49–66 (49).

present under the judges, and in its future under the monarchy. What has happened to the exilic community, the narrative says, happened many times to Israel in the past, and for exactly the same reason.

Yet while the master narrative may suggest that Israel is "a rapidly disintegrating society" and suffers the punishment that its actions deserve, trauma intrudes to throw this ethical explanation of history into doubt, subverting the master narrative's attempt to provide a totalizing explanation for the exiles' trauma. Part of the repetitive manifestation of trauma in the History, I argued in the chapter on Deuteronomy, is the intermittent confusion of generations that readers encounter. In the repetition of trauma, the time of trauma becomes all time, history becomes frozen at one event and collapses, and in Dtr, Israel can at times seem like a single generation who experiences the same event over and over. This repetition, however, subverts the logic in history that the master narrative is trying to use to explain the exiles' trauma. Generational confusion is apparent in the first two chapters of Judges. Judges 1:1 opens with the notice of the death of Joshua, and the narrative goes on to relate the failures of the individual tribes to exterminate the Canaanites who remain in the land, failures condemned by God in 2:1–5. Judges 2:6–10, however, returns readers to the situation during the lifetime of Joshua and his generation,[36] until, in 2:10, "all of that generation was gathered to their ancestors." There is a chronological ambiguity in this presentation, however, and it is unclear if the failures of Israel related in 1:1–2:5 are those of the generation that followed that of Joshua, or of the same one as the generation of Joshua's time, who appears in 2:6–10, describing their actions following his death. The former conclusion is the "usual solution" of exegetes, writes Barnabas Lindars, although he correctly states that there is no explicit evidence for this in the text, leading to his argument that 1:1–2:5 and 2:6–10 reflect events that occur simultaneously.[37] Klein and Jacobus Marais arrive at similar conclusions.[38]

These scholars have a point, for what drives the plot in Judges is Israel's initial failure to kill off the Canaanites, yet this is something

36. Lyle Eslinger describes 2:6 as "resumptive repetition" that brings readers back to the situation of Josh 24, since 2:8–9 is a verbatim repetition of Josh 24:29–30 (*Into the Hands of the Living God*, 66); Robert Polzin calls it a "temporal shift" (*Moses and the Deuteronomist*, 151); Webb a "flashback" (*The Book of the Judges*, 106).

37. Barnabas Lindars, *Judges 1–5: A New Translation and Commentary* (ed. A. D. H. Mayes; Edinburgh: T. & T. Clark, 1995), 95.

38. See Klein, *The Triumph of Irony*, 23–25; Jacobus Marais, *Representation in Old Testament Narrative Texts* (BIS 36; Leiden: Brill, 1998), 71–86. Both see 1:1–2:5 (1:1–36 for Klein) and 2:1/6–3:6 as two different perspectives on the same event.

already reported in Josh 13–17. It is simply unclear as to whether these failures occur during the time of the conquest generation or after their passing.[39] The confusion here points to the repetitive nature of trauma right at the beginning of Israel's settlement in the land in Dtr. There is no clear distinction between different generations of Israel here, and the text is vague enough to suggest both that the conquest generation was innocent of allowing Canaanites to survive (the "usual solution" of scholars) and that this was the generation that allowed the Canaanites to remain in the land and thus was to blame for the coming apostasy. The ambiguity can signal to readers that what is important in the cycle of apostasy that these passages introduce is not chronology but the single repetitive fate of Israel. The very opening of the story of Israel in the land throws the narrative's concept of history itself into question and renders it ambiguous. Trauma suggests that history is not related to chronology, and that the narrative is not interested in distinguishing between different generations, even though Judges is the first place in the History where we see cultic disloyalty repetitively punished with foreign invasion, a foreshadowing of the final trauma in Kings. Trauma suggests instead that each generation of Israel undergoes the same trauma as the result of foreign invasion as the exiles. The "one time only" of trauma collapses history and subverts the very notion of chronology.

But it is not simply the master narrative's understanding of history as chronological that trauma subverts here; more importantly, it subverts the narrative's concepts of God and justice. YHWH charges one generation in 2:2 with making a covenant (ברית) with the Canaanites, but it is not clear which one. The only generation that we know of who has made a covenant with the Canaanites was the conquest generation of Joshua's time in Josh 9, but it is not clear that this is the generation whom God is addressing in Judg 2. As a result of the charge, God leaves the Canaanites in the land so that their gods "might be a snare to you" (2:1–3). The possibility—although not certainty, for trauma subverts rather than offers a competing explanation—now exists that a generation who has not made any covenants with the Canaanites—the generation after the conquest generation—is charged by God with having done so and is punished for a crime of which they are innocent. It is certainly possible to read 1:1–2:5 as a whole as saying that the generation after Joshua's time made covenants with the Canaanites and that God is condemning this

39. Serge Frolov suggests that Judg 1:27–2:9 takes place at the same time as Josh 14–24 ("Joshua's Double Demise [Josh. xxiv 28–31; Judg. ii 6–9]: Making Sense of a Repetition," *VT* 58 [2008]: 315–23), although he admits that this "cannot, of course, be reconstructed with certainty" (p. 319).

generation—a reading in accord with the master narrative's understanding of God, justice, and punishment—but the text is simply not clear about this, and this absence of clarity is the intrusion of trauma. This is an uncanny foreshadowing of 2 Kgs 21–25, where, as we have already mentioned, trauma will suggest that a guiltless generation is forced to suffer the siege, destruction, mass death, and forced migration of 586.

Trauma intrudes also in the very punishment God chooses in order to respond to the crime of making a covenant with the Canaanites: "I will no longer drive them out from before you and they will be at your sides[40] and their gods will be a snare to you" (2:3). The result of the punishment is that later generations will be caught in this snare and suffer for the failure of an earlier generation. While the narrative in Judges attempts to explain to the exiles that the generations of Israel are judged by their loyalty to their divine suzerain—thus apostate generations are punished with warfare and cultically loyal ones experience rest in the land—trauma repeats and intrudes to subvert precisely this explanation for the exiles' trauma. Not only do we find a gap in the narrative's explanation for which generation has sinned; God's punishment of Israel by allowing the Canaanites to remain in the land does not affect only the sinful generation, it affects all of the following generations. Immediately after we hear of this punishment, the narrative in 2:11–3:6 introduces readers to the cycle of apostasy, telling readers that Israel intermarried with the Canaanites and worshipped their gods. Now that Canaanites remain in the land—and both Moses and Joshua have been clear that this leads to intermarriage, which leads to apostasy and punishment (Deut 7:1–6; 20:16–18; Josh 23:6–13)—the later generations are doomed. God's punishment of their ancestors becomes their punishment, despite the fact that Deut 7:9–10 and 24:16 make clear that children are not to be punished for the sins of their parents. Insofar as apostasy can be said to be the choice of these later generations, it is a choice that God forced them to make because he left the Canaanites in the land due to the sin of an earlier generation, as if God is unwilling or unable to distinguish between different generations of Israel. This subversion of the narrative's concepts

40. There is no consensus as to the original text here. The MT's לצדים is certainly the more difficult reading (the LXX, Vulgate, and Targum have the easier צרים "enemies"); I have followed the MT here and tried to translate it with something approaching the sense of מצד "next to, near, at the side of" (see Deut 31:26; Josh 3:16; 12:9; 1 Sam 6:8; etc.). The phrase לצנינם/לשטט בצדיכם in Josh 23:13 and Num 33:55 may be an attempt to gloss the unusual expression that we see here in the MT. Scholars have also argued for a connection to the Akkadian *ṣaddu* "snare" (e.g., Lindars, *Judges 1–5*, 79; Soggin, *Judges*, 25).

of Israel as a series of different generations and of justice as God's response to Israel's ethical choice is not a minor one for the exilic community. It suggests that God punishes them not because of their faults but because of actions of their ancestors over which they have no control. As we have already seen in the last two chapters, this uncannily foreshadows trauma's subversion of the narrative's explanation of the exiles' trauma in 2 Kgs 21–25, where it does not seem at all clear that God punishes the correct generation. It also suggests that God can remove the nation's ability to make a decision for vassal loyalty, and thus mocks the narrative's logic in history that explains God's justice on the basis of Israel's choices.

Given the claims of Moses and Joshua about the link between intermarriage with the Canaanites—or even simply leaving them alive—and committing apostasy, the claims in 2:22–23 and 3:4 that YHWH did not annihilate the Canaanites in order to test Israel's loyalty make no sense. Joshua had warned Israel in Josh 23:12–13 that God might refuse to exterminate the Canaanites[41] (although, in Judg 2:3, when God introduces the punishment with "I also said to you," he seems to take credit for the warning), although Joshua had said that this would happen only as punishment for intermarriage with the Canaanites, not for simply making covenants with them.[42] Since the whole point of commanding the extermination of the Canaanites was to avoid intermarriage and thus apostasy, punishing Israel's failure by replicating it contradicts the reason behind giving the command in the first place; this suggests, although does not claim outright, that God is making it impossible for future generations of Israel to obey. Judges 2:22–23 and 3:4 do not provide an explanation for God's punishment consonant with the narrative's understanding of God and justice—as far as readers can tell, this is a test that Israel will inevitably fail. It subverts the master narrative's claim that the different generations of Israel are responsible for their fate, just like the statements that Moses and Joshua have made at places like Deut 4:25–31; 29:3 [ET 4]; 30:1–10; and Josh 24:19, which claim that Israel is unable to obey. Would not foreign invasion, the punishment that dominates Judges, be better punishment for failing to annihilate the Canaanites? This would still leave the nation the option of deciding whether or

41. Besides the fact that Joshua says in Josh 23:13 that God will not exterminate the Canaanites from before Israel as punishment, a claim parallel with that of Judg 2:3, the words צדים and מוקש appear in both verses.

42. For Dtr's narrative, however, this is not an important difference, for Moses' warning in Deut 7:1–6 suggests that intermarriage will follow the making of covenants with Canaanites.

not to kill the Canaanites, an option that God has now removed, and thus leave open the possibility that the nation could still avoid future intermarriage and apostasy, and it would be a punishment that does not duplicate the crime. By refusing to rid the land of the Canaanites in 2:3, God promotes, perhaps virtually guarantees, the intermarriage, apostasy, and punishment of this and future generations of Israel. In this subversion of the narrative, the trauma the exilic community has suffered cannot be attributed, certainly not entirely, to their actions. Trauma repeats into the narrative as absence in its explanation of trauma, subverting its portrayals of God, punishment, and justice, suggesting that God does not care to distinguish between innocent and guilty generations, but makes all of the generations of Israel guilty and subjects all of them to punishment because he has stripped them of the ability to choose loyalty over disloyalty.

2. *The Subversion of the Narrative's Portrayal of God*

Dtr's master narrative clearly and in detail explains the link between apostasy and punishment in 2:11–3:6 that the following chapters relate in the cycle of apostasy. The stories of the individual judges refer back to this introduction and the sin of apostasy it articulates with the phrase "the Israelites continued to do/did evil in the eyes of YHWH," a phrase first introduced in 2:11, with an extended explanation in 2:11–13, 17, 19 of the apostasy of which that evil consists, and repeated at the beginning of the story of each major judge (3:7, 12; 4:1; 6:1; 10:6; 13:1). The narrative has already informed readers in Deut 4:30 and 30:1–5 of what action Israel must take when vassal loyalty has been so completely breached: repentance (שׁוב). In fact, God's failure utterly to destroy Israel after the various rounds of apostasy in Judges seems to point to mercy on his part, for throughout Judges God acts to save Israel from their foreign oppressors when they cry out to him, even though they neither express nor enact repentance (see 2:18; 3:9, 15; 4:3; 6:6), except in the case of the story of Jephthah. In 6:7–10 he sends a prophet to remind Israel of the vassal loyalty they owe him, but still acts to save Israel without the nation actually enacting that loyalty in repentance.[43] Yet trauma intrudes to question and subvert the way that the narrative conceives of and links repentance and salvation, a matter that ultimately derives from

43. Gideon destroys an apostate altar and constructs a Yahwistic one in its place, fulfilling a divine command to enact repentance (6:25–27), yet this act of repentance is opposed by the people of his town, who want to kill him for it (6:28–31). They see Baal, not YHWH, as their suzerain, and so act like "perfect Canaanites" (Butler, *Judges*, 206).

a continued subversion of the narrative's portrayal of God. The narrative's logic in history that tries to explain the exiles' trauma says that God punishes Israel's vassal disloyalty but saves when Israel turns or repents (שׁוב) from this, a perfectly logical position: disloyalty is punished; a return to loyalty is rewarded. Trauma, however, throws this into doubt. Readers might conclude from God's unwarranted acts of salvation that his mercy simply transcends justice—after all, these actions work to Israel's benefit—but this nonetheless subverts the narrative's portrayal of him as acting according to the concepts of justice and thus it subverts the narrative's attempt to portray God as the one who consistently and justly controls history. And, of course, if God's failure to be bound by the narrative's concept of justice can benefit Israel, it can also lead Israel to suffer a trauma that it does not justly deserve. Trauma will suggest precisely this in 2 Kgs 21–25 where, as we will discuss in more detail in Chapter 7, God does not punish the generations of Judah whom Manasseh, Amon, and Josiah (during the first 17 years of his reign) cause to sin, yet decides, for no explained reason, to inflict punishment and trauma on the people decades after Josiah returns them to cultic loyalty. Trauma's subversion of the narrative's concepts of God, justice, punishment, salvation, and repentance in Judges is no comfort for the exiles; it uncannily anticipates God's failure to be bound by the narrative's concept of justice in the ultimate explanation of the trauma.

Moreover, in the story of Jephthah, we see subversions of God, justice, punishment, salvation, and repentance that work to Israel's disadvantage, just as it will work to the exilic generation's disadvantage in 2 Kgs 21–25. When Israel for the first time admits of its wrongdoing in its apostasy, YHWH tells them to cry to the gods whom they have chosen to worship (10:10–14). When this admission of sin is followed by concrete forms of repentance in the turning aside of the foreign gods and renewed worship of YHWH (10:15–16a), the only time we witness such repentance in Judges on the part of all Israel, YHWH "became exasperated with Israel's evil" (10:16b).[44] After the narrative has clearly stated that repentance will

44. The NRSV translates ותקצר נפשו בעמל ישׂראל as "he [YHWH] could no longer bear to see Israel suffer," a positive response to Israel's plea and repentance that many scholars agree with. (See, e.g., the translations of the NIV and JPS, as well as those of Boling, *Judges*, 190; Soggin, *Judges*, 202; Elie Assis, *Self-Interest or Communal Interest? An Ideology of Leadership in the Gideon, Abimelech and Jephthah Narratives [Judg 6–12]* [VTSup 106; Leiden: Brill, 2005], 183; and Niditch, *Judges*, 120.) Others demur from this majority interpretation, noting that when the verb קצר is used to express emotion, it expresses exasperation. Robert Polzin translates "he grew annoyed [or impatient] with the troubled efforts of Israel" (*Moses and the Deuteronomist*, 177), and Webb provides a similar interpretation

lead to salvation, and after having shown that God is willing to deliver even without repentance on Israel's part, the divine response here subverts the ethical logic of repentance and salvation that the narrative asserts underlies history. The single most important idea in the master narrative is that the trauma the exiles or any generation of Israel has suffered can be explained through their disloyalty that God has punished. Having declared that God responds to repentance with salvation, a perfectly logical position, since repentance is an act of cultic loyalty, 10:6–16 subverts the notion that God is guided by such logic in his treatment of Israel. As in the earlier rotations of the cycle of apostasy, God acts not in accordance with the narrative's concept of justice but outside of that framework; now, however, God's failure to act as the master narrative says he does works to the detriment of Israel. This divine caprice introduces grave ambiguity into the narrative's attempt to explain the trauma of the exilic community and it uncannily foreshadows the way God will also ignore Josiah's perfect act of repentance that returns Judah to cultic loyalty. By throwing the master narrative's concepts of repentance and salvation into question in God's response to Israel's repentance, trauma subverts also the narrative's portrayal of a God who works justice, not to mention its understandings of justice and punishment, since punishment seems to arrive or be extended here in 10:6–16 precisely where the narrative has led us to expect salvation, a foreshadowing of the traumatic subversion of the narrative of Josiah's repentance.

As 10:6–16 is part of the Jephthah narrative, these verses raise the question of under what logic YHWH does in fact save Israel later on in this story, given his initial negative response to their repentance. The

(*The Book of the Judges*, 47–48). See also a similar translation in O'Connell, *The Rhetoric of the Book of Judges*, 172. They are correct in their reading of the verb, since it has the root meaning of "be short" and can be used in the sense of "be tired of, impatient with, discouraged," but nowhere means "be sorry for, show compassion." The verb applies to emotions elsewhere only in Num 21:4; Judg 16:16; Mic 2:7; Zech 11:8; and Job 21:4, and in all of these cases it has the sense of "be exasperated." Nowhere do we see a meaning of "feel sorry for." It is used in biblical Hebrew in the sense of someone's patience becoming short, somewhat in the same manner in which we can use the phrase "be short with" in English.

What does it mean to say that YHWH became exasperated with עמל ישׂראל? The word עמל here is somewhat ambiguous. It can refer to suffering (as it clearly does, given its parallels, in Deut 26:7; Pss 25:18; 90:10; Jer 20:18), but it makes little sense to suggest that God became exasperated with the suffering that God had inflicted. Instead, עמל has the sense here of "evil," as it does in Prov 24:2 (where it parallels שׁד, "violence"), Hab 1:13 (where it parallels רע, "evil"), and Isa 10:1 (where it parallels און, "iniquity"), among other places. YHWH's response to Israel's cry, then, is to become exasperated with the continual evil of the nation's apostasy.

narrative nowhere links this salvation to the repentance of 10:10, 15–16a. If, in fact, there is any trace of an explanation in the text as to why YHWH acts for Israel here it may be in Jephthah's mention of Chemosh during his negotiation with Ammon in 11:12–28. "Should you not possess what Chemosh your god has caused you to possess? And all that YHWH our God has caused us to possess we will possess" (11:24). This is the only non-pejorative reference to a foreign god in Judges, and Jephthah has suggested through this reference that there is another divine power who works in history.[45] If YHWH does not act after this public call for him to do so, the land Ammon has taken will now seem as if it is a gift to that nation from another god and not a punishment of Israel from YHWH. If YHWH, invoked by Jephthah to judge whether or not he has given the Transjordan to Israel (11:14, 27, esp. v. 27), fails to cause Israel to possess Gilead again, then, according to Jephthah's own statement, it would seem that Chemosh has caused Ammon to possess it.[46] This would appear to be the only obvious motivation that we find for YHWH's decision to save Israel after God has rejected Israel's repentance. And this is a situation much like those in Deut 9:25–29 and Josh 7:6–9 in which Moses and Joshua respectively appeal to the necessity for YHWH to appear strong before the nations as motivation to save Israel. YHWH is apparently willing to change his mind when his reputation is threatened. God appears to save Israel in this story not because of justice as defined by the narrative's ethical order in history (which would demand responding positively to Israel's repentance) or because of mercy (which is never mentioned in the story), but out of a need to demonstrate his power to the nations when Jephthah, like Moses and Joshua, has signaled that a rejection of Israel will make him appear weak.

The subversion of the narrative's portrayal of God as the guarantor of just rewards and punishments for Israel also interrupts the Samson narrative, wherein God seems interested not in salvation but in slaughter for its own sake. God designates Samson before his birth as a nazirite, and as

45. To some degree, Jephthah repeats God's claim in Deut 32:8 that "YHWH fixed the boundaries of the peoples according to the number of the gods" (reading with the more difficult LXX and 4QDeut[j]); cf. Dennis Olson, "The Book of Judges," in *The New Interpreter's Bible* (ed. Leander Keck; 12 vols.; Nashville: Abingdon, 1998–2005), 2:721–888 (830). But this verse, of course, assigns the power to establish this arrangement to YHWH alone.

46. As Klein points out, the fact that Jephthah misidentifies Chemosh as the god of Ammon (Chemosh was the god of Moab, not Ammon, and the narrator is well aware of this as 1 Kgs 11:7 shows) is simply another indication of his ignorance (*The Triumph of Irony*, 89), the most egregious example of which is his sacrifice of his daughter because of his ignorance of the law.

one who "will begin to save Israel from the hand of the Philistines" (13:3–5). It is unclear that Samson ever does begin to save Israel—as Yairah Amit notes, his narrative is marked by a sharp division between his tremendous power and potential and his absolute failure of leadership.[47] He exercises no military leadership whatsoever, unlike all of the other major judges; God's choice of him is a strange one, given that his character is "constitutionally asocial"[48]—unlike all of the other major judges, he works alone, never as a leader of an Israelite force. We might describe him as constitutionally violent as well as asocial, and God seems to take advantage of both qualities. It is notable that the spirit of God never comes upon Samson in order to enact salvation, but only in order to kill either an animal (14:6) or Philistines (14:19; 15:14–16). YHWH himself ignores one of the most important precepts of the law in this narrative, and is involved in Samson's attempt to marry a Philistine (14:2–4), violating the divine prohibition against the marriage of foreigners that the narrative has repeatedly presented as the root of Israel's apostasy.[49] Readers are told in 14:4 only that God causes Samson to violate the command "because he [God] was seeking an opportunity (תאנה) from the Philistines"—apparently the deaths of 1,030 Philistines that this leads to (14:19; 15:15–16), although no salvation of Israel results from it. The word תאנה certainly does not imply that God seeks any vengeance from the Philistines—their invasion, after all, is part of his punishment of Israel (13:1)[50]—or that God means to provoke them into a fight that will lead to salvation—for there is no salvation of Israel in this story[51]—so apparently his interest is in slaughter for its own sake. The

47. Amit, *The Book of Judges*, 266–75.

48. So Gregory Mobley, *Samson and the Liminal Hero in the Ancient Near East* (LHBOTS 453; New York: T&T Clark, 2006), 2.

49. Technically, Deut 7:1–4 does not list the Philistines as among the foreign nations with whom Israel is not to intermarry, but the Philistines are certainly one of the nations within Israel's borders in Dtr; after YHWH tells Israel that he will no longer drive out the nations (Judg 2:1–5), the narrative refers to the Philistines as one of them (3:1–6). As Gary Knoppers notes, Josh 23:12–13 extends the command in Deuteronomy to "the remnant of these nations who survive with you," allowing the narrative to condemn Solomon in 1 Kgs 11:1–2 for marrying foreign women who come from nations other than the seven listed in Deut 7 ("Solomon's Fall and Deuteronomy," in *The Age of Solomon: Scholarship at the Turn of the Millennium* [ed. Lowell K. Handy; SHCANE 11; Leiden: Brill, 1997], 392–410 [400–401]).

50. LXX^{A} translates תאנה here as ἀνταπόδομα "repayment," and LXX^{B} as ἐκδίκησιν "vengeance."

51. The NRSV translates תאנה הוא־מבקש מפלשתים as "a pretext to act against the Philistines," and the NJB translates the phrase as "seeking grounds for a quarrel with the Philistines." A number of commentators also specifically claim that the

entire story of Samson exhibits a great interest in killing but none in law and almost none in the pattern of history that the master narrative has so far pursued in Judges, where apostasy is followed by foreign oppression as punishment (the only reference to the cycle of apostasy is 13:1). As YHWH becomes more distant in this story, never intervening to save Israel, his interest in killing seems to increase and the interest in law and divine control of history to decrease. The Samson narrative carefully lists the body counts of the Philistines who die at Samson's hands (30 in 14:19; 1,000 in 15:15–16; 3,000 in 16:27; "a great slaughter" in 15:8) but never demonstrates either the judge's or God's intervention to save Israel from Philistine oppression. God's choice of someone so asocial and violent as judge suggests minimal interest in deliverance and maximal interest in carnage. And by the time we reach the end of the narrative in Judges, writes Hudson, God is entirely absent,[52] while the slaughter of Israel has taken center stage.

If we see here the narrative's point that poor leaders will fail Israel, we also see little divine interest in choosing good ones, or even using poor (yet divinely chosen) leaders to even attempt to deliver Israel. As we have seen in both Deuteronomy and Judges, at times God seems to want Israel to fail and violence to be visited upon the nation. Israel lacks leaders in these stories who lead the nation in cultic loyalty or who read the law as Moses commanded. Dtr's master narrative does not appear to view ignorance of the law as an excuse for failing to keep it,[53] and if God can send one prophet to remind the nation of the consequence of disloyalty in 6:7–10,[54] why can he not send others later in the narrative when the judges fail Israel? God's silence in the face of Jephthah's determined insistence to sacrifice his own daughter is as clear an example of this kind of traumatic subversion of the narrative as any in Judges. Cheryl Exum sees the tragedy of the Jephthah story specifically in this

"opportunity" that YHWH seeks here is to provoke the Philistines into a battle that will save Israel. See Daniel I. Block, *Judges, Ruth* (NAC 6; Nashville: Broadman & Holman, 1999), 426; Butler, *Judges*, 331–34; James A. Wharton, "The Secret of Yahweh: Story and Affirmation in Judges 13–16," *Int* 27 (1973): 48–65 (58).

52. Hudson, "Living in a Land of Epithets," 65.

53. Eslinger's claim that Israel's ignorance in Judg 2 of God's prior workings in history means that God is partly to blame for the punishments in Judges (*Into the Hands of the Living God*, 23–24) is not something that Dtr's master narrative argues, but it does get at my point here about the subversion of the narrative.

54. 4QJudg[a] omits 6:7–10, but this is not good evidence that the verses were added later. See the clear arguments for the original presence of these verses in Dtr in Wong, *Compositional Strategy*, 183 n. 118 and O'Connell, *The Rhetoric of the Book of Judges*, 147 n. 178.

silence and failure to intervene when the judge slaughters his own daughter.[55] One could certainly argue that, for the narrative, God can be silent here because the vow is so inappropriate and the offering of a child as a sacrifice to YHWH is so absurd that readers should not need guidance in seeing the sin on the part of all of the human parties, including the victim. God has already spoken at Horeb, and Moses has repeated this speech that unequivocally prohibits child sacrifice, and so the ethical framework of history here is so obvious that God need not speak again, and no editorial comment need be made to explain this silence; indeed, the narrative's silence invites readers to draw on the narrative's explanation of how history functions—and thus of how the exiles are to blame for the trauma they suffered—in order to condemn Jephthah and Israel. But the lack of explanation here, the narrative gap that we find, is precisely trauma's intrusion that asks a question that the narrative does not answer. Why is God silent when a divine word might save the daughter's life? After all, his condemnation of apostasy in 10:11–14 led to the repentance that we see in 10:15–16, and a word to Jephthah would save his daughter's life. Why does God not break this divine silence through prophetic activity as he did in 6:7–10? And it is not only that God is silent as Jephthah prepares to violate the law and sacrifice his child; we can point to the divine silence that pervades the cycle of apostasy in Judg 2–16 as part of trauma's absent presence. There is no record of Israel hearing the divine law since the conquest generation in Josh 8, and the last prophet God has sent (Judg 6:7–10) makes only the most cursory reference to the vassal loyalty on which the nation's life depends.[56]

So just as there is no divine intervention in the case of Jephthah's sacrifice that would explain that God's law forbids child sacrifice, so there is no divine intervention in Judges in general to communicate the law and its warnings to the sinful generations of Israel. The tragedy at the center of the story of Jephthah's daughter is at the center of Judges as a whole. Moses may have called each generation of Israel to a decision

55. J. Cheryl Exum, *Tragedy and Biblical Narrative: Arrows of the Almighty* (Cambridge: Cambridge University Press, 1992), 57–59. And Exum is not the only one to point to divine silence as related to tragedy; see also Tammi J. Schneider, *Judges* (BO; Collegeville, Minn.: Liturgical, 2000), 178; Phyllis Trible, "The Daughter of Jephthah: An Inhuman Sacrifice," in *Texts of Terror: Literary-Feminist Readings of Biblical Narratives* (OBT; Philadelphia: Fortress, 1984), 92–116 (101).

56. The ignorance that Gideon professes in 6:13 as to the explanation for the Midianite invasion certainly reflects his stupidity, but it also shows that the prophet of 6:7–10 is "ineffective" (Klein, *The Triumph of Irony*, 50). More, clearer, and more specific divine messages would help Israel in general, just as one such message here would help Jephthah's daughter in particular.

on vassal loyalty, but this, of course, depends on each generation knowing of what vassal loyalty consists. He also called for the law to be read "in the ears" of the people every seventh year (Deut 31:10–11), but that has not occurred, at least as far as readers know. It can seem as if the narrator and God believe that Israel is not a series of generations, each of whom needs to hear the stipulations of covenant and what they owe to God in order to remain alive in the land. God has chosen the judges to save Israel—or in Jephthah's case, at least approved him through inspiration (11:29)—but apparently failed to send prophets to give specific directions in regard to the law and failed to command that the law be read; divine silence here and elsewhere throughout Judges subverts the narrative's concept of Israel as a series of generations, each of whom needs to know what the covenant is before it can make a decision and act properly in vassal loyalty to God. The divine silence at the sacrifice itself that Exum identifies is thus not the only absence of divine activity that we can point to; God's silence in regard to the law throughout Judges is deafening, and subverts the narrative's portrayal of trauma as caused by foreign invasion as explainable through Israel's ethical choices. The tragedy of divine silence in the Jephthah story is rooted in the lack of explanation for this silence, a lack that subverts the master narrative's concepts of God, justice, Israel, and punishment throughout Judges.

It is not impossible that God has continually sent prophets to each generation of Israel in the land and that the narrative has simply not reported this; it is possible, in other words, to see Jephthah, his daughter, and all Israel as without excuse for their sin surrounding the sacrifice based on the master narrative's terms. Trauma, however, is present precisely in the absence of such narrative notices, and so tragically subverts the narrative's claims, particularly in the face of God's silence at Jephthah's intention to sacrifice his daughter. So there is a logic to and no tragedy in this story only if the characters willingly make bad ethical decisions, but there is no clear indication that they are aware of what makes their actions wrong. Because trauma's silence and ambiguity have impinged on the narrative, readers also do not understand why God has not spoken or instructed, and they can thus question the rational order of the cosmos that the master narrative presents. Because of this traumatic absence in narrative explanation, Israel appears here not as a generation who has never heard the law, but as the same people to whom Moses spoke, and so trauma subverts the narrative's concept of Israel as a succession of generations. It subverts also its concepts of God, justice, and punishment, since God does not justly punish a people whom God has neglected to inform of the law. The story's tragic vision is not just that Jephthah, his daughter, and Israel do not appear to know the logic that governs history and so are doomed by their own incorrect view of the cosmos, it is that even for exilic readers the narrative's explanation of these events is subverted through traumatic absence. God's silence cannot be controlled by Jephthah or Israel; trauma suggests, then, that the master narrative's logic that explains history and the exile is inadequate; it raises questions for which the narrative provides no answer. Trauma thus suggests that the suffering of Jephthah's daughter, and of Israel throughout Judges, is undeserved, an uncanny anticipation of the gap in the narrative's explanation of the suffering of the exilic generation whom Josiah returns to cultic loyalty.

In Dtr's narrative, Israel is clearly at fault for the sins the nation has committed, but traumatic interruptions and gaps suggest that God has intervened to promote the slaughter and punishment that Israel suffers in the foreign invasions throughout Judges by purposely leaving Canaanites in the land and by almost never informing Israel of the steps they could take to save themselves, and that he enjoys witnessing slaughter and is so disappointed on the single occasion when Israel does repent and cease its apostasy that he ignores the divine response to repentance that the narrative has led readers to expect. Since Dtr's narrative informs us that the presence of Canaanites leads to intermarriage, apostasy, and the slaughter of punishment, by the time readers reach the stories of Jephthah and Samson they might expect that God, who ignores repentance and evinces interest in slaughter, might have chosen to punish the tribes' failure to annihilate the Canaanites through the continued presence of the Canaanites in the land specifically to find a reason to repetitively induce slaughter in the land. Trauma will make a similar suggestion in 2 Kgs 21–25 when God, for no explained reason, ignores Josiah's perfect act of repentance. Trauma has thrown the narrative's attempt to explain the exilic community's trauma into an unresolved trial, for we have encountered serious doubts that God rules history according to justice as the narrative understands it, that history is the forum for God's justice, that there is any relationship between Israel's repentance and salvation—indeed, any relationship between Israel's acts of loyalty and disloyalty and God's treatment of the nation—and that the exilic community's trauma is something that will actually be clearly and unequivocally explained.

3. *Trauma and the Collapse of the Future*

Having discussed trauma's subversion of the narrative surrounding its portrayal of God, I return to the notion of traumatic repetition here to focus specifically on trauma's collapse of the future into the single time of trauma, since this draws from our observations about the subversion of the narrative's concepts of God and issues related to justice. By the time readers reach the end of Judges, they have encountered a trauma that Israel has repeatedly endured, the explanation of which has been repeatedly subverted, and a God who does not always act in accordance with the narrative's portrayal of him. As trauma intrudes into the narrative, then, the ethical knowability of history that the narrative promotes has been thrown into a radical questioning with no answer, and trauma itself can begin to feel like the essence of history in Judges. It is not difficult to see how someone traumatized by the experiences of siege, famine, mass death, and deportation (or at least how someone from a family and community who have experienced this) would portray Israel's history as an unending series of such traumas, regardless of whether or not he or she wanted to explain them. In Judges we see the single time of trauma subsuming the past into the uncontrollability and unknowability of 586. While the narrative has provided an ethical framework to explain and control the repetitive punishment in Judges—and thus to control and explain the exiles' trauma—this explanation and the concepts on which it relies has been subverted, as we have seen, and so thrown into unresolved doubt.

And just as all of Israel's history can appear like multiple repetitions of the same event, a sense of a future that can escape this repetition fades as Judges ends. As I discussed in section A above, the epilogues of Judg 17–21 offer Israel hope in a monarchy while the book as a whole subtly critiques that hope. The readers of the History are well aware that monarchy has also ended in failure, so it is difficult to read the end of Judges as anything more than false hope. Moreover, if God is mainly absent from the epilogues (but, contra Hudson, not entirely so), the traces of his presence that readers do see are more disturbing than a complete divine absence. God is present in the final five chapters only to respond by oracle to the requests of Israel as they prepare to attack Benjamin on two different occasions in order to bring the Benjaminite rapists and murderers to justice (20:18–28) and in a notice that he gave Israel victory over Benjamin in the third and final battle between nation and tribe (20:35). The first two of these battles, which Israel fights after inquiring of YHWH, result in the defeat of Israel at the hands of the much smaller Benjaminite force (20:16–18 says that Israel outnumbers Benjamin 400,000 to 26,000, a ratio of more than 15 to one). The text does not say, but readers might well assume, given such numerical disparity, that Benjamin's first two victories are due to God's intervention. Since God appears to grant Benjamin victory, and the divine oracles Israel receives in 20:18, 23 help Israel to decide to go into the battles that result in their defeats, should we see the death of 40,000 Israelites (20:21, 24) in battle reports (ones that, like the divinely given victories in Joshua, report no deaths among the victors) as a punishment of Israel? If so, for what particular sin? Klein correctly states that Israel interprets the oracles that precede its two defeats as the result of Israel's own misconception of true Yahwism.[57] But this hubris in itself is not disobedience to a specific commandment, let alone the apostasy that leads to national defeat elsewhere in Judges. There is an absence in the explanatory narrative where an explanation should be for what appears to be divine punishment of Israel in a war it launched out of a sense of justice. It is certainly possible to understand the two defeats of Israel and the deaths of 40,000 soldiers as God's disapproval and punishment of the nation's attempt to bring rapists and murderers to justice—as God's disapproval, in short, of Israel's attempt to enforce nomistic loyalty.

By this point, readers might assume that Israel is simply regularly punished for apostasy or for gross neglect of the law in the rape of the Levite's concubine in Judg 19 (although Israel as a whole is acting to right that wrong in Judg 20), but the narrative does not offer this as an explanation. At the moment when the nation appears interested in enacting justice, God seems to send them to defeat and slaughter with no clear explanation, a situation that mirrors his rejection of their repentance in 10:6–16. This is the absence and ambiguity of trauma, and it throws the narrative's concepts of justice, punishment, and God's control of history into question. Given trauma's subversion of the narrative's concepts of God, justice, and punishment so far in Judges, another possible explanation for the defeats of Israel and the slaughter of its soldiers in Judg 20 is that God is not overly interested in exercising just punishment on Israel, but is simply interested in witnessing slaughter for no clear reason. After all, if one wants to argue that God intervenes to punish both Israel and Benjamin in the battles of 20:18–48, why does he not intervene to protect Shiloh and its Yahwistic festival in 21:15–23, or Jabesh-gilead from the חרם that Israel inflicts on it in 21:8–12? If God is still intervening in history at this point, it is difficult to postulate definite ethical reasons that underlie his actions, an uncanny anticipation of the traumatic subversion of the narrative in 2 Kgs 21–25, where God appears to punish the innocent and ignore the sin of the guilty, the sin that Manasseh and his son and grandson cause them to sin. Trauma in Judg 19–21 does not definitively reject the narrative's portrayals of God, justice, and so on, nor does it provide its own explanatory logic—this would simply make it a counter-narrative—but it suggests and subverts, throwing the narrative's totalizing explanation into a trial with no resolution. If the stories of

57. Klein, *The Triumph of Irony*, 179–83.

Samson give readers a sense that God is acutely interested in slaughter and has forgotten his earlier promise to use Samson to begin to save Israel, Judg 19–21 can be read as displaying to readers a God who is interested specifically in the slaughter of Israel without any clear indication that this slaughter conforms to the ethical structure that Dtr's master narrative sees as the basis of history.

Trauma has so subverted the narrative's attempt to make sense of the exiles' experience of warfare and mass slaughter that it can seem impossible to explain history at all. This is not to say that it *is* impossible to make sense of history in Judges on the master narrative's terms, for we managed to do so in section A. The unanswered questions that trauma raises—Does God punish the correct generation in 2:1–5? Is the test of leaving Canaanites in the land one that it is possible for Israel to pass? Why does God reject Israel's repentance in 10:6–16?—can be explained using the narrative's definitions of God, justice, salvation, and so on. The difficulty, however, is that the answers to these questions are not clearly present in any totalizing way, and in these narrative absences that manifest trauma, God does not appear to be bound by the narrative's concept of justice, or to save in response to repentance, but seems at times rather to enjoy promoting and witnessing slaughter, and so history can be read as a repetition of the unexplainable traumatic events of the sixth century. By the end of Judges, that is to say, trauma has subverted the narrative's logic in history to such a degree that the trauma itself can be seen as the essence of history. Like Elie Wiesel's concentration camp language, it negates the language of untrammeled narrative explanation and takes its place, putting ambiguity in the place of certainty. From the reading of Judges, all of history might be open to a continual repetition of trauma without explanation.

Chapter 6

SAMUEL: THE TRAUMATIC TRIUMPH OF INJUSTICE

A. *The Master Narrative: Failures of Leadership*

1. *Failures of Priest and Prophet*

In the Deuteronomistic History's master narrative, the period of the judges does not entirely end with Samson, for both Samuel and his two sons also hold the office of judge (1 Sam 7:6, 15–17; 8:1–2). Yet by the end of the book of Judges the narrative has already portrayed this office as having failed to lead Israel properly, a foreshadowing of the kings whose poor leadership concludes with the ultimate failures of destruction and exile. The period of the monarchy begins in the book of Samuel, and the book continues the ambiguous view of the monarchy that we find in Judges. The opening chapters of 1 Samuel serve as a transition between the failed end of the period of the judges and the beginning of the monarchy. Structurally, the cycle of apostasy that begins in the story of Samson does not come to an end until Samuel's victory over the Philistines in 1 Sam 7.[1] In this transitional section we find that the judges are not the only leadership office that fails in Israel; the priests and the prophet Samuel lead Israel poorly as well. And while the narrative of 1–2 Samuel says little about the consequences of Israel's failures of loyalty to YHWH, its focus on Dtr's second theme of the failures of Israel's leadership prepares readers for its ultimate explanation of the exiles' trauma in Kings, where the monarchs will cause Israel to act in cultic disloyalty to their divine suzerain and thus guarantee the trauma the exilic community experiences. The book of Samuel, that is, transitions readers to the period of the monarchy and prepares them for the monarchy's failure that produces Israel's failure.

The transition to the monarchy in 1 Samuel is partially positive. Saul's victory over the Ammonites in 1 Sam 11, supported by the tribes, provides a successful conclusion to the transition story and seems to

1. See Frolov, "Rethinking Judges."

validate the Israelites' request for a monarchy in 1 Sam 8. The noted lack of a king in Judg 17–21 has been eliminated.[2] And while the narrative does have some positive things to say about the beginning of the monarchy, the first leadership office to which we are exposed in 1 Samuel is that of the priests. The sons of Eli, while they sacrifice to YHWH at Shiloh, do so improperly and steal from the offerings (2:12–16), their father makes only a weak attempt to put a stop to this (2:24–25), and these actions of cultic infidelity are punished with their deaths and the revocation of an eternal covenant of priesthood with Eli's family (2:27–36; 3:10–14; 4:17–18). "Therefore—the oracle of YHWH, the God of Israel—I had surely said that your house and the house of your father would go in and out before me forever (עד עולם), but now—the oracle of YHWH—far be it from me" (2:30).[3] The cultic disloyalty of the priests is punished in part with the covenant curse of death in battle. These poor cultic leaders simply continue Israel's abuse of the shrine at Shiloh that readers saw in Judg 21. We need not read the defeat of Israel by the Philistines in 4:3–22 in which Eli's two sons die, a defeat that is followed immediately by Eli's death, as only a punishment of this family's cultic infidelity, for Israel still has not repented of the apostasy in which they were engaged in the book of Judges. Yet, as readers have seen in Judges, without leaders who can promote absolute vassal loyalty to God, we cannot expect Israel as a whole to act or worship rightly.

It is Samuel who, in the narrative in 1 Sam 7 following the Philistines' victory over Israel in 1 Sam 4 that results in the death of Eli and his sons, leads this necessary repentance. In 1 Sam 7, Samuel calls the Israelites to cultic loyalty and repentance, and he rightly sacrifices to YHWH, resulting in divinely given victory over the Philistines (7:3–14), thereby concluding the cycle of apostasy begun in Judg 13. After 1 Sam 7, however, Samuel works solely in the office of prophet (see 9:9), and he is shown to be a leader with many flaws, one of the first of which is his own negative reaction to the nation's request for a monarchy. When his sons, whom he rather than God installs as judges, "took bribes and inclined away from justice" (8:1–3), Israel demands a king so that they may be "like all the nations" (8:5, 20) and have someone to lead them in battle

2. See Robert Polzin, *Samuel and the Deuteronomist: A Literary Study of the Deuteronomistic History*. Part Two, *1 Samuel* (ISBL; Bloomington: Indiana University Press, 1989), 110–14.

3. The judgment on the house includes a prophecy of the deaths of Hophni and Phinehas, a prophecy that is fulfilled in 1 Sam 4:10–18. Saul massacres the house in 1 Sam 22:6–19, and the final Elide, Abiathar, is removed from the priesthood in 1 Kgs 2:26–27, which explicitly fulfills the end of the prophecy in 1 Sam 2:35.

(8:20).[4] Some scholars see in God's response to this request—"they have rejected me as king over them" (8:7)—a negative divine reaction to the monarchy,[5] but God assents to their request and three times tells Samuel to "listen to their voice" (8:7, 9, 22). The narrative suggests that Israel's request "was evil in the eyes of Samuel" (8:6), but gives no such response from God. In fact, nowhere in 1 Sam 8–12 do we find God opposing the monarchy in and of itself.[6] What God thus appears to oppose is, first, the Israelite desire for a king due to the belief that their victories in battle will be dependent upon human and not divine effort (cf. 8:20)[7]—as we have already seen in Chapter 4 on Joshua, the narrative has been clear that victory in battle comes from God—and, second, the desire to be "like all the nations," which will be a desire that will culminate with apostasy. In Dtr's narrative, the very word גוים suggests Canaanites, and thus their worship practices that Israel must avoid.[8] The narrative's

4. In fact, Israel's request in 8:5 that it might have a king "to judge us" shows that the nation specifically wants someone to take the place of the judges (see Hans Wilhelm Hertzberg, *I & II Samuel: A Commentary* [trans. J. S. Bowden; OTL; Philadelphia: Westminster, 1964], 72; Lyle M. Eslinger, *Kingship of God in Crisis: A Close Reading of 1 Samuel 1–12* [BLS 10; Decatur, Ga.: Almond, 1985], 255–56).

5. E.g., Rolf Rendtorff, "Samuel the Prophet: A Link between Moses and the Kings," in *The Quest for Context and Meaning: Studies in Biblical Intertextuality in Honor of James A. Sanders* (ed. Craig A. Evans and Shemaryahu Talmon; BIS 28; Leiden: Brill, 1997), 27–36 (29); David M. Gunn, *The Fate of King Saul: An Interpretation of a Biblical Story* (JSOTSup 14; Sheffield: JSOT, 1980), 124–26; Eslinger, *Kingship of God in Crisis*, 262–64.

6. These chapters provide a reflection and even a debate on the form that the monarchy should take, but they cannot really be considered as anti-monarchical. So Artur Weiser, *Samuel: Seine geschichtliche Aufgabe und religiöse Bedeutung. Traditionsgeschichtlice Untersuchungen zu 1. Samuel 7–12* (FRLANT 81; Göttingen: Vandenhoeck & Ruprecht, 1962), 27, 34; Matitiahu Tsevat, "The Biblical Account of the Foundation of the Monarchy in Israel," in *The Meaning of the Book of Job and Other Biblical Studies: Essays on the Literature and Religion of the Hebrew Bible* (New York: Ktav, 1980), 77–99. The chapters warn of the potential dangers of the monarchy, but they also integrate it into Deuteronomistic theology (so Gerald E. Gerbrandt, *Kingship According to the Deuteronomistic History* [SBLDS 87; Atlanta: Scholars Press, 1986], 143, 145–54).

7. For this interpretation of 8:20, see also, e.g., Gerbrandt, *Kingship According to the Deuteronomistic History*, 148; Eslinger, *Kingship of God in Crisis*, 279–80; Ralph Klein, *1 Samuel* (WBC 10; Nashville: Thomas Nelson, 2008), 78; John Mauchline, *1 and 2 Samuel* (NCBC; London: Oliphants, 1971), 90.

8. In Dtr, we do find the word גוים (rather than the singular גוי) to refer to the nations of the world in general (e.g., Deut 26:19; 29:23 [ET 24]; 1 Kgs 5:11 [4:31]) or specifically to the nations among whom Israel would find itself in exile (Deut 4:27; 28:36, 49, 50, 65), but otherwise it almost always refers to the Canaanites.

explanations for the destructions of the Northern and Southern Kingdoms note explicitly that the people became like the nations in their cultic actions led by the monarchy (2 Kgs 17:8, 11, 15; 21:9, 11). From the narrative's point of view, the cultic disloyalty that it uses to explain the exilic community's trauma is not due to the mere choice of a monarchy; it is the result instead of a monarchy that makes Israel "like all the nations" in its worship. Israel ultimately receives a leadership that reflects the nation's ignorance of the logic that governs history: they do not need a leader to win their battles, since God already does that; they need a leader who will keep them from being like all the nations.

If neither the narrator nor God see anything wrong with the monarchy per se, how are we to explain Samuel's reaction? It is Samuel and not God who reacts angrily to the request, but he never acknowledges the leadership failures of his sons, whom he and not God has established as judges (8:1), and the narrative suggests that his response is self-interested, as if he wanted to concentrate power in his family's hands in order to create a dynasty. When readers encounter his son's abuses of power in office, they might be reminded of Eli's weak attempt to stop the poor leadership of his sons in 1 Sam 2,[9] and Samuel apparently does nothing at all to rein in his sons' poor leadership. His self-interest seems to damage his work as the prophet who transitions Israel's office of leadership to the monarchy as well. Seemingly more concerned about the position of his sons than the future of Israel, he does not faithfully relay God's response to Israel concerning their request for a king. When YHWH accedes to Israel's request, he tells Samuel to "solemnly enjoin them and tell them the law of the king (מִשְׁפַּט המלך)" (8:9). The most obvious referent to the law of which Samuel is to inform Israel is Deut 17:14–20, the law that permits a monarchy so long as the king is subject to the Torah. Since Israel's request for a king so that it might be "like all the nations" is a request that implies apostasy, this is not a matter of light interest in the master narrative. Given God's command, the law about the king in Deuteronomy, and the apostasy that the monarchy will lead, we might expect Samuel to report the law of Deut 17. But while 8:10 states that Samuel "spoke all the words of YHWH," the מִשְׁפַּט המלך that Samuel reports to Israel in 8:11–18 is much different from that of Deut 17, and

9. So Roy L. Heller, *Power, Politics, and Prophecy: The Character of Samuel and the Deuteronomistic Evaluation of Prophecy* (LHBOTS 440; New York: T&T Clark International, 2006), 55–56, 83–85; for other parallels between the Eli narrative and 8:1–3 see Eslinger, *Kingship of God in Crisis*, 251 and Shimon Bar-Efrat, *Das Erste Buch Samuel: Ein narratologisch-philologischer Kommentar* (trans. Johannes Klein; BWANT 176; Stuttgart: Kohlhammer, 2007), 143.

warns of an economic rape of the nation by its future king, something that sounds even worse than what his sons are already doing to Israel.[10] Samuel does not tell Israel that they do not need a king to fight their battles, nor does he warn them against their desire to be like the nations. As far as we can tell, then, Samuel does not emphasize what God would want to emphasize, but instead attempts to make the monarchy sound worse than the present leadership of his sons. So not only does Samuel's bias cause him to omit the true reasons why a monarchy is dangerous, his attempt to make a king sound worse than his sons is an obvious ploy that we might expect the Israelites in the story to see through, and thus is easily ignored by them. The monarchy will go on to lead Israel in the cultic failure that explains the exiles' trauma in the narrative, and Samuel's poor leadership is in part to blame.

Samuel's continuing place of leadership remains problematic for Israel because, in his final address to the nation in 1 Sam 12, he continues to misrepresent God. Samuel does, it is true, recite a salvation history of Israel to the nation in 12:6–15 that finally emphasizes the cultic and nomistic fidelity necessary to avoid destruction. But Samuel begins by referring to his own innocence in leading Israel when he opens his address in 12:1–5, saying nothing about his sons whom he set up as judges and who have stolen and perverted justice.[11] Here and in 12:12–13, where Samuel incorrectly claims that Israel asked for a monarchy when threatened by Ammon, he simply misrepresents their reasons for wanting a king, conveniently omitting the role of his own family's faulty leadership in motivating the request.[12] He never acknowledges the fact that God told him three times to listen to Israel's voice and establish a monarchy, a divine command that suggested God's approval of the nation's rejection of his sons' failed leadership. Even in reciting Israel's salvation history, Samuel refers to some of the figures whom God used to deliver Israel—Gideon, Jephthah, and himself[13] (12:11)—omitting

10. See Heller, *Power, Politics, and Prophecy*, 89–93.

11. Peter D. Miscall, *1 Samuel: A Literary Reading* (ISBL; Bloomington: Indiana University Press, 1986), 73; Eslinger, *Into the Hands of the Living God*, 87–88.

12. Heller, *Power, Politics, and Prophecy*, 113–15; David Jobling, *The Sense of Biblical Narrative: Structural Analyses in the Hebrew Bible*, vol. 2 (JSOTSup 39; Sheffield: JSOT, 1986), 65.

13. There are two text critical issues with the list of past saviors that Samuel provides in 12:11. First, in the MT Samuel makes reference to a "Bedan" whom God sent to Israel, but this figure is unknown in Dtr. For a list of attempts to identify Bedan with a figure known from Judges, see Serge Frolov, "Bedan: A Riddle in Context," *JBL* 126 (2007): 164–67 (164) and the bibliographic references there.

any mention of Gideon's idolatry, Jephthah's cultic disloyalty, and, of course, his own failures as a prophet. Indeed, the very way he links himself to flawed leaders of the past directs readers to reflect on Samuel's own shortcomings.

Samuel also misrepresents God in 1 Sam 15, his final rejection of Saul as king (at least while Samuel is still alive). When God tells Samuel that he repents (נחמתי) having made Saul king (15:11), Samuel does not pray for Saul, as he said he would in 12:23. Samuel is angry, "and he cried out (ויזעק) to YHWH all night" (15:11) following Saul's failure completely to do חרם to the Amalekites as God had ordered. It may be that this is an attempt by Samuel to intervene for Saul,[14] but 1 Samuel uses the verb זעק to indicate an action performed because of oppression or injustice, and the possibility exists that Samuel is crying out because of God's failure to announce an oracle of judgment against Saul for the king's disobedience.[15] In 15:16, Samuel says that he will tell Saul "what YHWH spoke to me last night," but the divine message he purportedly relays in 15:17–19 is not the one that the narrative records, although it would be fair to say that his judgment of Saul's actions accurately reflects the gist of the information that the narrator and YHWH have delivered in 15:1–10. However, Saul's repentance in 15:24–25 is met by Samuel with the response that, "because you have rejected the word of YHWH, YHWH has rejected you from being king" (15:26), which is not a judgment God has delivered to Samuel, or at least not one that the narrative reports. God has not delivered an oracle of judgment against Saul, but Samuel has devised the one that he had cried to God for. By having Samuel deliver divine words and judgment that it does not record, the narrative implicitly questions Samuel's reliability as a prophet. When, after delivering this judgment of rejection as if it were God's, Samuel twice tells Saul

The LXX has altered this reading to the easier "Barak." Second, the majority of the witnesses have Samuel include his own name at the end of the list (so the MT, LXX, Vulgate, and Targum). While some scholars alter "Samuel" to "Samson," following the Syriac, and thus have Samuel provide a list of figures known from Judges (e.g., P. Kyle McCarter, *1 Samuel: A New Translation with Introduction, Notes & Commentary* [AB 8; Garden City, N.Y.: Doubleday, 1980], 211; Peter R. Ackroyd, *The First Book of Samuel* [CBC; Cambridge: Cambridge University Press, 1971], 85), the majority reading here is still the more difficult one precisely because it does not follow an established list of saviors.

14. So, e.g., Hertzberg, *I & II Samuel*, 126; Mauchline, *1 and 2 Samuel*, 123; Klein, *1 Samuel*, 151.

15. So Heller, *Power, Politics, and Prophecy*, 127–28. In Dtr, the verb זעק is normally used when Israel cries to God to deliver them from oppression or disaster (e.g., Judg 3:9, 15; 6:6, 7; 10:10; 1 Sam 7:8; 8:18; 12:8).

that God does not "repent (נחם)" (15:29), the narrative's questioning of Samuel's fitness for office becomes more obvious; God already told Samuel in 15:11 that he has repented.[16]

Samuel at this point seems to be misrepresenting God and thus abusing his office in order to remove Saul from his leadership position. When, in the story of his anointing of David in 1 Sam 16, Samuel three times mistakes other sons of Jesse for God's king (16:8–10), one might wonder how well he understands God at all.[17] If Israel's monarchy is ultimately going to be a failure, the failures of the prophet who oversees the transition from judgeship to kingship do not help matters, especially given the prophet's initial failure to warn Israel of the law of the king and to remind them that cultic loyalty and not a monarchy is what will guarantee survival in the land. The master narrative in Judges pointed toward a monarchy only with ambiguity—the negative manner in which Samuel immediately portrays the monarchy in 1 Sam 8, however, reflects his own self-interest, not the true danger inherent in a monarchy from the narrative's point of view, and Israel can rightly ignore his objections as self-interested. Just like Moses' failures in Deuteronomy, some of Samuel's actions point to an inability of prophecy to deliver accurately divine instructions, a matter that we will investigate below in the section on traumatic intrusions into the narrative. Yet while readers might ask why God continues to use Samuel as an intermediary, we can point to his one great success as a judge: he leads Israel in repentance and a turning aside of their foreign gods (7:3–4) and sacrifices rightly (7:8–9), causing God to end the Philistine oppression (7:10–14) and the cycle of apostasy that began in Judg 13:1. Except for his installation of his sons as his successors, Samuel's work as a judge (as opposed to his work as a prophet) is a model of proper leadership.

2. *The Failure of Saul*

The story of Saul in Dtr is often described as tragic.[18] The tragedy of Saul's story in 1 Samuel that scholars identify largely seems to be rooted

16. See Heller, *Power, Politics, and Prophecy*, 129–31.

17. See Randall C. Bailey, "The Redemption of Yhwh: A Literary Critical Function of the Songs of Hannah and David," *BibInt* 3 (1995): 213–31 (224); Heller, *Power, Politics, and Prophecy*, 134; Klein, *1 Samuel*, 161; Antony F. Campbell, *1 Samuel* (FOTL 7; Grand Rapids: Eerdmans, 2003), 71.

18. So, e.g., Gunn, *The Fate of King Saul*, 23–31, 115–16; Yairah Amit, "The Delicate Balance in the Image of King Saul and Its Place in the Deuteronomistic History," in *Saul in Story and Tradition* (ed. Carol S. Ehrlich; FAT 47; Tübingen: Mohr Siebeck, 2006), 71–79 (71–74); von Rad, *Old Testament Theology*, 1:325;

within a lack of divine justice,[19] and this is a matter that I will discuss in the section below on traumatic intrusions into this part of Dtr's master narrative. His divine choice as king is demonstrated to Israel by lot (10:20–24), just as criminals are normally identified (see Josh 7:14–18; 1 Sam 14:40–42).[20] We have seen as well that the master narrative in Judges casts aspersions on Benjamin, Saul's tribe, and Gibeah, Saul's hometown. The insinuation of Saul's criminality is prescient, as he is almost immediately condemned of cultic disloyalty in 1 Sam 13. David Gunn argues that Saul's supposed cultic error in 13:8–9 is based on ambiguous instructions from Samuel in 10:8. Saul waits seven days at Gilgal to sacrifice as Samuel had instructed, but sacrifices before the prophet arrives. From Saul's point of view, Gunn argues, he has fulfilled the instructions, whereas from Samuel's he has not.[21] Although he had been instructed as part of "the word of God" (9:27) not to sacrifice at Gilgal before Samuel arrives, Saul believes that if he does not sacrifice immediately in order to begin the battle, his army will drift away from him and he will have inadequate forces left to confront the Philistines (13:8–12; cf. 9:27–10:8). In response to Samuel's demand for an explanation in regard to his wrongly timed sacrifice, Saul replies, "I said, 'Now the Philistines will descend against me at Gilgal, and the face of YHWH I have not appeased,' so I restrained myself[22] and I burned up the burnt offering" (13:12). Rather than fleeing like his army, Saul restrains himself and waits the seven appointed days before sacrificing. Samuel

Northrop Frye, *The Great Code: The Bible and Literature* (New York: Harcourt Brace Jovanovich, 1982), 181; Sarah Nicholson, *Three Faces of Saul: An Intertextual Approach to Biblical Tragedy* (JSOTSup 339; Sheffield: Sheffield Academic, 2002), 25–32, 36–112; Klaus-Peter Adam, "Nocturnal Intrusions and Divine Interventions on Behalf of Judah: David's Wisdom and Saul's Tragedy in 1 Samuel 26," *VT* 59 (2009): 1–33.

19. See, e.g., W. Lee Humphreys, "From Tragic Hero to Villain: A Study of the Figure of Saul and the Development of 1 Samuel," *JSOT* 22 (1982): 95–117 (102); Gunn, *The Fate of King Saul*, 115–16.

20. Steven L. McKenzie, "Saul in the Deuteronomistic History," in Ehrlich, ed., *Saul in Story and Tradition*, 59–70 (61–62); Polzin, *Samuel and the Deuteronomist*, 103–4.

21. Gunn, *The Fate of King Saul*, 38–40. See also Exum, *Tragedy and Biblical Narrative*, 27–28.

22. ואתאפק is sometimes translated here as "I forced myself," but as V. Philips Long points out, six out of seven appearances of the verb in the Hithpael have the sense of "to restrain oneself" (*The Reign and Rejection of King Saul: A Case for Literary and Theological Coherence* [SBLDS 118; Atlanta: Scholars Press, 1989], 89–90).

must now inform Saul that the point of sacrifice is not to entreat God's favor, but to signal loyalty and obedience to God (13:13), and even a minor violation of divine command is a sign of disloyalty.[23] As a result, Samuel informs Saul that "YHWH would have established your kingdom over Israel forever (עד עולם), but now your kingdom will not arise" (1 Sam 13:13–14). Saul's lapse in cultic fidelity may seem minor, but it foreshadows the ultimate cultic failure of the monarchy that the narrative will use to explain the trauma of the exilic community. In 1 Sam 8, the narrative points to a desire on Israel's part for a king, a desire not in any way rooted in the narrative's logic in history, since the nation believes that the point of a king is to win battles and be like all the nations, not to enforce vassal loyalty to YHWH. Israel has apparently received the king they deserve, for Saul also appears unaware of the absolute importance of cultic fidelity to God. He is merely the first of many kings whose failures to lead Israel in cultic loyalty to YHWH explain the exiles' trauma according to the narrative.

Nor does Saul seem to learn from his mistakes. In the story of 1 Sam 15 he again follows God's commands, but not completely, just as was the case in 1 Sam 13. Told to attack Amalek and "make חרם all that belongs to it," including all people and animals (15:3–4), Saul spares the king and the best of the animals (15:8–9). And as in 1 Sam 13, this story is made into a lesson about sacrifice. Saul justifies his claim that he has carried out the divine command (15:13, 20) by stating that animals were kept for Yahwistic sacrifice (15:15, 21), and Gunn argues that Saul and the people might not be aware of the difference between sacrifice and חרם.[24] The point that Samuel makes to Saul about sacrifice here, however, is the same one that he made in 1 Sam 13: absolute loyalty to the divine suzerain is necessary. "Obeying is better than sacrifice, to heed than the fat of rams" (15:22). For the master narrative, sacrifice is simply a way to enact cultic loyalty to YHWH, and in the narrative this demands complete obedience, a point Samuel makes here, regardless of his claims of the divine rejection of Saul. First Samuel 15:9 states that Saul and the people "did not want to make [the best of the animals] חרם," and we might wonder if Saul develops his claim that they were going to sacrifice

23. This is ultimately why Gunn's explanation does not work. The narrative's point in 13:8–14 is not that Saul is being punished for the wrong interpretation of Samuel's instructions, but that he has not followed God's instructions in regard to a cultic act: "You did not keep the commandment of YHWH your God" (13:13) is the charge Samuel lays against him. For similar interpretations, see, e.g., ibid., 87–90; McCarter, *1 Samuel*, 229–30.

24. Gunn, *The Fate of King Saul*, 47–49.

them only when confronted by Samuel (although the LXX includes an additional sentence in 15:12 which states that Saul sacrificed the spoil before Samuel arrived).[25] Yet even if the LXX's reading is correct, he still has not led Israel in following YHWH's instructions, and his claim to Samuel that "I feared the people and obeyed their voice" (15:24) only strengthens the argument against his leadership, since a good leader in the eyes of the narrative must enforce cultic and nomistic loyalty, not blindly follow disobedience initiated by Israel. Saul does not lead Israel in absolute obedience to their divine suzerain, but claims to follow their lead in disloyalty, a disloyalty that he and they were potentially about to express in sacrifice. Israel really does have the leader they deserve, and Saul here is a follower of the nation's poor impulses rather than a leader of cultic loyalty to God. His reign has not prevented the people from doing what is right in their own eyes. Samuel's proclamation that YHWH has removed Saul as a king (15:24, 28) is thus not surprising, for Saul's actions are a mere foreshadowing of the gross cultic disloyalty for which later monarchs will be responsible. Given Israel's complicity in this nomistic and cultic disloyalty, it is also not surprising that it is not only Saul who suffers. Following Samuel's leadership of repentance and right sacrifice, the narrative informs readers that "the hand of YHWH was against the Philistines all the days of Samuel" (7:13). Now that we are in the time of Saul's poor leadership, the Philistines are a constant menace (1 Sam 14; 17; 23; 28–29; 31), just as the invading nations were in Judges, a foreshadowing of the trauma that the exiles will suffer through foreign invasion because of poor royal leadership.

As Saul's failure in both cultic and nomistic loyalty is enough to lose him both eternal dynasty and kingship for himself, Israel's first foray into monarchy has been a failure from the narrative's point of view. Saul's failure in carrying out חרם among the Amalekites is ironically paralleled by his success in this act among the priests at Nob in 1 Sam 22, and the language used to describe his actions there—"Nob, the city of the priests, he struck with the edge of the sword, man and woman, children and infants, and oxen and donkey and sheep" (22:19)—almost

25. McCarter sees this sentence as original, arguing that the MT scribe omitted it due to homoioteleuton (*I Samuel*, 262–63). Of course, it is possible that the sentence's claim that Saul had just finished burning up the burnt sacrifices (ἀνάφερεν ὁλοκαύτωσιν τῷ κυρίῳ; from העלה עלות ליהוה) when Samuel arrived may be an insertion that parallels 13:10–11 (so, e.g., Jakob H. Grønbaek, *Die Geschichte vom Aufstieg Davids [1 Sam 15–2 Sam 5]: Tradition und Komposition* [Copenhagen: Munksgaard, 1971], 60 n. 8). If the verse is original, it is difficult to see how Samuel could then say in 15:14 that he can hear the sounds the animals are making.

exactly parallels the divine command against Amalek in 15:3 that he does not completely obey.[26] By 1 Sam 24–26, the fool Nabal who opposes David has become a type for Saul. The story of Nabal in 1 Sam 25 is bracketed by two stories of David passing up opportunities to kill Saul. The terms "good," "do good," "evil," and "do evil" appear twice as often in 1 Sam 25 as in any other chapter of the Saul narrative, and the whole point of the narrative in these three chapters appears to be the contrast between Saul's evil and David's goodness.[27] By his death, Saul's failed leadership has left Israel in much the same situation it was in at the end of the period of the judges. Saul has slaughtered the priests at Nob as Israel slaughtered at the Yahwistic shrine of Shiloh at the end of Judges; the Philistines occupy the land as far as Gilead (1 Sam 31:7), and so the land is under foreign occupation as it frequently was in the period of the judges; and the instability that follows within Israel leads to civil war and internecine Israelite slaughter (2 Sam 2:12–28, esp. 26–28), with particular notice of the killing within Benjamin (2 Sam 2:13, 24–25, 31), as was the case at the end of Judges. A monarchy with poor leadership will not guarantee that all Israelites will cease doing what is right in their own eyes and so avoid divine punishment; poor leadership of any office simply guarantees such punishment. Saul's failure is just one more example of a failure of leadership that the narrative can use to explain the exiles' trauma through the later failures of the monarchy.

3. *The Failures and Success of David*

While the master narrative in Judges deprecates Benjamin and Gibeah, it generally has better things to say there about the leadership of Judah. And while the narrative of Samuel generally presents the leadership of the Judean David as being better than that of the Benjaminite Saul, David is not a perfect leader, validating the subtle warnings about Southern leadership that we saw in the narrative of Judges. Sometimes David acts

26. See McKenzie, "Saul in the Deuteronomistic History," 65; Nicholson, *Three Faces of Saul*, 82.

27. So Gunn, *The Fate of King Saul*, 91–106, esp. 96. For others who point to Nabal as a reflection of or type for Saul, see Barbara Green, *How Are the Mighty Fallen? A Dialogical Study of King Saul in 1 Samuel* (JSOTSup 365; Sheffield: Sheffield Academic, 2003), 392–410; Diana Vikander Edelman, *King Saul in the Historiography of Judah* (JSOTSup 121; Sheffield: Sheffield Academic, 1991), 204–19; David Jobling, *1 Samuel* (BO; Collegeville, Minn.: Liturgical, 1998), 92–93; Polzin, *Samuel and the Deuteronomist*, 211–13. There are clear structural similarities between all three of the chapters of 1 Sam 24–26 (see Barbara Green, "Enacting Imaginatively the Unthinkable: 1 Samuel 25 and the Story of Saul," *BibInt* 11 [2003]: 1–23 [3–4]); we will discuss these chapters further below.

like a loyal vassal, sometimes he does not. In this sense his reign is a microcosm of those of his descendants whom readers encounter in Kings, some of whom receive a positive narrative judgment and some of whom do not,[28] and the narrative of his reign prepares readers for the narrative in Kings, where they will see that the limited loyalty of this house will not be enough to spare the exiles from their trauma. The narrative apparently has little to say in Samuel about the necessity of cultic loyalty, but the long narrative of which David is the center is hardly tangential to its explanation of trauma: the figure of David foreshadows the failure of his house to lead perfectly, and thus points exilic readers to the logical explanation of their trauma, which will centrally involve the failed leadership of the Davidides.

It is not clear in the narrative that David will necessarily be a better leader of Israel than his predecessors. He certainly takes pains to speak as if he is YHWH's loyal vassal, but the narrative suggests that his outward appearance of loyalty or piety in this regard belies baser and selfish motives that, like Samuel's self-interest, reduce the quality of his leadership. As I discuss David's desire for power here, something that helps to explain his failures as a leader in Israel, I will also take pains to point out cases where his pious speech conceals this desire. In the narrative, this contrast between pious speech of vassal loyalty and attempts to extend his control constructs a character who will also attempt to wrest power from God. For example, his pious words about protecting "YHWH's anointed," even when he has perfect opportunities to kill Saul (1 Sam 24:7, 11 [ET 6, 10]; 26:9, 11), contrast with Saul's many attempts on David's own life (although, to be fair, Saul does not know that Samuel anointed David, and David does not care to broadcast this).[29] While some scholars see his attitude in these situations as the upholding of an Israelite taboo against regicide,[30] such a taboo is mentioned in no

28. See Stephen McKenzie, "The Trouble with Kingship," in de Pury, Römer, and Macchi, eds., *Israel Constructs Its History*, 286–314 (308).

29. David seems at pains to tell Saul that he, David, is not worth the effort Saul is putting into his attempts to kill him. "After whom are you pursuing? After a dead dog? After a single flea?" (24:15 [ET 14]). "The king of Israel has gone out to seek a single flea, like one pursuing the partridge in the mountains" (26:20).

30. E.g., Charles Mabee, "David's Judicial Exoneration," *ZAW* 92 (1980): 89–107 (95); J. P. Fokkelman, "A Lie, Born of Truth, too Weak to Contain It: A Structural Reading of 2 Sam 1:1–16," in *Prophets, Worship, and Theodicy: Studies in Prophetism, Biblical Theology, and Structural Rhetorical Analysis, and on the Place of Music in Worship* (OTS 23; Leiden: Brill, 1984), 39–55 (49); P. Kyle McCarter, *II Samuel: A New Translation with Introduction, Notes, and Commentary* (AB 9; Garden City, N.Y.: Doubleday, 1984), 61.

biblical law, and no other biblical figure but David refers to it.[31] This legal innovation of David's reflects, rather, self-interest, since he is also YHWH's anointed, and aims at establishing a tradition that will protect him after Saul's death. This is perhaps clearest in 2 Sam 1:16, where David's first act after Saul's death is to kill the Amalekite who brings him the news. David justifies the killing of the Amalekite by saying, "Your blood is upon your head because your mouth answered against you, saying, 'I have killed YHWH's anointed'" (1:16); but, as Hugh Pyper points out, the Amalekite has said no such thing,[32] and, as readers know from 1 Sam 31:3–5, the Amalekite did not kill Saul. Rather than investigate the Amalekite's claim, or even honestly represent what the Amalekite has (falsely) reported, David twists his words in order to establish a tradition of capital punishment for royal assassins, a tradition that will protect him and his descendants. David may also hope that this act of recognizing an earlier divine choice for king will ingratiate himself with YHWH; he says, following his second sparing of Saul's life, "even as your life was valuable this day in my eyes, thus may my life be valuable in the eyes of YHWH" (26:24).

David can afford to make such pious assertions—even if it might be a feigned piety—despite the great advantage he would gain from Saul's death since he is aware that YHWH is with him and will remove Saul for him. The narrator tells us that YHWH is with David and protects and favors him (1 Sam 16:13; 18:14; 2 Sam 5:10), as do David (1 Sam 17:37; 2 Sam 22), Abigail (1 Sam 25:24–31), Saul's servant (1 Sam 16:18), and God himself (2 Sam 7:8–16). Whereas God designates Saul as a king "for them" in 8:22, he chooses David as a king "for me" in 16:1. To take 1 Sam 24–26 as an example of David's awareness that God favors and protects him, we find a chiasm that focuses, as we have seen, on the contrast of David's goodness and Saul's evil. In chs. 24 and 26 David twice spares Saul's life; in ch. 25, he is about to kill Nabal until Abigail tells him that God will do this for him. "If anyone should arise to pursue you and to seek your life, the life of my lord will be bound in the bundle of the living with YHWH your God, and the life of your enemies he will sling away in the hollow of the sling" (25:29). David realizes that he thus need not risk bloodshed (25:30–31), and her prediction concerning

31. So also Robert Alter, *The David Story: A Translation with Commentary of 1 and 2 Samuel* (New York: W. W. Norton, 1999), 197–98; Polzin, *Samuel and the Deuteronomist*, 210; Pamela Tamarkin Reis, "Killing the Messenger: David's Policy or Politics?," *JSOT* 31 (2006): 167–91 (176–77).

32. Hugh S. Pyper, *David as Reader: 2 Samuel 12:1–15 and the Poetics of Fatherhood* (BIS 23; Leiden: Brill, 1996), 14–27.

Nabal, David's enemy of the moment, comes to pass—"YHWH struck him down" (25:38)—validating Abigail's words and the lesson David has drawn from them (25:39). David then applies precisely the same lesson in 26:10 to Saul: "YHWH will strike him down."[33] The story of David and Nabal is a reflection of the story of David and Saul: Nabal, like Saul, has something that David wants; and in order to receive it, David need simply wait until God kills him.[34] These chapters certainly tell us something about God's attitude toward the protection of David, although they also show us that David is willing to kill Nabal and his men for the flimsiest of causes in 1 Sam 25—his decision to kill Nabal and wipe out his household arises from a failed attempt at extortion (25:4–22),[35] and he acknowledges to Abigail that had he carried out his plan to kill Nabal he would have borne "bloodguilt" (25:33).

David's interest in his own self-promotion couched in pious speech is actually presented immediately following his anointing. At his appearance at the battlefield in 1 Sam 17, he hears that the reward for the killing of Goliath is wealth and marriage into the king's family (17:25), and David's first speech of the chapter—of the entire History, in fact—is a question that asks for that information to be repeated (v. 26).[36] Only then

33. So also Polzin, *Samuel and the Deuteronomist*, 206; Gunn, *The Fate of King Saul*, 103; K. L. Noll, *The Faces of David* (JSOTSup 242; Sheffield: Sheffield Academic, 1997), 56–57.

34. For other similarities that the text draws between Nabal and Saul, and for arguments for Nabal as Saul's alter ego in this story, see Robert P. Gordon, "David's Rise and Saul's Demise: Narrative Analogy in 1 Samuel 24–26," *TynBul* 31 (1980): 37–64; Edelman, *King Saul*, 204–19; Jobling, *1 Samuel*, 92–93, 152–58; Steven L. McKenzie, *King David: A Biography* (Oxford: Oxford University Press, 2000), 96–97; Green, *How Are the Mighty Fallen?*, 392; Joseph Lorenzy, *Saul, Doeg, Nabal, and the "Son of Jesse": Readings in 1 Samuel 16–25* (LHBOTS 497; New York: T&T Clark, 2009), 51–83.

35. Jobling describes David in this story as a "bandit" (*1 Samuel*, 153), McKenzie as "Mafioso" (*King David*, 95–101).

36. This episode is recounted by the MT, but the much shorter LXX version of 1 Sam 17–18 omits 17:21–31, 41, 48b, 50, 55–18:6a, 10–12, 21b, 30. There is no consensus among scholars how to explain this textual critical problem. For a variety of perspectives on this issue, readers can consult the essays in Dominique Barthelémy et al., *The Story of David and Goliath: Textual and Literary Criticism* (OBO 73; Göttingen: Vandenhoeck & Ruprecht, 1986). The MT is the more difficult text since it contains putative contradictions that the shorter LXX has omitted. Since, however, it is possible to explain these contradictions and to see the LXX as an attempt to eliminate them, I read with the more difficult MT. For readings that make sense of the story in the MT, see D. W. Gooding, "An Approach to the Literary and Textual Problems in the David–Goliath Story," in Barthelémy et al., *The Story of David and Goliath*, 55–86 and Polzin, *Samuel and the Deuteronomist*, 161–78.

does he express the theological concern that Goliath defies God's army. His brother Eliab's response—"I know your presumption and the evil of your heart" (17:28)—can be taken as his expression of jealousy of David's courage and anointing,[37] but David's first expressed interest is in personal profit. David's own brother's initial observation concerning David's "heart" may well be accurate.[38] David's response to Eliab's outburst—"What have I done?" (17:29)—establishes a question that will seem more disingenuous each time he repeats it during his violent rise to power (1 Sam 20:1; 26:18; 29:8). In 20:1, for example, he asks the question in apparent shock that Saul should want to kill him, despite the fact that David has already accepted Jonathan's robe (18:4), married into the royal family (18:27), and developed a relationship with Samuel, who has protected him from Saul (19:18–24) and who has already told Saul that God will place another on the throne of Israel.[39] It is disingenuous speech that argues for his innocence while he is involved in a rise to power in replacing Saul as king.

The narrative, having established that David is greedy for power and that he attempts on numerous occasions to disguise this greed through pious speech, suggests as well that outward protestations of loyalty to the divine suzerain could also hide attempts to gain power at God's expense. While David has never breathed a word that would suggest that he is anything but his God's loyal vassal, readers are aware of his desire for power. After David finally "knew that YHWH had established him king over Israel" (2 Sam 5:12), he attempts to move the ark to Jerusalem, although God has given him no such command, and neither the narrator nor David explain his motivation in this regard. In this case, however, it makes most sense to see his move as an attempt to gain power at God's

37. So, e.g., J. P. Fokkelman, *Narrative Art and Poetry in the Book of Samuel: A Full Interpretation Based on Stylistic and Structural Analyses* (4 vols.; SSN 20, 23, 27, 31; Assen: Van Gorcum, 1981–1993), 2:63; Moshe Garsiel, *The First Book of Samuel: A Literary Study of Comparative Structures, Analogies and Parallels* (Ramat-Gan: Revivim, 1985), 109.

38. See Kenneth R. R. Gros Louis, "The Difficulty of Ruling Well: King David of Israel," *Semeia* 8 (1977): 15–23 (22); Lyle M. Eslinger, "A Change of Heart: 1 Samuel 16," in *Ascribe to the Lord: Biblical and Other Studies in Memory of Peter C. Craigie* (ed. Lyle M. Eslinger and Glen Taylor; JSOTSup 67; Sheffield: JSOT, 1988), 341–61 (357); Alter, *The David Story*, 105; Keith Bodner, *David Observed: A King in the Eyes of His Court* (Hebrew Bible Monographs 5; Sheffield: Sheffield Phoenix, 2005), 10–22.

39. For the other passages, see Marti J. Steussy, *David: Biblical Portraits of Power* (Studies on Personalities of the Old Testament; Columbia: University of South Carolina Press, 1999), 71–72; Bodner, *David Observed*, 18–22.

expense. In a similar story of Israel's movement of the ark to the place of battle with the Philistines in 1 Sam 4–6, it seems that Israel looks at the ark as a metonym for God, or as a sign of God's presence,[40] but certainly as a way in which God can be controlled. Despite the national failure in that story to repent of its apostasy—something that does not happen until 1 Sam 7—Israel believes that YHWH will grant them victory merely because the ark is in the vicinity: "Let us take the ark of the covenant of YHWH[41] from Shiloh to us that it might come into our midst and save us from the hand of our enemies" (1 Sam 4:3). There are a number of clear parallels between the story of David's moving of the ark to Jerusalem in 2 Sam 6 and that of the ark's journey from Philistia to Israel in 1 Sam 6: in both cases the ark is on a journey on a cart (1 Sam 6:10; 2 Sam 6:3); Israelites die during its movement (1 Sam 6:19; 2 Sam 6:6–7); and the movement is accompanied by rejoicing and sacrifices (1 Sam 6:13–15; 2 Sam 6:12–13, 17).[42] It is notable that David, so calculating in his struggle for power so far, attempts to move the ark only after he knows that God has established him as king and after God has twice given him victory in battle as the new king (2 Sam 5:17–20 and 22–25), the first time providing merely a positive response to David's inquiry, but the second giving specific instructions for how David is to conduct his military operations, and thus tightening his control over what David does.[43] So when David moves to bring the ark to Jerusalem, something that God has not commanded, it appears to be an attempt, like that of Israel in 1 Sam 4, to control divine power.[44]

For the narrative, however, the ark cannot be used to control God, but represents the covenant agreement mandating Israel's obedience:[45] in the

40. See Fokkelman, *Narrative Art and Poetry*, 4:201 for the former designation and Klein, *1 Samuel*, 42 for the latter.

41. The LXX reads "the ark of God" rather than the MT's "the ark of the covenant of YHWH." "The ark of God/YHWH" is the normal reference in 1–2 Samuel, which makes the MT the more difficult reading. It is possible that almost all of the witnesses are expansionistic (see McCarter, *I Samuel*, 103); "the ark of the covenant of YHWH" is a common Deuteronomistic expression (see below).

42. See Polzin, *Samuel and the Deuteronomist*, 68–71. For a short but clear chart of these and other parallels between 1 Sam 4–7 and 2 Sam 5–6, see Steussy, *David*, 54.

43. See Donald F. Murray, *Divine Prerogative and Royal Pretension: Pragmatics, Poetics and Polemics in a Narrative Sequence About David* (JSOTSup 264; Sheffield: Sheffield Academic, 1998), 98–103, 109–11.

44. See Lyle Eslinger, *House of God or House of David? The Rhetoric of 2 Samuel 7* (JSOTSup 164; Sheffield: Sheffield Academic, 1994), 23–24.

45. See Green, *How Are the Mighty Fallen?*, 138–39.

narrative, the ark is "the ark of the covenant of YHWH," in which Moses places the tablets from Horeb (Deut 10:2–5) and beside which is the people's copy of the law (Deut 31:26). The term "the ark of the covenant (of YHWH)" is one that the narrative has, in fact, used extensively so far in the History (Deut 10:8; 31:9, 25, 26; Josh 3:3, 6, 8, 11, 14, 17; 4:7, 9, 18; 8:33; Judg 20:27). The ark cannot be used to control God's power; it is instead a symbol of the treaty that God has established with Israel, something that presupposes God's ultimate control of history.[46] In 1 Sam 4–6, merely moving the ark to the site of the battle with the Philistines does not result in an Israelite victory; only the repentance and correct sacrifice of 1 Sam 7 accomplish that.

The ark does seem to represent YHWH's power in the narrative, but YHWH's absolute power in history cannot be controlled by any human and this power itself controls the sphere of human activity. YHWH's power can be manifest where the ark is present, as is clearly demonstrated to the Philistines in 1 Sam 5, where it seems to be responsible for the decapitation of Dagon and the plague within the Philistine cities. As "the ark of the covenant of YHWH," the ark represents the basis on which God judges and controls Israel's fate in history, the precise opposite of what the Israelites hope to accomplish with it in 1 Sam 4, where they seem to view it as a tool that will allow them to harness YHWH's power. Yet they cannot do so. Not only does the presence of the ark not result in victory in 1 Sam 4, its destructive power among the Philistines in 1 Sam 5 continues upon its return to Israel in 1 Sam 6, causing a plague-like slaughter in Israel in 6:19, reminiscent of the one God enacted among the Philistines, when Israelites attempt to look in the ark: "He [God] killed some of the people of Beth-shemesh because they looked into the ark;[47] he killed seventy men, fifty thousand men." The text presents the death of the fifty thousand as a kind of plague that begins with the death of

46. And it may be because, in Dtr, the tablets of the commandments are in the ark that "the ark of the covenant of YHWH" is its common name (Tigay, *Deuteronomy*, 106; Weinfeld, *Deuteronomy 1–11*, 421).

47. This reads with the more difficult MT. Scholars tend to read 6:19 with LXX^B: "But the sons of Jeconiah did not share in the joy of the men of Beth-shemesh when they greeted the ark of YHWH" (so, e.g., Hertzberg, *I & II Samuel*, 56; McCarter, *I Samuel*, 131; Patrick D. Miller and J. J. M. Roberts, *The Hand of the Lord: A Reassessment of the "Ark Narrative" of 1 Samuel* [Johns Hopkins Near Eastern Studies; Baltimore: The Johns Hopkins University Press, 1977], 58–59). LXX^B, however, simply seems to be trying to make sense of a difficult text, and so the MT is to be preferred here (see Barthelémy, *Critique textuelle*, 156; Campbell, *1 Samuel*, 78, and Serge Frolov, *The Turn of the Cycle: 1 Samuel 1–8 in Synchronic and Diachronic Perspectives* [BZAW 342; Berlin: de Gruyter, 2004], 135–36).

seventy people and quickly spreads, mimicking the one God has just visited on the Philistines (5:6, 9–12).[48] Israel cannot control God's power through manipulating the ark; their attempts to do so are met with destruction. And while God seems happy to fight on David's behalf in 2 Sam 5, as soon as David attempts to move the ark to Jerusalem, God "burst forth" and killed Uzzah (2 Sam 6:7–8), just as he had earlier "burst forth" against the Philistines to defeat them for David (5:20).[49] As in 1 Sam 4–6, God treats Israel like Philistines as soon as they attempt to control his power, thereby manifesting their complete ignorance of the logic and power that governs history.

David is now afraid of YHWH, but also expresses his true motivation: "How may the ark of YHWH come to me?" (6:9).[50] The fact that the house of Obed-edom flourishes while the ark resides there (6:11) might suggest that YHWH prefers it where it is, but David moves again to take the ark to Jerusalem, now accompanying its transfer with sacrifices (6:12–13, 17–18) that, for the narrative, signal cultic loyalty. This is, in fact, the first time in the narrative that we see David sacrifice, and perhaps this sign of loyalty reassures God. While David does bring the ark to his capital, God now explicitly prevents him from doing any more with it; the same night that David proposes building a house for it (7:2, 4)—and David's use of the word "house" rather than "temple" suggests an implicit parallel between himself and the deity, for he wants both of them to be in a "house" (7:2), suggesting an equality between them[51]—God communicates with him to indicate that he has not commanded such

48. The interpretation of "he [God] killed seventy men, fifty thousand men" as reflecting a plague spreading throughout Beth-shemesh is Frolov's (*The Turn of the Cycle*, 134–35). Scholars tend to eliminate the reference to the "fifty thousand men," in 6:19, sometimes by arguing for its insertion through redactional activity (e.g., Antony F. Campbell, *The Ark Narrative [1 Sam 4–6; 2 Sam 6]: A Form-Critical and Traditio-Historical Study* [SBLDS 16; Missoula: Scholars Press, 1975], 121–23) or as an invention of a glossator (David M. Fouts, "Added Support for Reading '70 Men' in 1 Samuel vi 19," *VT* 42 [1992]: 394) or as textual corruption (e.g., Fokkelman, *Narrative Art and Poetry*, 4:289, 575). But there is virtually no evidence from the textual witnesses for its removal from the original text and, as Frolov shows, the text makes perfect sense as it stands. The versions have tried to deal with the original text in different ways: the LXX joins the two numbers with a conjunction; the Syriac has inverted the two numbers and omitted the first איש in order to arrive at a normal complex number; and so on. See Barthelémy, *Critique textuelle*, 156–57.

49. As Murray notes, Uzzah's death for touching the ark at this point is surprising, since the ark had been touched when it was placed on the cart in 6:3, and will be again in 6:13 (*Divine Prerogative*, 125–26).

50. See Eslinger, *House of God or House of David?*, 14.

51. Cf. Fokkelman, *Narrative Art and Poetry*, 3:210.

a thing (7:5–7). The divine response, in fact, is aggressively negative.[52] Besides the equality between God and king the idea suggests, the act would have the added benefit for David of putting the deity under obligation to him,[53] completely undermining the suzerain–vassal relationship at the center of the master narrative's theology. God is not fooled by David's apparently pious concern that the ark dwells unworthily in a tent. Yet God, who has chosen David as a king for himself, continues to support him, and takes the opportunity of this overreaching for power on David's part to grant David an eternal (עד עולם) dynasty (7:14, 16), albeit one subject to punishment for disobedience (7:14). God does not reject this king he has chosen for himself as he rejected Saul, but he hardly gives David and his house *carte blanche*, since David has not proven himself entirely trustworthy, and God puts no limit on how severely the dynasty can be punished. So while a granting of an eternal dynasty to David immediately following his attempted power grab might seem an odd reaction, it is one that puts David in his place as a vassal utterly subject to his divine suzerain. David's recent expression of cultic loyalty through sacrifice suggests that he might be learning the lesson that pious speech is not enough.

So at this point in the narrative, David's rebellion against God's power is mild, at least in comparison with the examples of apostasy on display so far. Nonetheless, David's attempt to use a cultic apparatus to wrest some control from God points toward the apostate cultic apparatuses erected by Solomon, Jeroboam, and Manasseh that mark their disloyalty to God and that, in the latter two cases, are used to cause the people to sin and become like the nations, and so that are used by the narrative to explain the exiles' trauma. David is certainly not Manasseh as far as the narrative is concerned, but his portrayal here suggests to readers that he has a tendency to do what is right in his own eyes, an attitude that foreshadows the later failure of the monarchy.

While in 2 Sam 7 David is reminded of his vassal status while simultaneously reaping the benefits of God's unique concern for his continued leadership over Israel, in the story of Bathsheba and Uriah his reign continues to reflect the kind of royal overreaching that his movement of the ark suggests. When God tells David that, for this act of adultery and murder "the sword will not turn aside (תסור) from your house forever (עד עולם)" (12:10), he repeats the earlier language of promise—"my

52. Murray, *Divine Prerogative*, 165–67; Eslinger, *House of God or House of David?*, 24–35.

53. So Eslinger, *House of God or House of David?*, 24.

steadfast love will not turn aside (יסור) from him [David's son]" (7:15). David's eternal house is now one beset with eternal punishment. God interprets David's adultery and murder of Uriah by saying בזתני "You despised me" (12:10). The Elides were the last party in the narrative to be accused of "despising" (בזה) God (1 Sam 2:30). David is not stripped of either eternal dynasty or kingship as the Elides lost their eternal position as priests, and perhaps this is because, for the narrative, his sin is not cultic as the Elides' is. We have already seen that, since the book of Judges, the narrative focuses on Israel's cultic action as the basic standard by which God judges the nation's loyalty. The punishment of David, at least that which occurs during his lifetime, is not the revocation of the eternal covenant as was the case with the Elides (1 Sam 2:30), but does have certain parallels to his actions: the illegitimate child Bathsheba bears him will die (12:15–19); and just as he went on the roof to take Bathsheba, so will Absalom to take his concubines (16:2).[54] So while God does not annul the eternal covenant with David's house, he is quick to recognize that, without punishment to limit David and remind him of where ultimate control resides, David makes a poor leader. His failure of nomistic loyalty anticipates the failures of later kings in their loyalty to the divine suzerain. This is certainly not the last readers will see of divine punishment of monarchs.

Second Samuel 21–24, near the end of Dtr's narrative of David, forms a chiasm that highlights both David's failings and his one important Deuteronomistic success. These chapters begin with famine (21:1–14) and end with plague (24:1–25). Stories of David's warriors and their exploits form the next ring of the chiasm (21:15–22 and 23:8–39), and the central section consists of two psalms placed on David's lips (22:1–51 and 23:1–7).[55] In the psalms at the center of the chiasm, David praises God's actions in delivering him from enemies (22:2–20), but attributes these divine actions to his own righteousness in regard to his nomistic loyalty. "YHWH repaid me according to my righteousness,/according to the cleanness of my hand he gave back to me" (22:21); "For all of his judgments were before me,/and I did not turn aside from his statutes" (22:23). These statements are simply not true, unless one wishes to see

54. See D. M. Gunn, *The Story of King David: Genre and Interpretation* (JSOTSup 6; Sheffield: JSOT, 1978), 98–99; Gillian Keys, *The Wages of Sin: A Reappraisal of the "Succession Narrative"* (JSOTSup 221; Sheffield: Sheffield Academic, 1996), 127–41.

55. For the recognition of this chiasm, see Karl Budde, *Die Bücher Samuel* (KHAT 8; Tübingen: J. C. B. Mohr, 1902), 304; Childs, *Introduction*, 273.

the reference to God's repayment in 22:21 as ironically expressing God's punishment of David for his crimes. His further claim in 23:1–7 that YHWH made an "eternal covenant" with his house because of David's just rule (23:3–5), something he contrasts with the fate of the "worthless" (v. 6), shows that David either does not understand that he has committed any sins, or that he is simply lying about his relationship with his divine suzerain. His decision to view God's aid in battle as a sign of his own righteousness and cleanness of hands (22:21–28) may have been technically true when Saul was alive (22:1 reports that David spoke this psalm when he was delivered from Saul), but the narrative's placement of it near the end of his career causes it to reflect on his unrighteousness and ignorance or mendacity. The exploits of David and his warriors in the second ring of the chiasm, then, mean little in any ultimate terms of military success since it is God who has won David's battles for him and delivered him from his enemies. The military prowess of David and his warriors has, in fact, contributed no more to David's success as a king than David's own ethical actions have. This is not to say that leadership means nothing; the famine of 21:1–14 is caused by Saul's treatment of the Gibeonites, and the plague of 24:1–25 by David's census. Bad leadership can lead to disaster for Israel in Dtr's narrative, but David's right Yahwistic sacrifice at the end of the plague story that causes God to stop the destruction of Israel (24:18–25) assures God of the king's submission to divine authority. Despite all of his failures as a leader, there is one notable success of David in the narrative: he is always loyal to YHWH in his cultic activities. While the chiasm at the end of 2 Samuel highlights Saul's failure as a king and David's failures of theological awareness, it nonetheless ends with what is most important to the narrative's presentation of history: the necessity of cultic loyalty to avert the destruction of Israel. It is this necessity that David's descendants will ultimately fail to fulfill, and this failure that the narrative will use to explain the exiles' trauma.

By the time readers reach the end of Samuel they have seen a leader whose loyalty to his divine suzerain is imperfect despite his cultic successes. These successes and his status as God's choice as king may have won him an eternal dynasty, but his failures have earned his house eternal punishment. He is a model of his house in this way, for some of his descendants will be loyal to YHWH and some will not. The narrative of his career thus prepares readers for the successes and failures of the Davidides, and for the ultimate failure of Manasseh that explains the exiles' trauma.

B. *God, Saul, and Israel: A Traumatic Rejection of Justice*

1. *Introduction: God and Saul's Punishment*

I referred earlier to scholars who see Saul's story as tragic, and the tragic vision of his story seems especially evident when one compares the way God treats him with the way God treats David, a comparison that subverts Dtr's master narrative, as we shall see. One scholar who has pointed to the disparity in the divine treatment of the two kings is David Gunn, who argues that Saul's rejection as king for an apparently minor violation of God's command of חרם in the case of the Amalekites in 1 Sam 15 appears grossly unfair given David's many transgressions of God's law. In reference to the case of Saul's actions toward the Amalekites, writes Gunn,

> [t]he arbitrary disparity in God's treatment of the two figures is nowhere more manifest than here at the very culmination of the story. The thematic statement is plain. Good and evil come from God. He makes smooth the path of some; the path of others he strews with obstacles. He has his favourites; he has his victims. The reasons, if reasons exist, lie hidden in the obscurity of God's own being. Saul is one of God's victims.[56]

Northrop Frye argues that, at this point in Saul's story, God's opposition to him appears demonic.[57] What scholars like these see is unjust treatment of a character who, if not blameless in the story, is subject to a force—a divine force, specifically—beyond his control that shapes his destiny in a fearful way with little regard to Saul's own intentions and actions.[58] What Gunn and Frye point to is a divine force that exists outside of the calculations of justice—Frye's designation of God's actions as demonic actually present the divine actions in question as anti-justice. Like Gunn's observation that there is no explanation for the disparity in the divine treatments of Saul and David, this is, of course, an example of the eruption of trauma into Dtr's master narrative that attempts to explain the exile with reference to a divine judge who correctly responds to Israel's acts of nomistic and cultic loyalty and disloyalty, and that presents Saul as a foreshadowing of the worse monarchs who will lead

56. Gunn, *The Fate of King Saul*, 111.

57. Frye, *The Great Code*, 181.

58. And this is generally why scholars who refer to his story as tragic do so: Saul's suffering is ultimately due to a divine power that opposes him without clear or full explanation. See, e.g., Gunn, *The Fate of King Saul*, 115–16; von Rad, *Old Testament Theology*, 1:324–25. Even Yairah Amit, who refers to Saul's story as tragic because it appears to conform to the ancient Greek tragic pattern ultimately refers to Saul as tragic because he is unjustly condemned ("The Delicate Balance in the Image of Saul," 72–73).

Israel in the apostasy that will destroy it. The tragic vision of Saul's story lies in a portrayal of God that seems to match neither the narrative's conception of him nor its conception of justice that it attempts to use to explain the exilic community's trauma.

To prepare readers for these intrusions of trauma into the parts of the narrative involving Saul, Samuel, and Israel, I return briefly in this introduction to Gunn's and Frye's point about the portrayal of God in the story of Saul that subverts the narrative's concept of God and of justice. As we shall see in our discussion of the traumatic interruptions of the Samuel narrative, trauma suggests that it is possible that God's will cannot be known and that it does not conform to justice. If this is true in God's treatment of Saul, and if, as I will argue below, trauma suggests that God treats Israel like Saul, then it subverts the narrative's explanation of the trauma as the just, logical outcome of the people's own disloyalty, the same subversion of the narrative that we will see in 2 Kgs 21–25. We certainly see a traumatic subversion of the narrative's concepts of God and justice in the story of Saul; we have already noted the distinction that God makes between Saul, a king "for them" and David, a king "for me." The very fact that Saul is chosen by lot, as a criminal would be, suggests that God is predisposed to find fault in him. Saul does act wrongly in 1 Sam 13 and 15 by the master narrative's standards, which demand absolute obedience to the divine suzerain, yet Saul's explanations for his sacrifice in 13:11–12, his belief in 15:13, 20 that he has truly followed divine command, and his repentance and vow of cultic loyalty in 15:24–25 are pointedly ignored.

We can certainly read the stories of 1 Sam 13 and 15 as cohering with the narrative's logic—good intentions or not, disloyalty is disloyalty—but we see here an absence in narrative explanation. It is certainly possible to interpret these stories as pointing to Saul's ignorance and guilt, but the narrative is hardly clear about this. In this presence of traumatic absence, Saul's failing in 1 Sam 13 can be attributed to Samuel, who had failed to instruct him earlier in the necessity of absolute cultic obedience. When we read, moreover, that Saul "waited seven days, the appointed time that Samuel had said,[59] but Samuel did not come to Gilgal" (13:8), it is certainly possible to see the failure here as Samuel's, not Saul's. Saul waits seven days and sacrifices because he believes the sacrifice is necessary to entreat God's favor. Had Samuel told him that this is not the point of sacrifice before rather than after the act, the error might have been avoided. Instead, Samuel tells Saul in 10:7 to "do what your hand finds,

59. Adding אמר after אשׁר, following the LXX and Targum. Assumedly, the verb dropped out of the MT. See McCarter, *I Samuel*, 226.

because God is with you."[60] So one possible interpretation of 1 Sam 13 is that Saul suffers for Samuel's failure, rather as, trauma will suggest in 2 Kgs 21–25, the exilic generation suffers for the sins of their ancestors whom Manasseh and others caused to sin. God's failure to acknowledge Saul's repentance in 15:24–25,[61] which the king follows by a concrete act of lawful Yahwistic worship (15:31), provides an uncanny parallel with the divine failure to acknowledge Josiah's perfect act of repentance in 2 Kgs 23. If the narrative sends a message to Israel in 1 Sam 13 and 15 about the importance of absolute cultic loyalty to YHWH as the key to survival, part of the message that readers can take away from the gaps that trauma has left in the story is that YHWH will not always make the details of this loyalty clear, that people can suffer for sins others have committed, and that even repentance resulting from a true understanding of God's will may effect no corresponding act of divine salvation. As we have seen, it makes perfect sense that the narrative would present God as rewarding repentance with salvation, since the act of repentance is a returning to a recognition of God's authority as suzerain. God's refusal to acknowledge Saul's repentance is a jarring contrast with 1 Sam 7:3–11, where Samuel tells Israel that if they will repent and turn aside foreign gods, God "will rescue you from the hand of the Philistines," which is precisely what happens. It is his definitiveness about this cause and effect relationship—repentance leads to salvation—a definitiveness that reflects Moses' earlier statement on the issue in Deut 30:1–10, that makes the rejection of Saul's repentance so striking. After all, if God will not forgive a sin such as Saul's, why should exilic readers see him as anxious to forgive national apostasy? One can read this contrast as suggesting that the salvation of 1 Sam 7:3–11 was merely luck and that Moses misled Israel about the relationship between repentance and salvation.

The tragic vision of Saul's story is precisely this narrative and divine silence as to why God does not conform his actions to the narrative portrayals of divine justice, and it makes the story not just a tragedy for Saul but for the exiles. As we will discuss in some detail in the next

60. See Nicholson, *Three Faces of Saul*, 57.

61. Hertzberg argues that Saul shows in his repentance in 15:24–25 that the king believes that his sin can be removed by sacrifice, and this is why he asks Samuel to "lift" or forgive his transgression (שׂא נא את־חטאתי) and worship with him (*I & II Samuel*, 128). If this is in fact Saul's meaning, then he still has not properly learned the point of sacrifice according to the narrative—it does not forgive sins, it simply signals vassal loyalty—but the phrase "to lift one's sin" need not be understood this way. In fact, the phrase in Josh 24:19 clearly does not refer to sacrifice in the context of the forgiveness of sins.

chapter, the final narrative explanation of the trauma at the end of 2 Kings is not at all clear that justice has been done in God's refusal to acknowledge Josiah's repentance. There is no clear explanation in Saul's story as to why God does not react positively to his repentance; this is an absence, a gap in narrative explanation. Trauma does not argue that God is always unjust and dismissive of repentance—the salvation granted as a response to Israel's repentance in 1 Sam 7:3–11 suggests otherwise—since that would point to the establishment of a counter-narrative and alternative explanation. Trauma is present as a narrative absence that subverts explanation and suggests that if the cultic loyalty that Saul demonstrates in his repentance—and that Judah will demonstrate because of Josiah's leadership in repentance—does not change how God acts, then there is no point at all to attempt to explain history cultically. If God acts however he chooses, regardless of human attitudes and actions, and if he is willing to punish some people for sins that others have committed, then the point of presenting a history so that readers can find its covenantal logic to explain the exile is being subverted. This subversion throws into doubt the usefulness of using the narrative's logic to make any kind of totalizing statement about the past that explains the exiles' trauma. It is true that the punishments of Saul in 13:13–14 and 15:23, 26–29 are spoken by Samuel, an unreliable prophet, but God eventually does support them (1 Sam 16:1; 2 Sam 7:15), and it is to trauma's subversion of the narrative in the stories about Samuel that we now turn.

2. *The Traumatic Subversion of Prophecy*

Some of trauma's subversion of the narrative's portrayal of God appears at places where the narrative presents Samuel as a failure as a prophet. Trauma appears in absences of narrative explanation in these stories to subvert not only the narrative's portrayal of God, but of prophecy in general, for if prophets like Samuel do not rightly report God's word then, trauma suggests, no prophet, not even Moses, is to be fully trusted. The subversion of prophecy in the story of Samuel throws the narrative's explanation of trauma and the concepts on which it depends into grave doubt. We have seen that the narrative presents Samuel as a poor prophetic leader of Israel because his interest in maintaining his and his family's power within the nation causes him to fail to explain the proper role of a king. The economic rationale that he presents to Israel in 8:11–18 for rejecting a monarchy does not reflect the law of the king from Deut 17, nor does it reflect the narrative's concern that the monarchy will eventually make Israel like all the nations (cf. 8:4, 20) in the sense that the kings will cause Israel to worship idols and the gods of the nations. Samuel instead suggests that the monarchy will provide no more social or economic justice than his own corrupt sons do. His argument here, along with his anger in 8:6, is self-interested. The same point can be made when he tries to rewrite history in 12:12, claiming that Israel asked for a king during the Ammonites' invasion. This simply obscures the fact that Israel asked for a king earlier because of the failure of his own sons to judge properly.[62] When Samuel tells Saul in 15:29 that God does not change his mind (נחם), despite the fact that the narrative tells us that God has just done precisely that (15:11), readers may wonder how well Samuel really functions as a prophet. He appears to fail to relay God's concerns about a monarchy because of his own selfish interests, he lies about God, and brings a message about God's rejection of Saul from the kingship that God has not given, and so the prophet as an accurate intermediary for the divine is thrown into question.[63] It is certainly possible to make sense of some of these gaps in the narrative—for example, when Samuel says that God has rejected Saul from being king, readers might assume that God has told the prophet this and the narrative has simply not reported this divine speech. But it is precisely the absence of the report, combined with other clear failings of Samuel, that create the narrative gap and consequent ambiguity of trauma. A completely certain and totalizing explanation for why God punishes is out of the question here; as we will discuss in Chapter 7, the same traumatic ambiguity is present in 2 Kgs 21–25, the narrative's ultimate explanation of the exiles' trauma.

These intrusions that subvert the narrative explanation in the story of Samuel do not stem solely from his own failings, however; they arise also from God's failure to match the narrative's conception of him. In 16:2–3, God hides the purpose of Samuel's trip to Bethlehem from the prophet himself, and has him lie to the elders of Bethlehem. As in the case of 1 Kgs 22, which we will examine in the next chapter, this divine deception through a prophetic medium "undermines any facile delineation between categories such as 'true prophecy' and 'false prophecy.'"[64] The narrative says as well in 1 Sam 3:19, at the outset of Samuel's career, that God "was with him and he let none of his words fall to the ground." "He" may refer to Samuel,[65] although if it does, then it is potentially an inaccurate statement, depending on exactly what "he let none of his words fall to the ground" actually means, since Samuel does misrepresent and lie about God, as we have seen. On the other hand, "he" could just as

62. So Eslinger, *Into the Hands of the Living God*, 103–4,

63. See also Green, *How Are the Mighty Fallen?*, 261.

64. Heller, *Power, Politics, and Prophecy*, 133.

65. And this is perhaps the most common reading of the verse; see, e.g., Klein, *1 Samuel*, 34; Hertzberg, *I & II Samuel*, 42; Eslinger, *Kingship of God in Crisis*, 156.

easily refer to God here, and 3:19 would mean that God let none of Samuel's words fall to the ground. Precisely this appears to happen when Samuel rather than God informs Saul that God has rejected him as king (15:23, 26–29); God says nothing like this until after Samuel's judgment (16:1). With this reading of 3:19, we can see God as a "mirror" of a problematic prophet.[66] We see a similar relationship between Samuel and God in 1 Sam 12, when Samuel declares that Israel's mere request for the king is "evil…in the eyes of YHWH" (12:17), a pronouncement that corresponds neither to the allowance for a monarchy in Deut 17 nor to God's response to the request for one in 1 Sam 8. The prophet calls upon God to destroy the wheat harvest with rain (12:16–17), and God obliges (12:18), even though neither God nor narrator had said that such a request was evil in God's eyes, even though God's law permits such a request, and even though God commands Samuel three times to listen to Israel's request for a king. The narrative, however, does say that the request for a king "was evil in the eyes of Samuel" (8:6).

So the narrative's concept of prophecy as the true word of God has been thrown into a trial without resolution. What trauma suggests as it intrudes into the narrative of Samuel and his interactions with God, Saul, and Israel, then, is that Samuel misrepresents what God says, misrepresents the very character of God, leads and directs Israel and its king poorly because of his own character flaws, and can convince God to follow his lead in matters where his self-interest conflicts with justice. God can even instruct him to lie. While it is certainly possible to read the text and come to different conclusions on these issues, the very possibility of such readings is due to the absence of clear and full narrative explanation. The presence of trauma in narrative absence clearly subverts the narrative's concept of prophecy as a transparent communication of the divine will, something that is not a minor point for Dtr's narrative, because its whole logic in history works to explain trauma only if God's word and will can be truly and consistently known. The narrative explains the exiles' trauma to them as an understandable event that reflects vassal disloyalty into which the nation has been led by its kings, just as God had spoken through the prophets (2 Kgs 17:13, 23; 24:2). If the prophets' warnings cannot be trusted—and the story of Samuel suggests that this is a possibility—then the leadership and instruction of Moses, who describes himself as a prophet in Deut 18:15 and who, in Deuteronomy, originally presents the logic in history that explains the exiles' trauma, has also been thrown into question. When we remember, in fact, that

66. So Marti J. Steussy, "The Problematic God of Samuel," in Penchansky and Redditt, eds., *Shall Not the Judge of All the Earth Do What is Right?*, 127–61 (151).

Samuel's dialogue with God in 1 Sam 8:6–9 is the first dialogue between God and prophet readers have seen since Moses spoke with God,[67] then Samuel can appear to fit the bill of Moses' description of "a prophet like me" in Deut 18:15 more clearly than any other figure to this point in Dtr.[68] As we saw in Chapter 3, trauma intrudes into the narrative in Deuteronomy to question the reliability of Moses' instruction, and the traumatic subversions of the narrative of Samuel return readers to this problem. Even the merest suggestion of doubt here is a crucial subversion of Dtr's narrative, because if Samuel and Moses have failed to inform Israel and the exilic readers correctly of how God governs history—and trauma insists that this is a possibility—then the narrative's explanation of the exiles' trauma is thrown into unresolved doubt. What if Moses' word to Israel in the lawcode, as well as in the lawcode's introduction and conclusion, is no more transparent or accurate than Samuel's is to Israel and Saul? Since this is at least a possibility, then there is no absolutely clear and unchallenged explanation for 586.

The law of Deut 18:15–22, meant to distinguish false from true prophecy, does not resolve the ambiguity that trauma's absence has introduced into the narrative; the law is ineffectual on practical grounds, since Israel would not be in a position to wait to see if a prophecy that warned of destruction if Israel did not follow the prophet's instruction came true before the nation acted.[69] Since prophets lie, and since God instructs them to lie and can be understood to follow their self-interested decisions, how will Israel know whether or not to believe them? Can Israel believe Samuel when he tells them in 1 Sam 12:14–15, 24–25 that nomistic disloyalty will result in destruction, especially when he has misrepresented the facts about Israel's desire for a king in 12:12 in order to draw attention away from his family's poor leadership? When the existence of the nation demands knowing the word of God with certainty and acting on it, there must be a sure way of determining true prophecy before its judgment comes to pass, but the narrative has provided none.

67. See Rendtorff, "Samuel the Prophet," 28. Of course, Dtr's narrative also says in Deut 34:10 that YHWH knew Moses face to face, but this appears as one of the narrative's incomparability sayings ("there did not arise again in Israel a prophet like Moses"), and so we need not expect Samuel or any other prophet to attain that kind of intimacy with God.

68. I am not arguing that the narrative is specifically looking to Samuel with the phrase "a prophet like me," merely that there are some clear parallels between Moses and Samuel. The phrase in Deut 18:15 likely looks to the prophets in general.

69. See Robert P. Carroll, *When Prophecy Failed: Cognitive Dissonance in the Prophetic Traditions of the Old Testament* (New York: Seabury, 1979), 186; Tigay, *Deuteronomy*, 177.

In this traumatic absence of clear explanation, prophets are suspect intermediaries of divine command, and so there is no certain way, not even adhering to Moses' words, to know God's will, and the structure of history is unknowable and always open to an unexplainable repetition of trauma. The narrative's concepts of history and justice are subverted here along with its understanding of prophecy, for history can hardly be the realm in which prophecy is fulfilled and where justice is done if Israel cannot be certain that prophets truly bring God's word; the exilic readers can never know with certainty if prophetic instructions are lies or not, and thus God's word can never be certainly known. The possibility thus exists that the exilic community's trauma simply cannot be explained as divine punishment for vassal disloyalty.

3. *Saul and the Traumatic Torture of Israel*

The failure of prophetic leadership here thus threatens to subvert the narrative's entire ethical basis of history and explanation of its readers' trauma. The narrative's argument is not helped by the fact that God seems to hold David to an entirely different standard of justice from Saul, as we shall see. The traumatic subversion of Dtr's narrative is even stronger when we see that Saul's fate parallels that of Israel. Saul's reign is over almost as soon as it begins, and it is curious that he remains on the scene after David's anointing. Normally, once the narrative has finished with the story of a character, such as that of one of the judges, he or she disappears from the narrative. This is not the case, however, once God rejects Saul.[70] The rest of the time that Saul spends in Dtr's narrative is slow torture for him at God's hands, tormented by an evil spirit (16:14; 18:10).[71] Never aware that God has anointed David by Samuel, Saul is rejected by the people (1 Sam 18:6–7), his daughter (18:20; 19:8–17), and Jonathan, his heir (19:1–7; 20:1–42), all in favor of David. Only in 24:21 [ET 20] does he finally acknowledge that God prefers David to him and will make David king (although cf. 23:17, where Jonathan claims that Saul knows this).

The story of God's rejection of Saul as influenced by an unreliable and self-interested prophet, and the continuing story of Saul's torture and slow demise can seem like a summary of Israel's own history to the exiles, albeit a summary that subverts the narrative's concepts of God, prophecy, justice, punishment, and repentance. As Robert Polzin puts it, God's rejection of Saul anticipates God's rejection of Israel, and the

70. See Mark K. George, "Yhwh's Own Heart," *CBQ* 64 (2002): 442–59 (442–44).

71. Nicholson, *Three Faces of Saul*, 43, 78–79.

delay in removing Saul from the scene is reflected in Israel's own long demise in Dtr.[72] When God condemns Jeroboam for causing Israel to sin with his idols (1 Kgs 14:7–14), he says as well that the sin the king has caused the nation to commit will result also in Israel's destruction (14:15–16), yet it will take two war-filled centuries for this punishment to come to fruition in 2 Kgs 17. The bad prophecy and suspect word of God through Samuel that plagues Saul will also be Israel's problem, for in the narrative the fate of Israel since their entrance into the land up to their present exile depends on following the words of a prophet—Moses—the validity of whose direction, we have seen, has been subverted. The presentation of prophecy in Kings will add to the subversion of the narrative's conception of the institution and thus increase readers' doubts that prophetic leadership for Israel can be trusted. In the story of Saul and Samuel, readers see that God does not seem to distinguish between Samuel's failure to deliver the divine word properly and Saul's actions. While it is possible to read the story of Saul, as we did in section A, as providing an example of the divine punishment of disloyalty, it is also possible to read it as suggesting that the responsibility for his punishment can largely be laid at Samuel's door, just as it is possible to read 2 Kgs 21–25 as suggesting that an innocent exilic generation is subjected to trauma because of their ancestors' guilt. Since Moses is potentially a prophet like Samuel, Saul's fate of torment and death at God's hands, led by a prophet who misrepresents God, might be Israel's as well. Given trauma's subversion of the narrative's explanation for the exiles' trauma in 2 Kgs 21–25 that we will see in the following chapter, it will not be at all clear that Moses has rightly informed Israel of what actions on Israel's part bring salvation and punishment. This is particularly so when God ignores Josiah's perfect act of repentance despite Moses' claim in Deut 30:1–10 that God responds to repentance. In this regard, God's failure to acknowledge Saul's repentance and right worship in 1 Sam 15:24–31 is an uncanny parallel to the narrative failure to explain God's reaction to Josiah's repentance and reform.

Perhaps the clearest parallel between God's unjust treatment of Saul and Israel appears in the outer sections of the chiasm of 2 Sam 21–24. The story of 21:1–14 centers on the slaughter of Saul's house after his rejection and death because Saul killed the Gibeonites (21:1–2),[73] even

72. Polzin, *Samuel and the Deuteronomist*, 212–14.

73. In 21:1 we should read על־שׁאול ועל־ביתה דמים "there is bloodguilt on Saul and on his house." For על (as opposed to the MT's אל) and דמים in the context of bloodguilt, see Deut 19:10; 2 Sam 1:16; 1 Kgs 21:31–32. We should read ביתה דמים rather than the MT's בית הדמים since דמים does not require a definite article but בית

though that was precisely what Israel should have done in the conquest. Second Samuel 21:2 refers to the oath Israel swore to Gibeon in Josh 9:15, despite the fact that the narrative there in 9:14 questioned Israel's failure to inquire of YHWH before accepting the Gibeonites. God, as we have seen, punishes Israel by refusing to annihilate the Canaanites in Judg 2:1–3, referring to the ברית "covenant" that Israel has made with them, an apparent reference to the covenant with Gibeon, since that is the only covenant that the narrative records Israel making with Canaanites. Not content with killing Saul and removing his house from power, God seems to want to go on attacking his descendants, even though this punishment stands in direct contradiction to the command to annihilate the Canaanites given through Moses. For the exilic readers who see in Moses' presentation of divine commands the explanation of their trauma, this is narrative subversion indeed. The narrative does not clearly explain why Saul was wrong to follow God's command and ignore Israel's poorly conceived oath to the Gibeonites. The absence in the narrative's explanation of this apparent contradiction of justice is the presence of trauma, which undermines the narrative's concepts of God, justice, punishment, and prophecy when God can punish for no reason, or for a reason that stands in direct contradiction with an earlier command given through a prophet who has supposedly delivered to Israel the ethical logic on which, the narrative claims, the trauma of the exiles can be explained. Moreover, it is not Saul who dies here but his sons, despite the fact that Deut 24:16 prohibits the execution of children for the sin of their parents.[74]

This punishment is not merely unjust, it is anti-justice. At the corresponding outer side of this chiasm in 2 Sam 24 is the plague that slaughters 70,000 in Israel (24:15), a parallel to the body count of the seven Saulides who are killed in 21:5–9.[75] Nor does God appear to enact this slaughter with any just cause. Here, God is angry with Israel for no

does require a suffix, and we can read the ה- here as an archaic 3ms suffix. The text of the MT here would appear to result from incorrect word division. See Julius Wellhausen, *Der Text der Bücher Samuelis untersucht* (Göttingen: Vandenhoeck & Ruprecht, 1871), 208; McCarter, *II Samuel*, 437.

74. For the narrative's interpretation of Deut 5:9–10 in 7:9–10, an interpretation that makes clear that God punishes only the guilty and not their descendants, see Chapter 3.

75. Both chapters also display an interest in threes and sevens: three years of famine (21:1); 300 shekels (21:16); a punishment by threes in 24:13; seven dead Saulides in ch. 21; 70,000 dead Israelites in ch. 24. See Robert Polzin, *David and the Deuteronomist: 2 Samuel* (ISBL; Bloomington: Indiana University Press, 1993), 208–9.

stated reason; 24:1 merely says that "the anger of YHWH continued to burn against Israel." Readers can assume that Israel's disloyalty has deserved such anger, but the very fact that God "incited David against them" suggests that he is searching for a ruse to destroy Israel for no just cause. David's consequent census, done at God's command (24:1–2), thus results in the death of the 70,000 (24:15). The case of 2 Sam 21 is much like that of 2 Sam 24, in fact, for in both cases God punishes for the sin of a leader, although in the former case on a charge that makes no sense in the context of the master narrative, and in the latter for a crime that God himself has incited. This situation, in which David acts only according to divine command, with the result that God can punish David by punishing Israel, is no more just than the punishment of Beth-shemesh in 1 Sam 6. The choice that God offers David in 2 Sam 24 as to how he would like to see Israel punished—famine, warfare, or plague (24:13)—is really no choice at all, and in fact makes a mockery of the notion of ethical choice. God tortures Israel here outside of any logical basis that the narrative can explain, just as God tortured Saul. In foreshadowing Israel's unjust fate, the demise of Saul subverts the narrative's explanation of trauma as a just punishment. And this failure of divine justice in 2 Sam 21 does not only have parallels in 2 Sam 24, Judg 20–21, and 1 Sam 6, where Israel is punished for no explained reason, it has one in 2 Kgs 21–25 where God punishes Israel more than a generation after Josiah's perfect cultic reforms return Israel to cultic loyalty to YHWH—just as it is Saul's sons in 2 Sam 21 and not Saul who die for his alleged sin—thus subverting the narrative's final explanation for the exiles' trauma.

It is this lack of explanation for the supposed punishment that results in slaughter that makes the parallel between Saul and Israel a traumatic one. The failure of clear divine communication in prophecy is an important part of this trauma, since this too plays its part in the lacunae of explanation for trauma. And just as Saul's sons die for a sin that Saul putatively committed, a punishment that the law forbids, trauma will interrupt the narrative of 2 Kgs 21–25 to suggest that God there punishes the wrong generation. Saul's fate parallels Israel's, and the way God treats Saul is a microcosm of the way God treats Israel, a subversion of the narrative's attempt to make sense of the exile. The subversion of the narrative concepts of God, justice, punishment, repentance, salvation, and prophecy in Saul's story simply emphasizes their subversion in God's treatment of Israel. We have seen this where Saul's story overlaps with Samuel's; we will see it also in a somewhat different manner as Saul's story overlaps with and then is succeeded by David's.

C. *God and David: The Traumatic Triumph of Injustice*

1. *The Traumatic Subversion of the Portrayal of God*

Trauma interrupts Dtr's narrative in the David story by undermining its portrayal of God, and the most obvious example of this is the favoritism God shows to David that sets aside the punishment that David has earned. David, as we have seen, is God's king, while Saul is Israel's king. When David receives God's spirit, it does not simply turn aside from Saul, but Saul receives an evil spirit as well (1 Sam 16:14; 18:10). While God, prompted by Samuel, ultimately rejects Saul as king in 1 Sam 15 after ignoring Saul's repentance, David survives in power even after clear violations of the law, despite the fact that the law of the king insists that the monarch is subject to the law just as all Israelites are (Deut 17:19–20), and despite the fact that Moses stresses in Deuteronomy that Israel must obey all of the law, just as God stresses this point in Josh 1:7–8, as does Joshua in Josh 23:6 and Samuel in 1 Sam 12:14–15. David does not even repent of his adultery and murder as Saul repented of his wrongdoing once it was pointed out to him. Even after his power struggle with God when he moves the ark to Jerusalem, God does not remove him from power. Perhaps his action here is less serious in the narrative's eyes than Saul's sacrifice in 1 Sam 13, but the narrative does not make this case. God's gift to David of an eternal dynasty immediately following the power struggle seriously challenges the narrative's ethical structure of history.[76] Even though David seems to act as if bringing the ark to Jerusalem will help him use and direct divine power, trauma suggests at this point that God overlooks a potential challenge to his authority as suzerain that could be seen as a greater one than Saul ever presented with his incorrect actions, actions that appear to be due, at least in part, to Samuel's failures as a prophet. This very oversight subverts the narrative's concept of God as a just actor, and thus also its concepts of justice and punishment. One can argue that Saul's failure to be absolutely obedient in cultic matters is a grave sin in the eyes of the narrative, but the sequence of events in 2 Sam 5–7, where David seems to feel that he needs to take control of the ark so that he rather than God will control the military success of his kingdom points to a vassal who is unhappy with the control exercised by his suzerain. God refuses to make an eternal covenant with Saul's house because of a cultic sin, albeit one performed with good intentions and poor prophetic direction (1 Sam 13:13), and God strips Eli's house of its eternal covenant because of the intentional cultic sins of his sons, saying that "those who despise me will

76. So also Polzin, *David and the Deuteronomist*, 79.

be treated with contempt" (1 Sam 2:30). There is no explanation for the different way that God treats David, especially since he too "despised" God (2 Sam 12:9), at least not an explanation that we can clearly see in Dtr's master narrative. This is, then, a manifestation of trauma's absent presence.

The Bathsheba and Uriah story is a clear example of the preferential treatment that David receives. The divine condemnation for David's adultery and murder begins with Nathan's story of the rich man who stole and killed the poor man's lamb to feed a visitor, causing David to respond that the rich man must repay the lamb fourfold[77] (2 Sam 12:1–6). David seems to be fooled by Nathan's parable because he treats it as a legal case. In such a reading, Nathan's whole point has been to allow David, as the guilty party, to distance himself from the case so that he can apply an objective verdict.[78] Yet Nathan has arranged the story so as to avoid charging David with murder; the rich man in the story is guilty only of theft. This is not simply a case of a prophet failing truly to relate divine intention, for the oracle that follows in 12:7–12 does refer to David's murder of Uriah in v. 9, but the divine punishment David receives in v. 11—an enemy will sleep with his wives—is reciprocity only for David's adultery, and even this does not follow the law for adultery of Deut 22:22, which commands death for both parties. Nathan, that is, ignores the murder in his story of 12:1–6 just as God ignores it in the oracle of 12:7–14, and the punishment God decrees for adultery does not even follow the law he has given. Second Samuel 12:14 does explicitly state that Bathsheba's child will die because of David's sin, but in this whole case, God does not only ignore the law for murder in Deut 19:11–13, but also the commandment in Deut 24:16, which states that children are not to die for the sins of their parents. And God even lessens the punishment that he does pronounce on David, since Absalom will sleep with David's concubines, not his wives (cf. 2 Sam 16:20–22).[79]

77. The LXX has David command a sevenfold rather than a fourfold repayment. It is difficult to determine a more difficult reading in this case, and so I read with the MT and the majority of the ancient witnesses. For the most thorough defense of the LXX here, see R. A. Carlson, *David, the Chosen King: A Traditio-Historical Approach to the Second Book of Samuel* (trans. Eric J. Sharpe and Stanley Rudman; Stockholm: Almqvist & Wiksell, 1964), 153–57.

78. So Uriel Simon, "The Poor Man's Ewe Lamb: An Example of a Juridical Parable," *Bib* 48 (1967): 207–42.

79. The biblical writings are not overly clear as to the difference between a wife and a concubine, but concubines appear to have held a lower social status than a wife. For a discussion of this difference and the relevant evidence, see K. Engelkar, "פִּלֶגֶשׁ," *TDOT* 11:549–51.

God's preference for David, in short, causes him to set aside the principles of justice that the narrative presents as underlying divine action in history. So there is no explanation for why, when David has "despised" God, his house is not treated the same way the last house to despise God—the Elides—is treated, and stripped of its eternal covenant. I suggested in section A above that perhaps the important difference for Dtr's narrative between the sins of David and the Elides is that David's sin is not cultic, but this is not actually a justification provided by the narrative itself. There is no explanation for why God ignores the laws of murder and its punishment when it comes to David's treatment of Uriah. In the story of David and his treatment of Bathsheba and Uriah, we see trauma intervene to subvert the narrative's concepts of God, justice, and punishment. It becomes difficult to argue that God justly evaluates and punishes all wrong actions in history in such cases, and so it is possible to say that he has his favorites and his victims, as Gunn suggests, and his justice and punishment in the stories of Saul and David appear to be divided along those lines rather than by adherence to the law. The narrative's logic in history is undermined again in this story, since God does not seem interested in enforcing the regulations of the covenant when it does not suit him to do so. While it is possible to make sense of these stories as contrasting a leader who fails in his cultic loyalty to God with one who is successful in this regard (as we did in section A above), thus clarifying for readers the key failing of the monarchs in Kings, the narrative never actually makes this case, and so trauma intervenes here as a gap in the logic or explanation of history in the narrative. So while we could argue that, for Dtr's narrative, Saul's cultic disloyalty in 1 Sam 13 and his disobedience in 1 Sam 15 (which involved an attempted sacrifice) are worse sins than David's adultery and murder, the very fact that God sets aside the demands of the law to deal with that adultery and murder subverts the narrative's portrayal of him as a just actor. The portrayal of David and God here subverts the narrative's earlier claim that strict obedience to the law is necessary for Israel to remain in the land, and so subverts its explanation of the exiles' trauma.

This would be good news for the exiles only if God intends to extend them unexplained favorable treatment as he does to David, but the mass death, destruction, and forced migration that they have witnessed and undergone suggest that this is not the case. When we look at the story of Saul, we see that God is willing, in some cases, to ignore repentance and even potentially to punish some for the shortcomings of others, precisely what trauma will suggest in 2 Kgs 21–25. When we compare Saul's story to David's, we see an unjust, unequal divine treatment of the two characters as God overlooks many of David's sins, or at least does not punish

David as the narrative's logic requires, just as, trauma suggests, God overlooks the faults of the generations whom Manasseh, Amon, and Josiah (at least for the first 17 years of his reign) cause to sin. Trauma in these stories of David questions the narrative's logic in history because it subverts the very concepts that the narrative depends on to support its logic. God, trauma suggests, is not bound by justice and does not punish equitably. Present as an absence in the narrative's explanation of the trauma of the exilic community, trauma suggests that there is nothing at all that can explain the difference between the way God treats David and the way God treats Saul, and thus it undermines the narrative's attempt to explain the exilic community's trauma. The parallels that we traced between Saul and the exilic community suggest that the exiles, like Saul, are among the victims of God's unexplained actions that do not wholly seem to correspond to the narrative's explanation of the trauma as just.

So the failings of David in Dtr's master narrative ultimately point to failings of the divine suzerain that the narrative does not clearly explain. God may tell Samuel, as he reveals David as his choice for king, that he "looks to the heart" rather than outward appearance as humans do (1 Sam 16:7), but David is physically impressive (16:12), just like Saul (9:2; 10:23), and one wonders if God does in fact look at physical attributes when choosing a king.[80] The first thing that we hear about David's heart is Eliab's claim that it is "evil" (17:28), a statement that has some merit, as we have seen. There is some ambiguity here as to just what God cares about when choosing a king, and the wisdom of God's choice, given David's actions, is in some doubt. Once, in short, we come to the end of the stories of David and we have a good sense of his character, there is simply no good explanation for why God might favor him, as we saw Gunn arguing above. Trauma interrupts the narrative's attempt to frame history in an ethical logic that depends on God's justice by subverting its concepts of God and justice. And when we see the moral weakness exhibited by Amnon in his rape of Tamar and Absalom in his premeditated murder of Amnon (2 Sam 13), it seems that David's own ethical failings have been passed on to his sons, and that his whole house is a bad one to make an eternal covenant with.[81] When the story of Amnon's rape and Absalom's murder follows immediately upon the story of Bathsheba and Uriah, and when God does not revoke the eternal covenant with David's house as he did in the case of the Elides, the gap in the

80. See Frank H. Polak, "David's Kingship: A Precarious Equilibrium," in Reventlow, Hoffman, and Uffenheimer, eds., *Politics and Theopolitics*, 119–47 (146–47).

81. Keys, *The Wages of Sin*, 144–46.

narrative's logic of explanation is great. God rewards David by maintaining the eternal covenant with his house for no perceptible reason, certainly for no reason that Dtr's narrative actually explains. There is an uncanny parallel here with 2 Kgs 21–25: the unpunished generations of Judah whom Manasseh, Amon, and Josiah caused to sin so grievously are rather like David, who literally gets away with murder. We could argue that David's absolute cultic loyalty might explain why God does not remove him from the throne, but this kind of explanation severs the connection between keeping the law and sacrificing rightly that Dtr's narrative has maintained since Deuteronomy, and it cannot paper over the gap that trauma has left in the narrative's explanation, which has thrown the narrative's concepts of God, justice, and punishment into unresolved trial. David's cultic loyalty is one way to explain God's treatment of David; it is the absence of explanation, however, that manifests the presence of trauma. Since, as we have seen, God treats the exilic generation like Saul, ignoring repentance and punishing the innocent in place of the guilty, we see an uncanny foreshadowing of trauma's subversion of the narrative's ultimate explanation of the readers' trauma in 2 Kgs 21–25.

2. *David's Subversive Interpretation of History and His Parallel with God*
David's interpretation of history, particularly in regard to the role that God and his justice play in it, subverts the conclusion that the master narrative has come to in its logic in history. His conclusions about these matters, in fact, allow him to act as a parallel figure for the subversive portrayal of God that David's interpretation of history embraces, thereby emphasizing God's own lack of justice in the story and the subversion of the narrative's explanation of the exiles' trauma as the expression of God's justice. We actually come across David providing an explanation for history as he has experienced it in 2 Sam 22:1–23:7, although this interpretation does not really match that of the master narrative, but of trauma's subversion of it. We have noted already in the first part of this chapter in regard to these psalms that David either completely misunderstands the narrative's logic in history or he understands it but lies about it. We did not note there, however, that in 23:1 the narrator refers to 23:2–7 as a whole, or at least to 23:2–4, as an "oracle," and that David himself says in 23:2 that his interpretation of history comes from "the spirit of YHWH [that] speaks through me." We can limit David's inspired speech only to 23:2–4,[82] which says merely that a just ruler is a good

82. So, e.g., Antony F. Campbell, *2 Samuel* (FOTL 8; Grand Rapids: Eerdmans, 2005), 200; H. N. Richardson, "The Last Words of David: Some Notes on II Samuel

ruler, and thus take the claim in 23:5–7 as merely David's own incorrect assertion that his eternal covenant is due to his putatively just rule. Yet even in this case, David's rhetorical question, "All my salvation and all desire will he not cause to prosper?"[83] points to the fact that God has saved him, rewarded his desire for kingship, and caused him to prosper, an unexplained support that at times appears to contradict the commands of the law. His oracle and his own reflection on it draw readers' attention to the fact that, despite his actions, God has largely treated him as if he were perfect, an unexplained subversion of the narrative's logic in history.

So 23:1–7 presents the ancestor of Manasseh, whose cultic leadership explains the exiles' trauma according to the narrative, glibly lying about his actions of justice, thus pointing to the fact that God has, without explanation, supported and rewarded him anyway, largely overlooking his faults and refusing to annul his eternal covenant. Indeed, the fact that God fails to end the covenant with David as he did with the Elides, or remove David as he removed Saul suggests that he largely agrees with David's positive evaluation of his rule as just, and this subverts the narrative as well. David's interpretation of history in 23:1–7 is one that subverts the narrative's claim that God applies the covenant curses equitably to the guilty. We will find the same subversion in 2 Kgs 21–25, where the guilty generations whom Manasseh, Amon, and Josiah cause to sin are left unpunished, while the generations that Josiah returns to cultic loyalty are subject to the trauma of 586.

It is perhaps because David rightly understands that the concepts of God and justice as the narrative presents them simply do not always hold that he seems suspicious of God's eternal covenant in 2 Sam 7. David's response in 7:18–29 to Nathan's oracle of 7:4–17 is, we might say, a place where we see David applying what he knows about God, and it is a place where he demonstrates little trust that God will actually do what he has promised. Second Samuel 7:18–29 begins with self-abasement, perhaps in an attempt to soothe God's anger over David's desire to build a temple,[84] but David then goes on to demand four times that God

23:1–7," *JBL* 90 (1971): 257–66 (259–60); McCarter, *II Samuel*, 480; Noll, *The Faces of David*, 160–61.

83. I read here with the MT rather than attempting to reconstruct a text on the basis of evidence from LXX^L (cf. McCarter, *II Samuel*, 478; Noll, *The Faces of David*, 167–68 n. 51), which does not correspond to the majority of the witnesses.

84. David begins his response to the oracle in 7:18–19 by suggesting that he and his house are of little weight in comparison with YHWH. Eslinger also argues that David begins this way in order to make up for his effrontery in trying to build a

establish the covenant that he has already promised (7:25, 29).[85] The phrase עד עולם appears six times in the chapter, and three of the occurrences are from David: one to flatter God by connecting the greatness of the divine name to the eternal covenant with David (7:26); one to wrongly refer to an eternal covenant that God has supposedly made with Israel (v. 24); and one in the context of his fourfold request that God actually establish the covenant that he has promised (v. 25), a context in which David also twice uses the word לעולם (v. 29). David may or may not know that God made and then dissolved an eternal covenant with the Elides, but he seems unsure that God will actually do what he has promised for his house. God has left the language of the punishment of David's house suspiciously vague in 7:14–15—he promises only that it will not meet the fate of complete removal as Saul's house did[86]—and, from encountering the story of the Elides, readers know, even if David does not, that עד עולם is not a promise that God binds himself to.[87] David's reading of history has left him suspicious as to how God will act. He may say to YHWH himself (cf. 2 Sam 22:1) that "the word of YHWH is pure (צרופה)" (22:31), in the sense of lacking any evil dross,[88] but in 2 Sam 7 he seems to know that this kind of claim, the claim that the master narrative makes, sometimes fails.

David's interpretation of history in places like 2 Sam 7:18–29 and 23:1–7 show that he is truly a man after God's own subversive heart. God tells Samuel right before David is anointed that God "looks to the heart" when he chooses kings (1 Sam 16:7), and this can be seen as pointing to David as a parallel figure for a God who sometimes subverts the system of justice, reward, and punishment that he has established.

temple, and also notes that David's self-abnegation here echoes YHWH's "belittling tone" earlier in 7:5, 8 (*House of God or House of David?*, 67–68). David, that is, quickly realizes his subordinate place as vassal, and follows his suzerain's lead in that regard.

85. David uses the imperatives of קום and עשׂה in 7:25 and יאל and ברך in 7:29. See Eslinger, *House of God or House of David?*, 65–68.

86. See ibid., 57–64.

87. Polzin (*Samuel and the Deuteronomist*, 44–49) argues that the fall of the Elides with their eternal covenant foreshadows that of the Davidides.

88. This part of the tricolon of 22:31 is sometimes taken as a later addition (e.g., McCarter, *II Samuel*, 469; Hertzberg, *I & II Samuel*, 390; Anderson, *2 Samuel*, 265), but there is no textual evidence for this. McCarter translates the final word as "refined silver," arguing that the metal here is simply implied (*II Samuel*, 469), but since the verb צרף is used to refer to the refining and purification of various types of metal in Biblical Hebrew, it is preferable to render only the passive participle in the translation.

One could argue that what David has learned from history, in short, is that God does not always act as the narrative says he does, and that justice is not always what the narrative claims it to be. Since God favors David, something that itself falls outside of justice as the narrative understands it, David can afford to act like God does, and his own anomistic acts parallel those of God and emphasize this subversion of the narrative's concepts of God and justice. Just as God at times sets aside the law in dealing with David, so David sets it aside when dealing with Amnon, whom he does not punish in any way for his rape of Tamar.[89] David's interest in protecting his own life by declaring that harming God's anointed is a crime reflects God's own interest in protecting his divine status, for we have seen how sensitive he is to appearing weak in the eyes of Israel and the nations. Of course, the self-interest of both here is manifested through actions that subvert the narrative; David simply invents a law or custom that benefits him, and God ignores the narrative's requirements for punishment when the divine reputation is at stake. He is one of God's favorites, even when such favoritism can be seen as subverting the master narrative's concepts of God and justice, and David seems to know this. What trauma will suggest in 2 Kgs 21–25, however, is that Israel, like Saul, is one of God's victims, a victimization that subverts these concepts as well.

89. The explanation for David's failure to punish Amnon in 2 Sam 13:21—"he would not punish his son Amnon because he loved him because he was his first-born"—is present in the LXX and 4QSam^{a}, but the MT has omitted it due to homoioarchton. The MT scribe skipped from ולא at the beginning of this section to the same word at the beginning of 13:22. See McCarter, *II Samuel*, 319–20.

Chapter 7

KINGS: THE END OF NARRATIVE

A. *Dtr's Master Narrative and Its Collapse in Kings*

1. *Introduction*

The narrative of the final book of the Deuteronomistic History continues the book of Samuel's focus on the failures of Israel's monarchy but, in a final coalescence of the two main themes, shows how this monarchy leads the people in the cultic disloyalty that explains the exilic community's trauma. The cultic influence of the monarchy is clear, and the results of its failures catastrophic, because they become Israel's failures: the kings of the North, and eventually of Judah, cause the people to sin in cultic disloyalty to their divine suzerain. Yet the narrative provides readers with one example of perfect repentance; Josiah undoes all of the cultic sins of his predecessors, acting as God commands in Deut 12 and imitating Moses' actions in Deut 9:21 towards the golden calf, and he alone in Dtr reads the law "in the ears" of the people (2 Kgs 23:2) as Moses commanded (Deut 31:11). Of all the characters in the History, he alone is said to said to act in loyalty to God "with all his heart and with all his soul and with all his might" as Moses had commanded (2 Kgs 23:25; cf. Deut 6:5),[1] and the narrative presents his perfect cultic actions—his repentance (שׁוב), as 23:25 calls his reforms—as leadership done "according to all of the law of Moses" (23:25). His perfect cultic loyalty in his repentance is interpreted as perfect nomistic loyalty as well.

Nor is Josiah the only king lauded by the master narrative. Hezekiah also carries out a religious reformation praised by the narrative, and, just as no king compares to Josiah in his act of repentance (23:25), Hezekiah is incomparable among the monarchs for his trust in God. The master

1. See Friedman, *The Exile and Biblical Narrative*, 5–10 and Steven L. McKenzie, *The Trouble with Kings: The Composition of the Book of Kings in the Deuteronomistic History* (VTSup 42; Leiden: Brill, 1991), 129.

narrative places the notice of his cultic reform (2 Kgs 18:3–4) next to the one concerning his trust—"he trusted in YHWH the God of Israel, so that after him there was none like him among all the kings of Judah, nor among those who were before him" (18:5)[2]—but the clearest proof of his trust is in his response to the Assyrian's threat of a siege of Jerusalem. When the Rabshakeh arrives to speak for the Assyrian king and negotiate for the surrender of the city, he ridicules trust (בטח) in the power of Egypt to save in 18:19–21, 24, and then in the power of YHWH (18:28–30, 32b–35). He refers, in fact, specifically to Hezekiah's correct cultic reforms as one of the reasons why YHWH will not save Jerusalem (v. 22); the fact that YHWH does deliver Jerusalem in this narrative shows, of course, that this cultic loyalty is precisely what God wants to see.[3] The master narrative's point is that perfect trust by Israel's leader has led to right cultic action which has led to divine protection.[4] In fact, the Rabshakeh's use of "Thus says the great king, the king of Assyria" (so 18:19, with variations in 18:29, 31) contrasts with Isaiah's use of "Thus says YHWH" in 19:6, 20, 32; 20:5. Hezekiah trusts in the true suzerain who can deliver Jerusalem and in his true prophet, and his deliverance proves that "you, YHWH, are God alone" (19:19).

These and other royal success, however, do not prevent the exiles' trauma. The narrative's focus on Saul and David in Samuel prepares readers for the focus on the monarchs in Kings. The monarchy that Israel chose is now in charge of Israel's cultic life; by the end of Kings it will make Israel "like all the nations," although not in the sense that Israel intended when it asked for a king in 1 Sam 8. The control that the monarchy exercises over the nation's cultic life is what ultimately explains the exiles' trauma, the narrative argues, for Manasseh causes Judah to sin, and so we can see why the narrative has made leadership failures one of its two main themes throughout the History. The narrative's presentation of the kings in the North, all of whom cause the people to sin, explains the siege, destruction, and exile that Samaria and the North

2. This incomparability statement may seem to contradict the one given to Josiah in 2 Kgs 23:25, where his repentance is said to exceed that of any king before or after him, but, as Gary Knoppers and other scholars point out, the issues on which Hezekiah and Josiah are compared are different. For Hezekiah, the issue is trust, and the bulk of the narrative devoted to his reign is about trust in God during the Assyrian siege. For Josiah, on the other hand, the narrative focuses on his cultic repentance and the perfection with which he executes it. See Knoppers, '"There Was None Like Him'"; Gerbrandt, *Kingship According to the Deuteronomistic History*, 53.

3. See Robert L. Cohn, *2 Kings* (BO; Collegeville, Minn.: Liturgical, 2000), 130–31.

4. For this as the point of the story, see Sweeney, *I & II Kings*, 409, 417.

suffer as a precursor to the trauma of 586. The Davidides in the South are not perfect, but they do not cause the people to commit apostasy until the reign of Manasseh, and this failure of leadership dooms Judah and is the final part of the narrative's explanation of the exilic community's trauma. Our examination of the narrative's presentation of Solomon, which opens the narrative of Kings, shows that while he is far from a perfect leader, and while he actually builds high places for his wives, he does not cause the people to sin there. His actions warrant the continued punishment of David's house that God promised and began in 2 Samuel, but his sin is qualitatively different than that of all of the Northern kings and of Manasseh. Only when the people sin under the influence of the kings whom they have chosen does God punish them, and Solomon's sin helps to throw this narrative explanation of trauma into relief.

It is not clear, however, how the narrative deals with the eternal covenant with the Davidides which, unlike the eternal covenant with the Elides, is never explicitly annulled. There is a striking lack of narrative clarity at the close of the History on this and a number of other issues, including God's failure to acknowledge Josiah's repentance, the delay of punishment until decades after Josiah's reforms, and the significance of 2 Kgs 25:27–30, which reports that Jehoiachin is released from prison. In a narrative that means to explain the exiles' trauma on the basis of a logic in history that claims that vassal disloyalty leads to destruction, there are some glaring narrative gaps at the culmination of that explanation. The narrative does not explain why the disloyal generations of Manasseh's 55 year apostate reign (and of the 19 years between his death and Josiah's reforms) are not punished for the sin that he, Amon, and even Josiah for the first part of his reign cause them to commit, even though that sin was worse than that of the Canaanites; why Josiah's repentance, which reinstitutes the nation's loyalty to God, is not rewarded; nor what future awaits the exilic community and its deposed Davidic king. Moses' insistence in Deuteronomy that each generation must make the same decision for loyalty to God indicates that, for the narrative, the same logic that explains the exiles' trauma consistently underlies history, yet what future the exiles can expect is ambiguous to say the least. There is no scholarly consensus as to what the narrative communicates about this in 2 Kgs 25:27–30. Martin Noth believed that these verses' report is notable for the lack of hope that it foresees in the future, while Gerhard von Rad saw the History's narrative communicating a glimmer of hope for Israel's future return to the land.[5] A third

5. Noth, *The Deuteronomistic History*, 97–98 and Gerhard von Rad, *Studies in Deuteronomy* (trans. David Stalker; SBT 9; London: SCM, 1953), 90–91.

and mediating position is that of Hans Walter Wolff, who argued that the Deuteronomistic History is clear in its insistence that repentance must precede return from exile, although his analysis of the History's end concludes merely that "God is still acting for his people,"[6] and that there is no specific hope at the end of the History since there is no account of repentance among the exiles. This scholarly ambiguity in interpretation, as we shall see, is simply a reflection of the ambiguity that trauma introduces to seal off a conclusive final word of the History's narrative. At the end of Kings, narrative explanation collapses into the ambiguity of traumatic anti-narrative. We will, of course, have much more to say about these and other traumatic subversions of the narrative in section B, but, unlike the previous chapters, I will begin to discuss these main traumatic subversions of the narrative in section A. Second Kings 21–25 is so central to the narrative's ultimate explanation of the exilic community's trauma that we need to see how trauma puts an end to the narrative's totalizing certainty at this key point before exploring other ways trauma subverts the narrative.

2. *Solomon's Failures*

As the narrative moves from the founding of the Davidic dynasty in Samuel to the succession of Solomon, the story of the latter's consolidation of power and construction of the temple might seem to herald at least a brief "Golden Age"[7] in Israel. The narrative will blame the Davidides' loss of the kingdom on Solomon's marriages to foreign women and the inevitable apostasy that thereby results in 1 Kgs 11. Solomon thus does not live up to his father's cultic perfection, but he does at least construct the temple, a great cultic success. This apparent bifurcation of his reign often leads scholars to see a narrative that has its main structural division between 1 Kgs 1–10 and the apostasy of 1 Kgs 11.[8] The narrative of his reign, however, is not so simply structured. There is a "muted subtheme" of royal failure in the opening chapters of the Solomon narrative, as

6. Hans Walter Wolff, "The Kerygma of the Deuteronomic Historical Work," trans. Frederick C. Prussner in *The Vitality of Old Testament Traditions* (ed. Walter Brueggemann; Atlanta: John Knox, 1982), 83–100; quote from p. 99.

7. This is the term that David Jobling uses to describe 1 Kgs 3–10 (since he sees negative comments on Solomon's reign only in 1 Kgs 2 and 11). See his '"Forced Labor': Solomon's Golden Age and the Question of Literary Representation," in *Poststructuralism as Exegesis* (ed. David Jobling and Stephen D. Moore; Semeia 54; Atlanta: Scholars Press, 1992), 57–76 (60).

8. So Marc Brettler, "The Structure of 1 Kings 1–11," *JSOT* 49 (1991): 87–97 (87).

Richard Nelson puts it,[9] a description that some studies of the structure of 1 Kgs 1–11 have made more specific.[10]

We need not discuss the details of the structure of 1 Kgs 1–11 here; I merely wish to point to the fact that the narrative provides readers with warnings early on in the narrative of Solomon's reign that he is not a perfect monarch, but is as flawed a leader as his father. Indications of his imperfections, in fact, are available very early on in 1 Kgs 1–11, as Jerome Walsh points out. The notice of his marriage to Pharaoh's daughter in 3:1–3, for example, uses the verb חתן in the Hithpael, which the biblical writers always employ pejoratively for marriages, in order to foreshadow Solomon's apostasy of 1 Kgs 11;[11] in 4:1–5:8 [ET 4:1–28] Solomon taxes the North but not Judah, and this passage also suggests that the forced labor he raises in 5:27–32 [ET 13–18] is a burden placed exclusively on the North.[12] The attention paid to Solomon's construction of his own palace in ch. 7 while he appears negligent in building the temple,[13] to his ceding of Israelite land to a foreign power in 9:10–14, to the notice that he employed Canaanites left in the land as forced labor (מס)[14]—a virtual repetition of the notices of Judg 1 that the narrative of Judg 2–3 uses to explain the apostasy of the Israelites upon their settlement in the land—all subtly prepare readers for his cultic failure in 11:1–8. Indeed, Brettler's observation that 9:26–11:10 draws close parallels between the prohibitions in Deut 17:14–20 on the king's ability to

9. Richard D. Nelson, *First and Second Kings* (Interpretation; Louisville: John Knox, 1987), 42.

10. See Brettler, "The Structure of 1 Kings 1–11"; John W. Olley, "Pharaoh's Daughter, Solomon's Palace, and the Temple: Another Look at the Structure of 1 Kings 1–11," *JSOT* 27 (2003): 355–69; Amos Frisch, "Structure and Significance: The Narrative of Solomon's Reign (1 Kings 1–12:24)," *JSOT* 51 (1991): 3–14; Jerome T. Walsh, *1 Kings* (BO; Collegeville, Minn.: Liturgical, 1996), 150–56; Kim Parker, "Repetition as a Structuring Device in 1 Kings 1–11," *JSOT* 42 (1988): 19–27; and David Williams, "Once Again: The Structure of the Narrative of Solomon's Reign," *JSOT* 86 (1999): 49–66.

11. Jerome T. Walsh, "The Characterization of Solomon in First Kings 1–5," *CBQ* 57 (1995): 471–93 (486); see pp. 482–92 for the details of the negative portrayals of Solomon in 1 Kgs 1–5.

12. Ibid., 489, 492.

13. A number of scholars point to the fact that the notice in 3:1–3 that Solomon and the people sacrifice at the high places because Solomon had not yet built the temple implicitly criticizes his failure still to have not yet built the temple. See, e.g., Siebert, *Subversive Scribes*, 161–64; Iain W. Provan, *1 and 2 Kings* (NIBC; Peabody, Mass.: Hendrickson, 1995), 45.

14. Judg 1:28, 30, 33, 35 also use the term מס to describe the role of the remaining Canaanites in Israel.

acquire excessive horses, wives, and wealth[15] demonstrates that Solomon has already shown himself ready to forego the nomistic loyalty he owes his divine sovereign, and thus readers should be unsurprised when he displays cultic disloyalty in 1 Kgs 11. Marvin Sweeney argues that the law of the king in Deut 17:14–20 seems to have been composed with the censure of Solomon in mind: Solomon acquires many wives who turn him away from loyalty to God (1 Kgs 11:1–8; cf. Deut 17:17); he has many chariots that he receives from Egypt (1 Kgs 10:26–29; cf. Deut 17:16); and he has much gold and silver (1 Kgs 10:1–27; cf. Deut 17:17). His cultic sin in regard to the high places results in the establishment of the Northern Kingdom and its idolatry, and, argues Sweeney, the narrative presents him as Josiah's foil.[16]

So despite Solomon's construction of the temple in 1 Kgs 6, the divine wisdom he receives and uses in 1 Kgs 3, and the prosperous state of Israel during his reign (4:20), his failures, and most especially his cultic failure in 1 Kgs 11, provide readers with a cautionary note in regard to his leadership. Gary Knoppers's argument that Solomon's reign is the "apex of Israelite history" in Dtr's narrative, most particularly in his construction of the temple,[17] overestimates somewhat his position in the narrative's hierarchy of behavior. His cultic and nomistic failures make him a worse leader than his father, further justifying God's proclamation of the eternal punishment of the house in 2 Sam 12:10. As important and influential for the history of Israel and the Davidides as Solomon's construction of the temple is for the narrative, the high places Solomon establishes in 1 Kgs 11:1–8 are equally so. The two main themes of the narrative appear in this story, not to mention the distinctly Deuteronomistic motif of intermarriage leading to apostasy: Solomon constructs the high places for his foreign wives and sacrifices to their gods (11:1–8); this cultic infidelity in and of itself is understood by God as a rejection of "my covenant and my statutes" (11:11); and this failure of Israel's leader causes the split of the kingdom that results in further and worse apostate leadership in the North. There is no reference in God's condemnation of Solomon to the other sins that the previous chapters document; 11:10 specifies only that YHWH had commanded Solomon "about this matter, not to go after other gods."

15. For specific parallels between Deut 17:14–20 and 1 Kgs 9:26–11:10, see Brettler, "The Structure of 1 Kings 1–11," 90–95.

16. Marvin A. Sweeney, "The Critique of Solomon in the Josianic Edition of the Deuteronomistic History," *JBL* 114 (1995): 607–22 (615–17, 621–22); idem, *King Josiah of Judah*, 93–96.

17. Knoppers, *Two Nations Under God*, 1:59–60, 121–22.

His apostasy results in the Davidides' loss of the kingdom—they retain only Judah as a "fief" (ניר)[18]—and only once Josiah destroys Solomon's high places is he able to re-enter the land of the Northern tribes of which the Davidides were stripped as punishment (see 2 Kgs 23:13–15).[19] Sweeney's argument that the narrative portrays Solomon as the "quintessential example of monarchic rule" in the most negative sense[20] does not really work given the narrative's more negative evaluations of Ahab and Manasseh,[21] but the narrative does portray Solomon with ambivalence. The cultic loyalty and leadership Solomon manifests in the construction of the temple is greatly compromised in the narrative's eyes by his construction of high places, which leads to the loss of the North and its apostasy and eventual destruction. This, of course, is why the oracles warning of punishment of the Davidides, oracles that refer to God's warning in 2 Sam 7:14 that God will punish David's son when he is disobedient, occur within the narrative of his reign (1 Kgs 2:3–4; 8:25; 9:4–5). These three passages warn of a potential loss of "the throne of Israel/your kingdom" for the crime of apostasy, and this is precisely what happens. As Baruch Halpern argues, these conditional statements deal with the schism in the kingdom following Solomon's reign, not with the exile. The narrative makes clear at places like 1 Kgs 11:11–13, 31–36 that God plans on taking the kingdom from Solomon's son and giving it to Jeroboam, whom God calls "king over Israel" in 11:37 (and cf. 12:20). After Solomon is said to sit on "the throne of Israel" in 1 Kgs 1:46; 10:9, the phrase is used later in Dtr only for Northern kings (2 Kgs 10:30; 15:12). His apostasy does indeed result in the loss of the "throne" and "kingdom" as God promises, leaving the Davidides with only a fief.[22] These events fit as well with the eternal (עד עולם) punishment of the house that God promised David in 2 Sam 12:10, for they continue it. The narrative suggests that for David's son,

18. For this translation of ניר, see Ben Zvi, "Once the Lamp Has Been Kindled…" Since the word means "cultivated land" in Mishnaic Hebrew, and since this meaning fits the appearance of the word in non-Deuteronomistic passages, the sense of "fief" would seem the most likely translation.

19. On this, see Knoppers, "'There Was None like Him,'" 428–29; idem, *Two Nations Under God*, 2:195.

20. Sweeney, *King Josiah of Judah*, 176.

21. The narrative describes Ahab as doing "more to provoke YHWH, the God of Israel, than all the kings of Israel who were before him" (1 Kgs 16:33) and Manasseh as doing "more evil than the Amorites did who were before him" (2 Kgs 21:11), so by comparison, Solomon is not as evil as they are. We will have more to say below about the kinds of evil the narrative sees kings as committing.

22. Halpern, *The First Historians*, 157–74.

as for David himself, punishment is necessary to temper the grant of an eternal dynasty. While Solomon does not directly lead the people in apostasy, his failure in cultic loyalty causes the establishment of the first Northern dynasty, which promotes the worship of other gods, an act of cultic disloyalty that all the rest of the Northern kings and dynasties will continue. As in Judges and Samuel, there is little narrative focus on the necessity of nomistic loyalty in Kings, for while the narrative presents Solomon as disobeying non-cultic laws from Deuteronomy, particularly in his leadership in allowing Canaanites to remain alive in the land and his flagrant disregard for the Law of the King of Deut 17, it passes no judgment in that regard, explicitly directing readers' attention only to his cultic lapses. The narrative presents Solomon, like his father, as an Israelite leader with many flaws, but David has at least never failed in his cultic loyalty to the divine suzerain. This failure on Solomon's part strips Israel from the control of the Davidides; only once Josiah destroys Solomon's apostate high places do we see the Davidides return to the North (2 Kgs 23:13–20).[23] First Kings 11:11–13, 31–36 suggest that only the eternal covenant with David prevents the Davidides' complete loss of power.

3. *The Failures of the Northern Monarchy and People*

The History's narrative of the North during the Divided Monarchy focuses even more forcefully and clearly than the story of Solomon on the two main themes of the failures of cultic loyalty and leadership. In structure it shares similarities with the cyclical narrative of the judges, as David Jobling notes, for in the North the narrative presents a cycle of dynasties and individual monarchs that God raises up to rule Israel.[24] As in Judges, foreign invasion continues to punish cultic disloyalty, culminating with the final invasion that will destroy the North,[25] and in 2 Kgs 13:1–6 we even see a repetition of the typical language that the narrative uses in the cycle of apostasy in Judges.[26] This tells readers that, despite

23. So also ibid., 154–55 and Knoppers, *Two Nations Under God*, 2:68–69, 195.

24. David Jobling, "The Salvation of Israel in 'The Book of the Divided Kingdoms', or, Was there any 'Fall of the Northern Kingdom?,'" in *Redirected Travel: Alternative Journeys and Places in Biblical Studies* (ed. Roland Boer and Edgar W. Conrad; JSOTSup 382; London: T&T Clark International, 2003), 50–61 (56–58).

25. For the invasions in the context of the cultic sins of Israel and Judah and their kings, see 1 Kgs 14:22–26; 20:1–34; 2 Kgs 6:8–23; 6:24–7:20; 13:1–6, 22–24; 15:19, 29; 17:1–23; 24:1–4, 8–17; 25:1–26.

26. As in Judges, the "evil in the eyes of YHWH" (13:2) leads to a foreign invasion (v. 3), a call for divine intervention without repentance (v. 4), and a "savior" who delivers Israel (v. 5). Assumedly, however, the savior is Joash, who does not

Jehu's elimination of Ahab's Baalism in 2 Kgs 10, the situation in the North with poor leadership, even it if is better leadership than Ahab and his house could offer, still makes Israel no better than it was with no leadership at all. As we saw in the narrative of Judges, once Israel's disloyalty makes it like the nations it was supposed to annihilate, the nation itself can become the means of its own punishment in civil war, and the narrative of Kings is full of references to wars between Israel and Judah in the midst of the sin of the people.[27] Unlike the narrative in Judges, however, we never hear of the people crying out to God because of war and foreign invasion. Once Israel makes the choice for the monarchy, in fact, we hear little at all about the people. The narrative's focus on Saul and David in Samuel has prepared readers for the narrative's conclusion in Kings that it is the monarchy that the people have chosen that becomes responsible for Israel's cultic life, and that it is the kings who lead the people to disaster. It is ultimately the cultic disloyalty in which the kings lead the people that explains the exilic community's trauma in the narrative.

It has long been clear that the "sin(s) of Jeroboam," which Frank Cross identified as one of the major themes of Kings, is the focus of the narrative's negative evaluation of the kings of the North. In announcing to Jeroboam that he will receive the kingdom of which the Davidides have been deprived because of Solomon's sin, God promises Jeroboam a "sure house" (1 Kgs 11:38)—that is, an enduring dynasty—just as God had promised one to David (2 Sam 7:16), so long as Jeroboam acts like David (11:29–39). However, the narrative concludes that Jeroboam's construction of "two calves of gold," along with their new sanctuaries, festivals, and priests "was a sin, and the people went before the one at Bethel and before the one as far as Dan" (12:30). The narrative interprets Jeroboam's actions as amounting to making "other gods" (14:9), and notes that he did this specifically to stop the people of the North from worshiping in Jerusalem (12:26–27). And because no Northern king ever removes Jeroboam's shrines and calves, "the sin that Jeroboam sinned and that he caused Israel to sin (ואשׁר החטיא את־ישׂראל)" (14:16) becomes the basis of the narrative's evaluations of the Northern monarchs. In this replication of the idolatry that the Israelites committed with the golden

appear until 13:10, after the reign of Jehoahaz (13:1–9), in the narration of whose reign 13:1–6 appears. It is Joash who defeats Aram (13:22–25), the nation sent by God to oppress Israel in 13:3. See Sweeney, *I & II Kings*, 355.

27. For the wars between Israel and Judah, see 1 Kgs 14:30; 15:6, 16–22; 2 Kgs 13:12; 14:1–14; 15:37–16:9. Note also 1 Kgs 16:17, which refers to a civil war within Israel.

calf in the wilderness (Deut 9:8–10:11) and that Micah and the tribe of Dan commit in the land (Judg 17–18),[28] readers see the beginning of the realization of the prophecy of the nation's destruction found in Deut 4:25–31, the first passage in Dtr's narrative to warn of the consequences of apostate idolatry. Only now do readers truly see what God meant when he told Samuel that a choice for a king was a choice against divine leadership (1 Sam 8:7–8). The people want a king so that they can be "like all the nations" (1 Sam 8:5, 20) and, by the time of the exile of the North, they have become precisely that. In their apostasy, "they sacrificed on every high place *like the nations* whom YHWH exiled from before them" (2 Kgs 17:11), "they walked in the statutes *of the nations*" (v. 8), and "they rejected his [YHWH's] statutes and his covenant…and they went…*after the nations* who were around them" (v. 15). By demanding a king, Israel wished to be like the nations; the kings, ironically, have made them so.

Technically, the narrative distinguishes between the sins of the monarchs and the sins of the people, but states that the kings of the North have compelled the people to sin—hence the causative use of חטא—something that goes far beyond a merely personal transgression on the part of the individual monarchs. A clear example of the way in which the narrative emphasizes the distinction between the power of the monarch to affect the cultic lives of his subjects and the guilt that the people bear for actually committing the sins that the Northern kings have forced upon them is 2 Kgs 17:7–23. Second Kings 17:7–18 explains why God found it necessary to punish the North with exile, and these verses find cause in the wrongful cultic actions in which the Northerners had been engaged for the past 200 years. Verses 21–23 provide a summary of the cultic history of the Northern Kingdom, and explain its collapse this way: "Jeroboam drove Israel from after YHWH, and he caused them to sin a great sin (והחטיאםחטאה גדולה). And the Israelites walked in all the sins of Jeroboam, which he did; they did not turn aside from it until YHWH

28. The construction of a calf (or calves) made out of gold in Deut 9:8–10:11 and 1 Kgs 12:28–29 is an obvious parallel. We can also see a parallel with Micah's idol in Judg 17–18 that the tribe of Dan steals. Both Micah and Jeroboam appoint false priests (cf. Judg 18:30 and 1 Kgs 12:31), and both create an idol that ends up in Dan (cf. Judg 18:30–31 and 1 Kgs 12:29). See Nadav Na'aman, "The Danite Campaign Northward (Judges xvii–xviii) and the Migration of the Phocaeans to Massalia (Strabo iv 1,4)," *VT* 55 (2005): 47–60 (48–51). Moreover, the term מסכה/ות "molten image/s" appears in Dtr only to refer to the sin of Jeroboam (1 Kgs 14:19; 2 Kgs 17:16) and Micah's idol (Judg 17:3, 4; 18:14, 17, 18). See E. Theodore Mullen, Jr., "The Sins of Jeroboam: A Redactional Assessment," *CBQ* 49 (1987): 212–32 (214 n. 5).

turned them aside from before him." As in 2 Kgs 17:21, the verb חטא appears in the Hiphil in the evaluation of every king in the North, with only two exceptions.[29] The narrative refers to "the sin(s) of Jeroboam" in the evaluations of fourteen of the nineteen Northern kings.[30] When it comes to describing the sin of the kings of Israel, the narrative clearly lets readers know that the sin of Jeroboam, which every succeeding king commits, has the effect of causing the people to sin. This is true even of Zimri (1 Kgs 16:19), who reigns only seven days and who founds no dynasty; the appearance of this evaluation even for his reign speaks to its importance in the narrative's cultic interpretation of history and its understanding of the sin and punishment of the Northern monarchs. This also speaks to a development of the narrative's theme of leadership in Israel, for while past leaders' sins had impacted the nation negatively—Joshua's covenant with Gibeon, for example, or Gideon's ephod, which he used to lead Israel in idolatry—Israel's cultic life is now presented as uncompromisingly under the control of the monarchs. The monarchs may be the cause of the sin, but because they control the nation's cultic life, Israel will suffer the consequences. In the absence of royal leadership in Judg 17–21, "everyone did what was right in their own eyes"; in Kings, poor royal leadership in the North only leads to Israel doing what is right in the eyes of the monarchs.

This explanation for the destruction of the North is a clear exposition of the narrative's logic in history and its two main themes that point to the results of the people's failures in loyalty and the contributions of the leaders of Israel to that failure. Second Kings 17:7–23 mainly explains the siege, destruction, and exile of Samaria and the North that foreshadow the exile of 586, but 17:19–20 directly points readers in the Babylonian exile to their own trauma that is to follow only eight chapters later. As poor as Solomon's cultic choice is at the end of his reign, he

29. It appears for the evaluations of Jeroboam (1 Kgs 14:16); Nadab (15:30); Baasha (15:34; 16:2); Elah (16:13); Zimri (16:19); Omri (16:26); Ahab (21:22); Ahaziah (22:52); Jehoram (2 Kgs 3:3); Jehu (10:29, 31); Jehoahaz (13:2); Jehoash (13:11); Jeroboam II (14:24); Zechariah (15:9); Menahem (15:18); Pekahiah (15:24); and Pekah (15:28). The only two Northern kings for whom the History does not use חטא in the Hiphil are Shallum, who reigns only one month, and Hoshea, the last king in the North. The narrative says nothing, however, to suggest that they did not continue Jeroboam's sin.

30. Jeroboam (1 Kgs 14:16); Nadab (15:30); Baasha (15:34); Omri (16:26); Ahab (16:31); Jehoram (2 Kgs 3:3); Jehu (10:29, 31); Jehoahaz (13:2); Jehoash (13:11); Jeroboam II (14:24); Zechariah (15:9); Menahem (15:18); Pekahiah (15:24); and Pekah (15:28).

never causes the people to sin. His cultic failure is not cultic leadership. While his high places result in further punishment of the Davidides, Solomon does not force the people to join his wives in their worship of foreign gods; because it does not affect the people, they are not punished along with his family. It is the consistently poor leadership of the North that dooms its population. In only one case in Kings are the people said to take the lead in cultic disloyalty, and that occurs in Judah in 1 Kgs 14:22–24[31] and is immediately punished in 14:25–26 with foreign invasion, precisely the pattern that the narrative in Judges has conditioned readers to expect. While it is the people here who do "evil in the eyes of YHWH" with their apostasy, just as they did in Judges (Judg 2:11–13; 3:7, 12; 4:1; 6:1; 10:6; 13:1), from now on it is the kings, who are in charge of Israel's cultic life, who will be said to do "evil in the eyes of YHWH" (1 Kgs 11:6; 15:26, 34; 16:19, 25, 30; 22:52; 2 Kgs 3:2; 8:18, 27; 13:2, 11; 14:24; 15:9, 18, 24, 28; 17:2; 21:2, 20; 23:32, 37; 24:9); leadership of the kings, in short, is often no better than Israel is without leadership. According to the narrative's logic that explains the exilic community's trauma, when the people sin they are punished, even when that sin is caused by their leaders. Perhaps if Samuel had properly warned Israel of this possibility when Israel demanded a king this eventuality could have been avoided, but he failed to do so. As we have seen in Judges, however, the narrative does not suggest that a leaderless Israel is a viable alternative, and this is true also in Kings. When the people of Judah of their own accord erect apostate institutions in 1 Kgs 14:22–24, Asa undoes this damage that Rehoboam and Abijam tolerated (15:11–13)[32]—this, the narrative suggests, is precisely the leadership the people need, but of which they have far too little.

31. This reads with the MT of 14:22 ("Judah did evil in the eyes of YHWH") rather than with the LXX and the textual witnesses to 2 Chr 12:14, which attribute the evil to Rehoboam. Because this is the only place in Kings where the people and not a king is the subject of the phrase, the MT has the more difficult reading. And even the LXX uses plural verb forms in 14:23–24 when describing the apostasy that was committed, rather than the singular verb forms we would expect if only one person were responsible for the sin, which suggests that the scribe altered 14:22 to conform to the standard formula in Kings of the monarchs' leadership in cultic loyalty.

32. Asa's reform, in fact, anticipates that of Josiah (Sweeney, *I & II Kings*, 193). It is interesting that the narrative says that Asa "did what was just in the eyes of YHWH like David his father" (15:11), even while it claims that Asa's reforms did not eliminate the high places. Like David, he is not perfect, but also like David he does not permit non-Yahwistic worship on the part of the people.

4. *The Failures of Judah and the Future of Israel*

The narrative's logic in history is clear enough in the way that the narrative explains the destruction of the North. By the time we reach the end of the History and the ultimate explanation for the exilic community's own trauma, however, the narrative certainty that God punishes sinful generations for their disloyalty, even the disloyalty that the monarchy causes them to commit, has been subverted by ambiguity, and in this part of the chapter we will investigate this traumatic ambiguity alongside of our investigation of the master narrative's presentation of the Judean monarchy. Why does God not punish the sinful generations during the 55 years of Manasseh's reign, or even during the 19 years between his death and Josiah's reforms, since during this time their sin exceeds that even of the Canaanites?[33] Why does God pointedly ignore Josiah's perfect act of repentance, since he returns Judah to cultic loyalty, but instead punish the nation when it is more than a generation removed from the sin that the nation was forced to commit?[34] Will the eternal covenant with David guarantee salvation for the exilic community in a return to the land or not? We begin with this last point of ambiguity, since it involves a discussion of the first two as well.

It is clear in the narrative of the Northern kings that the fact that they cause the people to act in cultic disloyalty to their suzerain explains the destruction of the North, not to mention the annihilation or, at least, the removal from power of the Northern dynasties. As I have argued elsewhere, comparing the fate of the Northern dynasties (rather than the fate of the individual kings who found no royal house) to that of the Davidides provides readers with a number of templates that they can use to make sense of the future that awaits Judah's royal house after the exile.[35] Of the five dynasties who rule in the North—those of Jeroboam, Baasha, Ahab, Jehu, and Menahem—all of them continue the sin of

33. The narrative does not tell readers when Manasseh began his cultic reforms, and even leaves open the possibility that he caused Judah to sin for the full 55 years of his reign (2 Kgs 21:1). The apostasy that he causes Judah to sin continues during the two-year reign of Amon (21:19–22) and for the first 17 years of Josiah's reign, since he does not begin his reforms until his eighteenth year (22:1–3).

34. Josiah enacts his perfect cultic reform in his eighteenth year as king (22:1–3), and there is no further reference to any Judean king causing the people to sin. It thus appears as if Judah lives in cultic loyalty to God for the last 13 years of Josiah's 31-year reign as well as for the 22 years between his death and the destruction of Jerusalem (see 23:31, 36; 24:8, 18 for the length of the reigns of the last four Judean kings), or 35 years in total. We will discuss this issue at more length below.

35. David Janzen, "An Ambiguous Ending: Dynastic Punishment in Kings and the Fate of the Davidides in 2 Kings 25:27–30," *JSOT* 33 (2008): 39–58.

Jeroboam, and God wipes out all of the males of the first three (see 1 Kgs 14:7–11; 15:29; 16:1–4, 11–13; 20:21–24; 2 Kgs 9:7–10; 10:1–14) and permanently removes Jehu's house from power so that it cannot rule again (2 Kgs 10:30; 15:12). Neither fate is said to befall the house of Menahem (2 Kgs 15:17–26), but since it is removed from power only 29 years before the Northern exile, it obviously does not rule again. Yet, in our present discussion of what the narrative does or does not signal about the fate of the Davidides following the exile, we cannot simply assume that because Manasseh has also caused Judah to sin that David's house will be treated like the Northern dynasties. The Davidides potentially pose an exception to the logic that the narrative applies to the disloyal Northern houses, since God has promised David an eternal dynasty. If David's descendants will always reign in Jerusalem, then they must have a country—or at least a fief—to reign over, so if this eternal promise holds true for them it should also hold true for Judah. At key points in the narrative where the rule of the Davidides might seem to warrant their removal from power—when Solomon first sins (1 Kgs 11:36), when three consecutive Davidides do evil (15:4–5), and in the midst of the reigns of two Davidides who are compared to Ahab (2 Kgs 8:19)—the narrative states that God, "because of David," had given the Davidides a ניר "fief" forever.[36] In the last of these cases, in fact, the narrative says that "YHWH was not willing to destroy Judah because of David," thus linking the eternal covenant with the Davidides to the continued existence of their fief. The History concludes, however, with the destruction of Jerusalem and the Davidide Jehoiachin in exile. Clearly, one way to make sense of 2 Kgs 25 is simply to conclude that God annulled the eternal covenant with David's house, since Manasseh not only causes Judah to sin as all of the Northern kings caused Israel to sin, but makes their sin worse than even that of the Canaanites (2 Kgs 21:9), meaning that the evil he forces the people to commit exceeds that of the North, which, the narrative says, only equaled that of the Canaanites (17:8, 15). In fact, Manasseh is the first and only Davidide who is the subject of the verb חטא in the Hiphil in the History (21:11, 16).

Having concluded that the sin of Judah is now even worse than that of the Canaanites, the narrative states that the sin that Manasseh caused the nation to sin explains the destruction of Judah and Jerusalem and the exilic community's trauma (2 Kgs 21:11–15; 23:26–27; 24:2–4), and we

36. The reference to a ניר appears in all three of these passages; for the translation of ניר as "fief," see Ben Zvi, "Once the Lamp Has Been Kindled." Only 1 Kgs 11:36 and 2 Kgs 8:19 specifically state that YHWH had told David that his descendants would be given this fief כל הימים "forever."

have thus arrived at the explanatory culmination of the master narrative. Israel chose the monarchy, the monarchy caused the cultic disloyalty of the North and of Judah, and destruction resulted. This explanation of the trauma, however, seems to have left a number of important elements in the narrative unaccounted for, most notably the eternal covenant with David, which the narrative never reports that God annuls, and the hope that the possibility of the continuation of this covenant provides to Judah in exile. For some scholars the conclusion to the History in 2 Kgs 25:27–30, where Evil-Merodach releases Jehoiachin from prison and allows him to eat at the royal table, combined with the eternal promise to David, suggests hope for the exiles' future.[37] God has promised to establish the throne of the kingdom of David's son, as well as David's house and kingdom, עד עולם "forever" (1 Sam 7:13, 16). God does reserve the right to rebuke David's son (v. 14), but says that divine חסד will not be removed from him as it was from Saul (v. 15). We have seen in the narrative that God can make and then break eternal covenants, for God responds to the sins of the Elides by declaring, "Indeed I said, 'Your house and the house of your father will go about before me forever (עד עולם),' but now—the oracle of YHWH—far be it from me" (1 Sam 2:30), yet we find no such explicit negation of the eternal covenant with David.

However, in response to Manasseh's sin, God does condemn Judah and the Davidides by stating that "I will stretch over Jerusalem the measuring line for Samaria and the plummet for the house of Ahab" (2 Kgs 21:13). This appears to be a double condemnation: what happened to Samaria will happen to Jerusalem; and what happened to the house of Ahab (see God's promise to annihilate all male members of Ahab's house in 1 Kgs 20:21–24 and 2 Kgs 9:7–10 and its fulfillment in 2 Kgs 10:1–14) will happen to the house of David. Because a Davidide causes the people to sin, both dynasty and people will be punished. One

37. While not phrasing his approach to 25:27–30 in precisely this way, von Rad believed that the promise to David held out hope for the future, and others agree with his more optimistic interpretation of these verses. For such interpretations, see the citations in Murray, "Of All the Years," 245 n. 5; see also Christof Hardmeier, "King Josiah in the Climax of the Deuteronomic History (2 Kings 22–23) and the Pre-Deuteronomic Document of a Cult Reform at the Place of Residence (23:4–15): Criticism of Sources, Reconstruction of Literary Pre-Stages and the Theology of History in 2 Kings 22–23," in Grabbe, ed., *Good Kings and Bad Kings*, 123–63 (141–42); Rainer Albertz, "Wer waren die Deuteronomisten? Das historische Rätsel einer literarischen Hypothese," *ET* 57 (1997): 319–38 (325); Halpern, *The First Historians*, 158; John Gray, *I & II Kings: A Commentary* (2d ed.; OTL; Philadelphia: Westminster, 1970), 773.

could interpret 21:13 as God's rejection of the unconditional covenant; on the other hand, however, the Davidides are not completely wiped out as the house of Ahab was, since Jehoiachin remains alive in exile. Isaiah's prophecy of 2 Kgs 20:12–19 prepares readers for that difference, for in this story the prophet informs Hezekiah that one day his descendants will serve as eunuchs in the Babylonian court. Moreover, as we have seen, the narrative informs us at three critical junctures where Davidides prove to be disloyal that God is not inclined to abrogate the covenant with David.

The ambiguity as to the fate of the Davidides and any potential hope communicated to the exiles in 2 Kgs 25:27–30 is not lessened when we consider God's treatment of the Davidides after the reigns of Jehoram, who marries a daughter of Ahab, and his son Ahaziah, whose mother is the Omride Athaliah. Jehoram "walked in the way of the kings of Israel, even as the house of Ahab did, because he took the daughter of Ahab as a wife" (2 Kgs 8:18). Ahaziah "walked in the way of the house of Ahab, and did evil in the eyes of YHWH like the house of Ahab because he was a son-in-law of the house of Ahab" (8:27). The phrase "walked in the way of the kings of Israel" is quite similar to "walked in the way of Jeroboam," an evaluation applied to six of the eight kings of Israel between Jeroboam and the Davidide Jehoram, and it is a phrase that is almost always closely linked in the evaluation with the charge of causing the people to sin.[38] Yet the narrative does not use חטא in the Hiphil in the evaluation of either of these two Davidic kings, and so their transgressions in the narrative remain like that of Solomon, who builds his high places solely for the use of his foreign wives (1 Kgs 11:7–8) and thus does not cause Israel to sin, rather than Jeroboam's. At this point, the narrative records a punishment of the Davidides that approaches that of the Northern dynasties whom God destroys for causing Israel to commit apostasy, or at the very least removes from power so that the house cannot rule again: all of the male Davidides, save for Joash, are murdered in

38. "He walked in the way of Jeroboam" (or, in the case of Nadab, "in the way of his father") is found in the evaluations of Nadab (1 Kgs 15:26), Baasha (15:34; and cf. 16:2), Zimri (16:19), Omri (16:26), Ahab (16:31, which actually says "sins of Jeroboam" rather than "way of Jeroboam"), and Ahaziah (22:53). These evaluations are normally accompanied by a statement that the king "did evil in the eyes of YHWH" (see 15:26, 34; 16:19, 25, 30; 22:53) and by a reference to חטא in the Hiphil (15:30, 34; 16:19, 26; 22:53), although this evaluation of Ahab appears in 21:22. The reference to the house of Ahab in both of the evaluations, especially that of Ahaziah, who "walked in the way of the house of Ahab," suggests also the crime of introducing Baalism to Judah (a conclusion bolstered by the fact that in 11:18–19 the people remove the Baal cult from Judah following the installation of Joash).

a coup; and the house is removed from power for six years as the Omride Athaliah takes the throne (2 Kgs 11:1–3).

The Davidides Jehoram and Ahaziah have acted, to some degree, like the Northern kings, although the narrative does not actually use חטא in the Hiphil for their actions. Nonetheless, given the judgment formula used for the two kings that referred to the cultic sins of the Northern kings, it would not be surprising had the narrative announced the annihilation of the Davidides here. But one male Davidide survives the pogrom and the removal from power is only temporary, unlike the cases of the Northern dynasties. Moreover, it is in this story that we find the final ניר statement. For Iain Provan, this story forms the pattern that 25:27–30 follows: what happened to the Davidides in the time of Joash will happen to them after the exile.[39] Just as the story of Isaiah's prophecy to Hezekiah in 2 Kgs 20:16–18, in which he tells the kings that his descendants will serve in the Babylonian court, appears to prepare us for the fate of the Davidides in exile, the story of Jehoram, Ahaziah, Athaliah, and Joash can be read in the same manner. The punishment of the exile, like the punishment during the reign of Athaliah, is yet another example of the eternal punishment that God promised David's house in 2 Samuel. If one privileges this story in the interpretation of 2 Kgs 25, then Dtr's final verses point to restoration. In this scenario, the narrative explains the exiles' trauma by means of Manasseh's sin but maintains that, "because of David," the destruction and exile of 586 of the people and the Davidide are merely a more severe version of the punishment during the time of Athaliah, not a complete end to the nation.

However, this is not the only story in the narrative of the monarchy with which one can draw a comparison with 25:27–30. Some scholars see here a parallel to the story of David's treatment of Saul's son Mephibosheth in 2 Sam 9. Like Mephibosheth, Jehoiachin is the surviving male scion of a dethroned house; like David, the Babylonian Evil-Merodach shows regard for his defeated enemy, and seats him at his table and provides him with food.[40] This interpretive possibility means that the

39. Iain Provan, "The Messiah in the Book of Kings," in *The Lord's Anointed: Interpretation of Old Testament Messianic Texts* (ed. Philip Satterthwaite et al.; Carlisle: Paternoster, 1995), 67–85 (74–76); idem, *1 & 2 Kings*, 279–81. See also McKenzie, "The Divided Kingdom," 141.

40. E.g., Jeremy Schipper, "'Significant Resonances' with Mephibosheth in 2 Kings 25:27–30: A Response to Donald F. Murray," *JBL* 124 (2005): 521–29; Polzin, *David and the Deuteronomist*, 103–6; Jan Jaynes Granowski, "Jehoiachin at the King's Table: A Reading of the Ending of the Second Book of Kings," in *Reading Between Texts: Intertextuality and the Bible* (ed. Danna Nolan Fewell; LCBI; Louisville: Westminster John Knox, 1992), 173–88 (183–84).

future of the house of David in 25:27–30 is potentially not an optimistic one, for the Davidides would thus appear like the Saulides, a defeated house that will not rule again. On the other hand, after Manasseh causes the people to sin, God seems to promise the Davidides the same fate of annihilation as the house of Ahab (2 Kgs 21:13), although this is not exactly what happens, as 25:27–30 shows us. The survival of at least one male Davidide in captivity can seem to point toward the (at least somewhat) hopeful prophecy of Isaiah to Hezekiah, to a parallel with the restoration of Joash, and to the ניר passages.

Based on what we can see in the narrative's presentation of the punishment of the Northern kings and dynasties and on what it has and has not said about the unconditional covenant with David, readers are left with the following options as real possibilities for the interpretation of 25:27–30:

A Davidide caused the people to sin. The narrative has clearly shown in its evaluations of the Northern dynasties that royal houses that so act will, at the very least, be removed from power, if not completely destroyed. Notably, it says nothing about the survival of Jehoiachin's sons.[41] The narrative claims that God can annul eternal covenants, and this appears to be the case here. Perhaps the line will survive, but it will not rule again. The punishment that was temporary during the reign of Athaliah will be permanent now. The prophecy of 2 Kgs 21:13 and the parallel with Mephibosheth take precedence in this interpretation.[42]

The Davidides are a special case for Dtr's narrative. True, Manasseh caused the people to sin, but nowhere does God explicitly annul the unconditional covenant. Exilic readers can thus expect the dynasty's restoration to power, just as occurred after the punishment in the reign of Athaliah. The ניר statements that refer to David, the prophecy of 2 Kgs 20:12–19, and the parallel with Joash take precedence in this interpretation.

41. Yair Hoffman, "The Deuteronomist and the Exile," in *Pomegranates and Golden Bells: Studies in Biblical, Jewish, and Near Eastern Ritual, Law, and Literature in Honor of Jacob Milgrom* (ed. David P. Wright et al.; Winona Lake, Ind.: Eisenbrauns, 1995), 659–75 (667–68). As Hoffman notes, however, they are mentioned in the Babylonian document that refers to Jehoiachin's rations (p. 668 n. 22).

42. One could also add here a parallel with the fate of the house of Menahem, if one interprets the fate of the Menahemides as being exiled and removed from power forever. As we have seen, the narrative is not entirely clear as to their fate, and this would be a best case scenario reading of what happens to them. Since this dynasty is removed from power only 29 years before the exile of the North, however, the narrative might simply assume that this house will not rule again.

It is, however, not possible to choose with absolute certainty between these two interpretations. The narrative is clear enough in setting out a relationship between the cultic failures of the Northern kings and the destruction or, at least, removal from power of the Northern dynasties. In the North, dynasties that cause the people to be cultically disloyal are, at a minimum, removed from power, and in three out of five cases completely destroyed. It is the clarity of this logic in history that relies on the cultic loyalty of the kings as regards the North that makes the vagueness at the end of the book so strikingly ambiguous. The narrative clearly states that God can abrogate eternal covenants, yet does not say explicitly that this has occurred in the case of the Davidides; yet neither does it go out of the way to make a reference to the covenant with David, as is done in 1 Kgs 11:36, 15:4–5, and 2 Kgs 8:19, where in each case Davidic sin might seem to threaten the future of the house. Despite the perfection of Josiah's repentance—and 2 Kgs 23:25 is the only place in the History where anyone is said to express loyalty to God with heart, soul, and mind—this perfect return to cultic loyalty is not met with a corresponding divine repentance of the punishment of Judah announced in 21:10–15. On the contrary, 23:26–27 is clear that the return of the people to cultic loyalty makes no difference as to how God will treat Judah: "YHWH did not repent (שׁב) from the burning of his great anger that burned against Judah." There is, in fact, no fulfillment passage in 25:27–30 at all, either in reference to the covenant or to an earlier prophecy of punishment, although the narrative could have cited 2 Sam 7, 2 Kgs 21:13, or 20:16–18. Unsurprisingly, a number of scholars have pointed out that what is omitted in the final four verses of Kings seems as important as what is included. There is no reference to repentance or to the lack of it; no reference to any action on the part of God, either for or against Jehoiachin; no reference to the covenant with David, either upholding or breaking it; and not even any indication as to whether or not Jehoiachin's children survived in exile to carry on the line.[43]

And even beyond this ambiguity in regard to the future of the Davidides, the History says nothing about the fate of the exiles themselves. We can return to the observation in Deut 30 that repentance must precede return and to Wolff's point that this condition has not been satisfied by the end of the narrative, but not only has this idea recurred in Kings only as a possibility in Solomon's prayer (1 Kgs 8:33–34, 46–51), but the

43. Respectively, these are the observations of Murray, "Of All the Years," 264–65; Christopher T. Begg, "The Significance of Jehoiachin's Release: A New Proposal," *JSOT* 11 (1986): 49–56 (50); Rose, "Deuteronomistic Ideology," 431; and Hoffman, "The Deuteronomist and the Exile," 667–68.

whole notion that God meets repentance with salvation is subverted by the narratives of Jephthah and Saul, where the repentance of Israel and of a leader of Israel meet with divine refusal (Judg 10:15–16; 1 Sam 15:24–31). The very fact that the master narrative can refer to the futility of Josiah's unequalled repentance in 2 Kgs 23:25–27 unsettles that earlier assertion still further. The narrative does not so much as mention a link between salvation and repentance anywhere in or around the stories of the destructions of Israel and Judah or the story of Josiah's repentance. It is true, of course, that if one interprets 2 Kgs 25:27–30 as foreshadowing a restoration of Davidic power, then that would imply the restoration of the people, since a king needs subjects to rule. On the other hand, the pessimistic interpretation does not rule out the possibility that the people could repent and be restored to the land independently of Davidic rule. There is no reason to believe that the narrative presents the monarchy as a necessary form of leadership for Israel, since in the History's narrative it appears as simply one form of failed leadership among others.

Our discussion of the ambiguity that trauma has introduced into the way the narrative handles the fate of the Davidides here has led us to other unresolved questions, most clearly the future of the exilic community. Moses has promised that repentance will lead to return, but we have seen God explicitly reject Josiah's perfect act of repentance. As I have mentioned in earlier chapters, a link between repentance and salvation makes perfect sense from the narrative's point of view, since repentance returns the nation to cultic loyalty, and so for God to ignore the act said to be done for him with all of Josiah's heart, soul, and might—the only such act in the whole History—is to suggest that acts of cultic loyalty can have no effect on how God treats Israel. This is a traumatic subversion of the narrative that goes to the core of its explanation of history and trauma, an explanation based on the logic that God punishes acts of disloyalty and rewards acts of loyalty. Yet there is no punishment at all for the generations of the days of Manasseh, Amon, and the first 17 years of Josiah's reign whose sin is worse than the Canaanites; it is only 35 years after Josiah returns Judah to cultic loyalty that God punishes the nation. A disloyal generation—and potentially multiple disloyal generations, since this apostasy could have lasted as long as 74 years—is not punished, while a generation who is loyal is.

It is not simply that God appears to punish the wrong generation of Israel, as if he is unable to distinguish between them, it is the fact that trauma's subversion of the narrative's concepts of God, justice, punishment, repentance, salvation, and Israel all undermine the narrative's ultimate explanation of the exiles' trauma. It is still possible to explain the trauma on the narrative's terms; we could argue, for example, that although none of the four kings who follow Josiah are said to cause the people to sin, they are all said to do evil like their ancestors (23:32, 37; 24:9, 19–20),[44] which could be understood to mean that they continue Manasseh's sin. This reading is most likely in the case of Jehoiakim, who is said to do "evil in the eyes of YHWH like all that his fathers did" (23:37); it is possible, even if it is not entirely clear, to see this notice as suggesting that he imitated all of the evil that all of the Davidides did, including Manasseh's evil of causing Judah to sin.[45] Second Kings 24:19–20, in fact, specifies that the final king does evil and that YHWH was angry with Judah and Jerusalem. It is not precisely clear why he was angry—the text does not specify that the king's sin caused the anger, and we saw in 2 Sam 24:1 a case where unexplained divine anger with no reference to any sin that led to destruction within Israel—but it is certainly possible that the anger is due to sin that Zedekiah potentially caused Judah to commit. In this interpretation we can argue that God does not recognize Josiah's repentance because his successors returned Judah to the sin of Manasseh.

The difficulty with this explanation, however, is that the alternative case—God ignores gross sin of the people for up to 74 years, ignores Josiah's perfect act of repentance, and then punishes an innocent generation 35 years after Judah has been returned to cultic loyalty—is just as likely. It is more likely, in fact, since the text specifies only Manasseh's sin, and not the sin of any of the kings after Josiah, as the cause of the exiles' trauma. The fact that all of the last four kings are said to do "evil in the eyes of YHWH" certainly implies that they were worshipping foreign gods, but the phrase by itself does not mean that they were working to cause Israel to sin—it certainly does not mean this when it appears in Judges.[46] So at the place where we might expect the clearest

44. Jehoahaz and Jehoiakim are at least said to do evil like their ancestors (23:32, 37), and since Jehoiakim is said to act this way, the statements that Jehoiachin and Zedekiah act like Jehoiakim (24:9, 19) imply that they act like their ancestors as well.

45. See also Sweeney, *King Josiah of Judah*, 35–36.

46. As we saw in Chapter 1, some members of the Cross school of redaction point to the regnal evaluations in 2 Kgs 23:26–25:30 as one piece of evidence to argue for an exilic redactor, particularly because the accusation that Jehoiakim "did evil in the eyes of YHWH like all that his fathers did" (23:37) can seem to contradict the perfect evaluation of Josiah. See Nelson, *Double Redaction*, 36–41; A. D. H. Mayes, *The Story of Israel Between Settlement and Exile: A Redactional Study of the Deuteronomistic History* (London: SCM, 1983), 123; O'Brien, *The Deuteronomistic History Hypothesis*, 268–70; Vanoni, 'Beobachtungen zur deuteronomistischen Terminologie," 359. However, the narrative says that Josiah is loyal to YHWH "with all his heart, with all his soul, and with all his might" only in regards to his

explanation of the exiles' trauma, we find no use of חטא in the Hiphil after the story of Manasseh, no explanation for why God does not punish Judah for the cultic disloyalty it commits while Manasseh, Amon, and Josiah (at least for the first 17 years of his reign) cause them to commit it, no explanation for why God ignores Josiah's repentance or inflicts trauma on a whole nation more than a generation after readers can be certain that the people sinned, and no clear explanation of whether or not the "evil" that the last four kings committed involved causing the people to sin. The future of the exilic community is also unclear; it is possible, but not certain, that it is tied to the future of the Davidides, but their future is ambiguous. Moses has promised that repentance will lead to salvation, but we hear nothing about repentance after God refuses to acknowledge Josiah's. This not only subverts Moses' statement, it subverts the basis of the narrative's explanation of history and trauma, which is that God rewards cultic loyalty and punishes cultic disloyalty. The ambiguity we have surveyed can be explained, but trauma intrudes into the narrative to deny any kind of clear and totalizing explanation. It has thrown the narrative's language into unresolved trial. We will have more to say about trauma's subversion of the narrative in Kings in section B below, but we move first to the narrative of the prophets.

5. *The Failure of the Prophets*

It is when Northern apostasy reaches its nadir with Ahab's addition of Baalism to Jeroboam's sin (see 1 Kgs 16:31–33) that the focus of the narrative shifts to the prophets in 1 Kgs 17–2 Kgs 8. The king's introduction of Baal worship is met with Elijah's announcement of famine in 1 Kgs 17:1, reminiscent particularly of the curse of Deut 28:23–24. He leads Israel in a rejection of Ahab's foreign worship in 1 Kgs 18 and confronts the king's participation in social injustice in 1 Kgs 21. In 1 Kgs 20, other prophets intervene to save Israel from invasion and to condemn Ahab for his disobedience of divine command, and, in 1 Kgs 22, God acts through the prophets to kill Ahab as Elijah had prophesied in 21:19–21. Ahab's re-introduction of Canaanite worship in 16:31–33 is followed by a notice of Hiel's rebuilding of Jericho in 16:34, notes Sweeney, as if the narrative is signaling that Canaanite worship will be paralleled by

repentance (23:25). He is inimitable this way just as Hezekiah has no rival among the kings in terms of trust (18:5), like Solomon is unequalled in terms of his wisdom (1 Kgs 5:9–11 [ET 4:29–31]), and Moses is unrivalled among the prophets for knowing God face to face (Deut 34:10). Yet, although the narrative does not explicitly say so, Josiah, like his father and grandfather, caused the people to sin before he began his reformation in the eighteenth year of his reign. His repentance is perfect; his entire reign is not.

the re-establishment of the Canaanite cities, with Israelites acting like Canaanites within them.[47] As Elijah is succeeded by Elisha, the narrative seems to be drawing a parallel between them and Moses and Joshua. Elijah, like Moses, encounters God at Horeb (1 Kgs 19); Elijah is taken to heaven in the Transjordan (2 Kgs 2:1–12) just as Moses dies there; his successor, like Moses', then crosses the Jordan and, argues Philip Satterthwaite, initiates a new conquest of Israel, but this time to eliminate Canaanite worship practices rather than Canaanites.[48] The Elisha stories that most closely parallel stories of Elijah—miraculously providing oil and a son for a widow (cf. 1 Kgs 17:8–24 and 2 Kgs 4:1–37)—take place within Israel, whereas the parallel stories in the Elijah narrative take place in Sidon.[49] When the monarchy fails, the prophets do not replace them, but they do become the narrative focus of the History until the elimination by Jehu of Ahab's house and the Baalism it introduced in 2 Kgs 9–10. They parallel the judges who arose during the apostasy of Israel's first period in the land. Just as God raised up judges to deal with the problems caused by Israel's apostasy earlier, God here appoints prophets to lead in the apostate vacuum created by Ahab and his house, and there is no need to argue that the Elijah–Elisha block of material is a post-Deuteronomistic insertion.[50]

Yet even these figures are not complete successes as leaders in the History's narrative. Elijah, the first of the prophets to be the focus of this

47. Marvin A. Sweeney, "On the Literary Function of the Notice Concerning Hiel's Re-Establishment of Jericho in 1 Kings 16:34," in *Seeing Signals, Reading Signs: The Art of Exegesis: Studies in Honor of Antony F. Campbell, SJ for His Seventieth Birthday* (ed. Mark A. O'Brien and Howard N. Wallace; JSOTSup 415; T&T Clark International, 2004), 104–15 (109–10). For other parallels between Ahab and Hiel, see Charles Conroy, "Hiel Between Ahab and Elijah–Elisha: 1 Kgs 16,34 in Its Immediate Literary Context," *Bib* 77 (1996): 210–18.

48. Philip E. Satterthwaite, "The Elisha Narratives and the Coherence of 2 Kings 2–8," *TynBul* 49 (1998): 1–28 (see esp. 8–9). For other arguments that the Historian is deliberately paralleling Moses and Joshua with Elijah and Elisha, see Burke O. Long, *2 Kings* (FOTL 10; Grand Rapids: Eerdmans, 1991), 31; Provan, *1 and 2 Kings*, 173.

49. See Satterthwaite, "The Elisha Narratives," 8 n. 17. For an examination of the parallels between their miracles, see Nachman Levine, "Twice as Much of Your Spirit: Pattern, Parallel and Paronomasia in the Miracle of Elijah and Elisha," *JSOT* 85 (1999): 25–46.

50. This, nonetheless, is still maintained by some scholars, even if scholarship still largely sees 1 Kgs 17–2 Kgs 8 as a Deuteronomistic insertion. For a survey of the state of the question see Susanne Otto, *Jehu, Elia und Elisa: Die Erzählung von der Jehu-Revolution und die Komposition der Elia-Elisa-Erzählungen* (BWANT 8/12; Stuttgart: Kohlhammer, 2001), 11–25.

section of the narrative, is actually portrayed as disingenuous, argues Russell Gregory, and is "a prophet plagued by his own ego and exaggerated importance."[51] Elijah's self-confidence collapses, notes Paul Kissling, the moment a figure in the narrative—Jezebel—challenges his authority in 1 Kgs 19:2, and Elijah never does dare to meet or deal with her. He presents his own word in 17:1 rather than YHWH's, and he does not allow God's victory over the prophets of Baal in 1 Kgs 18 to sway his "defeatist attitude," claiming in 18:22 and 19:10, 14 that he alone is left of YHWH's prophets, even though both he and readers know this not to be true, since the narrative has assured us otherwise in 18:3–4, 13.[52] Elijah seems intent, in fact, on supplanting God's authority and initiative despite the prophet's own lack of courage—as John Olley notes, his initial proclamation of 1 Kgs 17:1 may well be his own word rather than God's, and "the word of YHWH" comes to Elijah only three times. Only in 1 Kgs 17:16 and 2 Kgs 1:17 do we read of something occurring "according to the word of YHWH that Elijah had spoken." Even the contest between YHWH and the prophets of Baal in 1 Kgs 18 is undertaken entirely on Elijah's initiative. Only in 2 Kgs 1 and 1 Kgs 17:13–14 is Elijah's message exactly as YHWH gave it to him.[53]

As the narrative presents Elisha as a parallel to Joshua, it emphasizes that his activities take place mainly within the boundaries of Israel, unlike many of those of Elijah (who, again, is associated with Moses who dies outside of the land). Yet once inside Israel, Elisha does little to actually remove apostasy from the nation, and, in the part of the narrative that deals with him, only 2 Kgs 3:1–3 refers to conflict with the house of Ahab and the worship of Baal, and this reference does not even mention Elisha. Satterthwaite argues that the Elisha narratives show the prophet working to benefit the faithful within Israel and to punish the unfaithful—for example, upon first crossing the Jordan as Elijah's successor he acts to bless the faithful by healing the water of Jericho to permit agriculture there (2:19–22), and then curses the children who mock him as God's prophet, resulting in their deaths (2:23–24), a result reminiscent of the curses of Deut 28:32.[54] Yet, although the prophets appear precisely because of the failure of leadership in the North with Ahab's new cultic innovation of Baalism that adds to Jeroboam's sin, Elisha does virtually

51. Russell Gregory, "Irony and the Unmasking of Elijah," in Alan J. Hauser and Russell Gregory, *From Carmel to Horeb: Elijah in Crisis* (JSOTSup 85; BLS 19; Sheffield: Almond, 1990), 91–169 (99, 102).

52. Kissling, *Reliable Characters*, 97–124.

53. John Olley, "Yhwh and His Zealous Prophet: The Presentation of Elijah in 1 and 2 Kings," *JSOT* 80 (1998): 25–51 (33–37, 45).

54. This example from Satterthwaite, "The Elisha Narratives," 8–10.

nothing to lead in this situation. His narrative is marked by no climactic scene of confrontation with apostate cult leaders; there is virtually no confrontation between him and the apostate Omrides. The Elisha narrative, argues Wesley Bergen, provides "a negative judgment on prophetism"—his miracles seem unnecessary, and God is largely absent from the stories the narrative tells about him.[55] Like his predecessor, Elisha pursues activities on his own rather than divine initiative. There is no direct divine speech in the Elisha stories, and we frequently find the phrase "according to the word of Elisha" rather than "according to the word of YHWH."[56] These stories are, in the end, "a belittling portrayal of the prophet and of prophetism in general," as Elisha fails to eliminate Baalism and ultimately accommodates rather than confronts a monarchy that causes Israel to sin.[57]

By comparing Elijah and Elisha to Moses and Joshua, the narrative suggests that the two prophets have far greater leadership flaws than the first two leaders of Israel. The prophets act and speak on their own behalves when they should be intermediaries for the divine will; Elijah has either a tenuous grasp on reality, or else simply misrepresents his role as prophet, even before God; neither prophet fulfills the command God gives them in 1 Kgs 19:15–17. The prophet Elisha actually seems unnecessary at points in his narrative. To take the story of the Shunamite woman (2 Kgs 4:1–37; 8:1–6) as an example, his interaction with her is marked by so many miscommunications and ambiguous statements (e.g., 4:13–15) and unnecessary intermediaries (e.g., the prophet's unnecessary use of Gehazi in 4:12, 25–27) that readers must question how well the prophet can communicate with God, or even whether or not the prophet is not an otiose intermediary much like Gehazi is in these stories;[58] some scholars, in fact, see 4:8–37 as praising the woman at the expense of the prophet and his role.[59] Prophets do not become the perfect leaders that

55. Wesley J. Bergen, *Elisha and the End of Prophetism* (JSOTSup 286; Sheffield: Sheffield Academic, 1999), 11, 104, 175.

56. Ibid., 43–44.

57. Ibid., 42, 45, 177–78. For similar comments, see David Jobling, "A Bettered Woman: Elisha and the Shunamite in the Deuteronomic Work," in *The Labour of Reading: Desire, Alienation, and Biblical Interpretation* (ed. Fiona C. Black, Roland Boer, and Erin Runions; SBLSS 36; Atlanta: Society of Biblical Literature, 1999), 177–92.

58. So also Mark Roncace, "Elisha and the Woman of Shunem: 2 Kings 4:8–37 and 8:1–6 Read in Conjunction," *JSOT* 91 (2000): 109–27 (112–20).

59. E.g., Burke O. Long, "A Figure at the Gate: Readers, Reading, and Biblical Theologians," in *Canon, Theology, and Old Testament Interpretation: Essays in Honor of Brevard S. Childs* (ed. Gene M. Tucker, David L. Petersen, and Robert R.

Israel needs to survive, according to the narrative, and after the story of Jehu's extermination of the house of Ahab and the worshipers of Baal in 2 Kgs 9–10, the narrative returns to the status quo with a monarchy following in Jeroboam's sin. The narrative certainly does not present the prophets as worse leaders than the monarchy, but their failures lead to a continuance of the same kind of apostasy that, according to the narrative, explains the exiles' trauma.

B. *The Traumatic End of Narrative in Kings*

1. *Solomon as a Traumatic Parallel for God*

Our examination of the narrative of Kings has already brought a number of traumatic subversions of the narrative to light. It is not clear why God does not punish and destroy the sinful generations of the long period under Manasseh, Amon, and the first 17 years of Josiah when the cultic disloyalty of the nation exceed that of the Canaanites and the North for up to 74 years. It is not clear why God waits for 35 years after Josiah's perfect repentance that restores the nation to cultic loyalty to impose siege, famine, mass death, destruction, forced migration, and trauma on the people. Not only is it not clear why God ignores Josiah's act of repentance, it is unclear in the final verses of the History if the narrative's logic in history, specifically the link it draws between repentance and salvation, is still functioning, and if Moses' promise of restoration following repentance is even still a possibility. The total failure of the dynasty with whom God chose to make an eternal covenant to save the people, not to mention the failures of Jeroboam (whom God also chose) and his successors in the North, and the failure of virtually every leader whom God chose, including the prophets, suggests that God may have little aptitude for choosing leaders for Israel, and so suggests that he might share some of the blame for the exiles' trauma, rather than being simply the objective dispenser of justice. And the fact that God explicitly ignores the perfect repentance of Josiah suggests further that he is not bound by the narrative's portrayal of him or of its concepts of justice, punishment, salvation, or repentance. With the collapse of the master narrative through the subversion of trauma, the usefulness of the narrative's logic for interpreting history has been gravely undermined. Exilic readers can hardly view it as an unchallenged guide to making sense of the community's trauma. It is now impossible to read the future of Israel

Wilson; Philadelphia: Fortress, 1988), 166–86; Jobling, "A Bettered Woman," 178–80; Yairah Amit, "A Prophet Tested: Elisha, the Great Woman of Shunem, and the Story's Double Message," *BibInt* 11 (2003): 279–94.

with any sort of clarity since the absence of trauma has subverted the explanatory capacity of the narrative. While it is still possible to make sense of 2 Kgs 21–25 on the master narrative's terms, the intrusion of trauma introduces absences and ambiguity into the narrative to create not a competing counter-narrative with its own clear explanations but a subversive anti-narrative.

So the future for the exiles is unclear. The narrative does not use its logic in history to define it more clearly, despite a few weak attempts early in the History in Deut 4 and 30. Near the beginning of Solomon's prayer in 1 Kgs 8:22–53, the king asks in vv. 33–34 that repentance be followed by return to the land, but by vv. 46–51, as if he is downgrading his expectations, merely asks God that exiles receive mercy from their enemy (although this could, of course, imply that his petition here is that the exiles be returned to the land).[60] The wordplay between שׁוב "to repent" and שׁבה "to be captive" is a well-known feature of 1 Kgs 8:46–51;[61] as J. G. McConville points out, it is present also in Deut 30:1–10, but there the root שׁבה appears only once.[62] That is, by the time we reach Solomon's prayer in the final book of the History, there is more emphasis on captivity than on repentance, and repentance itself might seem to have less of an effect than Moses promises in Deut 30. There is also certainly no guarantee that God will listen to the plea of the (eventually) apostate Solomon and bestow any kind of mercy on the exiles. Concepts such as God, punishment, repentance, and salvation have been thrown into unresolved question. There is, that is, no clear or unchallenged sense that God will rightly guide history to meet disloyalty with punishment and repentance in exile with salvation, a promise from Moses that seems to be in the process of disappearing by the time we reach the end of the History. The punishment of trauma, rather than being simply God's just response to Israel's vassal disloyalty, now can be seen as the nation's permanent fate, the essence of its history. Trauma's subversion of the narrative through its ambiguity, the ambiguity that rejects totalizing explanations, intervenes to strip history of meaning for the exilic readers.

Solomon is not, as far as we hear in Dtr, a man after God's own heart as David was, although he is imbued with God's wisdom. His plea for wisdom, which God grants in the vision of 1 Kgs 3:3–15, is quickly

60. So Cogan, *1 Kings*, 287.

61. See Jon D. Levenson, "The Paronomasia of Solomon's Seventh Petition," *HAR* 6 (1982): 135–38; Sweeney, *I & II Kings*, 135; Walsh, *1 Kings*, 114; Gwilym H. Jones, *1 and 2 Kings* (NCBC; Grand Rapids: Eerdmans, 1984), 204.

62. J. G. McConville, "1 Kings viii 46–53 and the Deuteronomic Hope," *VT* 42 (1992): 65–79 (75–76).

demonstrated in the case of the two prostitutes and the two babies in 3:16–28, in the conclusion of which the narrative states that "they [all of Israel] saw that the wisdom of God was in him, to do justice" (3:28), and his sagacity is lauded by foreign monarchs (5:21 [ET 7]; 10:1–10) and by the narrator (5:9–14 [ET 4:29–34]). It is, of course, most concretely demonstrated in the case of the two prostitutes immediately following his theophany in 1 Kgs 3, where his ability to solve a crime with no witnesses allows readers to see just how much wiser Solomon is than they, as some scholars conclude.[63] Given the narrative's claim that God has given Solomon wisdom, that the people recognize that Solomon does in fact have God's wisdom in him, and its own paean to the king's wisdom in 5:9–14 [ET 4:29–34], however, we might expect it to be a bit clearer as to the success of Solomon's judgment in the case. When Solomon announces his intention to cut the remaining living child in half for distribution to the two mothers, "the woman whose son was alive said to the king—because her compassion for her son grew warm—she said, 'Please, my lord, give the living child to her; certainly do not kill him,' and the other said, 'It will belong neither to me nor to you. Cut!'" (3:26). Solomon responds by saying, "Give the living child to her; certainly do not kill him. She is his mother" (3:27). The text, that is, in reporting only that Solomon says, "Give the living child *to her*," is not precisely clear as to which woman Solomon believes should receive the child, a problem noted by the LXX translators who expanded the original text and have Solomon say, "Give the child to the one who said, 'Give him to her.'"[64]

63. So, e.g., Meir Sternberg, *The Poetics of Biblical Narrative: Ideological Literature and the Drama of Reading* (ISBL; Bloomington: Indiana University Press, 1985), 169 and Stuart Lasine, "The Riddle of Solomon's Judgment and the Riddle of Human Nature in the Hebrew Bible," *JSOT* 45 (1989): 61–86 (76–77).

64. There are many differences between the MT and LXX in Dtr's narrative of Solomon's reign, and there is no consensus in scholarship as to the relationship between these two texts. D. W. Gooding, for example, has argued strenuously in many works for the priority of the MT, and more recently his arguments for MT's priority have been supported by, e.g., Zvi Talshir, *The Alternative Story of the Division of the Kingdom: 3 Kingdoms 12:24a–z* (JBS 6; Jerusalem: Simor, 1993) and Percy S. F. van Keulen, *Two Versions of the Solomonic Narrative: An Inquiry into the Relationship Between MT 1 Kgs. 2–11 and LXX 3 Reg. 2–11* (VTSup 104; Leiden: Brill, 2005). Others, such as Julio Trebolle Barrera and Adrian Schenker, argue for the superiority of LXX; see, e.g., Trebolle Barrera's *Salomón y Jeroboan: Historia de la recensión y redacción de 1 Reyes 2–12, 14* (Bibliotheca Salmanticensis. Dissertationes 3; Salamanca: Universidad Pontificia, 1980) and Schenker's *Septante et texte massorétique dans l'histoire la plus ancienne du texte de 1 Rois 2–14* (CRB 48; Paris: Gabalda, 2000). Regardless of which tradition should have

In the original wording, however, Solomon's command to "give the living child to her" would most reasonably refer to the last woman who spoke, the woman whom readers—unlike Solomon and those in the story who observe the trial—know is not the true mother of the living child.[65] That is, the most reasonable interpretation of Solomon's response is that he has the baby given to the wrong woman. To be fair to Solomon, it is not out of the question that the one who says "Cut!" could not be the true mother; after all, writes George Mendenhall, one could argue that "the true mother would rather see her child killed than give him up to an unscrupulous bitch."[66]

The text does not even make it clear whether the plaintiff or defendant is the true mother. The plaintiff, who opens the proceedings before the king, claims that the other woman stole her (the plaintiff's) child at night, "and your maidservant was asleep" (3:20); the LXX omits this phrase since it is patently impossible for someone who slept through this crime to be the sole witness to it. Gary Rendsburg rejects the argument that Solomon should have been able to tell from this presentation that the woman was lying, since it would put readers in the position of "out-Solomoning Solomon," which, he argues, cannot be authorial intent.[67] The question of intent aside, it is clear that there are a number of important gaps in the narrative of this story. If Solomon does notice the absurd testimony on the part of the plaintiff, the narrator does not tell readers that he has, and so doubt has been cast on his ability to judge and on the quality of "the wisdom of God" in general. And right when the narrative could have made it absolutely clear that Solomon did give the baby to the correct mother—by using, for example, a phrase like the one the LXX translators inserted—it does not. It is not at all clear that Solomon has done a good job in distributing justice here; it is possible that the correct woman receives the child, but not certain. It is possible that the wisdom of God in Solomon has justly decided the case, but trauma is present in the absence of clear and full explanation to suggest

overall priority, however, each individual passage must be examined in and of itself, and in the case of 1 Kgs 3:27, the MT is clearly the more difficult and thus preferred text, since the LXX resolves the ambiguity of Solomon's pronouncement.

65. So Walsh, "The Characterization of Solomon," 488–89.

66. George E. Mendenhall, "The Shady Side of Wisdom: The Date and Purpose of Genesis 3," in Bream, Heim, and Moore, eds., *A Light unto My Path*, 319–34 (324).

67. Gary A. Rendsburg, "The Guilty Party in 1 Kings iii 16–28," *VT* 48 (1998): 534–41 (535). The position Rendsburg takes his stand against is advanced by E. Leibowitz and G. Leibowitz, "Solomon's Judgment" (Hebrew), *Beth Mikra* 35 (1989–1990): 242–44.

that this may not be true and that the wisdom of God in Solomon might have failed.

It can seem odd to read that the narrator and Israel sees this as "the wisdom of God"—although they are apparently correct in this view, since God tells Solomon in 3:12 in response to the king's plea for wisdom in judgment that "I have given you a wise and discerning heart"—not merely because the case has not been solved beyond a reasonable doubt, but also because Solomon decides to threaten the use of deadly force on an innocent child in order to reach a verdict. Not only is the text vague as to whether or not justice is administered, it makes no comment on what would have happened if the women had frozen in terror when Solomon said he would kill the child and neither one of them had spoken. This administration of justice by terror here—precisely the way the narrative explains the siege, mass killing, destruction, and forced migration in Kings—has found an ambivalent reception at least since the compilation of midrash, one of which quotes a rabbi as saying, "If I had been there, I would have put a rope around Solomon's neck, for one child dead was apparently not enough for him" (*Midrash Tehillim* 72:2). This is the example par excellence of Solomon's manifestation of divine wisdom in the master narrative, and it is uncomfortably reminiscent of the trauma that will close the book. Divine wisdom, we learn, threatens the innocent with death to reach a verdict, the justice of which is unclear. Here indeed we would seem to see trauma intruding into Dtr's narrative that undermines the narrative's attempt to communicate the justice of the judgment against Jerusalem and Judah in 2 Kgs 25 and thus to explain the exilic community's trauma. This uncanny parallel between Solomon and God thus subverts the narrative's concepts of God and justice, and the consequent punishment or salvation that should result from divine justice. In both cases it seems at least just as likely that the exercise of divine wisdom has resulted in injustice rather than justice; the narrative logic in history is subverted by ambiguity here.

A clear bridge between the ambiguous terror that passes for judgment in 1 Kgs 3 and the exiles' trauma in 2 Kgs 25 is 2 Kgs 6:24–7:20, the story of the Aramean siege of Samaria while Jehoram is king and Elisha is the main prophetic figure. The story begins with a case of two women who come before the king arguing over one dead and one living child, sounding much like the case brought before Solomon in 1 Kgs 3, although Jehoram, unlike Solomon, does not resolve his legal conundrum even in an unsatisfactory way. Second Kings 6:24–7:20 is also a clear parallel to the story of the final destruction of Jerusalem in 25:1–11 since it, like 2 Kgs 25, reflects the covenant curses of Deut 28:49–57 of invasion, siege, and famine.[68] Second Kings 6–7, in fact, includes the covenant curse of cannibalism of one's children (something that 25:1–11 does not report), since the dispute between the two women in 6:24–29 that opens the story is that they had agreed that they would each kill one of their sons and share the flesh as food, but one of the women, after having shared in the consumption of the child of the other, has now reneged on that deal and hidden her own son. The case is a perverse version of the one that Solomon decided, and 2 Kgs 6:24–7:20 as a whole points closely to the exilic community's own trauma as a realization of the curses of Deut 28.

Since the story of 2 Kgs 6:24–7:20 occurs during the reign of a son of Ahab who continues the sin of Jeroboam (3:1–3), we could see this siege story, which reflects the curses of Deut 28, as the master narrative's control of the meaning of the trauma of 586. Here, after all, the narrative's logic in history seems to provide an explanation for the siege of an Israelite city and the resulting famine of its inhabitants, which Deut 28 predicts and 2 Kgs 25 realizes in regard to Jerusalem. And in the story itself, it is not the king and his army who provide salvation for the city, but God. This salvation is discovered by lepers (7:3–10), social outcasts, and the apostate king himself does not even believe that divine salvation has actually been provided (7:12). The story's "subplot," as Volkmar Fritz puts it, is that God's control of history is truly revealed through the prophets, since Elisha correctly prophesies the end of the siege and famine (7:1), and the man who doubts his word (7:2) is killed at the end of the story (7:17–20).[69]

One can see in this story a contrast between Jehoram's utter failure to decide the case of the two women and Solomon's wisdom that decides the similar case in 1 Kgs 3, but the story creates an unflattering parallel between Solomon's poor judgment in 1 Kgs 3 and God's poor judgment in 2 Kgs 6–7. In 1 Kgs 3:16–28, Solomon displays "the wisdom of God

68. In regard to the famine in the story of 6:24–7:20, 6:25 says that a donkey's head sold for 80 shekels and one quarter qab of "dove's dung" (reading חרי יונים with the MT's ketib, LXX, Vulgate, Syriac, and Targum) cost five shekels. The dove's dung may be a reference to the seed of a carob or inedible husks—the Akkadian terms *zê summati* or *hallā summati*, literally meaning "dove's dung," have such a meaning (see *CAD* 15:380). Israel Eph'al, *The City Besieged: Siege and Its Manifestations in the Ancient Near East* (CHANE 36; Leiden: Brill, 2009), 60–61 n. 67 notes that the carob and its husk were considered to be food for animals, not humans.

69. See Volkmar Fritz, *1 & 2 Kings: A Continental Commentary* (trans. Anselm Hagedorn; Minneapolis: Fortress, 2003), 271; Cogan and Tadmor, *II Kings*, 83; T. R. Hobbs, *2 Kings* (WBC 13; Waco, Tex.: Word, 1985), 92; Sweeney, *I & II Kings*, 313–14.

to do justice" in a case where it is unclear that justice has actually been done, where innocent life is threatened, and where greater judicial investigation into the claims of the plaintiff should have been exercised. Jehoram actually appears as a sympathetic character in the story in 2 Kgs 6–7, for his initial reaction to the complaint of the cannibal mother is to tear his clothes and reveal the sackcloth that he is wearing (6:30). His second reaction, a vow to separate Elisha's head from his body (6:31), is understandable.[70] Elisha has previously kept Israelites alive with food and water (2 Kgs 2:19–22; 4:1–7), brought a child back to life (4:18–37),[71] and prevented an Aramean attack altogether, placing the enemy army helpless before the Israelite king (6:8–23). It is not clear why Elisha does not now act to help end the siege, or at least the famine that has led the Samarians to consume their own children, either through a miracle that he enacts himself or through prayer for divine intervention as was the case in 6:17, 18, and 20. Jehoram is a leader in demonstrating mourning with his sackcloth who moves to kill a prophet who, for some unknown reason, does not act to save Israel from invaders as he has in the past.[72]

Yet the failure to save Samaria here is not only Elisha's, it is God's, and not just because Elisha is God's choice as prophet. The story says nothing about the siege as punishment for apostasy; in fact, it supplies no reason for it. We could argue that the apostasy of a son of Ahab is simply assumed, although we are told in 3:1–3 that Jehoram, while still committing the sin of Jeroboam, was actually a better king (by the narrative's cultic standards) than his father, since he removes Ahab's Baal pillar. There is simply no clear reason why such horror should happen during Jehoram's time and not during that of Ahab's son Ahaziah, who followed his father's cultic lead entirely (1 Kgs 22:51–53). If God wishes to visit such punishment upon the dynasty and the nation that it has caused to sin, why not do it when the sin is at its nadir? Why do it to a king who

70. This is not the conclusion of all commentators. Jones argues that no reason is given for the king's anger (*1 and 2 Kings*, 434). Neither the king nor narrator provide a reason, and so readers have to fill one in. Gray argues that the king is simply trying to draw attention away from himself (*I & II Kings*, 471). See below for my response.

71. Although 8:4–5 at least suggests that Jehoram did not know of this specific incident before the siege.

72. So given the context of the story, the king's anger toward the prophet is understandable. The king is not trying to draw attention away from himself, he is bringing attention to bear upon the prophet who had been responsible for saving Israel from Aram and who now does nothing. See Sweeney, *I & II Kings*, 311; Hobbs, *2 Kings*, 80; Bergen, *Elisha and the End of Prophetism*, 139.

has enacted cultic reform, even if such reform makes him no better (but certainly no worse) than the other Northern kings? Perhaps the narrative's point is that God saves through Elisha in 6:8–23 because the current king has repudiated Ahab's Baalism, if not Jeroboam's apostasy (3:1–3); that is, perhaps 6:8–23 is a reward for Jehoram's partial reform, and 6:24–7:20 a punishment for not taking that reform further. The narrative, however, never says this. It is not impossible to explain this story through the narrative's logic in history as a punishment of cultic disloyalty, but there is just no clear sense here, in this story so reminiscent of 2 Kgs 25, that God is actually punishing the correct generation of Israelites with siege, famine, and mass death, since the apostasy during the 24 years of Ahab and Ahaziah was worse than that under Jehoram, whose (admittedly partial) reform God has apparently ignored, as he will ignore Josiah's and fail to punish the sinful generations of the reigns of Manasseh and Amon. It is this absence of narrative clarity that manifests trauma. There is no clear sense that this siege has been well thought out by God for a specific purpose, nor is any reason given for its miraculous end. So as in 1 Kgs 3 it is not clear at the end of the story that the right decision has been made, since there is no clear explanation for the siege, famine, and suffering in the first place. God's judgment in this story can appear even worse than Solomon's in 1 Kgs 3, since innocent life has not just been threatened, it has been ended, and there is no investigation at all into the crimes that warrant the decision of siege and famine that God has mandated. In a scene that sounds much like that of 2 Kgs 25, divine wisdom, just as in 1 Kgs 3, threatens the innocent with death to reach a verdict, the justice of which is unclear.[73] The traumatic subversion of these narratives uncannily foreshadows the subversion of the narrative's explanation of the exiles' trauma.

"The wisdom of God" that Solomon exercises in 1 Kgs 3 subverts the narrative's concepts of God and justice, and 2 Kgs 6:24–7:20, which looks back to the story of 1 Kgs 3 and forward to the fulfillment of the divine curses of Deut 28 in 2 Kgs 25, links this subversion to that of 2 Kgs 21–25. If Solomon has "the wisdom of God to do justice," trauma suggests that this divine justice has nothing in common with the narrative's view of it. As both 1 Kgs 3 and 2 Kgs 6–7 show, "the wisdom of God to do justice" is subverted by what we could see as the willingness of the judge to destroy the innocent and by the judge's failure to investigate the crime adequately or provide a rationale for punishment,

73. For 2 Kgs 6:24–31 as a reflection of and comment on 1 Kgs 3, see Hugh S. Pyper, "Judging the Wisdom of Solomon: The Two-Way Effect of Intertextuality," *JSOT* 59 (1993): 25–36.

and it is not clear in either story that the judge's actions have actually resulted in justice, just as it is not clear in 2 Kgs 21–25. Neither the portrayal of God nor those of justice and punishment in this story clearly and unambiguously match those of the master narrative since it is unclear as to why God has allowed the Arameans to besiege the city and why God and Elisha have not ended the siege before famine set in, in contrast to Elisha's salvation of the land in 6:8–23. All of these concepts are subverted in the story. And despite Jehoram's sackcloth in 6:30, there is also no clear indication here that there is any true repentance among king or people that can explain the city's salvation.

In regard to this last point, the possibility exists, of course, that God brings the siege upon Samaria simply to demonstrate his ability to save and to validate the word of his prophet. This is not the only possibility—perhaps God really does respond to the repentance Jehoram's sackcloth might manifest—but it is certainly one of them. We could plausibly see the emphasis of the conclusion to the story, in fact, not as 7:16, which states that plundering of the Aramean camp ended the famine "according to the word of YHWH" that Elisha spoke in 7:1, but as 7:17–20, the ultimate part of the conclusion that takes up most of its space, and which deals with the death of the man who rejected Elisha's prophecy of 7:1. The conclusion pays much more attention to this incident than to the salvation of the city and the food available to the survivors. We can see here, as we have elsewhere, a traumatic intrusion into the narrative that suggests that God is interested not in justice but in his reputation, even if, in proving his power, he must kill the innocent.[74] Since the narrative lacks a clear explanation both for the siege and the salvation of the city, it is possible to see the larger point of this story not as emphasizing that cultic disloyalty leads to punishment, but that God can prove his control of history. The realization of the curses of Deut 28 in this reading is a horrendous indictment of divine justice, and as if to emphasize God's lack of concern with the innocent who suffer, the cannibal mothers disappear from the story with no resolution to their dispute or even a note as to the fate of the one surviving child (if in fact he is still alive).[75] Besides a further subversion of the narrative's concepts of God and justice, the conclusion subverts the narrative's concepts of repentance

74. Bergen contrasts 7:16 as the fulfillment of God's oracle with 7:17–20 as the fulfillment of Elisha's "personal vendetta against a particular officer," a contrast that, he writes, reflects poorly on the prophetic office (*Elisha and the End of Prophetism*, 147–48).

75. See Walter Brueggemann, *Testimony to Otherwise: The Witness of Elijah and Elisha* (St. Louis: Chalice, 2001), 69–70.

and salvation and the link between them. We can see God as saving Samaria not because of any overt act of repentance but, as the conclusion of the story seems to emphasize, merely to demonstrate his power in history as communicated through his prophet. Acting as a bridge between 1 Kgs 3 and 2 Kgs 25, the story subverts the narrative's explanation for the exilic community's trauma.

2. *Trauma in the Stories of the Prophets*

As the kings in the narrative of the North lead the people in apostasy and the narrative turns to the leadership of the prophets, it presents them as failures of leadership as well, and in doing so actually raises the problem as to whether divine leadership can be trusted. This goes beyond the failures of Elijah and Elisha as they apparently act on their own initiatives or fail to fulfill their divine missions. To take the story of 2 Kgs 6:24–7:20 as an example again, we can certainly say that no explanation is given for Elisha's failure to save the city when he has previously acted to save individuals and towns. If we wish to see in his inconsistency another narrative example of the failure of Israelite leadership, we might also note that it corresponds to a failure of the narrative to provide any overt explanation for the siege and famine at all. That is, in the absence of narrative explanation, Elisha's failure here, like Solomon's bizarre application of "the wisdom of God" in 1 Kgs 3, can be read as paralleling a divine failure to judge rightly in bringing the Aramean siege upon Samaria in the first place; Elisha's failure to act or explain in 2 Kgs 6–7 parallels and draws attention to God's failure in these matters.

It is no wonder that, upon hearing the case of the cannibal mothers, Jehoram wants to kill Elisha in 6:31, for he apparently cannot understand the prophet's failure to relieve the siege when he has previously saved the nation. In 6:8–23, for example, Elisha works with the power of God to save Israel from Aramean attacks, and even leads an Aramean army, miraculously struck blind, into Samaria. Jehoram asks if he can kill the Arameans, but Elisha forbids it. Prophet and God work in tandem to save Israel and Samaria, but it is unclear why they have not both prevented the siege. Since the prophet works with the power of God, however, this inexplicable failure is not his alone. God and his prophet have saved Israel, Samaria, and the apostate king for no explained reason in 6:8–23; now God punishes and then saves for no explained reason. Again, we need not read the story this way, but in this gap in complete narrative explanation that is trauma, the chilling possibility exists that God punishes and saves for no clearly understood reasons. It is possible to read this story as saying that neither God nor his prophet is acting in any consistent manner in the punishment or salvation of Samaria. The narrative

provides us with no explanation as to how God could permit this horror to occur, and the story of siege, famine, and cannibalism caused by a foreign invasion is a striking contrast to 6:8–23. In this interpretation, God either acts capriciously in sending foreigners to invade the land and torture the people, or he sometimes does not control history at all. In a case like 2 Kgs 6:24–7:20, which mirrors the siege situation of 2 Kgs 25, trauma throws basic concepts of Dtr's narrative—God, justice, punishment, and salvation—that the narrative attempts to use to explain the exiles' trauma, a trauma foreshadowed by this very story, into unresolved ambiguity. While it is not impossible to explain it in terms of the narrative's logic in history, trauma is present precisely in the gaps in the narrative here that create the ambiguity of traumatic anti-narrative that puts the narrative's concepts into a trial without resolution.

The story of Micaiah in 1 Kgs 22 also subverts the narrative's concepts of God, justice, and punishment, but it does so within the context of subverting the narrative's concept of prophecy, something we have already seen in Deuteronomy and Samuel. In 1 Kgs 22, Ahab's prophets are deliberately misled by God in order to lure the king to his death, and Micaiah provides Ahab and readers an insight into the deception of the divine world. God's actions here hardly match up to his own claim in Deut 32:4 that he is "a God of faithfulness; and there is no deceit" in him, for he has deliberately sent a lying spirit into the mouths of Ahab's prophets.[76] The story results in Ahab's death—he does go out to battle (22:29) and is killed (22:34–37)—as prophesied in 1 Kgs 21:19, although even this prophecy is not precisely fulfilled in the king's death.[77] If God can lie to prophets—hardly something foreseen in the law of Deut 18:20–22, which addresses only lies prophets devise themselves—and

76. Some scholars try to argue that God remains truthful since the lying spirit itself is responsible for misleading Ahab's prophets (22:20–22; e.g., P. J. Williams, "Lying Sprits Sent by God? The Case of Micaiah's Prophecy," in *The Trustworthiness of God: Perspectives on the Nature of Scripture* [ed. Paul Helm and Carl R. Trueman; Grand Rapids: Eerdmans, 2002], 58–66 [65–66]; Walter C. Kaiser, *Toward Old Testament Ethics* [Grand Rapids: Zondervan, 1983], 256). This, however, ignores Micaiah's interpretation of the situation in 22:23, which attributes ultimate control of the lying spirit to God: "And now, look, YHWH has given a lying spirit in the mouth of all of these your prophets, and YHWH has spoken evil against you."

77. Elijah prophesies to Ahab in 1 Kgs 21:19 that "in the place where the dogs licked Naboth's blood, the dogs will lick your blood as well," and 21:1–14 is clear that Naboth was killed in Jezreel, his hometown. The dogs do lick Ahab's blood following his death at Ramoth-gilead, but they do so in Samaria, not Jezreel, although this is said to be "according to the word of YHWH that he spoke" (22:38).

if God does not even work to fulfill precisely things that have already been prophesied, then we see a fear that prophecy cannot be trusted and that the divine judge is willing to work unethically and sloppily, perhaps reminding readers of Solomon's sloppy judgment in 1 Kgs 3. One could argue that, from the master narrative's point of view, God's lie acts merely to fulfill an earlier prophecy, and so should not be seen as a regular occurrence, but the narrative does not assure readers of this. In this traumatic absence of explanatory assurance, then, another possibility that trauma's subversion of the narrative raises in 1 Kgs 22 is that if God has lied to Ahab's prophets, he may have lied to the prophet Moses. If so, then Moses' presentation of the narrative's logic in history in Deuteronomy is thrown into doubt and may not be able to explain the exiles' trauma. The suggestion that Israel's fate does not always depend on its actions of cultic loyalty and disloyalty, despite Moses' claims, uncannily anticipates the subversion of the narrative in God's failure to recognize Josiah's repentance or to punish Judah directly during the time when it committed Manasseh's sin. Moses, after all, has claimed that God "does not delay" to punish the guilty and that he punishes the sinner "to his face" (Deut 7:9–10). He has also claimed that God has made a law forbidding that children be punished for the sins of their parents (24:16), and has said that God recognizes repentance (30:1–5). These ambiguities in the narrative are not certainties, for Moses' claims about Israel's vassal loyalty are largely proven true in the narrative, but it is precisely the absence of explanation in the story of Micaiah for God's actions that would make the story fully cohere with the master narrative that manifests the presence of trauma to subvert narrative certainties and cast them into doubt.

The same traumatic fear that God does not speak truthfully to the prophets is also found in 1 Kgs 19:15–18, where God tells Elijah what will happen in the future: Elijah will anoint Hazael, Jehu, and Elisha; and all three of these will kill the apostate within Israel. "And it will be that the one who escapes from the sword of Hazael, Jehu will kill, and the one who escapes from the sword of Jehu, Elisha will kill" (1 Kgs 19:17). Yet much of what God prophesies here does not come to pass. Elijah does not anoint Hazael, Jehu, or Elisha.[78] Hazael does defeat Israel in

78. We could, of course, attribute Elijah's failure to do this to his own flaws (so, e.g., Hauser and Gregory, *From Carmel to Horeb*, 73). This is certainly a possible interpretation in regard to the commands to anoint in 19:15–16; in these verses, God gives Elijah a series of commands (the initial imperatives לך שׁוב in 19:15 are followed by a series of verbs in 19:15–16 in the perfect and imperfect that simply continue the imperative mood in 19:15; see *IBHS* ¶32:2:2), and God cannot be

battle, although his killings are not specifically directed against the apostate (2 Kgs 10:32; 12:17–18; 13:3, 22), and while the narrative makes a point of saying that Jehu slaughters the worshippers of Baal (2 Kgs 9:24–10:28), Elisha's killing is limited to children who deride his baldness (2 Kgs 2:23–24). These killings certainly do not happen in the order that God says that they will in 1 Kgs 19:17. God has either lied to Elijah for no conceivable reason, or cannot accurately predict what will happen in the future in terms of prophecy and judgment, or has simply changed his mind about punishment and slaughter and given no warning of this. The narrative's whole notion of prophecy as something that supports and reveals a consistent logic in history through its instruction and warning of divine punishment is subverted. And, once again, if the instructions of the prophets cannot be trusted because God lies to them or changes his mind without warning after the prophecy has been delivered, then the logic Moses has drawn between cultic disloyalty and destruction is also thrown into unresolved doubt. So again, the explanation of trauma in 2 Kgs 21–25 has been uncannily anticipated, for there God exercises judgment against a seemingly innocent generation, while the cultically disloyal generations are not punished.

A somewhat similar questioning of the master narrative occurs in 1 Kgs 13. In 13:1–10, a man of God prophesies the destruction of Jeroboam's altar by Josiah at Bethel, telling the king also that YHWH has commanded him (the man of God) not to eat or drink during his prophetic mission in the North. On his return from Bethel, he is waylaid by a prophet who tells him that this command has been revoked, and who invites him to eat at his house (13:11–18). After the man of God eats with the prophet, he is attacked and killed by a lion that eats neither him nor his donkey (13:19–25), and the prophet sees this as confirmation that the man of God's prophecy against Bethel will in fact come true (13:26–32). Scholars do not agree as to the point of the story,[79] although the prophet's conclusion at the end of the story is that the word of the

blamed if Elijah does not carry them out. This possibility, however, does not alter the fact that, in 19:17, God prophesies events that do not occur entirely as he predicts they will; 19:17 begins not with a verb that continues the imperative mood of the previous verses but with והיה "and it will be…."

79. Different scholars see it as dealing primarily with true and false prophecy; the fulfillment of God's word; an example of prophetic disobedience; and general theological implications of prophetic words and actions. For a short bibliography of works that explore each of these themes, see James K. Mead, "Kings and Prophets, Donkeys and Lions: Dramatic Shape and Deuteronomistic Rhetoric in 1 Kings xiii," *VT* 49 (1999): 191–205 (191–92).

man of God that he spoke to Jeroboam was in fact God's word. Since the manner of his death proves that God indeed told him not to eat in the North as the man of God had told Jeroboam, his prophecy to Jeroboam regarding the altar at Bethel must also in fact be legitimate (13:26–32). So in the master narrative of 1 Kgs 13, God's word through his prophetic messengers appears completely reliable, particularly in regard to the punishments for violations of divine commands that they foretell.[80]

Yet if the whole point of 13:11–32 is to confirm the prophetic word the man of God spoke to Jeroboam, the story undermines trust in prophecy itself and thus is subverted. The man of God's word to Jeroboam is certainly true as far as the narrative is concerned—Josiah fulfills it in 2 Kgs 23:15–18—but the prophet's word was not. The prophet tells the man of God that the word of YHWH that he, the prophet, has received revokes the earlier command to the man of God not to eat in the North, and then the narrator adds as an aside that כחש לו "he lied to him" (13:18). Are readers to take this to imply that the prophet lies to the man of God, or that God lied to the prophet? There is no sure way to tell. The conclusion of the story suggests the prophet thought up the lie in order to test the veracity of the man of God's word, but it is certainly possible that God lied to the prophet, just as he will lie to Ahab's prophets in 1 Kgs 22, and told him to invite the man of God to eat. The possibility that God has lied clearly subverts the narrative's concepts of God, justice, and punishment; and if God has not lied, then the prophet has lied, just as Micaiah initially does in 1 Kgs 22:15, and this possibility is a further subversion of the narrative's presentation of prophecy as the forum of clear divine instruction and warning. As at other places in the History—the undermining of Moses' veracity, Samuel's lies and self-interest, the story of Micaiah and Ahab's prophets—this story makes it impossible to distinguish between true and false prophecy. The narrative may claim that the destruction of Judah took place "according to the word of YHWH which he spoke through the hand of his servants the prophets" (2 Kgs 24:3), just as was the case for the destruction of the

80. As D. W. van Winkle points out, the somewhat odd use of the word מצוה in 13:21 in the condemnation of the man of God makes a connection with the "commandment" of Deuteronomy, which Moses tells Israel must be obeyed absolutely ("1 Kings xiii: True and False Prophecy," *VT* 39 [1989]: 31–43 [40–41]), and thus points out that Jeroboam has violated Deuteronomic law (idem, "1 Kings xii 25–xiii 34: Jeroboam's Cultic Innovations and the Man of God from Judah," *VT* 46 [1996]: 101–14). So what happens to the man of God will happen to Israel. See also Robert L. Cohn, "Literary Technique in the Jeroboam Narrative," *ZAW* 97 (1985): 23–35 (32–34).

Northern Kingdom (2 Kgs 17:13, 23), but trauma subverts the narrative's very concept of prophecy, and with it the narrative's concepts of God, justice, and punishment. In these stories, trauma intrudes into and subverts the narrative, suggesting that since God or his prophets can lie, God's will for Israel and the reasons why he acts in history—whether to kill the man of God in 1 Kgs 13 or a multitude of Samarians in 2 Kgs 6–7 and Judeans in 2 Kgs 25—cannot be clearly and unambiguously known. If God lied to Moses, or if Moses lied, then the narrative's logic that links cultic disloyalty to punishment is thrown into doubt, a doubt that uncannily foreshadows the presence of trauma's absence in the explanation of 2 Kgs 21–25. In these prophetic stories, then, trauma subverts the narrative's totalizing explanation of the exilic community's trauma. God can lie to prophets (1 Kgs 22, and possibly 1 Kgs 13) and make misstatements to them about the future (1 Kgs 19:15–18), and prophets can lie in a matter of life and death (another possible interpretation of 1 Kgs 13:11–32) and can lie to protect God's lies (as Micaiah does in 1 Kgs 22:15).

After readers encounter the story of Micaiah and learn that God lies to prophets, and that prophets can lie to protect God's lies, they encounter the story of 2 Kgs 3:4–27, which begins in much the same way as Micaiah's story does: an Israelite king calls upon Jehoshaphat to join him in reconquering lost territory (2 Kgs 3:7 and 1 Kgs 22:3–4); Jehoshaphat responds by saying, "My people are your people, my horses are your horses" (2 Kgs 3:7; 1 Kgs 22:4); and Jehoshaphat says, early in both stories, "Is there not here a prophet of YHWH? Let us inquire of YHWH from him" (2 Kgs 3:11; 1 Kgs 22:7).[81] The similarities between the openings of 2 Kgs 3 and 1 Kgs 22 actually lead readers to expect that God will lie through Elisha in 2 Kgs 3 as he did through Ahab's 400 prophets in 1 Kgs 22:6, 11, 19–23. Yet Elisha's prophecy of 3:15–19 seems to come true in 3:20–25: water is miraculously provided to keep the armies of Israel, Judah, and Edom alive (3:16–17, 20); and the Israelites block up the springs of Moab and spoil the land with stones, and cut down its trees (3:25), all just as Elisha had said (3:19). But Elisha had also said, "You will strike (הכיתם) every fortified city and every choice city" (3:19), and we find in 3:25 that although Israel "*overturned* the cities (וערים יהרסו)," the slingers can only futilely *strike* (ויהכוה) Kir-haresheth (3:25), a city that Israel fails to conquer altogether. So by

81. This is Jehoshaphat's phrasing in 2 Kgs 3:11. In 1 Kgs 22:7, since the 400 prophets of Ahab have already begun to prophesy, he says, "Is there not here another prophet of YHWH? Let us inquire from him."

the end of the story, Elisha's prophecy has only been partially fulfilled, for Israel overturns (הרס) Moab's cities, and the only one they strike (נכה) is the one where their failure forces them to withdraw.[82]

Paul Kissling argues that of the prophecy of 3:16–19, only 3:16–17, dealing with the miraculous provision of water to the armies, is really from God, since only here does Elisha say, "Thus says YHWH"; the continuation of the prophecy in 3:18–19, in Kissling's view, does not reflect God's word.[83] The fact of the matter is, however, given the similarities with the story of Micaiah, we now expect God to lie through the prophets, and these similarities suggest, although not unequivocally, that God has lied to the king of Israel and his allies to bring defeat to Israel, just as was the case in 1 Kgs 22. Of course, it does not really matter to the Israelite army if God or the prophet is responsible for the lie. The story subverts Dtr's master narrative, just as 1 Kgs 22 does, but it now accustoms readers to expect God to lie through his prophets, or at the very least to expect the prophets to lie, and thus to mislead hearers as to the divine word that could lead to salvation. The narrative's concepts of God, justice, and prophecy have been subverted again. As readers become accustomed to lies from the prophets, of either divine or prophetic origin, they are uncannily prepared for trauma's subversion of the narrative's explanation of the exiles' trauma in 2 Kgs 21–25, where God does not really act as the prophet Moses had said he would.

The final failure of Elisha's prophecy in 3:26–27 contains a subversion of Dtr's narrative that readers have not previously encountered (at least not so openly as here), since it is in these verses that the king of Moab, pressed by the Israelites and their allies, sacrifices his son on the wall of Kir-haresheth, "and great wrath came upon Israel, and they pulled back from him and returned to the land." This "is one of the most perplexing items in Scripture,"[84] since one of the obvious ways to interpret it is that the Moabite king has sacrificed his son to Chemosh, and the wrath of this god now forces the Israelites to withdraw. One could, of course, argue that the wrath in question is from YHWH, and Richard Nelson says that the narrative has already established in 1 Kgs 18, the story of Elijah and

82. This distinction of הרס and נכה is thus important to the presentation of this story and the ultimate failure of Elisha's prophecy to come true. So also Jesse C. Long, Jr., "Elisha's Deceptive Prophecy in 2 Kings 3: A Response to Raymond Westbrook," *JBL* 126 (2007): 168–71, who rightly makes this argument against Raymond Westbrook, "Elisha's True Prophecy in 2 Kings 3," *JBL* 124 (2005): 530–32.

83. Kissling, *Reliable Characters*, 185–86.

84. So Cogan and Tadmor, *II Kings*, 47.

the prophets of Baal, that YHWH alone acts in history,[85] but that case was a contest between YHWH and Baal, not YHWH and Chemosh. Scholars have also argued that the Israelites withdraw here because they are simply terrified by the human sacrifice,[86] or disgusted by it,[87] or that the wrath is really YHWH's, and Elisha has enticed Jehoram to defeat, just as Micaiah enticed Ahab.[88] But one of the possibilities that the lack of narrative explanation leaves available is that the god of Moab has acted in history to force the Israelite withdrawal, and some scholars read the text this way.[89] The very fact that we see ambiguity on this issue at all reflects new traumatic intrusion into Dtr's narrative, for trauma, like the master narrative itself, has never before questioned in such an open way God's power to rule history absolutely; ambiguity here directly conflicts with the narrative's assertion that YHWH alone controls history, and thus opens the door to the suggestion that this is not the only divine will that can bring punishment and salvation. If it is at least possible that YHWH is not the only divine being who controls history, then perhaps that explains why, in 2 Kgs 21–25, a generation who appears righteous is subjected to trauma while disloyal generations were spared: YHWH, despite what the narrative says, is not alone in his control of history and so cannot always do what the narrative says he will.

In the stories of the prophets that we have just surveyed, we see trauma subvert the narrative's concept of a God who acts justly to punish and save the people and who clearly reveals the logic that he uses to control history. God can apparently punish and save for no explained reason, as in the story of the siege of Samaria in 2 Kgs 6:24–7:20, which parallels the siege, famine, and mass death the exilic community experiences and

85. Nelson, *First and Second Kings*, 169–70.

86. So, e.g., James A. Montgomery, *A Critical and Exegetical Commentary on the Books of Kings* (ICC; Edinburgh: T. & T. Clark, 1951), 364; Long, *2 Kings*, 44.

87. So Sweeney, *I & II Kings*, 279–80, 284. Sweeney argues that the wrath that comes over Israel in 3:27 could not be YHWH's, since that would leave Elisha's prophecy of 3:19 unfulfilled, and so the wrath is actually Israel's own.

88. So Jesse C. Long, Jr. and Mark Sneed, "'Yahweh Has Given these Three Kings into the Hand of Moab': A Socio-Literary Reading of 2 Kings 3," in *Inspired Speech: Prophecy in the Ancient Near East. Essays in Honor of Herbert B. Huffmon* (ed. John Kaltner and Louis Stulman; JSOTSup 378; London: T&T Clark International, 2004), 253–75 (266–67). In a somewhat similar way, David Noel Freedman says that Dtr allows Jehoram to have the victory over Moab that fulfills Elisha's prophecy, but because of his continued apostasy, God makes him retreat immediately (communication cited in Cogan and Tadmor, *II Kings*, 52 n. 8).

89. E.g., Jones, *1 and 2 Kings*, 400; Gray, *I & II Kings*, 439; John Barclay Burns, "Why Did the Besieging Army Withdraw? (II Reg 3,27)," *ZAW* 102 (1990): 187–94.

witnesses in 2 Kgs 25. God can lie through the prophets, as in the story of Micaiah in 1 Kgs 22, and prophets like Micaiah can lie to protect his lies. In stories like 1 Kgs 13 involving the prophet and the man of God, or 2 Kgs 3 involving Elisha and the invasion of Moab, it is not clear whether God or his prophet lies, although there is no practical difference between the two options for readers, since the truth of God's will is obscured in either event. God does not always fulfill what he announces to the prophets, as in the case of 1 Kgs 19:15–18, nor does he always seem interested in acting according to the narrative's claims in regard to the link between cultic disloyalty and punishment. Trauma has even suggested in 2 Kgs 3 that YHWH is not the only divine power who controls history. While it is possible also to interpret these stories in ways that cohere with the narrative's explanatory logic in history, all of these cases reflect trauma's intrusion as explanatory absence that subverts the narrative's claim that God acts consistently and for just and predictable reasons in history, and trauma's subversion of the narrative in 2 Kgs 21–25 bears out these doubts that the exiles' trauma can be absolutely explained on the narrative's terms.

3. *The Subversion of the Narrative's Foreshadowings of 586*

In fact, when we turn to three passages in Kings—Solomon's prayer of 1 Kgs 8; the explanation for the destruction of Samaria in 2 Kgs 17; and the siege and salvation of Jerusalem in 2 Kgs 18–19—where the narrative refers either explicitly or implicitly to 586 itself and thus foreshadows and attempts to explain this trauma, we find the same subversions of the narrative's portrayal of a God who justly distributes punishment and salvation to Israel.[90] In 1 Kgs 8, Solomon, who has been given God's wisdom, suggests that God does not always live up to the narrative's conception of him as responding to repentance, an act of loyalty, with salvation. In 8:46–51, the prayer's seventh petition, Solomon refers specifically to the possibility of exile and asks that God respond to Israel's repentance in exile and to forgive, apparently not trusting God to live up to the standards previously enunciated in Deut 30:1–5. Solomon does not even bother to ask that God return Israel to the land as Moses promises in Deut 30:6–10, but only that they receive compassion from their captors, even though in the second petition (8:33–34) he does make the link between repentance (שׁוב) and return (שׁוב) to the land. It is always possible to see the narrative here as merely reinforcing through

90. 2 Kgs 6:24–7:20 is also a clear parallel to the destruction of Jerusalem in 2 Kgs 25, but since we have already examined trauma's subversion of the narrative there, I do not include it in the discussion here.

Solomon's mouth claims that it has already made, but trauma is present in the explanatory absence here that makes other interpretations possible. The insecurity that YHWH will not recognize repentance at all can be seen as built into the framework of this prayer, and not only in vv. 46–51, but throughout. In the second and third petitions (vv. 33–36), Solomon asks that God relent from punishment in the face of repentance, something that the fourth petition (vv. 37–40), with its use of סלח "to forgive," also implies. Solomon, in short, feels a need to ask God to respond to repentance with salvation throughout his prayer, even though, based on the master narrative's portrayals of God, justice, punishment, repentance, and salvation, we might expect such an idea to be so basic that there is no point in asking. Yet the prophetic stories that we have just examined suggest that Solomon is wise to ask, as does 2 Kgs 21–25 where God seems to respond to repentance and renewed cultic loyalty with punishment. These stories and Solomon's prayer manifest the same traumatic subversion of the narrative's assertion that God acts justly and, therefore, that history is knowable and controllable. If, as trauma suggests at these points, history does not operate according to the logic by which the narrative claims it does, then neither history nor the trauma in which the exiles live can be explained.

And by the time we reach the little that the narrative does say directly in 2 Kgs 25 about the siege, famine, mass death, and destruction of Jerusalem and Judah of 586, we learn that "the anger of YHWH was against Jerusalem and Judah until he cast them away from before him" (24:20). There is no precise listing of sins here, one could argue, because the narrative has already explained the exile in reference to the sins of Manasseh in 21:1–16, although this argument does not deal with the fact that God does not punish even one of the generations who sins during the extreme disloyalty of Judah during the reigns of Manasseh, Amon, and the first 17 years of Josiah, but only 35 years after Josiah returns the nation's cultic loyalty to YHWH. When we turn to another passage that foreshadows 586, 2 Kgs 17:1–23, we find a pericope that is much more precise in regard to the sins that caused the final siege and destruction of Samaria and the exile of the North, making this invasion, siege, and exile a prototype of 586. The long explanation of 17:7–23 lists sins that are almost all entirely cultic in nature, and so would seem to provide a just explanation for the destruction of Samaria and Israel in accordance with the narrative's logic in history. Yet even here, at one of the most important validations of the narrative's portrayal of history, trauma intrudes. Some of the sins listed in 2 Kgs 17 have been ascribed only to Judah and its kings (e.g., the worship of the host of heaven [17:16; cf. 21:3, 5], or the practice of passing children through fire [17:17; cf. 16:3; 21:6]), and others practiced in the North but mainly ascribed to Southerners in Dtr (e.g., the worship at high places and pillars [17:9–11]). The passage, in short, "fails to make a very good case that the fall of northern Israel was justified."[91]

For these reasons, Pauline Viviano argues that 2 Kgs 17 is really directed against the sins of Judah and constructed with the fall of the South in mind.[92] Other scholars argue that readers will assume that Israel has committed all of these sins just as Judah has.[93] Both assumptions are reasonable, but the problem lies with the very point that they are assumptions, and that the passage can leave readers with the uncanny feeling that Israel is being judged for crimes that it did not commit, or that at the very least that it has committed less than its Southern neighbor. God's judgment here, like Solomon's in 1 Kgs 3, seems sloppy and poorly articulated by the master narrative. It is precisely the gaps in the narrative at this extremely important realization of its logic in history that throws its explanation of trauma into doubt. Trauma has again subverted the narrative's concepts of God, justice, and punishment with ambiguity. The ambiguity derives from these lacunae in the narrative, and these derive from the powerful absence that is trauma. Second Kings 17:1–23, describing the destruction of Samaria and the Northern Kingdom, including a three-year siege of the capital that the narrative covers in fourteen words,[94] is for the narrative a clear warning of what could happen to Judah and Jerusalem, and yet it suggests here that God is willing to punish for sins that the recipients of the punishment have not actually committed, or have committed less than others who are not punished. These gaps of narrative explanation are echoed in the depiction of the destruction of Judah during the generations after Josiah returns the nation to cultic loyalty rather than during the time of the generations whom Manasseh, Amon, and the young Josiah cause to sin.

When, of course, the perfect act of repentance by Josiah makes no discernable difference in the fate of Judah, the exiles might well ask themselves if the future holds anything open for them except a repetition of trauma. God's failure to respond to repentance with salvation, as was

91. Jobling, "The Salvation of Israel," 55.

92. Pauline A. Viviano, "2 Kings 17: A Rhetorical and Form-Critical Analysis," *CBQ* 49 (1987): 548–59. See also Provan, *Hezekiah and the Books of Kings*, 72–73.

93. See Knoppers, *Two Nations Under God*, 2:64 n. 36; 2:197; Cogan and Tadmor, *2 Kings*, 206–14; Marc Zvi Brettler, "Ideology, History and Theology in 2 Kings 17:7–23," *VT* 39 (1989): 268–82 (275).

94. ויעל שמרון ויצר עליה שלש שנים בשנת התשיעית להושע לכד מלך־אשור את־שמרון "And he went up to Samaria and he besieged it three years. In the ninth year of Hoshea, the king of Assyria captured Samaria."

the case with Israel's repentance in Judg 10:10–16 and Saul's in 1 Sam 15:24–31, is a clear subversion of the concepts of repentance and salvation in the narrative. And it is not simply the story of Josiah where we see this particular subversion of Dtr's master narrative; the same can be said for the story of Hezekiah's cultic reform as well. Following the destruction of the North for its cultic sins in 2 Kgs 17, one could argue that, in the third and final passage that we will examine here, God's salvation of Jerusalem from Sennacherib's siege in 2 Kgs 18–19 in the context of a proper Deuteronomistic cultic reform by Hezekiah is really a place where we can see Dtr's narrative taking control of the trauma of 586.[95] That is, in comparison to the situation of the Northern Kingdom, whose kings caused the people to sin like the nations, God does not destroy but saves Jerusalem because its Davidic king exercises proper cultic loyalty towards the divine suzerain. This fits nicely into the way that the master narrative demonstrates how God controls history in response to the actions of Israel and its leaders. In the narrative contrast of 2 Kgs 17 with 2 Kgs 18–19, the exiles can clearly see that cultic disloyalty leads to punishment while cultic loyalty leads to salvation.

This narrative assertion seems particularly obvious when we pay attention to the narrative's emphasis on the salvation of Jerusalem in the context of Hezekiah's trust in YHWH. After all, what is at stake in the Rabshakeh's speech to Jerusalem in 18:19–35 and the letter of Sennacherib in 19:9–13 is trust (בטח) in God's ability to deliver (נצל). Hezekiah, who removes Solomon's apostate high places and other earlier acts of cultic disobedience (18:3–5) "trusted in YHWH" like no other king before or after (18:5). This trust to which the narrative refers in its recounting of Hezekiah's cultic reforms is also linked to his observance of the "commandments that YHWH commanded Moses" (18:6). Second Kings 18:9–12 even reminds us that the destruction of the North occurred "because they did not listen to the voice of YHWH their God and transgressed his covenant, all that Moses the servant of YHWH commanded" (v. 12).[96] As we have already seen at the beginning of this chapter, the Rabshakeh

95. For the argument that the Hezekiah narrative was produced in 588 to speak directly to the siege of Jerusalem, see Christof Hardmeier, *Prophetie im Streit vor dem Untergang Judas: Erzählkommunikative Studien zur Entstehungssituation der Jesaja- und Jeremiaerzählungen in II Reg 18–20 und Jer. 37–40* (BZAW 187; Berlin: de Gruyter, 1990).

96. As Cohn points out, when the Rabshakeh begins to ridicule the notion of trust in Egypt in 18:19–25, it is not clear at first that Egypt is actually the object of his derision, since he does not mention the country until v. 21. As a result, the kind of trust that readers, at first, will think he refers to is Hezekiah's trust in YHWH, which the narrative has just praised (*2 Kings*, 129–30).

uses the verb בטח six times in 18:19–21, 24 in reference to Judah's vain trust in Egypt to deliver them from Assyria. He uses it again in 18:22 in reference to what he sees as vain trust in YHWH since Hezekiah has enacted his cultic reform that removed Yahwistic shrines that were outside of the temple, and again in 18:30, part of the Rabshakeh's larger argument in vv. 29–35 that YHWH will not deliver, for no god has delivered any other nation from Sennacherib's army. The root נצל occurs eight times in 18:29–35. Sennacherib also uses both בטח and נצל in his letter of 19:9–13 to repeat the Rabshakeh's argument that no god so far has delivered any nation from the power of Assyria. As we discussed at the beginning of the chapter, in a story that lauds Hezekiah as exhibiting perfect trust in YHWH, the king is faced with a choice between trusting in the power of his God to control history and the power of "the great king, the king of Assyria," and he chooses correctly. He would appear to be a fine example of leadership in the eyes of the master narrative. Obeying the law God commanded through Moses and exhibiting true vassal loyalty through his cultic actions and trust, he is a stark contrast to the kings of the North who followed in the sins of Jeroboam and caused their people to sin. If any part of Kings might seem to validate the narrative's explanation for the destruction of Jerusalem and its logic in history, this would appear to be it.

Trauma, however, subverts the master narrative's explanation of history even here. There is, first, the question of why Hezekiah's great trust and proper cultic reform of 18:1–6—an act of repentance, although the narrative does not explicitly call it that—is met with invasion and siege. The story ultimately ends well for Hezekiah and Jerusalem, but readers might wonder why God did not spare Jerusalem the siege in the first place, given the great trust and cultic loyalty that Hezekiah demonstrates. Siege and destruction of the land through foreign invasion, after all, are realizations of the curses of Deut 28, and the narrative has continually presented invasion as a punishment for cultic disloyalty (Judg 2:11–3:6; 3:7–8, 12–14; 4:1; 6:1–5; 10:6–9; 13:1; 1 Sam 7:3–13; 1 Kgs 11:14–25; 14:22–26; 2 Kgs 13:1–3; 15:17–20, 28–29; 16:1–9; 17:1–23), and while it is possible to see how the North has earned such a fate, it is difficult to see why Judah during the time of Hezekiah has. Second, we should note that in 18:19–35, the Rabshakeh actually provides six reasons why Jerusalem should surrender: (1) Trust in the help of Egypt is futile (18:19–21); (2) Hezekiah has removed Yahwistic altars, and so trust in YHWH is futile (18:22); (3) Judah does not have the forces to resist a full-scale invasion (18:23–24); (4) YHWH has ordered Assyria to invade Judah (18:25), a claim that the Rabshakeh sets up in 18:22, when he says that Hezekiah has destroyed Yahwistic altars throughout the land;[97] (5) The people in Jerusalem will be forced "to eat their dung and drink their urine" during a siege, which warns of famine conditions (18:27); and (6) No god has delivered any nation from Assyria, so Jerusalem should not expect YHWH to do so (18:32b–35). It is this last argument that Sennacherib repeats in his letter in 19:9–13. Notably, as we shall see below, both Hezekiah and YHWH think that only one of these arguments will really compel God to act, and that is the last one. As we have seen so frequently before in our examinations of traumatic intrusions to the master narrative, YHWH can be seen to be willing to abandon any kind of just rule of history in regards to punishment and salvation when he feels his reputation as the one who controls history is threatened.

Both of these issues—the lack of explanation for the siege and God's sole concern with his reputation for power—clearly subvert the narrative's view of justice. The first suggests that God allows history to wander out of control, or that he punishes king and nation for no stated reason, which is precisely what trauma suggests in 2 Kgs 21–25, where Judah is punished only some decades after Josiah returns the people to cultic loyalty. The fact that the cultic reform of Hezekiah is immediately followed by an invasion and siege indicts the narrative's logic in history that tries to explain trauma, just as surely as God's failure to reward Josiah's repentance does. By the narrative's logic, repentance, which returns the people to vassal loyalty, should be met with salvation, and when loyalty is met with destruction instead then there seems to be no way to explain what YHWH does. One could argue that the ultimate salvation of Jerusalem merely justifies the master narrative's points in regard to loyalty and leadership, but the absence in explanation is still an absence, and one that manifests the presence of trauma.

The second issue of God's sole concern with his reputation for power is subversive for a somewhat different reason. It is in fact possible to understand the Rabshakeh's sixth and final reason why Jerusalem should surrender (and the only reason that Sennacherib repeats in his letter) as the claim that YHWH will not save Jerusalem, not that YHWH cannot save Jerusalem, especially given his claims in 18:22 and 25 that YHWH supports the Assyrian attack since Hezekiah destroyed his altars, but YHWH himself interprets the issue in Isaiah's oracle of 19:21–34 as the Assyrian claim that they and not he control history. This is odd, since we would expect YHWH to react first, if not solely, to the idea that the destruction of places of worship that his law forbids angers him, but he and his prophet never refer to this. And again, the narrative might simply

97. So also Hobbs, *2 Kings*, 258; Sweeney, *I & II Kings*, 416.

see Hezekiah's loyalty as the primary motivating factor behind the salvation of Jerusalem here, but such an explanation is lacking. Instead, according to Isaiah's oracle of salvation for Jerusalem, the reason why God will save the city is because of Sennacherib's boasts of power (19:23–24) through which "you taunted the Lord." The Assyrian rejection of trust in YHWH's ability to deliver is met in this oracle with the assertion that their taunting (חרף in 19:22, 23), reviling (גדף in 19:22), and raging against (רגז in 19:27, 28) YHWH is the reason why God will defeat them:

> Because you have raged against me and your arrogance has gone up in my ear,
> I have set my hook in your nose and my bit in your lips
> and I will turn you back on the way in which you have come (19:28).

Isaiah provides oracles of deliverance for Jerusalem in 19:6–7 and 20–34, but not once does God say that he will deliver because Hezekiah has returned the people to cultic loyalty to him. As far as readers can see, he acts only because of his reputation. The cultic loyalty has not only failed to stop the invasion in the first place, but in the absence of Assyria's arrogance—in the absence, in short, of the Rabshakeh's sixth argument, which claims that YHWH would not save Jerusalem and that YHWH interprets to mean that he cannot save—one wonders if God would even bother to save Jerusalem at all. Perhaps, trauma suggests, God allows the Babylonian destruction of Jerusalem not to punish Judah justly —after all, if justice were being done here we might expect some explanation as to why God does not respond to Josiah's repentance that returns the people to cultic loyalty—but simply because justice as the narrative defines it is not his interest.

Hezekiah himself seems to see a desire on God's part to bolster his reputation, and his approach to Isaiah in 19:2–4 and his prayer of 19:15–19 refer specifically and solely to Assyria's arrogance in challenging YHWH's power as motivation for deliverance. His prayer, in fact, picks up on the Rabshakeh's and Sennacherib's references to the failures of other gods to save other lands (18:33–35; 19:12–13), and Hezekiah tells YHWH that the Assyrians are comparing YHWH to these other gods, although "they are not gods but the work of human hands, wood and stone" (19:18). "Save us from his hand," Hezekiah concludes his prayer in response to Sennacherib's letter, "so that all the kingdoms of the earth might know that you, YHWH, are God alone" (19:19). His prayer suggests that the only thing that matters about the Assyrian invasion is the claim, verbalized through the Rabshakeh and Sennacherib, that YHWH does not control history. This is the only idea on which YHWH fixates also, and the oracle concludes with God saying that "I will defend this city to save it, for my sake and for the sake of David my servant" (19:34). As far as readers can tell, what motivates him is the threat to his reputation to control history and so to keep his promise to David. Given the word God sends to Isaiah, God shows no interest in cultic loyalty or concern about those who might be condemned to eat their dung and drink their urine during a siege. The story suggests, as do others we have already discussed, that God does not act here according to the logic that rules history that the narrative presents, nor to distribute punishment and salvation when they have been earned, and he does not act out of compassion for Jerusalem's suffering. He acts for himself, regardless of whether or not such actions might be in accordance with the narrative's concepts of justice or punishment or salvation.

So in trauma's subversion of the narrative here, there is no sense for the exiles that God will act any differently in their case, for 2 Kgs 21–25 has also reported that God did not punish the generations whom Manasseh caused to sin and that he ignored Josiah's actions that returned Judah to cultic loyalty. His guidance of history, trauma suggests, is not really a response to Israel's ethical actions and cannot really be predicted, and so if God does not feel his honor mocked by the Babylonians he might let the exilic community's suffering go on forever. It is simply not clear in 2 Kgs 18–19 or in 2 Kgs 21–25, the story it uncannily foreshadows, that God cares about or is willing to recognize repentance. So the case may simply be that God will not respond to the exiles' repentance any more than he did to Josiah's. Even if he were to return them from exile, he might let them repeat the trauma for no just reason if by doing so he could prove his power to the nations. This subversion suggests that Israel cannot really know why God acts, and that God does not care about what happens to Israel when he does act.

Of course, we need not read 2 Kgs 18–19 this way; simply because the text does not say directly that YHWH responds to Hezekiah's cultic reform when he saves Jerusalem does not rule this out as a possible reading of these chapters. But it is this absence of explanation that trauma introduces in its eruption into the narrative that subverts its concepts of God, justice, punishment, repentance, and salvation, and that suggests that we can find no logic in history. Trauma resists and subverts the narrative's explanatory claims for trauma, and so sees no future at all. As we saw at the end of the discussion of the narrative of the monarchy in section A, it is trauma that has closed off the narrative at the end of Kings—or, perhaps, left it without an ending—in its refusal to allow explanatory logic to unambiguously dictate the future. At the narrative's final collapse and its final failure to explain the failure of Josiah's repentance, or God's failure to punish the sinful generations during the reigns of Manasseh, Amon, and the first 17 years of Josiah, or to give any sense as to which part or parts of the story in Kings should be the key interpretive guide(s) to the exilic community's future, it points to nothing except an absence of explanation, which is precisely what trauma is. Trauma has subverted the concepts that the narrative uses to explain history, and by throwing them into unresolved ambiguity and trial it undermines the narrative's attempt to control it. If readers cannot decide what future awaits the exiles, that is because trauma sees no future. There is no predictive, logical pattern on which to base such prophecy for trauma; this is precisely what the gaps and absences its intrusions into Dtr's explanatory narrative have pointed to all along. If God does not act justly but works in disregard of the law, if he does not clearly command and warn through the law and the prophets, if his actions of punishment and salvation bear no relation to justice or repentance, then history itself and the trauma that the exilic community, and perhaps the author of the History him or herself, have undergone are not explainable or containable in narrative. The narrative's ethical dictionary, still sitting on the shelves of the Garden of Eden and containing clear concepts that are put to use in an explanatory history, cannot capture or provide a totalizing account of trauma, but then no dictionary or concepts can.

Chapter 8

CONCLUSION: TRAUMA AND THE SUBVERSION OF DTR'S NARRATIVE

Beginning with Deut 1, where a generation of Israel dies outside of the land, the Deuteronomistic History appears fixated on the fate of the exiles. This is, of course, because its narrative is trying to explain their suffering to them by presenting an explanatory framework of history, showing how disloyalty to God leads again and again to destruction and suffering. Ensconced as these notices of vassal failure tend to be in clear ethical explanations for suffering and trauma, the very vehicle our author has chosen for explanation suggests also a traumatic fixation on events that he or she cannot truly know, understand, or explain. Trauma repeats in the literary works of survivors and their descendants because it is unknowable and yet very powerful, a force that survivors thus need and yet are unable to possess intellectually, and so one which they subject to constant questioning that produces no real insight. The author could have written a book of only a few chapters to relate and explain the destruction of Jerusalem and the exile; instead, readers encounter a 181-chapter history that continually repeats the exiles' suffering throughout Israel's past. And throughout the narrative's attempt in these chapters to provide a clear and totalizing explanation to explain the trauma of 586, it suffers gaps that subvert its explanation through ambiguity of interpretation, gaps that witness to the presence of this absent yet powerful trauma. Rather than discovering a series of intertwined but competing explanations for suffering such as the book of Job provides, we find in Dtr that trauma undermines the narrative's certainties through a lack of explanation, throwing the narrative's truths and concepts into an unending trial that reaches no verdict. Again and again we came across passages in Dtr that would admit of a reading that would cohere with the master narrative, but that are also rent through with enough ambiguity that they can be read in ways that directly challenge the explanation that the narrative presents as true.

Readers have perhaps noticed that, throughout Chapters 3 through 7, I spend roughly half of each chapter discussing the master narrative and half of each discussing trauma's subversion of it. This structure is misleading to some degree, for it can suggest that narrative and its traumatic subversion receive equal weight in Dtr. This is not really so; the narrative and its explanation of suffering and exile predominate while the ambiguity of trauma, so to speak, nibbles around its edges. As I hope to have shown, however, trauma is present enough in Dtr to throw the narrative's explanatory claims into questions that receive no answers. Trauma does not truly present a coherent counter-narrative, for it is present only in the ambiguity of narrative absence, and these absences can generally be filled in ways that make sense on the basis of the narrative's terms or definitions of things such as God, punishment, repentance, Israel, and so on. What this presence of traumatic ambiguity does provide is a lack of unambiguous and totalizing explanation.

And because of this, we cannot explain these gaps through some kind of theory of redaction, whether it be an existing or newly invented one. Trauma appears as a questioning of a coherent and totalizing narrative, and this means that, when we are able to read a passage as making sense on the terms of the master narrative that we have been tracking, we need not posit a redactional hand to explain it. I do not venture to guess as to whether or not the author knowingly left the narrative absences that we have found in the text in order promote a kind of internal theological dialogue; whether or not he or she intended them, the absences that subvert narrative explanation are present, undermining the violent gift that the narrative presents to its readers. Trauma's own gift to readers is merely violence that fractures this explanatory gift while being unable to replace it. Its powerful presence as literary absence mirrors its psychological manifestation in its readers; its violence to narrative explanation mirrors that of psychological trauma's alienation from the sense of self.

The use of trauma theory in the field of biblical studies is still in its infancy, and has largely been confined to the application of observations of the study of trauma in the fields of mental health to help make sense of biblical writings.[1] My use of trauma as a literary tool has, I hope, made clear that biblical writings produced by individuals and within

1. See, e.g., Daniel L. Smith-Christopher, *A Biblical Theology of Exile* (OBT; Minneapolis: Fortress, 2002), 89–104; William Morrow, "Post-Traumatic Stress Disorder and Vicarious Atonement in the Second Isaiah," in *Psychology and the Bible: A New Way to Read the Scriptures* (ed. J. Harold Ellens and Wayne G. Rollins; 4 vols.; Psychology, Religion, and Spirituality; Westport, Conn.: Praeger, 2004), 1:167-83; David G. Garber, Jr., "Traumatizing Ezekiel, the Exilic Prophet," in Ellens and Rollins, eds., *Psychology and the Bible*, 2:213–35. Garber's essay, however, is an example of a work in biblical studies that largely uses trauma theory as a method from literary criticism in his approach to the book of Ezekiel.

communities that have undergone terrible suffering have hidden depths to them that trauma theory can point to, if not elucidate. The depths of trauma are hidden because survivors and their descendants themselves cannot truly know them, but this does not mean that they do not leave traces in the biblical writings. On the contrary, they are remarkably powerful because they are unknowable, resulting in a search that can seem unending because the traces that they leave are ones of absences. Trauma is forever subverting attempts to make sense of it, yet its powerful and controlling unknowability forces survivors and their descendants to return again and again to this controlling yet incomprehensible force. Using trauma theory cannot bring this trauma to light anymore than the master narrative of the Deuteronomistic History or any other writing can; it can only point to the power of its absent presence.

Bibliography

Aaron, David. *Etched in Stone: The Emergence of the Decalogue.* New York: T&T Clark, 2006.

Ackroyd, Peter R. *The First Book of Samuel.* CBC. Cambridge: Cambridge University Press, 1971.

Adam, Klaus-Peter. "Nocturnal Intrusions and Divine Interventions on Behalf of Judah: David's Wisdom and Saul's Tragedy in 1 Samuel 26." *VT* 59 (2009): 1–33.

Albertz, Rainer. "In Search of the Deuteronomists: A First Solution to a Historical Riddle." Pages 1–17 in Römer, ed., *The Future of the Deuteronomistic History.*

———. *Israel in Exile: The History and Literature of the Sixth Century* B.C.E. Translated by David Green. SBL Studies in Biblical Literature 3. Leiden: Brill, 2004.

———. "Wer waren die Deuteronomisten? Das historische Rätsel einer literarischen Hypothese." *ET* 57 (1997): 319–38.

———. "Why a Reform Like Josiah's Must Have Happened." Pages 27–49 in Grabbe, ed., *Good Kings and Bad Kings.*

Alter, Robert. *The David Story: A Translation with Commentary of 1 and 2 Samuel.* New York: W. W. Norton, 1999.

Amit, Yairah. "The Delicate Balance in the Image of King Saul and Its Place in the Deuteronomistic History." Pages 71–79 in Ehrlich, ed., *Saul in Story and Tradition.*

———. *Hidden Polemics in Biblical Narratives.* Translated by Jonathan Chipman. BIS 25. Leiden: Brill, 2000.

———. "Literature in the Service of Politics: Studies in Judges 19–21." Pages 28–40 in Reventlow, Hoffman, and Uffenheimer, eds., *Politics and Theopolitics.*

———. "A Prophet Tested: Elisha, the Great Woman of Shunem, and the Story's Double Message." *BibInt* 11 (2003): 279–94.

Anderson, Bernhard W. *Understanding the Old Testament.* 4th ed. Englewood Cliffs, N.J.: Prentice Hall, 1986.

Assis, Elie. "The Choice to Serve God and Assist His People: Rahab and Yael." *Bib* 85 (2004): 82–90.

———. *Self-Interest or Communal Interest? An Ideology of Leadership in the Gideon, Abimelech and Jephthah Narratives (Judg 6–12).* VTSup 106. Leiden: Brill, 2005.

Auerhahn, Nanette C., and Dori Laub. "Intergenerational Memory of the Holocaust." Pages 21–42 in Danieli, ed., *International Handbook.*

Auld, A. G. "Judges 1 and History: A Reconsideration." *VT* (1975): 261–85.

Bailey, Randall C. "The Redemption of Yhwh: A Literary Critical Function of the Songs of Hannah and David." *BibInt* 3 (1995): 213–31.

Bar-Efrat, Shimon, *Das Erste Buch Samuel: Ein narratologisch-philologischer Kommentar.* Translated by Johannes Klein. BWANT 176. Stuttgart: Kohlhammer, 2007.

———. *Narrative Art in the Bible.* Sheffield: T&T Clark International, 2004.

Barocas, Harvey A., and Carol B. Barocas. "Wounds of the Fathers: The Next Generation of Holocaust Victims." *International Review of Psycho-Analysis* 6 (1979): 331–41.

Barthélemy, Dominique. *Critique textuelle de l'Ancien Testament: 1. Josué, Juges, Ruth, Samuel, Rois, Chroniques, Esdras, Néhémie, Esther*. OBO 50/1. Göttingen: Vandenhoeck & Ruprecht, 1982.

Barthelémy, Dominique et al. *The Story of David and Goliath: Textual and Literary Criticism*. OBO 73. Göttingen: Vandenhoeck & Ruprecht, 1986.

Begg, Christopher T. "The Significance of Jehoiachin's Release: A New Proposal." *JSOT* 11 (1986): 49–56.

Ben Zvi, Ehud. "Once the Lamp Has Been Kindled...: A Reconsideration of the MT *Nîr* in 1 Kgs 11:36; 15:4; 2 Kgs 8:19 and 2 Chr 21:17." *ABR* 39 (1991): 19–30.

Bergen, Wesley J. *Elisha and the End of Prophetism*. JSOTSup 286. Sheffield: Sheffield Academic, 1999.

Black, Fiona C., Roland Boer, and Erin Runions, eds. *The Labour of Reading: Desire, Alienation, and Biblical Interpretation*. SBLSS 36. Atlanta: Society of Biblical Literature, 1999.

Block, Daniel I. *Judges, Ruth*. NAC 6. Nashville: Broadman & Holman, 1999.

Bodner, Keith. *David Observed: A King in the Eyes of His Court*. Hebrew Bible Monographs 5. Sheffield: Sheffield Phoenix, 2005.

Boling, Robert G. "In Those Days There Was No King in Israel." Pages 33–48 in Bream, Heim, and Moore, eds., *A Light Unto My Path*.

———. *Judges: A New Translation with Introduction and Commentary*. AB 6A. Garden City, N.Y.: Doubleday, 1975.

Braulik, Georg. "Die Ausdrücke für 'Gesetz' im Buch Deuteronomium." Pages 1–38 in *Studien zum Deuteronomium*. SBA 2. Stuttgart: Katolisches Biblewerk, 1988.

———. *Deuteronomium 1–16,17*. NEBAT 15. Würzburg: Echter, 1986.

———. *Die Mittel deuteronomischer Rhetorik: Erhoben aus Deuteronomium 4,1–40*. AnBib 68. Rome: Biblical Institute, 1978.

Bream, Howard N., Ralph D. Heim, and Carey A. Moore, eds. *A Light Unto My Path: Old Testament Studies in Honor of Jacob M. Myers*. GTS 4. Philadelphia: Temple University Press, 1974.

Brekelmans, C. "Joshua xxiv: Its Place and Function." Pages 1–9 in *Congress Volume: Leuven 1989*. Edited by J. A. Emerton. VTSup 43. Leiden: Brill, 1991.

Breslau, Naomi, and Glenn C. Davis. "Posttraumatic Stress Disorder: The Etiologic Specificity of Wartime Stressors." *American Journal of Psychiatry* 144 (1987): 578–83.

Brettler, Marc Zvi. *The Book of Judges*. OTR. London: Routledge, 2002.

———. "The Book of Judges: Literature as Politics." *JBL* 108 (1989): 395–418.

———. "Ideology, History and Theology in 2 Kings 17:7–23." *VT* 39 (1989): 268–82.

———. "Jud 1,1–2,10: From Appendix to Prologue." *ZAW* 101 (1989): 433–35.

———. "Predestination in Deuteronomy 30:1–10." Pages 171–88 in Schearing and McKenzie, eds., *Those Elusive Deuteronomists*.

———. "The Structure of 1 Kings 1–11." *JSOT* 49 (1991): 87–97.

Briere, John. *Psychological Assessment of Adult Posttraumatic States: Phenomenology, Diagnosis, and Measurement*. 2d ed. Washington: American Psychological Association, 2004.

Bright, John. *The Authority of the Old Testament*. Nashville: Abingdon, 1967.

Brueggemann, Walter. *Testimony to Otherwise: The Witness of Elijah and Elisha*. St. Louis: Chalice, 2001.

Budde, Karl. *Die Bücher Samuel*. KHAT 8. Tübingen: J. C. B. Mohr, 1902.

Burns, John Barclay. "Why Did the Besieging Army Withdraw? (II Reg 3,27)." *ZAW* 102 (1990): 187–94.

Butler, Trent C. *Joshua*. WBC 7. Waco, Tex.: Word, 1983.

———. *Judges*. WBC 8. Nashville: Thomas Nelson, 2009.

Campbell, Antony F. *1 Samuel*. FOTL 7. Grand Rapids: Eerdmans, 2003.

———. *2 Samuel*. FOTL 8. Grand Rapids: Eerdmans, 2005.

———. *The Ark Narrative (1 Sam 4–6. 2 Sam 6): A Form-Critical and Traditio-Historical Study*. SBLDS 16. Missoula: Scholars Press, 1975.

Campbell, Antony F., and Mark A. O'Brien. *Unfolding the Deuteronomistic History: Origins, Upgrades, Present Text*. Minneapolis: Fortress, 2000.

Carlson, R. A. *David, the Chosen King: A Traditio-Historical Approach to the Second Book of Samuel*. Translated by Eric J. Sharpe and Stanley Rudman. Stockholm: Almqvist & Wiksell, 1964.

Carroll, Robert P. *When Prophecy Failed: Cognitive Dissonance in the Prophetic Traditions of the Old Testament*. New York: Seabury, 1979.

Caruth, Cathy, ed. *Trauma: Explorations in Memory*. Baltimore: The Johns Hopkins University Press, 1995.

Childs, Brevard S. *Introduction to the Old Testament as Scripture*. Philadelphia: Fortress, 1979.

Christensen, Duane L. *Deuteronomy 1:1–21:9*. WBC 6A. Thomas Nelson, 2001.

———. *Deuteronomy 21:10–34:12*. WBC 6B. Nashville: Thomas Nelson, 2002.

Clements, R. E. "Achan's Sin: Warfare and Holiness." Pages 113–26 in Penchansky and Redditt, eds., *Shall Not the Judge of All the Earth Do What is Right?*

Cogan, Mordechai. *1 Kings: A New Translation with Introduction and Commentary*. AB 10. New York: Doubleday, 2001.

Cogan, Mordechai, and Hayim Tadmor. *II Kings: A New Translation with Introduction and Commentary*. AB 11. New York: Doubleday, 1988.

Coggins, Richard. "What Does 'Deuteronomistic' Mean?" Pages 22–35 in Schearing and McKenzie, eds., *Those Elusive Deuteronomists*.

Cohn, Robert L. *2 Kings*. BO. Collegeville, Minn.: Liturgical, 2000.

———. "Literary Technique in the Jeroboam Narrative." *ZAW* 97 (1985): 23–35.

Collins, John J. *Introduction to the Hebrew Bible*. Minneapolis: Fortress, 2004.

Conroy, Charles. "Hiel Between Ahab and Elijah–Elishah: 1 Kgs 16,34 in Its Immediate Literary Context." *Bib* 77 (1996): 210–18.

Cortese, Enzo. "Lo schema deuteronomistico per i re di Giuda e d'Israele." *Bib* 56 (1975): 37–52.

Cross, Frank Moore. "The Theme of the Book of Kings and the Structure of the Deuteronomistic History." Pages 274–89 in *Canaanite Myth and Hebrew Epic: Essays in the History of the Religion of Israel*. Cambridge, Mass.: Harvard University Press, 1973.

Danieli, Yael, ed. *International Handbook of Multigenerational Legacies of Trauma*. New York: Plenum, 1998.

Des Pres, Terrence. "The Authority of Silence in Elie Wiesel's Art." Pages 49–57 in Rosenfeld and Greenberg, eds., *Confronting the Holocaust*.

deVries, Simon J. *Yesterday, Today, and Tomorrow: Time and History in the Old Testament*. Grand Rapids: Eerdmans, 1975.

Dietrich, Walter, "David in Überlieferung und Geschichte." *Verkündigung und Forschung* 22 (1977): 44–48.

———. "Martin Noth and the Future of the Deuteronomistic History." Pages 153–75 in McKenzie and Graham, eds., *The History of Israel's Traditions*.

———. *Prophetie und Geschichte: Eine redaktionsgeschichtliche Untersuchung zum deuteronomistischen Geschichtswer*. FRLANT 108. Göttingen, Vandenhoeck & Ruprecht, 1972.

Edelman, Diana Vikander. *King Saul in the Historiography of Judah*. JSOTSup 121. Sheffield: Sheffield Academic, 1991.

Ehrlich, Carol S., ed. *Saul in Story and Tradition*. FAT 47. Tübingen: Mohr Siebeck, 2006.

Ellens, Harold, and Wayne G. Rollins, eds. *Psychology and the Bible: A New Way to Read the Scriptures*. 4 vols. Psychology, Religion, and Spirituality. Westport, Conn.: Praeger, 2004.

Eph'al, Israel. *The City Besieged: Siege and Its Manifestations in the Ancient Near East*. CHANE 36. Leiden: Brill, 2009.

Erikson, Kai. *A New Species of Trouble: Explorations in Disaster, Trauma, and Community*. New York: W. W. Norton, 1994.

———. "Notes on Trauma and Community." Pages 183–99 in Caruth, ed., *Trauma*.

Eslinger, Lyle M. "A Change of Heart: 1 Samuel 16." Pages 341–61 in *Ascribe to the Lord: Biblical and Other Studies in Memory of Peter C. Craigie*. Edited by Lyle M. Eslinger and Glen Taylor. JSOTSup 67. Sheffield: JSOT, 1988.

———. *House of God or House of David? The Rhetoric of 2 Samuel 7*. JSOTSup 164. Sheffield: Sheffield Academic, 1994.

———. *Into the Hands of the Living God*. JSOTSup 84. BLS 24. Sheffield: Almond, 1989.

———. *Kingship of God in Crisis: A Close Reading of 1 Samuel 1–12*. BLS 10. Decatur, Ga.: Almond, 1985.

Exum, J. Cheryl. "The Centre Cannot Hold: Thematic and Textual Instabilities in Judges." Pages 578–600 in Knoppers and McConville, eds., *Reconsidering Israel and Judah*.

———. *Tragedy and Biblical Narrative: Arrows of the Almighty*. Cambridge: Cambridge University Press, 1992.

———. "The Tragic Vision and Biblical Narrative: The Case of Jephthah." Pages 59–83 in *Signs and Wonders: Biblical Texts in Literary Focus*. Edited by J. Cheryl Exum. Semeia. Atlanta: Scholars Press, 1989.

Eynikel, Erik. *The Reform of King Josiah and the Composition of the Deuteronomistic History*. OTS 33. Leiden: Brill, 1996.

Felman, Shoshana. "Education and Crisis, or the Vicissitudes of Teaching." Pages 1–56 in Felman and Laub, eds., *Testimony*.

Felman, Shoshana, and Dori Laub, eds. *Testimony: Crises of Witnessing in Literature, Psychoanalysis, and History*. New York: Routledge, 1992.

Felsen, Irit. "Transgenerational Transmission of Effects of the Holocaust: The North American Research Perspective." Pages 58–63 in Danieli, ed., *International Handbook*.

Fine, Ellen S. "Transmission of Memory: The Post-Holocaust Generation in the Diaspora." Pages 185–200 in Sicher, ed., *Breaking Crystal.*

Finkelstein, Israel. "The Archaeology of the Days of Manasseh." Pages 169–87 in *Scripture and Other Artifacts: Essays on the Bible and Archaeology.* Edited by Michael D. Coogan, J. Cheryl Exum, and Lawrence E. Stager. Louisville: Westminster John Knox, 1994.

Fitzmyer, Joseph A., and Daniel J. Harrington. *A Manual of Palestinian Aramaic Texts: Second Century B.C.–Second Century A.D.* BibOr 34. Rome: Biblical Institute, 1978.

Fokkelman, J. P. "A Lie, Born of Truth, too Weak to Contain It: A Structural Reading of 2 Sam 1:1–16." Pages 39–55 in *Prophets, Worship, and Theodicy: Studies in Prophetism, Biblical Theology, and Structural Rhetorical Analysis, and on the Place of Music in Worship.* OTS 23. Leiden: Brill, 1984.

———. *Narrative Art and Poetry in the Book of Samuel: A Full Interpretation Based on Stylistic and Structural Analyses.* 4 vols. SSN 20, 23, 27, 31. Assen: Van Gorcum, 1981–1993.

Fouts, David M. "Added Support for Reading '70 Men' in 1 Samuel vi 19." *VT* 42 (1992): 394.

Freud, Sigmund, *Beyond the Pleasure Principle.* Pages 18:7–64 in *SE.*

———. "Charcot." Pages 3:11–39 in *SE.*

———. "The Uncanny." Pages 17:219–52 in *SE.*

Fridman, Lea Wernick. *Words and Witness: Narrative and Aesthetic Strategies in the Representation of the Holocaust.* Albany: State University of New York Press, 2000.

Friedman, Richard Elliott. *The Exile and Biblical Narrative: The Formation of the Deuteronomistic and Priestly Works.* HSM 22. Chico, Calif.: Scholars Press, 1981.

Frisch, Amos. "Structure and Significance: The Narrative of Solomon's Reign (1 Kings 1–12:24)." *JSOT* 51 (1991): 3–14.

Fritz, Volkmar. *1 & 2 Kings: A Continental Commentary.* Translated by Anselm Hagedorn. Minneapolis: Fortress, 2003.

———. *Das Buch Josua.* HAT I/7. Tübingen: J. C. B. Mohr, 1994.

Frolov, Serge. "Bedan: A Riddle in Context." *JBL* 126 (2007): 164–67.

———. "Joshua's Double Demise (Josh. xxiv 28–31; Judg. ii 6–9): Making Sense of a Repetition." *VT* 58 (2008): 315–23.

———. "Rethinking Judges." *CBQ* 71 (2009): 24–41.

———. *The Turn of the Cycle: 1 Samuel 1–8 in Synchronic and Diachronic Perspectives.* BZAW 342. Berlin: de Gruyter, 2004.

Frye, Northrop. *The Great Code: The Bible and Literature.* New York: Harcourt Brace Jovanovich, 1982.

Garber, David G., Jr. "Traumatizing Ezekiel, the Exilic Prophet." Pages 2:213–35 in Ellens and Rollins, eds., *Psychology and the Bible.*

Garsiel, Moshe. *The First Book of Samuel: A Literary Study of Comparative Structures, Analogies and Parallels.* Ramat-Gan: Revivim, 1985.

George, Mark K. "Yhwh's Own Heart." *CBQ* 64 (2002): 442–59.

Gerbrandt, Gerald E. *Kingship According to the Deuteronomistic History.* SBLDS 87. Atlanta: Scholars Press, 1986.

Gooding, D. W. "An Approach to the Literary and Textual Problems in the David–Goliath Story." Pages 55–86 in Barthelémy et al., *The Story of David and Goliath.*

Gordon, Robert P. "David's Rise and Saul's Demise: Narrative Analogy in 1 Samuel 24–26." *TynBul* 31 (1980): 37–64.

Gorman, Frank H., Jr. *The Ideology of Ritual: Space, Time and Status in the Priestly Theology*. JSOTSup 91. Sheffield: Sheffield Academic, 1990.

Gottwald, Norman K. *The Hebrew Bible: A Socio-Literary Introduction*. Philadelphia: Fortress, 1985.

Grabbe, Lester L., ed. *Good Kings and Bad Kings*. LHBOTS 393. ESHM 5. London: T&T Clark International, 2005.

Granowski, Jan Jaynes. "Jehoiachin at the King's Table: A Reading of the Ending of the Second Book of Kings." Pages 173–88 in *Reading Between Texts: Intertextuality and the Bible*. Edited by Danna Nolan Fewell. Literary Currents in Biblical Interpretation. Louisville: Westminster John Knox, 1992.

Gray, John. *I & II Kings: A Commentary*. 2d ed. OTL. Philadelphia: Westminster, 1970.

Green, Barbara. "Enacting Imaginatively the Unthinkable: 1 Samuel 25 and the Story of Saul." *BibInt* 11 (2003): 1–23.

———. *How are the Mighty Fallen? A Dialogical Study of King Saul in 1 Samuel*. JSOTSup 365. Sheffield: Sheffield Academic, 2003.

Green, Bonnie L., et al. "Posttraumatic Stress Disorder: Toward DSM–IV." *Journal of Nervous and Mental Disease* 173 (1985): 406–11.

Gregory, Russell. "Irony and the Unmasking of Elijah." Pages 91–169 in Hauser and Gregory, *From Carmel to Horeb*.

Grønbaek, Jakob H. *Die Geschichte vom Aufstieg Davids (1 Sam. 15–2 Sam. 5): Tradition und Komposition*. Copenhagen: Munksgaard, 1971.

Gros Louis, Kenneth R. R. "The Difficulty of Ruling Well: King David of Israel." *Semeia* 8 (1977): 15–23.

Gunn, David M. *The Fate of King Saul: An Interpretation of a Biblical Story*. JSOTSup 14. Sheffield: JSOT, 1980.

———. *The Story of King David: Genre and Interpretation*. JSOTSup 6. Sheffield: JSOT, 1978.

Halpern, Baruch. *The First Historians: The Hebrew Bible and History*. University Park, Pa.: Pennsylvania State University Press, 1988.

Halpern, Baruch, and David S. Vanderhooft. "The Editions of Kings in the 7th–6th Centuries B.C.E." *HUCA* (1991): 179–244.

Hardmeier, Christof. "King Josiah in the Climax of the Deuteronomic History (2 Kings 22–23) and the Pre-Deuteronomic Document of a Cult Reform at the Place of Residence (23:4–15): Criticism of Sources, Reconstruction of Literary Pre-Stages and the the Theology of History in 2 Kings 22–23." Pages 123–63 in Grabbe, ed., *Good Kings and Bad Kings*.

———. *Prophetie im Streit vor dem Untergang Judas: Erzählkommunikative Studien zur Entstehungssituation der Jesaja- und Jeremiaerzählungen in II Reg 18–20 und Jer. 37–40*. BZAW 187. Berlin: de Gruyter, 1990.

Hauser, Alan J., and Russell Gregory. *From Carmel to Horeb: Elijah in Crisis*. JSOTSup 85. BLS 19. Sheffield: Almond, 1990.

Hawk, L. Daniel. *Every Promise Fulfilled: Contesting Plots in Joshua*. LCBI. Louisville: Westminster John Knox, 1991.

———. "The Problem with Pagans." Pages 153–63 in *Reading Bibles, Writing Bodies: Identity and the Book*. Edited by Timothy K. Beal and David M. Gunn. Biblical Limits. London: Routledge, 1997.

Heller, Roy L. *Power, Politics, and Prophecy: The Character of Samuel and the Deuteronomistic Evaluation of Prophecy*. LHBOTS 440. New York: T&T Clark International, 2006.

Herman, Judith Lewis. *Trauma and Recovery*. New York: Basic, 1992.

Herrmann, Siegfried. "Die konstruktive Restauration: Das Deuteronomium als Mitte biblischer Theologie." Pages 155–70 in *Probleme biblischer Theologie: Gerhard von Rad zum 70. Geburtstag*. Edited by Hans Walter Wolff. Munich: Kaiser, 1971.

Hertzberg, Hans Wilhelm. *I & II Samuel: A Commentary*. Translated by J. S. Bowden. OTL. Philadelphia: Westminster, 1964.

———. *Die Bücher Josua, Richter, Ruth*. ATD 9. Göttingen: Vandenhoeck & Ruprecht, 1985.

Hirsch, Marianne. "Marked by Memory: Feminist Reflections on Trauma and Transmission." Pages 71–91 in Miller and Tougaw, eds., *Extremities*.

Hobbs, T. R. *2 Kings*. WBC 13. Waco, Tex.: Word, 1985.

Hoffman, Yair. "The Deuteronomist and the Exile." Pages 659–75 in *Pomegranates and Golden Bells: Studies in Biblical, Jewish, and Near Eastern Ritual, Law, and Literature in Honor of Jacob Milgrom*. Edited by David P. Wright et al. Winona Lake, Ind.: Eisenbrauns, 1995.

Hoffmann, Hans-Detlef. *Reform und Reformen: Untersuchungen zu einen Grundthema der deuteronomistischen Geschichtsschreibung*. ATANT 66. Zurich: Theologischer Verlag, 1980.

Hudson, Don Michael. "Living in a Land of Epithets: Anonymity in Judges 19–21." *JSOT* 62 (1994): 49–66.

Humphreys, W. Lee. "From Tragic Hero to Villain: A Study of the Figure of Saul and the Development of 1 Samuel." *JSOT* 22 (1982): 95–117.

Janet, Pierre. *Psychological Healing: A Historical and Clinical Study*. Translated by Eden Paul and Cedar Paul. 2 vols. London: George Allen & Unwin, 1925.

Janzen, David. "An Ambiguous Ending: Dynastic Punishment in Kings and the Fate of the Davidides in 2 Kings 25:27–30." *JSOT* 33 (2008): 39–58.

———. *The Social Meanings of Sacrifice in the Hebrew Bible: A Study of Four Writings*. BZAW 344. Berlin: de Gruyter, 2004.

———. "Why the Deuteronomist Told about the Sacrifice of Jephthah's Daughter." *JSOT* 29 (2005): 339–57.

Japhet, Sara. *I & II Chronicles*. OTL. Louisville: Westminster John Knox, 1993.

———. *The Ideology of the Book of Chronicles and Its Place in Biblical Thought*. BEATAJ 9. Frankfurt am Main: Lang, 1989.

Jastrow, Marcus. *Dictionary of the Talmud, Babli, Yerushalmi, Midrashic Literature and Targumim*. New York: Pardes, 1950.

Jobling, David. *1 Samuel*. Berit Olam. Collegeville, Minn.: Liturgical, 1998.

———. "A Bettered Woman: Elisha and the Shunamite in the Deuteronomic Work." Pages 177–92 in Black, Boer, and Runions, eds., *The Labour of Reading*.

———. "'Forced Labor': Solomon's Golden Age and the Question of Literary Representation." Pages 57–76 in *Poststructuralism as Exegesis*. Edited by David Jobling and Stephen D. Moore. Semeia 54. Atlanta: Scholars Press, 1992.

———. "The Salvation of Israel in 'The Book of the Divided Kingdoms', or, Was there any 'Fall of the Northern Kingdom?'" Pages 50–61 in *Redirected Travel: Alternative Journeys and Places in Biblical Studies*. Edited by Roland Boer and Edgar W. Conrad. JSOTSup 382. London: T&T Clark International, 2003.

———. *The Sense of Biblical Narrative: Structural Analyses in the Hebrew Bible*, vol. 2. JSOTSup 39. Sheffield: JSOT, 1986.

Jones, Gwilym H. *1 and 2 Kings*. NCBC. Grand Rapids: Eerdmans, 1984.

Joüon, Paul. *A Grammar of Biblical Hebrew*. Translated and revised by T. Muraoka. 2 vols. SubBib 14. Rome: Pontificio Istituto Biblica, 1991.

Kaiser, Otto. *Der Gott des Alten Testaments*. Uni-Taschenbücher 1747. Göttingen: Vandenhoeck & Ruprecht, 1993.

Kaiser, Walter C. *Toward Old Testament Ethics*. Grand Rapids: Zondervan, 1983.

Kalaidjian, Walter. *The Edge of Modernism: American Poetry and the Traumatic Past*. Baltimore: The Johns Hopkins University Press, 2006.

Kaminsky, Joel S. *Corporate Responsibility in the Hebrew Bible*. JSOTSup 196. Sheffield: Sheffield Academic, 1995.

Kelly, Brian E. *Retribution and Eschatology in Chronicles*. JSOTSup 211. Sheffield: Sheffield Academic, 1996.

Keulen, Percy S. F. van. *Manasseh Through the Eyes of the Deuteronomists: The Manasseh Account (2 Kings 21:1–18) and the Final Chapters of the Deuteronomistic History*. OTS 38. Leiden: Brill, 1996.

———. *Two Versions of the Solomonic Narrative: An Inquiry into the Relationship Between MT 1 Kgs. 2–11 and LXX 3 Reg. 2–11*. VTSup 104. Leiden: Brill, 2005.

Keys, Gillian. *The Wages of Sin: A Reappraisal of the "Succession Narrative"*. JSOTSup 221. Sheffield: Sheffield Academic, 1996.

Kissling, Paul J. *Reliable Characters in the Primary History: Profiles of Moses, Joshua, Elijah and Elisha*. JSOTSup 224. Sheffield: Sheffield Academic, 1996.

Klein, Lillian. *The Triumph of Irony in the Book of Judges*. JSOTSup 68. BLS 14. Sheffield: Almond, 1988.

Klein, Ralph W. *1 Chronicles: A Commentary*. Hermeneia. Minneapolis: Fortress, 2006.

———. *1 Samuel*. WBC 10. Nashville: Thomas Nelson, 2008.

Knauf, Ernst Axel. "Does 'Deuteronomistic Historiography' (DtrH) exist?" Pages 388–98 in de Pury, Römer, and Macchi, eds., *Israel Constructs Its History*.

Knoppers, Gary. "Is There a Future for the Deuteronomistic History?" Pages 117–34 in Römer, ed., *The Future of the Deuteronomistic History*.

———. "Prayer and Propaganda: Solomon's Dedication of the Temple and the Deuteronomist's Program." Pages 370–96 in Knoppers and McConville, eds., *Reconsidering Israel and Judah*.

———. "Solomon's Fall and Deuteronomy." Pages 392–410 in *The Age of Solomon: Scholarship at the Turn of the Millennium*. Edited by Lowell K. Handy. SHCANE 11. Leiden: Brill, 1997.

———. "'There Was None Like Him': Incomparability in the Book of Kings." *CBQ* 54 (1992): 411–31.

———. *Two Nations Under God: The Deuteronomistic History of Solomon and the Dual Monarchies*. 2 vols. HSM 52–53. Atlanta: Scholars Press, 1993–1994.

Knoppers, Gary N., and J. Gordon McConville, eds. *Reconsidering Israel and Judah: Recent Studies on the Deuteronomistic History*. SBTS 8. Winona Lake, Ind.: Eisenbrauns, 2000.

Kogan, Ilany. *The Cry of Mute Children: A Psychoanalytic Perspective of the Second Generation of the Holocaust*. London: Free Association, 1995.

Kolk, Bessel A. van der. “Trauma and Memory.” Pages 279–302 in *Traumatic Stress: The Effects of Overwhelming Experience on Mind, Body, and Society*. Edited by Bessel A. van der Kolk, Alexander C. McFarlane, and Lars Weisaeth. New York: Guilford, 1996.

Kolk, Bessel A. van der, and Onno van der Hart. “The Intrusive Past: The Flexibility of Memory and the Engraving of Trauma.” Pages 158–82 in Caruth, ed., *Trauma*.

Kratz, Richard G. *The Composition of the Narrative Books of the Old Testament*. Translated by John Bowden. London: T&T Clark, 2005.

Langer, Laurence L. *Admitting the Holocaust: Collected Essays*. Oxford: Oxford University Press, 1995.

———. “Aharon Appelfeld and the Language of Sinister Silence.” Pages 125–38 in *Admitting the Holocaust*.

———. “Beyond Theodicy: Jewish Victims and the Holocaust.” Pages 25–30 in *Admitting the Holocaust*.

———. *Holocaust Testimonies: The Ruins of Memory*. New Haven: Yale University Press, 1991.

———. “Introduction.” Pages 3–12 in *Admitting the Holocaust*.

———. “Myth and Truth in Cynthia Ozick’s ‘The Shawl’ and ‘Rosa’.” Pages 139–44 in *Admitting the Holocaust*.

———. “The Literature of Auschwitz.” Pages 89–107 *Admitting the Holocaust*.

———. “A Tainted Legacy: Remembering the Warsaw Ghetto.” Pages 31–40 in *Admitting the Holocaust*.

Lasine, Stuart. “The Riddle of Solomon’s Judgment and the Riddle of Human Nature in the Hebrew Bible.” *JSOT* 45 (1989): 61–86.

Laub, Dori. “An Event Without a Witness: Truth, Testimony and Survival.” Pages 75–92 in Felman and Laub, eds., *Testimony*.

Leibowitz, E., and G. Leibowitz. “Solomon’s Judgment” (Hebrew). *Beth Mikra* 35 (1989–1990): 242–44.

Lenchak, Timothy A. *“Choose Life!”: A Rhetorical-Critical Investigation of Deuteronomy 28,69–30,20*. AnBib, 129. Rome: Pontificio Istituto Biblico, 1993.

Levenson, Jon D. “The Paronomasia of Solomon’s Seventh Petition.” *HAR* 6 (1982): 135–38.

Levine, Nachman. “Twice as Much of Your Spirit: Pattern, Parallel and Paronomasia in the Miracle of Elijah and Elisha.” *JSOT* 85 (1999): 25–46.

Lind, Millard C. *Yahweh is a Warrior: The Theology of Warfare in Ancient Israel*. Scottdale, Pa.: Herald, 1980.

Lindars, Barnabas. *Judges 1–5: A New Translation and Commentary*. Edited by A. D. H. Mayes. Edinburgh: T. & T. Clark, 1995.

Lipschits, Oded. *The Fall and Rise of Jerusalem: Judah Under Babylonian Rule*. Winona Lake, Ind.: Eisenbrauns, 2005.

Lohfink, Norbert. “Die Bedeutungen von hebr. *jrš qal* und *hif.*” *BZ* 27 (1983): 14–33.

———, ed. *Das Deuteronomium: Entstehung, Gestalt, und Botschaft*. BETL 68. Leuven: Peeters, 1985.

———. “Die ‘*ḥuqqîm umišpāṭîm*’ im Buch Deuteronomium und ihre Neubegrenzung durch Dtn 12:1.” *Bib* 70 (1989): 1–30.

———. *Das Hauptgebot: Eine Untersuchung literarischer Einleitungsfragen zu Dtn 5–11*. AnBib 20. Rome: Pontifical Biblical Institute, 1963.

Long, Burke O. *1 Kings with an Introduction to Historical Literature*. FOTL 9. Grand Rapids: Eerdmans, 1984.

———. *2 Kings*. FOTL 10. Grand Rapids: Eerdmans, 1991.

———. "A Figure at the Gate: Readers, Reading, and Biblical Theologians." Pages 166–86 in *Canon, Theology, and Old Testament Interpretation: Essays in Honor of Brevard S. Childs*. Edited by Gene M. Tucker, David L. Petersen, and Robert R. Wilson. Philadelphia: Fortress, 1988.

Long, Jesse C., Jr. "Elisha's Deceptive Prophecy in 2 Kings 3: A Response to Raymond Westbrook." *JBL* 126 (2007): 168–71.

Long, Jesse C., Jr., and Mark Sneed. "'Yahweh Has Given these Three Kings into the Hand of Moab': A Socio-Literary Reading of 2 Kings 3." Pages 253–75 in *Inspired Speech: Prophecy in the Ancient Near East: Essays in Honor of Herbert B. Huffmon*. Edited by John Kaltner and Louis Stulman. JSOTSup 378. London: T&T Clark International, 2004.

Long, V. Philips. *The Reign and Rejection of King Saul: A Case for Literary and Theological Coherence*. SBLDS 118. Atlanta: Scholars Press, 1989.

Lorenzy, Joseph. *Saul, Doeg, Nabal, and the "Son of Jesse": Readings in 1 Samuel 16–25*. LHBOTS 497. New York: T&T Clark, 2009.

Mabee, Charles. "David's Judicial Exoneration." *ZAW* 92 (1980): 89–107.

MacDonald, Nathan. *Deuteronomy and the Meaning of "Monotheism."* FAT 2/1. Tübingen: Mohr Siebeck, 2003.

Marais, Jacobus. *Representation in Old Testament Narrative Texts*. BIS 36. Leiden: Brill, 1998.

Mason, Rex. *Propaganda and Subversion in the Old Testament*. London: SPCK, 1997.

Mauchline, John. *1 and 2 Samuel*. NCB. London: Oliphants, 1971.

Mayes, Andrew D. H. "Deuteronomistic Ideology and the Theology of the Old Testament." *JSOT* 82 (1999): 57–82.

———. *Deuteronomy*. NCBC. Grand Rapids: Eerdmans, 1979.

———. "Deuteronomy 4 and the Literary Criticism of Deuteronomy." Pages 195–224 in *A Song of Power and the Power of Song: Essays on the Book of Deuteronomy*. Edited by Duane L. Christensen. SBTS 3. Winona Lake, Ind.: Eisenbrauns, 1993.

———. "Deuteronomy 29, Joshua 9, and the Place of the Gibeonites in Israel." Pages 321–25 in Lohfink, ed., *Das Deuteronomium*.

———. *The Story of Israel Between Settlement and Exile: A Redactional Study of the Deuteronomistic History*. London: SCM, 1983.

Mazar, Amihay. *The Archaeology of the Land of the Bible, 10,000–586 B.C.E.* ABRL. New York: Doubleday, 1992.

McCarter, P. Kyle. *I Samuel: A New Translation with Introduction, Notes & Commentary*. AB 8. Garden City, N.Y.: Doubleday, 1980.

———. *II Samuel: A New Translation with Introduction, Notes, and Commentary*. AB 9. Garden City, N.Y.: Doubleday, 1984.

McConville, J. G. "1 Kings viii 46–53 and the Deuteronomic Hope." *VT* 42 (1992): 65–79.

———. "Narrative and Meaning in the Book of Kings," *Bib* 70 (1989): 31–49.

McConville, J. G., and J. G. Millar. *Time and Place in Deuteronomy*. JSOTSup 179. Sheffield: Sheffield Academic, 1994.

McGlothin, Erin. *Second-Generation Holocaust Literature: Legacies of Survival and Perpetration*. Studies in German Literature, Linguistics, and Culture. Rochester, N.Y.: Camden House, 2006.

McKenzie, Steven L. "Deuteronomistic History." *ABD* 2:160–68.

———. "The Divided Kingdom in the Deuteronomistic History and in Scholarship on It." Pages 135–45 in Römer, ed., *The Future of the Deuteronomistic History*.

———. *King David: A Biography*. Oxford: Oxford University Press, 2000.

———. "Saul in the Deuteronomistic History." Pages 59–70 in Ehrlich, ed., *Saul in Story and Tradition*.

———. *The Trouble with Kings: The Composition of the Book of Kings in the Deuteronomistic History*. VTSup 42. Leiden: Brill, 1991.

———. "The Trouble with Kingship." Pages 286–314 in de Pury, Römer, and Macchi, eds., *Israel Constructs Its History*.

McKenzie, Steven L., and M. Patrick Graham, eds. *The History of Israel's Traditions: The Heritage of Martin Noth*. JSOTSup 182. Sheffield: Sheffield Academic, 1994.

Mead, James K. "Kings and Prophets, Donkeys and Lions: Dramatic Shape and Deuteronomistic Rhetoric in 1 Kings xiii." *VT* 49 (1999): 191–205.

Mendenhall, George E. "The Shady Side of Wisdom: The Date and Purpose of Genesis 3." Pages 319–34 in Bream, Heim, and Moore, eds., *A Light unto My Path*.

Milgrom, Jacob. *Cult and Conscience: The Asham and the Priestly Doctrine of Repentance*. SJLA 18. Leiden: Brill, 1976.

———. *Leviticus 1–16: A New Translation with Introduction and Commentary*. AB 3. New York: Doubleday, 1991.

Millar, J. Gary, *Now Choose Life: Theology and Ethics in Deuteronomy*. NSBT 6. Leicester: Apollos, 1998.

Miller, Nancy K., and Jason Tougow, eds. *Extremities: Trauma, Testimony, and Community*. Urbana, Ill.: University of Illinois Press, 2002.

Miller, Patrick D. *Deuteronomy*. Interpretation. Louisville: John Knox, 1990.

Miller, Patrick D., and J. J. M. Roberts, *The Hand of the Lord: A Reassessment of the "Ark Narrative" of 1 Samuel*. Johns Hopkins Near Eastern Studies. Baltimore: Johns Hopkins University Press, 1977.

Miscall, Peter D. *1 Samuel: A Literary Reading*. ISBL. Bloomington: Indiana University Press, 1986.

Mitchell, Gordon. *Together in the Land: A Reading of the Book of Joshua*. JSOTSup 134. Sheffield: JSOT.

Mobley, Gregory. *Samson and the Liminal Hero in the Ancient Near East*. LHBOTS 453. New York: T&T Clark, 2006.

Möhlenbrink, Kurt. "Die Landnahmensagen des Buches Josua." *ZAW* 56 (1938): 250–54.

Montgomery, James A. *A Critical and Exegetical Commentary on the Books of Kings*. ICC. Edinburgh: T. & T. Clark, 1951.

Moran, William L. "The Ancient Near Eastern Background of the Love of God in Deuteronomy." Pages 170–81 in *The Most Magic Word: Essays on Babylonian and Biblical Literature*. Edited by Ronald S. Hendel. CBQMS 35. Washington: The Catholic Biblical Association of America, 2002.

Morrow, William. "Post-Traumatic Stress Disorder and Vicarious Atonement in the Second Isaiah." Pages 1:167–83 in Ellens and Rollins, ed., *Psychology and the Bible*.

Mueller, Aydeet. *The Micah Story: A Morality Tale in the Book of Judges*. StBL 34. New York: Lang, 2001.
Mullen, E. Theodore, Jr. "Judges 1:1–3:6: The Deuteronomistic Reintroduction of the Book of Judges." *HTR* 77 (1984): 33–64.
———. "The Sins of Jeroboam: A Redactional Assessment." *CBQ* 49 (1987): 212–32.
Murray, Donald F. *Divine Prerogative and Royal Pretension: Pragmatics, Poetics and Polemics in a Narrative Sequence About David*. JSOTSup 264. Sheffield: Sheffield Academic, 1998.
———. "Of All the Years the Hopes—or Fears? Jehoiachin in Babylon (2 Kings 25:27–30)." *JBL* 120 (2001): 245–65.
Na'aman, Nadav. "The Danite Campaign Northward (Judges xvii–xviii) and the Migration of the Phocaeans to Massalia (Strabo iv 1,4)." *VT* 55 (2005): 47–60.
———. "Death Formulae and the Burial Places of the Kings of the House of David." *Bib* 85 (2004): 245–54.
———. "Population Changes in Palestine Following Assyrian Deportations." *TA* 20 (1993): 104–24.
Nelson, Richard D. *Deuteronomy: A Commentary*. OTL. Louisville: Westminster John Knox, 2002.
———. *The Double Redaction of the Deuteronomistic History*. JSOTSup 18. Sheffield: JSOT, 1981.
———. "The Double Redaction of the Deuteronomistic History: The Case is Still Compelling." *JSOT* 29 (2005): 319–37.
———. *First and Second Kings*. Interpretation. Louisville: John Knox, 1987.
———. *Joshua: A Commentary*. OTL. Louisville: Westminster John Knox, 1997.
———. "Josiah in the Book of Joshua." *JBL* 100 (1981): 531–40.
Nicholson, Sarah. *Three Faces of Saul: An Intertextual Approach to Biblical Tragedy*. JSOTSup 339. Sheffield: Sheffield Academic, 2002.
Niditch, Susan. *Judges: A Commentary*. OTL. Louisville: Westminster John Knox, 2008.
Noll, K. L. "Deuteronomistic History or Deuteronomic Debate? (A Thought Experiment)." *SJOT* 31 (2007): 311–45.
———. *The Faces of David*. JSOTSup 242. Sheffield: Sheffield Academic, 1997.
North, Robert. "The Theology of the Chronicler." *JBL* 82 (1963): 369–81.
Noth, Martin. *Das Buch Josua*. HAT 1/7. Tübingen: J. C. B. Mohr, 1938.
———. *The Deuteronomistic History*. Translated by Jane Doull et al. JSOTSup 15. Sheffield: JSOT, 1981.
O'Brien, Mark A. *The Deuteronomistic History Hypothesis: A Reassessment*. OBO 92. Göttingen: Vandenhoeck & Ruprecht, 1989.
O'Connell, Robert H. *The Rhetoric of the Book of Judges*. VTSup 63. Leiden: Brill, 1996.
O'Dowd, Ryan. *The Wisdom of Torah: Epistemology in Deuteronomy and the Wisdom Literature*. FRLANT 225. Göttingen: Vandenhoeck & Ruprecht, 2009.
Olley, John W. "Pharaoh's Daughter, Solomon's Palace, and the Temple: Another Look at the Structure of 1 Kings 1–11." *JSOT* 27 (2003): 355–69.
———. "Yhwh and His Zealous Prophet: The Presentation of Elijah in 1 and 2 Kings." *JSOT* 80 (1998): 25–51.
Olson, Dennis T. "The Book of Judges." Pages 2:721–888 in *The New Interpreter's Bible*. Edited by Leander Keck. 12 vols. Nashville: Abingdon, 1998–2005.

———. *Deuteronomy and the Death of Moses: A Theological Reading*. OBT. Minneapolis: Fortress, 1994.

Otto, Susanne. *Jehu, Elia und Elisa: Die Erzählung von der Jehu-Revolution und die Komposition der Elia-Elisa-Erzählungen*. BWANT 8/12. Stuttgart: Kohlhammer, 2001.

Parker, Kim. "Repetition as a Structuring Device in 1 Kings 1–11." *JSOT* 42 (1988): 19–27.

Penchansky, David, and Paul L. Redditt, eds. *Shall Not the Judge of All the Earth Do What is Right? Studies in the Nature of God in Tribute to James L. Crenshaw*. Winona Lake, Ind.: Eisenbrauns, 2000.

Perry, Campbell, and Jean-Roch Laurence. "Mental Processing Outside of Awareness: The Contributions of Freud and Janet." Pages 9–48 in *The Unconscious Reconsidered*. Edited by Kenneth S. Bowers and Donald Meichenbaum. New York: John Wiley & Sons, 1984.

Person, Raymond F., Jr. *The Deuteronomic School: History, Social Setting, and Literature*. SBL Studies in Biblical Literature 2. Leiden: Brill, 2002.

Polak, Frank H. "David's Kingship: A Precarious Equilibrium." Pages 119–47 in Reventlow, Hoffman, and Uffenheimer, eds., *Politics and Theopolitics*.

Polzin, Robert. *David and the Deuteronomist: 2 Samuel*. ISBL. Bloomington: Indiana University Press, 1993.

———. *Moses and the Deuteronomist: A Literary Study of the Deuteronomic History*. New York: Seabury, 1980.

———. *Samuel and the Deuteronomist: A Literary Study of the Deuteronomistic History*. Part 2, *1 Samuel*. ISBL. Bloomington: Indiana University Press, 1989.

Preuss, Horst Dietrich. *Old Testament Theology*. Translated by Leo G. Purdue. 2 vols. OTL. Louisville: Westminster John Knox, 1995.

Provan, Iain W. *1 and 2 Kings*. NIBC. Peabody, Mass.: Hendrickson, 1995.

———. *Hezekiah and the Books of Kings: A Contribution to the Debate about the Composition of the Deuteronomistic History*. BZAW 172. Berlin: de Gruyter, 1988.

———. "The Messiah in the Book of Kings." Pages 67–85 in *The Lord's Anointed: Interpretation of Old Testament Messianic Texts*. Edited by Philip Satterthwaite et al. Carlisle: Paternoster, 1995.

Pury, Albert de, Thomas C. Römer, and Jean-Daniel Macchi, eds. *Israel Constructs Its History: Deuteronomistic Historiography in Recent Research*. JSOTSup 306. Sheffield: Sheffield Academic, 2000.

Pyper, Hugh S. *David as Reader: 2 Samuel 12:1–15 and the Poetics of Fatherhood*. BIS 23. Leiden: Brill, 1996.

———. "Judging the Wisdom of Solomon: The Two-Way Effect of Intertextuality." *JSOT* 59 (1993): 25–36.

Rad, Gerhard von. *Deuteronomy: A Commentary*. Translated by Dorothea Barton. OTL. Philadelphia: Westminster, 1966.

———. *Das Geschichtsbild des Chronistischen Werkes*. BWANT 54. Stuttgart: Kohlhammer, 1930.

———. *Old Testament Theology*. Translated by D. M. G. Stalker. 2 vols. New York: Harper & Row, 1962–1965.

———. *The Problem of the Hexateuch and Other Essays*. Translated by E. W. Trueman Dicken. London: SCM, 1984.

———. *Studies in Deuteronomy*. Translated by David Stalker. SBT 9. London: SCM, 1953.

Regev, Eyal. "Priestly Dynamic Holiness and Deuteronomic Static Holiness." *VT* 51 (2001): 243–61.

Rendsburg, Gary A. "The Guilty Party in 1 Kings iii 16–28." *VT* 48 (1998): 534–41.

Rendtorff, Rolf. "Samuel the Prophet: A Link Between Moses and the Kings." Pages 27–36 in *The Quest for Context and Meaning: Studies in Biblical Intertextuality in Honor of James A. Sanders*. Edited by Craig A. Evans and Shemaryahu Talmon. BIS 28. Leiden: Brill, 1997.

Reventlow, Henning Graf, Yair Hoffman, and Benjamin Uffenheimer, eds. *Politics and Theopolitics in the Bible and Postbiblical Literature*. JSOTSup 171. Sheffield: JSOT, 1994.

Richards, Kent Harold. "Deuteronomist." Page 219 in *Harper's Bible Dictionary*. Edited by Paul J. Achtemeier. San Francisco: Harper & Row, 1985.

Richardson, H. N. "The Last Words of David: Some Notes on II Samuel 23:1–7." *JBL* 90 (1971): 257–66.

Richter, Wolfgang. *Die Bearbeitung des "Retterbuches" in der deuteronomistischen Epoche*. BBB 21. Bonn: Hanstein, 1964.

Römer, Thomas C. "The Book of Deuteronomy." Pages 178–212 in McKenzie and Graham, eds., *The History of Israel's Traditions*.

———. "The Form-Critical Problem of the So-Called Deuteronomistic History." Pages 240–52 in *The Changing Face of Form Criticism for the Twenty-First Century*. Edited by Marvin A. Sweeney and Ehud Ben Zvi. Grand Rapids: Eerdmans, 2003.

———, ed. *The Future of the Deuteronomistic History*. BETL 147. Leuven: Peeters, 2000.

———. *The So-Called Deuteronomistic History: A Sociological, Historical and Literary Introduction*. London: T&T Clark, 2005.

Römer, Thomas C., and Albert de Pury. "Deuteronomistic Historiography (DH): History of Research and Debated Issues." Pages 24–141 in de Pury, Römer, and Macchi, eds., *Israel Constructs Its History*.

Roncace, Mark. "Elisha and the Woman of Shunem: 2 Kings 4:8–37 and 8:1–6 Read in Conjunction." *JSOT* 91 (2000): 109–27.

Rose, Martin. "Deuteronomistic Ideology and Theology of the Old Testament." Pages 424–55 in de Pury, Römer, and Macchi, eds., *Israel Constructs Its History*.

Rösel, Hartmut N. "Does a Comprehensive 'Leitmotif' Exist in the Deuteronomistic History?" Pages 195–211 in Römer, ed., *The Future of the Deuteronomistic History*.

Rosenfeld, Alvin H. "The Problematics of Holocaust Literature." Pages 1–30 in Rosenfeld and Greenberg, eds., *Confronting the Holocaust*.

Rosenfeld, Alvin H., and Irving Greenberg, eds. *Confronting the Holocaust: The Impact of Elie Wiesel*. Bloomington: Indiana University Press, 1978.

Rosenthal, Gabriele, ed. *The Holocaust in Three Generations: Families of Victims and Perpetrators of the Nazi Regime*. Translated by Catherine Johnson. London: Cassell, 1998.

Rosenthal, Gabriele et al. "The Collective Trauma of the Lodz Ghetto: The Goldstern Family." Pages 51–68 in Rosenthal, ed., *The Holocaust in Three Generations*.

Rothberg, Michael. "Between the Extreme and the Everyday: Ruth Klüger's Traumatic Realism." Pages 55–70 in Miller and Tougow, eds., *Extremities: Trauma*.

Rüterswörden, Udo. "Die Liebe zu Gott im Deuteronomium." Pages 229–38 in *Die deuteronomistischen Geschichtswerke: Redaktions- und religionsgeschichtliche Perspektiven zur 'Deuteronomismus'-Diskussion in Tora und Vorderen Propheten.* Edited by Markus Witte et al. BZAW 365. Berlin: de Gruyter, 2006.

Satterthwaite, Philip E. "The Elisha Narratives and the Coherence of 2 Kings 2–8." *TynBul* 49 (1998): 1–28.

Schade, Waltraud et al. "Shared and Divided Worlds: The Stern Family." Pages 95–117 in Rosenthal, ed., *The Holocaust in Three Generations.*

Schearing, Linda S., and Steven L. McKenzie, eds. *Those Elusive Deuteronomists: The Phenomenon of Pan-Deuteronomism.* JSOTSup 268. Sheffield: Sheffield Academic, 1999.

Schenker, Adrian. *Septante et texte massorétique dans l'histoire la plus ancienne du texte de 1 Rois 2–14.* CRB 48. Paris: Gabalda, 2000.

Schipper, Jeremy. "'Significant Resonances' with Mephibosheth in 2 Kings 25:27–30: A Response to Donald F. Murray." *JBL* 124 (2005): 521–29.

Schmidt, Konrad. *Erzväter und Exodus: Untersuchungen zur doppelten Begründung der Ursprünge Israels innerhalb der Geschichtsbücher des Alten Testaments.* WMANT 81. Neukirchen–Vluyn: Neukirchener Verlag, 1999.

Schmidt, Ludwig. "P in Deuteronomium 34." *VT* 59 (2009): 475–94.

Schmidt, Werner H. *Old Testament Introduction.* Translated by Matthew J. O'Connell. 2d ed. New York: de Gruyter, 1995.

Schmitt, Götz. *Der Landtag von Sichem.* Stuttgart: Calwer, 1964.

Schneider, Tammi J. *Judges.* BO. Collegeville, Minn.: Liturgical, 2000.

Seters, John Van. *In Search of History: Historiography in the Ancient World and the Origins of Biblical History.* New Haven, Conn.: Yale University Press, 1983.

Sherwood, Aaron. "A Leader's Misleading and a Prostitute's Profession: A Re-examination of Joshua 2." *JSOT* 31 (2006): 43–61.

Efraim, Sicher. "The Burden of Memory: The Writing of the Post-Holocaust Generation." Pages 19–88 in Sicher, ed., *Breaking Crystal.*

———, ed. *Breaking Crystal: Writing and Memory after Auschwitz.* Urbana, Ill.: University of Illinois Press, 1998.

Siebert, Eric A. *Subversive Scribes and the Solomonic Narrative: A Rereading of 1 Kings 1–11.* LHBOTS 436. New York: T&T Clark, 2006.

Simon, Uriel. "The Poor Man's Ewe Lamb: An Example of a Juridical Parable." *Bib* 48 (1967): 207–42.

Sjöberg, Mikael. *Wrestling with Textual Violence: The Jephthah Narrative in Antiquity and Modernity.* The Bible in the Modern World 4. Sheffield: Sheffield Phoenix, 2006.

Slater, Susan. "Imagining Arrival: Rhetoric, Reader, and Word of God in Deuteronomy 1–3." Pages 107–22 in Black, Boer, and Runions, eds., *The Labour of Reading.*

Smend, Rudolf. "The Law and the Nations: A Contribution to Deuteronomistic Tradition History." Pages 95–110 in Knoppers and McConville, eds., *Reconsidering Israel and Judah.*

Smith-Christopher, Daniel L. *A Biblical Theology of Exile.* OBT. Minneapolis: Fortress, 2002.

Soggin, J. Alberto. *Introduction to the Old Testament: From Its Origins to the Closing of the Alexandrian Canon.* Translated by John Bowden. 3d ed. OTL. Louisville: Westminster John Knox, 1989.

———. *Joshua: A Commentary*. Translated by R. A. Wilson. OTL. London: SCM, 1972.

———. *Judges: A Commentary*. Translated by John Bowden. OTL. London: SCM, 1981.

Speed, Nancy et al. "Posttraumatic Stress Disorder as a Consequence of the POW Experience." *Journal of Nervous and Mental Disease* 177 (1989): 147–53.

Spieckermann, Hermann. "Mit der Liebe im Wort: Ein Beitrag zur Theologie des Deuteronomiums." Pages 190–205 in *Liebe und Gebot: Studien zum Deuteronomium*. Edited by Richard G. Kratz and Hermann Spieckermann. FRLANT 190. Göttingen: Vandenhoeck & Ruprecht, 2000.

Stern, Ephraim. *Archaeology of the Land of the Bible*. Vol. 2, *The Assyrian, Babylonian, and Persian Periods*. ABRL. New York: Doubleday, 2001.

Sternberg, Meir. *The Poetics of Biblical Narrative: Ideological Literature and the Drama of Reading*. ISBL. Bloomington: Indiana University Press, 1985.

Steussy, Marti J. *David: Biblical Portraits of Power*. Studies on Personalities of the Old Testament. Columbia: University of South Carolina Press, 1999.

———. "The Problematic God of Samuel." Pages 127–61 in Penchansky and Redditt, eds., *Shall Not the Judge of All the Earth Do What is Right?*

Sutherland, Roy K. "Israelite Political Theories in Joshua 9." *JSOT* 53 (1992): 65–74.

Sweeney, Marvin A. *I & II Kings: A Commentary*. OTL. Louisville: Westminster John Knox, 2007.

———. "The Critique of Solomon in the Josianic Edition of the Deuteronomistic History." *JBL* 114 (1995): 607–22.

———. *King Josiah of Judah: The Lost Messiah of Israel*. Oxford: Oxford University Press, 2001.

———. "On the Literary Function of the Notice Concerning Hiel's Re-Establishment of Jericho in 1 Kings 16:34." Pages 104–15 in *Seeing Signals, Reading Signs: The Art of Exegesis. Studies in Honor of Antony F. Campbell, SJ for His Seventieth Birthday*. Edited by Mark A. O'Brien and Howard N. Wallace. JSOTSup 415. New York: T&T Clark International, 2004.

Sznycer, Maurice. *Les passage puniques en transcription latine dans le "Poenulus" de Plaute*. Études et commentaires 65. Paris: Klincksieck, 1967.

Tal, Kalí. *Worlds of Hurt: Reading the Literatures of Trauma*. Cambridge: Cambridge University Press, 1996.

Talshir, Zvi. *The Alternative Story of the Division of the Kingdom: 3 Kingdoms 12:24a–z*. JBS 6. Jerusalem: Simor, 1993.

Talstra, E. "Deuteronomy 9 and 10: Synchronic and Diachronic Observations." Pages 187–210 in *Synchronic or Diachronic? A Debate on Method in Old Testament Exegesis*. Edited by Johannes C. de Moor. OTS 34. Leiden: Brill, 1995.

Tamarkin Reis, Pamela. "Killing the Messenger: David's Policy or Politics?" *JSOT* 31 (2006): 167–91.

Task Force on DSM–IV. *Diagnostic and Statistical Manual of Mental Disorders*. 4th ed. text revision. Washington: American Psychiatric Association, 2000.

Tigay, Jeffrey H. *Deuteronomy: The JPS Torah Commentary*. Philadelphia: Jewish Publication Society, 1996.

Trebolle Barrera, Julio. *Salomón y Jeroboan: Historia de la recensión y redacción de 1 Reyes 2–12, 14*. Bibliotheca Salmanticensis. Dissertationes 3. Salamanca: Universidad Pontificia, 1980.

Trible, Phyllis. "The Daughter of Jephthah: An Inhuman Sacrifice." Pages 92–116 in *Texts of Terror: Literary-Feminist Readings of Biblical Narratives*. OBT. Philadelphia: Fortress, 1984.

Tsevat, Matitiahu. "The Biblical Account of the Foundation of the Monarchy in Israel." Pages 77–99 in *The Meaning of the Book of Job and Other Biblical Studies: Essays on the Literature and Religion of the Hebrew Bible*. New York: Ktav, 1980.

Ulrich, Eugene. "4QJoshua[a] and Joshua's First Altar in the Promised Land." Pages 89–104 in *New Qumran Texts and Studies: Proceedings of the First Meeting of the International Organization for Qumran Studies, Paris 1992*. Edited by George J. Brooke. STDJ 15. Leiden: Brill, 1994.

Ulrich, Eugene et al. *Qumran Cave 4—IX: Deuteronomy, Joshua, Judges, Kings*. DJD 14. Oxford: Clarendon, 1995.

Vanoni, Gottfried. "Beobachtungen zur deuteronomistischen Terminologie in 2 Kön 23,25–25,30." Pages 357–62 in Lohfink, ed., *Das Deuteronomium*.

Veijola, Timo. *Die ewige Dynastie: David und die Entstehung seiner Dynastie nach der deuteronomistischen Darstellung*. AASF B/193. Helsinki: Suomalainen Tiedakatemia, 1975.

———. *Das Königtum in der Beurteilung der Deuteronomistischen Historiographie: Eine redaktionsgeschichtliche Untersuchung*. AASF B/198. Helsinki: Suomalainen Tiedakatemia, 1977.

Viviano, Pauline A. "2 Kings 17: A Rhetorical and Form-Critical Analysis." *CBQ* 49 (1987): 548–59.

Walsh, Jerome T. *1 Kings*. BO. Collegeville, Minn.: Liturgical, 1996.

———. "The Characterization of Solomon in First Kings 1–5." *CBQ* 57 (1995): 471–93.

Webb, Barry G. *The Book of the Judges: An Integrated Reading*. JSOTSup 46. Sheffield: JSOT, 1987.

Weinfeld, Moshe. *Deuteronomy 1–11: A New Translation with Introduction and Commentary*. AB 5. New York: Doubleday, 1991.

———. *Deuteronomy and the Deuteronomic School*. Oxford: Clarendon, 1972.

———. "Judges 1:1–2:5: The Conquest Under the Leadership of the House of Judah." Pages 388–400 in *Understanding Poets and Prophets: Essays in Honor of George Wishart Anderson*. Edited by A. Graeme Auld. JSOTSup 152. Sheffield: Sheffield Academic, 1993.

Weippert, Helga. "Das deuteronomistische Geschichtswerk: Sein Ziel und Ende in der neueren Forschung." *Theologische Revue* 50 (1985): 213–49.

———. "Die 'deuteronomistischen' Beurteilungen der Könige von Israel und Juda und das Problem der Redaktion der Königsbücher." *Bib* 53 (1972): 301–39.

Weiser, Artur. *Samuel: Seine geschichtliche Aufgabe und religiöse Bedeutung. Traditionsgeschichtlice Untersuchungen zu 1. Samuel 7–12*. FRLANT 81. Göttingen: Vandenhoeck & Ruprecht, 1962.

Wellhausen, Julius. *Der Text der Bücher Samuelis untersucht*. Göttingen: Vandenhoeck & Ruprecht, 1871.

Westbrook, Raymond. "Elisha's True Prophecy in 2 Kings 3." *JBL* 124 (2005): 530–32.

Westermann, Claus. *Theologie des Alten Testaments in Grundzügen*. ATD Ergänzungsreihe 6. Göttingen: Vandenhoeck & Ruprecht, 1978.

Wharton, James A. "The Secret of Yahweh: Story and Affirmation in Judges 13–16." *Int* 27 (1973): 48–65.

Wiesel, Elie. "Why I Write." Pages 200–206 in Rosenfeld and Greenberg, eds., *Confronting the Holocaust.*

Williams, David. "Once again: The Structure of the Narrative of Solomon's Reign." *JSOT* 86 (1999): 49–66.

Williams, P. J. "Lying Spirits Sent by God? The Case of Micaiah's Prophecy." Pages 58–66 in *The Trustworthiness of God: Perspectives on the Nature of Scripture.* Edited by Paul Helm and Carl R. Trueman. Grand Rapids: Eerdmans, 2002.

Wilson, Robert R. "Unity and Diversity in the Book of Kings." Pages 293–310 in *"A Wise and Discerning Mind": Essays in Honor of Burke O. Long.* Edited by Saul M. Olyan and Robert C. Culley. BJS 325. Providence: Brown Judaic Studies, 2000.

Winkle, D. W. van. "1 Kings xii 25–xiii 34: Jeroboam's Cultic Innovations and the Man of God from Judah." *VT* 46 (1996): 101–14.

———. "1 Kings xiii: True and False Prophecy." *VT* 39 (1989): 31–43.

Wiseman, D. J. *The Vassal-Treaties of Esarhaddon.* Iraq 20. London: The British School of Archaeology in Iraq, 1958.

Wolff, Hans Walter. "The Kerygma of the Deuteronomic Historical Work." Translated by Frederick C. Prussner. Pages 83–100 in *The Vitality of Old Testament Traditions.* Edited by Walter Brueggemann. Atlanta: John Knox, 1982.

———. "The Kerygma of the Deuteronomistic Historical Work." Pages 62–78 in Knoppers and McConville, eds., *Reconsidering Israel and Judah.*

Wong, Gregory T. K. *Compositional Strategy of the Book of Judges: An Inductive Rhetorical Study.* VTSup 111. Leiden: Brill, 2006.

Yaez, Hanna. "Inherited Fear: Second-Generation Poets and Novelists in Israel." Pages 160–69 in Sicher, ed., *Breaking Crystal.*

Yamada, Frank M. *Configurations of Rape in the Hebrew Bible: A Literary Analysis of Three Rape Narratives.* StBL 109. New York: Lang, 2008.

Yee, Gale. "Ideological Criticism: Judges 17–21 and the Dismembered Body." Pages 138–60 in *Judges and Method: New Approaches in Biblical Studies.* Edited by Gale Yee. 2d ed. Minneapolis: Fortress, 2007.

Younger, K. Lawson, Jr. "The Configuring of Judicial Preliminaries: Judges 1:1–2:5 and Its Dependence on the Book of Joshua." *JSOT* 68 (1995): 75–92.

———. "Judges 1 in Its Near Eastern Literary Context." Pages 207–27 in *Faith, Tradition, and History: Old Testament Historiography in Its Near Eastern Context.* Edited by A. R. Millard, James K. Hoffmeier, and David W. Baker. Winona Lake, Ind.: Eisenbrauns, 1994.

Zakovitch, Yair. "Humor and Theology or the Successful Failure of Israelite Intelligence: A Literary-Folkloric Approach to Joshua 2." Pages 75–98 in *Text and Tradition: The Hebrew Bible and Folklore.* Edited by Susan Niditch. SBLSS. Atlanta: Scholars Press, 1990.

Zimmerli, Walther. *Grundriss der alttestamentlichen Theologie.* Theologische Wissenschaft 3. Stuttgart: Kohlhammer, 1972.

INDEXES

INDEX OF REFERENCES

Index of Authors